尾田栄一郎

Eiichiro Oda

"Teacher!!! AfrOda's lost his lunch money!!!"
"What!!? Is that true!!?
AfrOda!!! No lunch for you!!!!"

—Eiichiro Oda, 2000

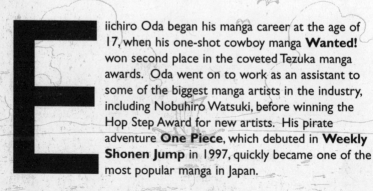

Eiichiro Oda began his manga career at the age of 17, when his one-shot cowboy manga **Wanted!** won second place in the coveted Tezuka manga awards. Oda went on to work as an assistant to some of the biggest manga artists in the industry, including Nobuhiro Watsuki, before winning the Hop Step Award for new artists. His pirate adventure **One Piece**, which debuted in **Weekly Shonen Jump** in 1997, quickly became one of the most popular manga in Japan.

ONE PIECE VOL. 16
The SHONEN JUMP Manga Edition

This volume contains material that was originally published in English in SHONEN JUMP #56-58. Artwork in the magazine may have been slightly altered from that presented here.

STORY AND ART BY EIICHIRO ODA

English Adaptation/Lance Caselman
Translation/JN Productions
Touch-up Art & Lettering/Vanessa Satone
Design/Sean Lee
Editor/Urian Brown

Editor in Chief, Books/Alvin Lu
Editor in Chief, Magazines/Marc Weidenbaum
VP of Publishing Licensing/Rika Inouye
VP of Sales/Gonzalo Ferreyra
Sr. VP of Marketing/Liza Coppola
Publisher/Hyoe Narita

Published by VIZ Media, LLC
P.O. Box 77010
San Francisco, CA 94107

SHONEN JUMP Manga Edition
10 9 8 7 6 5 4 3 2 1
First printing, November 2007

www.viz.com

THE WORLD'S MOST POPULAR MANGA
www.shonenjump.com

SHONEN JUMP MANGA

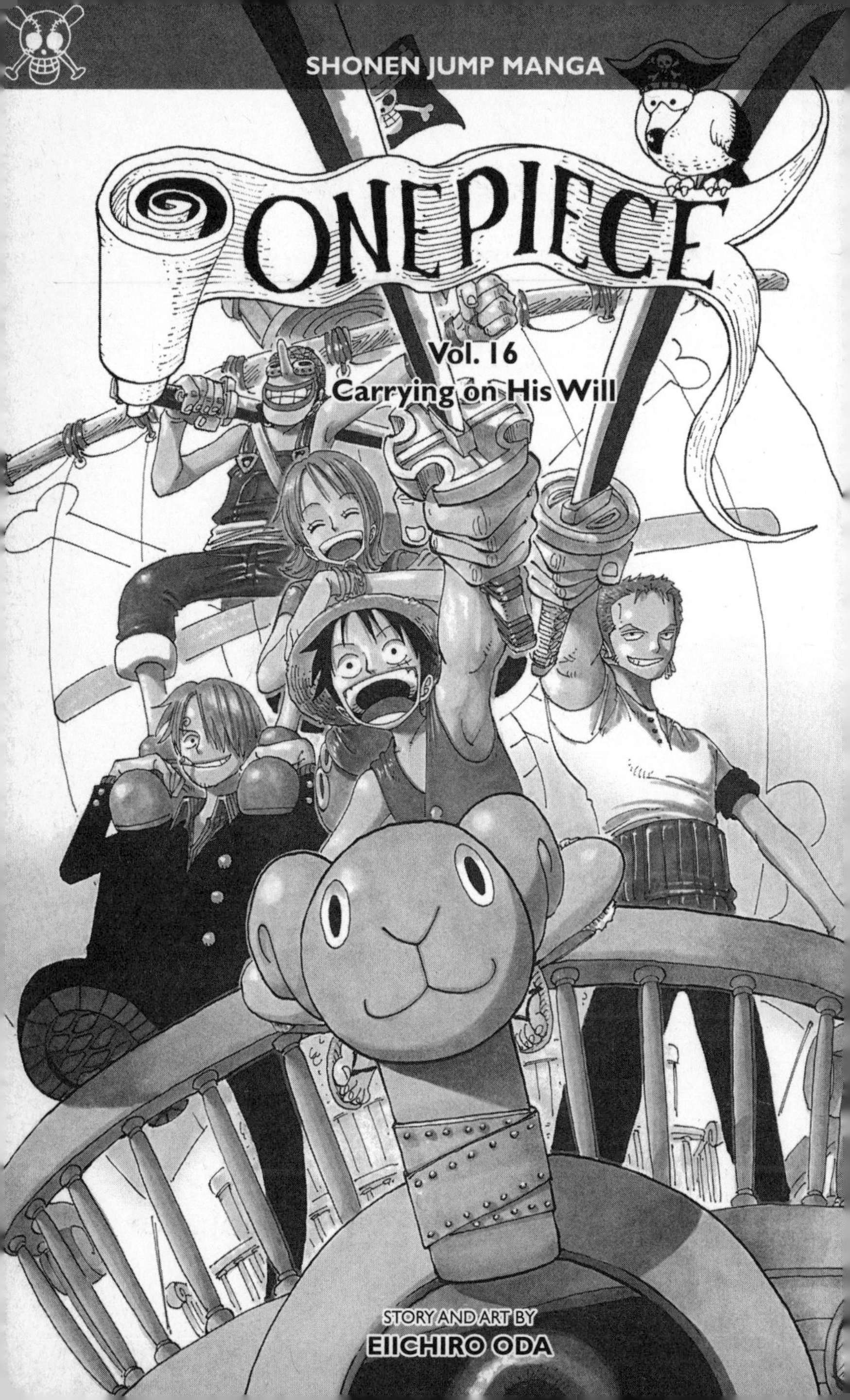

ONE PIECE

Vol. 16
Carrying on His Will

STORY AND ART BY
EIICHIRO ODA

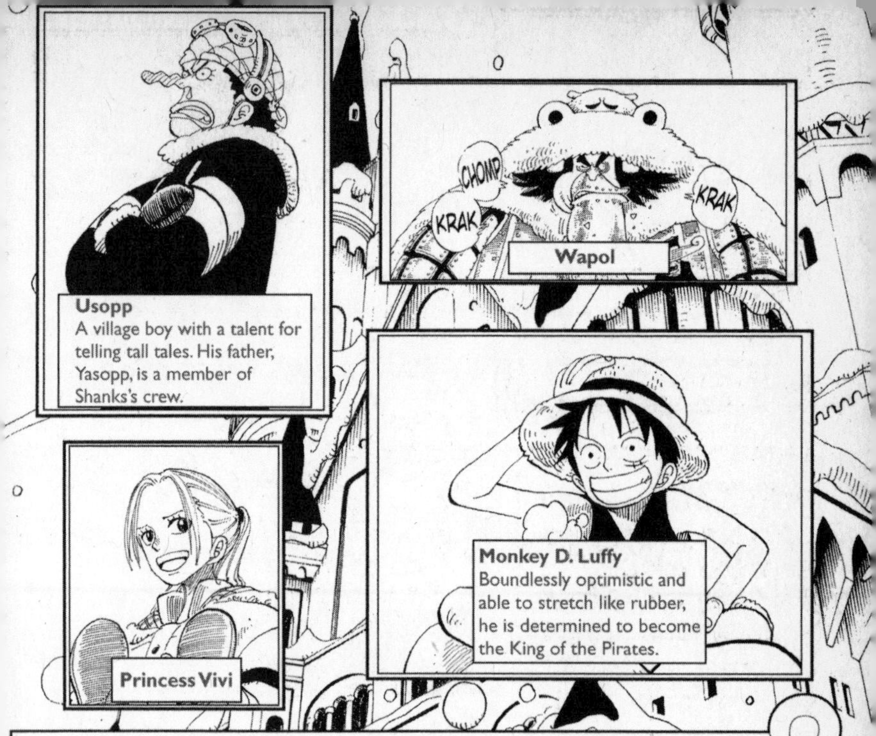
KRAK
CHOMP
KRAK
Wapol
Usopp
A village boy with a talent for telling tall tales. His father, Yasopp, is a member of Shanks's crew.
Monkey D. Luffy
Boundlessly optimistic and able to stretch like rubber, he is determined to become the King of the Pirates.
Princess Vivi

Monkey D. Luffy started out as just a kid with a dream—and that dream was to become the greatest pirate in history! Stirred by the tales of pirate "Red-Haired" Shanks, Luffy vowed to become a pirate himself. That was before the enchanted Devil Fruit gave Luffy the power to stretch like rubber, at the cost of being unable to swim—a serious handicap for an aspiring sea dog. Undeterred, Luffy set out to sea and recruited some crewmates: master swordsman Zolo, treasure-hunting thief Nami, lying sharpshooter Usopp, and Sanji, the high-kickingchef.

Having reached the Grand Line, Luffy and crew are escorting Princess Vivi to the Kingdom of Alabasta in order to prevent its takeover by the secret crime organization Baroque Works. But having overheard the true identity of Mr. Zero (Sir Crocodile, one of the Seven Warlords of the Sea), Luffy and the others find themselves fighting for their lives against his formidable agents. After a fierce battle on a prehistoric island of giants, they set sail for Alabasta, but Nami suddenly develops a high fever. In search of a doctor, the crew arrives at Drum Island, land of perpetual snow. This kingdom was recently plundered by pirates, and its king fled the island, taking all the physicians with him. Now the only remaining doctor lives in a castle high atop the island's tallest mountain—but she's rumored to be a witch! Undaunted, Luffy straps Nami to his back and he and Sanji begin the perilous ascent to the castle, only to find themselves in the path of a deadly avalanche!!

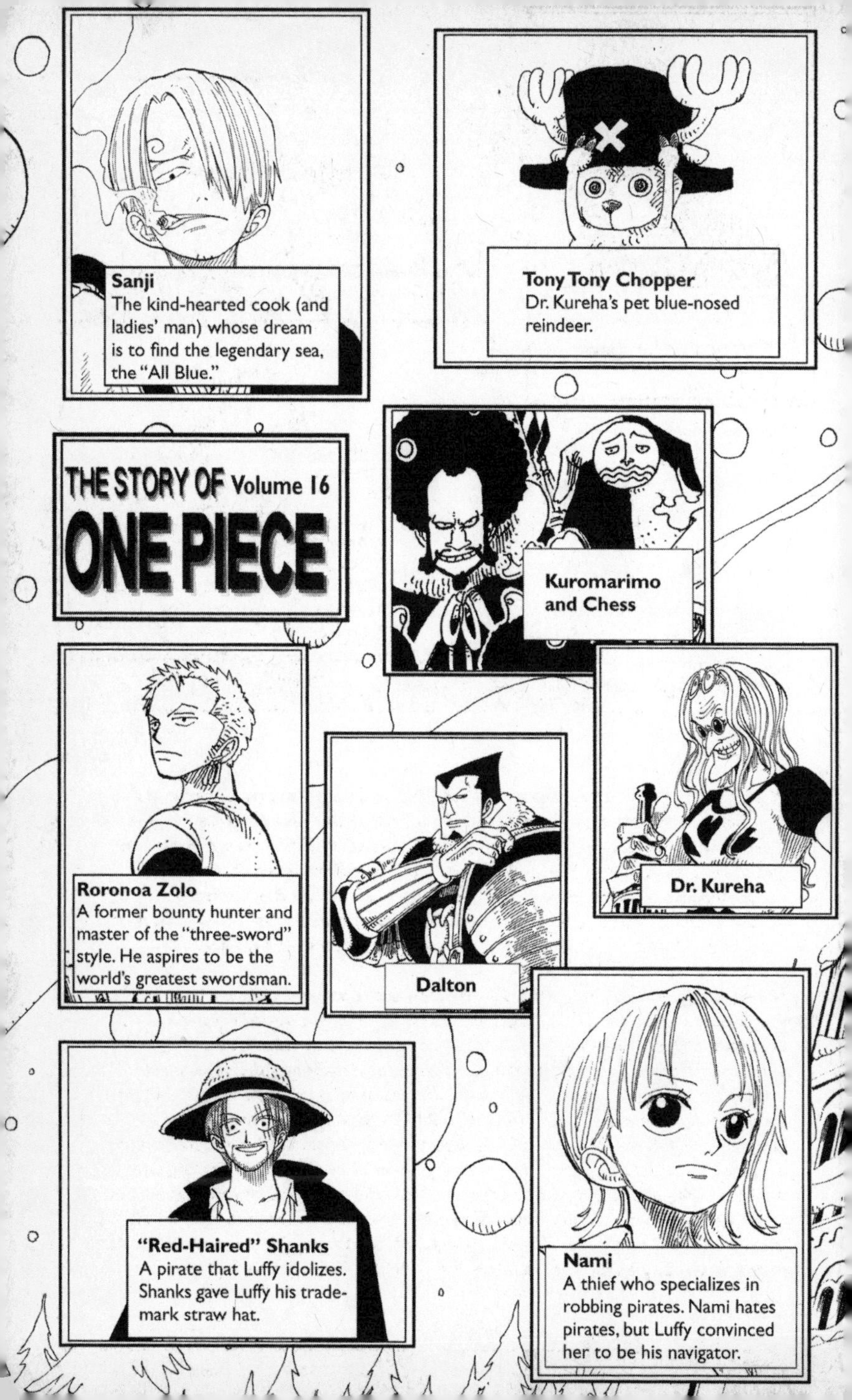
Tony Tony Chopper
Dr. Kureha's pet blue-nosed reindeer.
Sanji
The kind-hearted cook (and ladies' man) whose dream is to find the legendary sea, the "All Blue."
Kuromarimo and Chess
THE STORY OF Volume 16
ONE PIECE
Dr. Kureha
Dalton
Roronoa Zolo
A former bounty hunter and master of the "three-sword" style. He aspires to be the world's greatest swordsman.
Nami
A thief who specializes in robbing pirates. Nami hates pirates, but Luffy convinced her to be his navigator.
"Red-Haired" Shanks
A pirate that Luffy idolizes. Shanks gave Luffy his trade-mark straw hat.

Vol. 16
CARRYING ON HIS WILL

CONTENTS

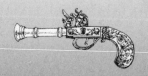

Chapter 137: AVALANCHE

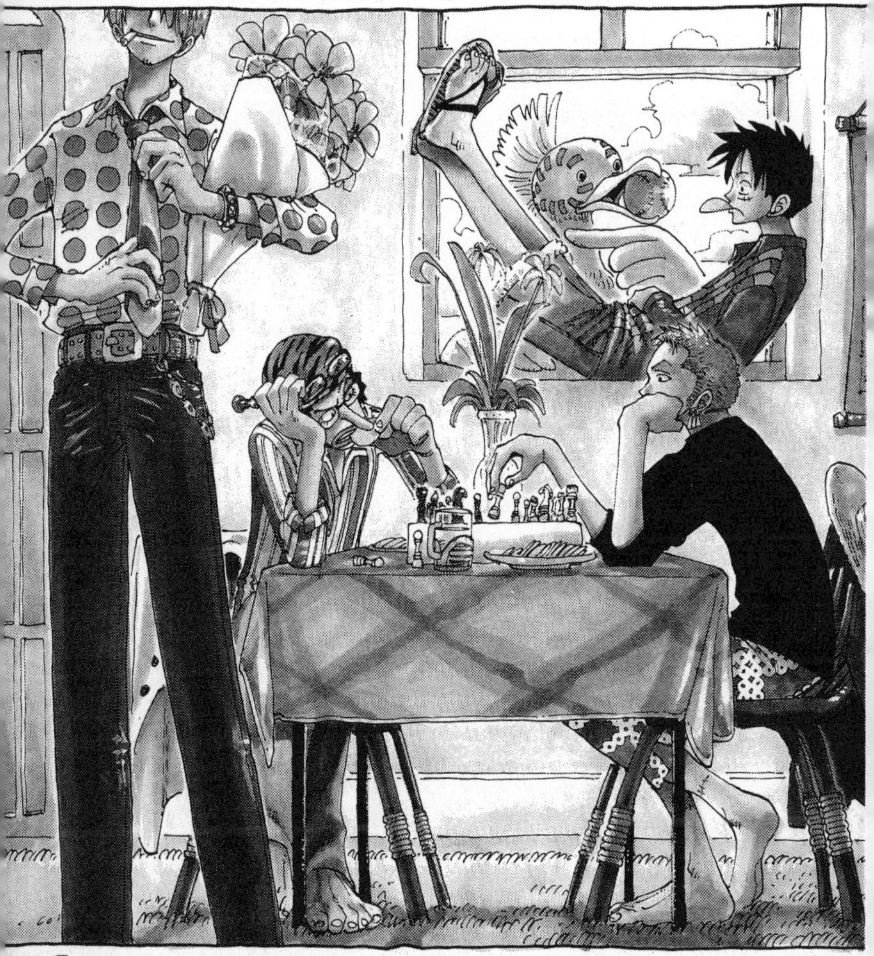

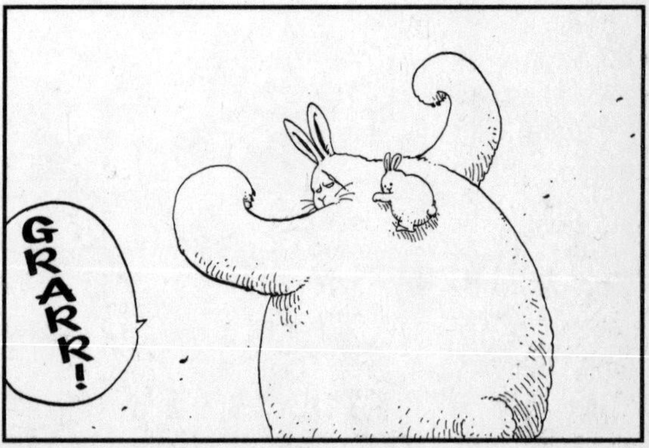
GRARR!

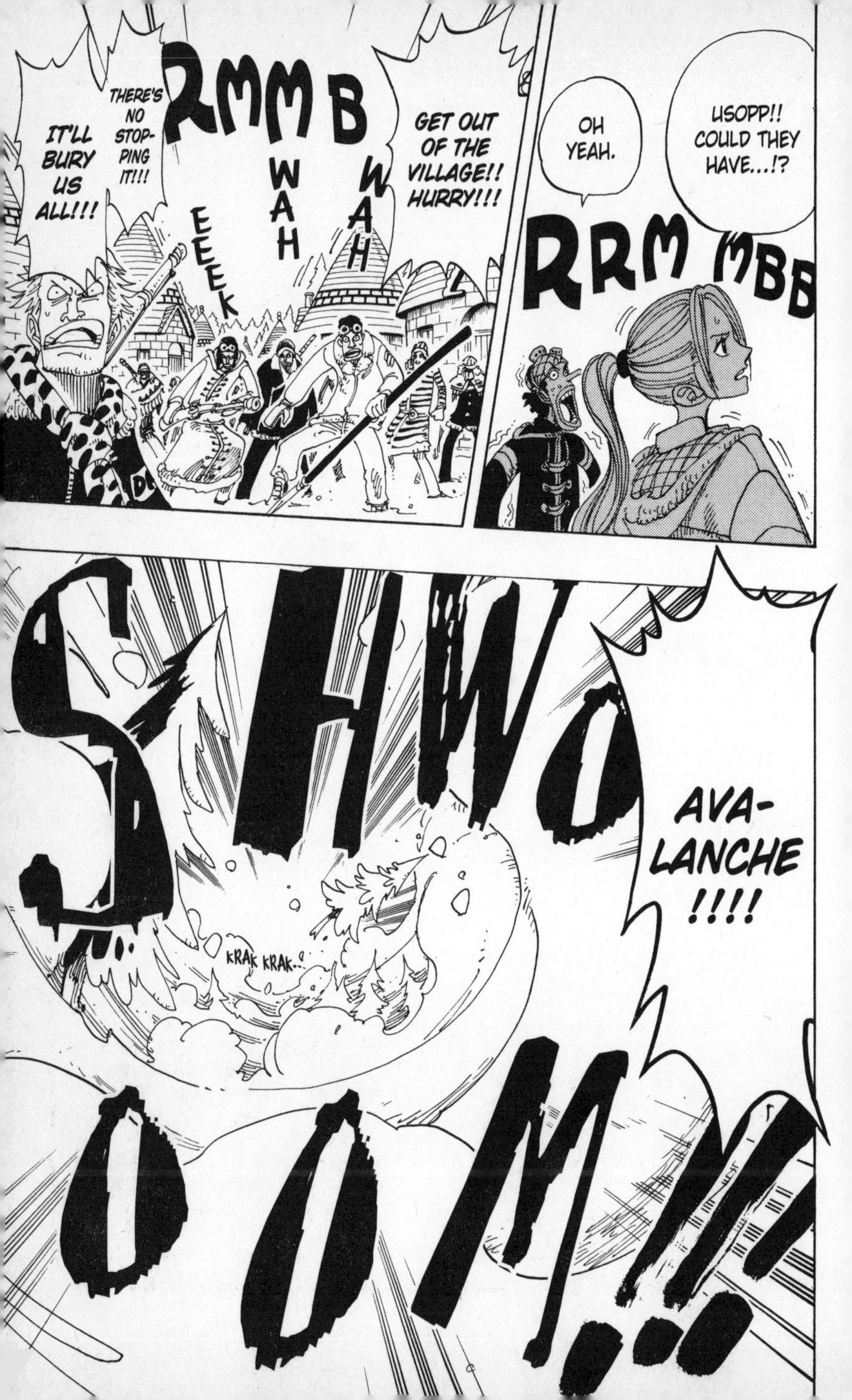
USOPP!! COULD THEY HAVE...!?
OH YEAH.
RRM MBB
GET OUT OF THE VILLAGE!! HURRY!!!
WAH
WAH
RMM B
EEEK
THERE'S NO STOP-PING IT!!!
IT'LL BURY US ALL!!!
AVA-LANCHE !!!!
SHWO
KRAK KRAK..
OOM!!

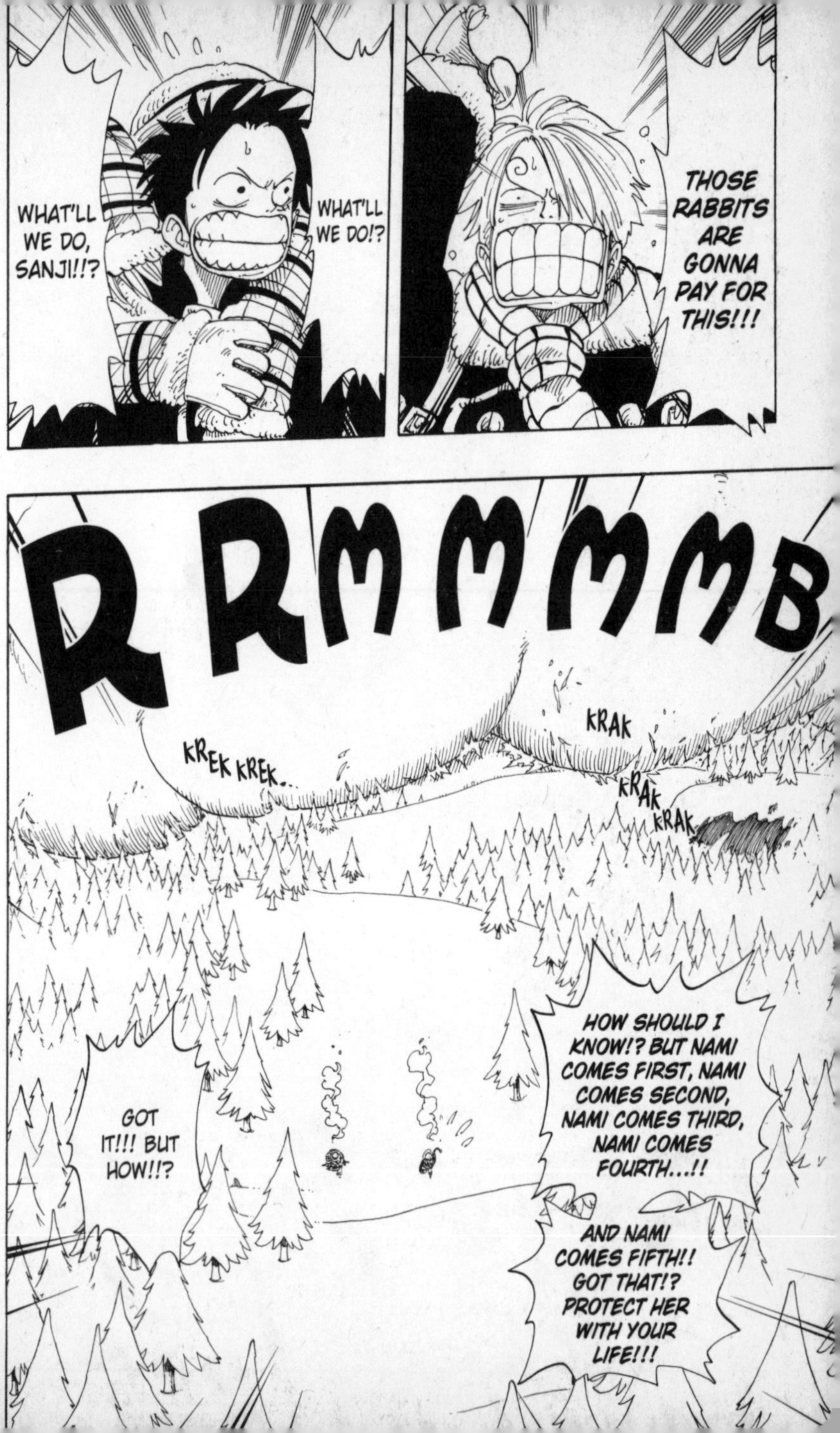
THOSE RABBITS ARE GONNA PAY FOR THIS!!!
WHAT'LL WE DO!?
WHAT'LL WE DO, SANJI!!?
RRMMMMB
KRAK
KREK KREK...
KRAK KRAK
HOW SHOULD I KNOW!? BUT NAMI COMES FIRST, NAMI COMES SECOND, NAMI COMES THIRD, NAMI COMES FOURTH...!!
AND NAMI COMES FIFTH!! GOT THAT!? PROTECT HER WITH YOUR LIFE!!!
GOT IT!!! BUT HOW!!?

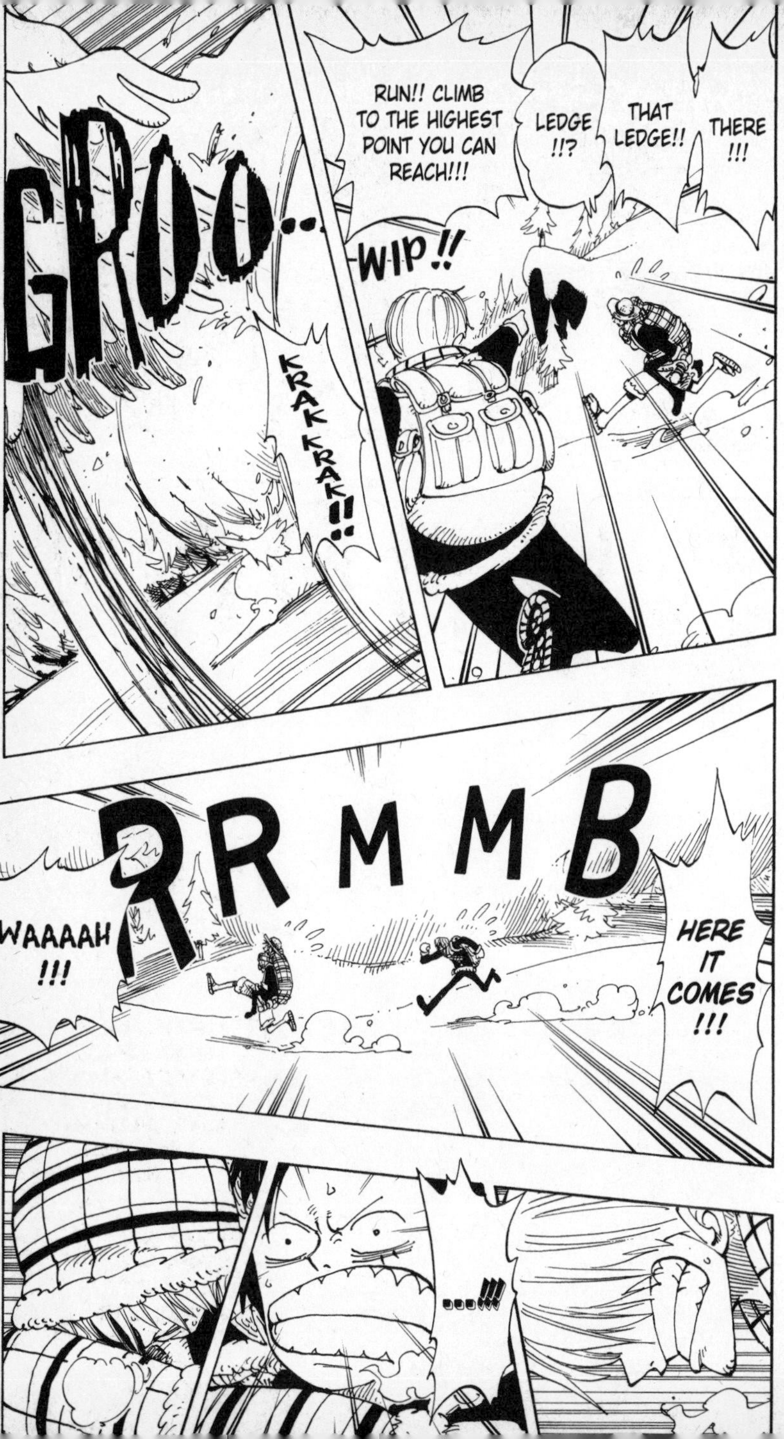
RUN!! CLIMB TO THE HIGHEST POINT YOU CAN REACH!!!
LEDGE !!?
THAT LEDGE!!
THERE !!!
WIP!!
GROO...
KRAK KRAK!!
HERE IT COMES !!!
RRMMB
WAAAAH !!!
...!!!

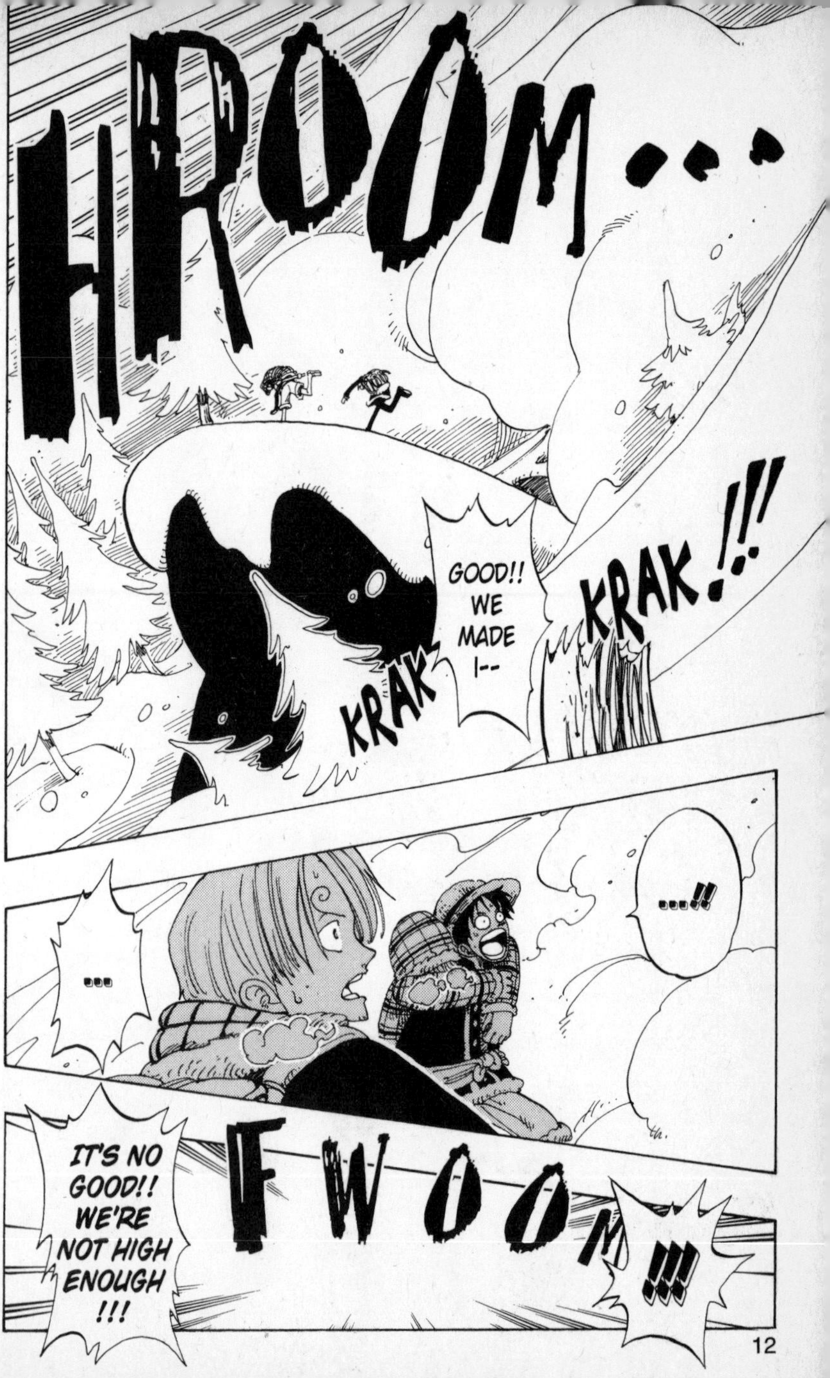
HROOM...
KRAK!!!
GOOD!! WE MADE I--
KRAK
...!!
...
FWOOM!!!
IT'S NO GOOD!! WE'RE NOT HIGH ENOUGH!!!

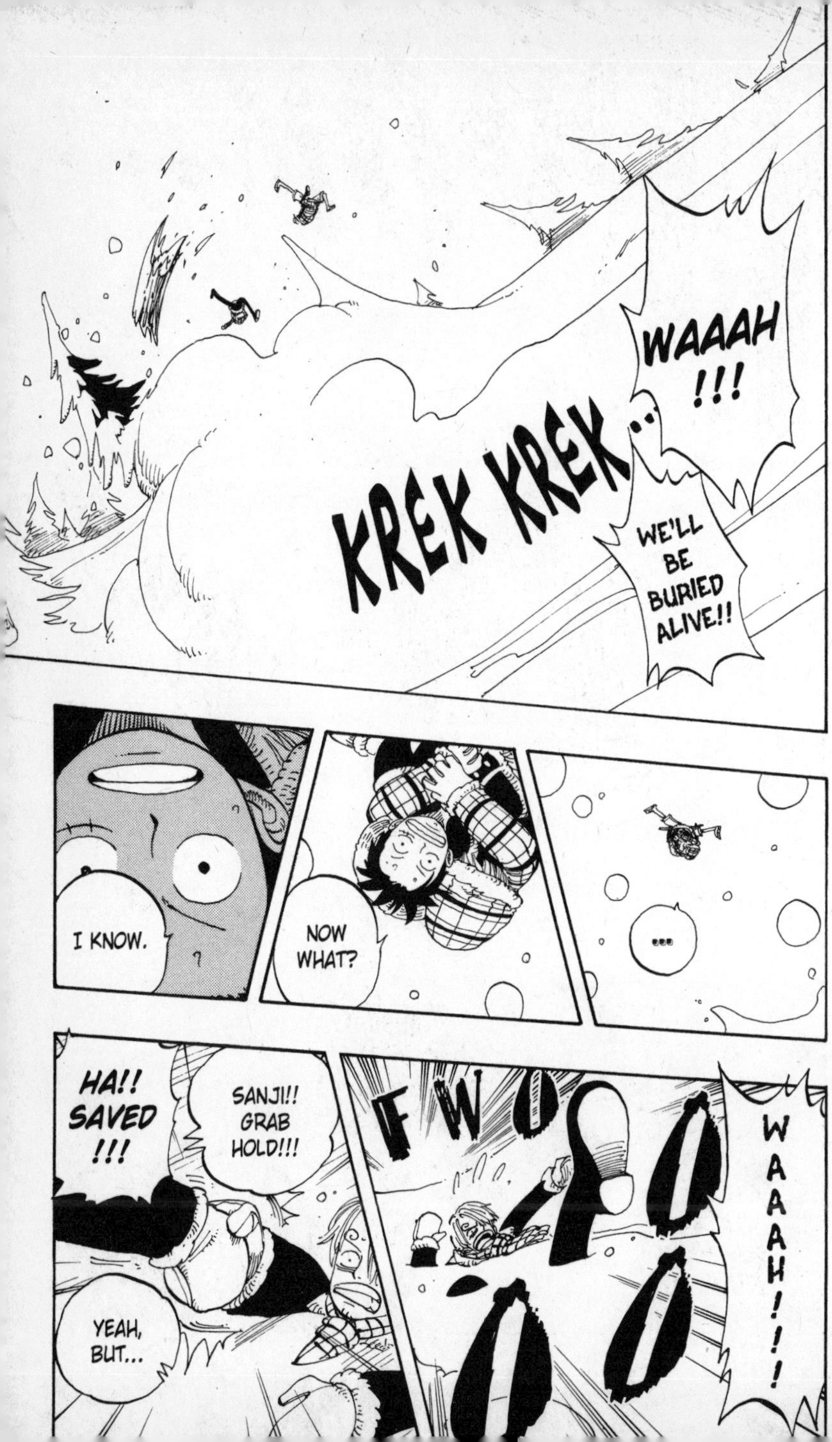
WAAAH!!!
WE'LL BE BURIED ALIVE!!
KREK KREK...
...
NOW WHAT?
I KNOW.
FWOOO
WAAAAH!!!!!
SANJI!! GRAB HOLD!!!
HA!! SAVED!!!
YEAH, BUT...

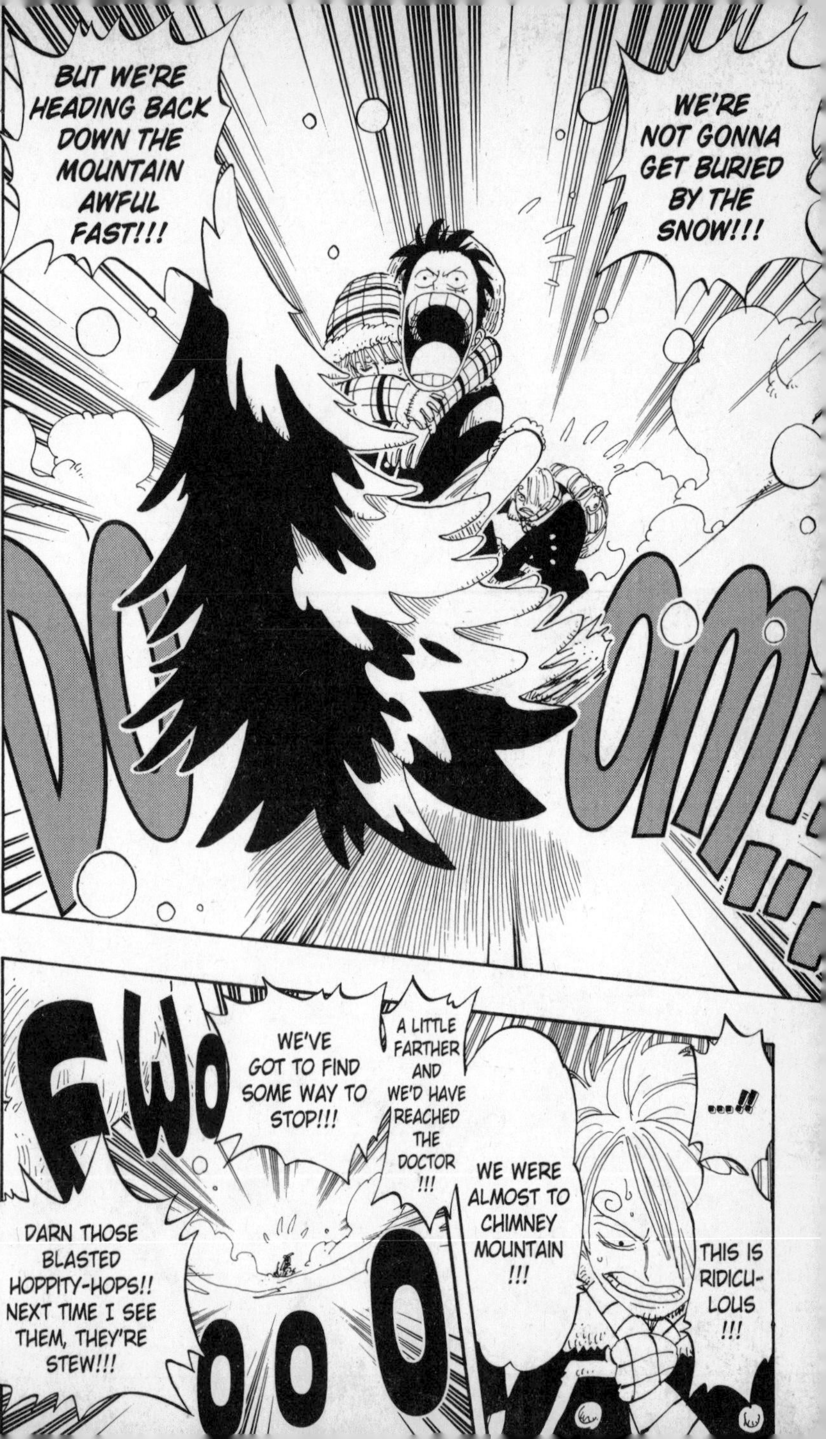
WE'RE NOT GONNA GET BURIED BY THE SNOW!!!
BUT WE'RE HEADING BACK DOWN THE MOUNTAIN AWFUL FAST!!!
DOOM...
...!!
THIS IS RIDICU-LOUS!!!
WE WERE ALMOST TO CHIMNEY MOUNTAIN!!!
A LITTLE FARTHER AND WE'D HAVE REACHED THE DOCTOR!!!
WE'VE GOT TO FIND SOME WAY TO STOP!!!
FWOOOO
DARN THOSE BLASTED HOPPITY-HOPS!! NEXT TIME I SEE THEM, THEY'RE STEW!!!

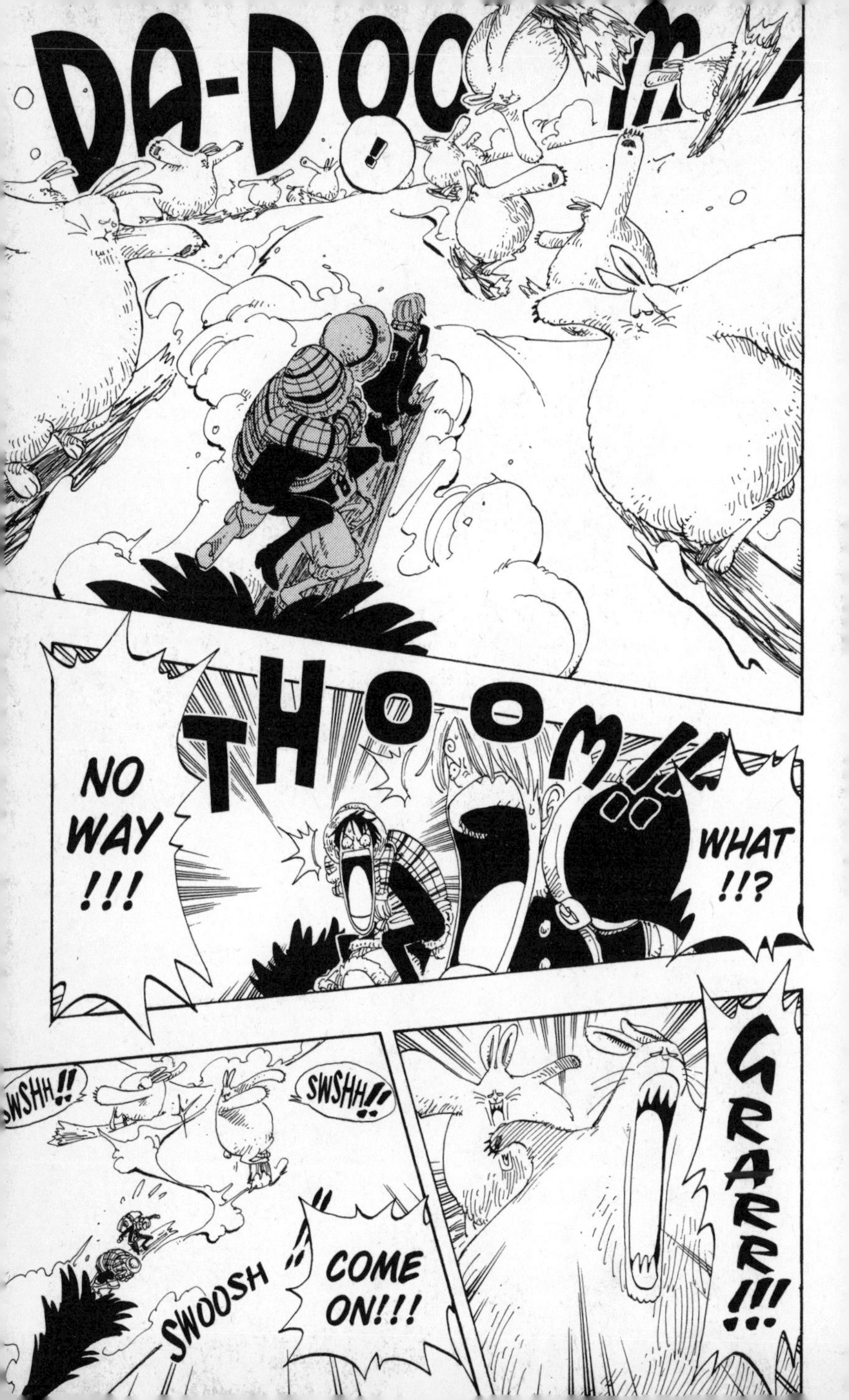
DA-DOOM
!
THOOM!!
WHAT!!?
NO WAY!!!
GRARR!!!
SWSHH!!
SWSHH!!
COME ON!!!
SWOOSH

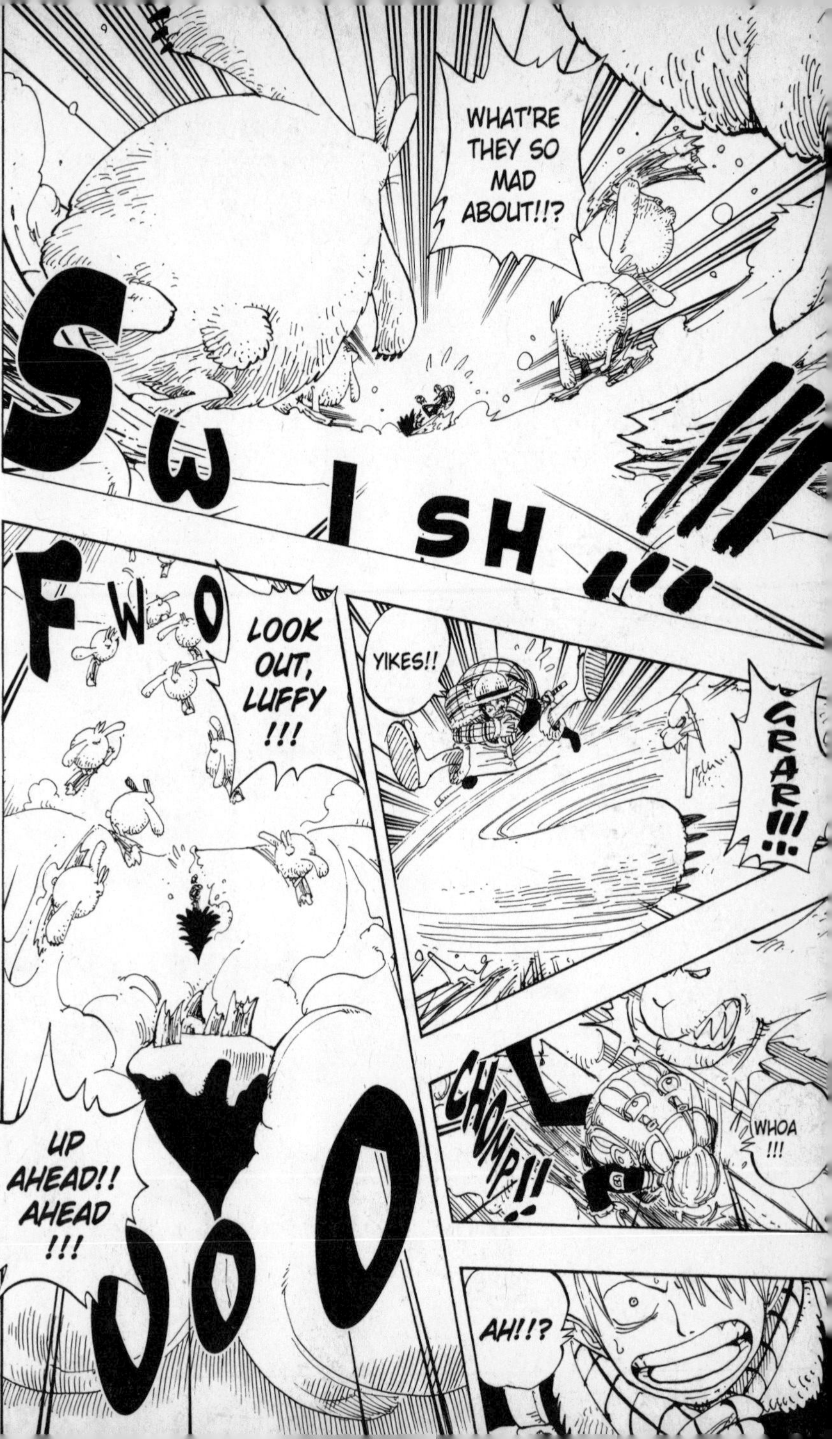
WHAT'RE THEY SO MAD ABOUT!!?
SWISH!!!
YIKES!!
GRAR!!!
CHOMP!!
WHOA!!!
AH!!?
FWOOOO
LOOK OUT, LUFFY!!!
UP AHEAD!! AHEAD!!!

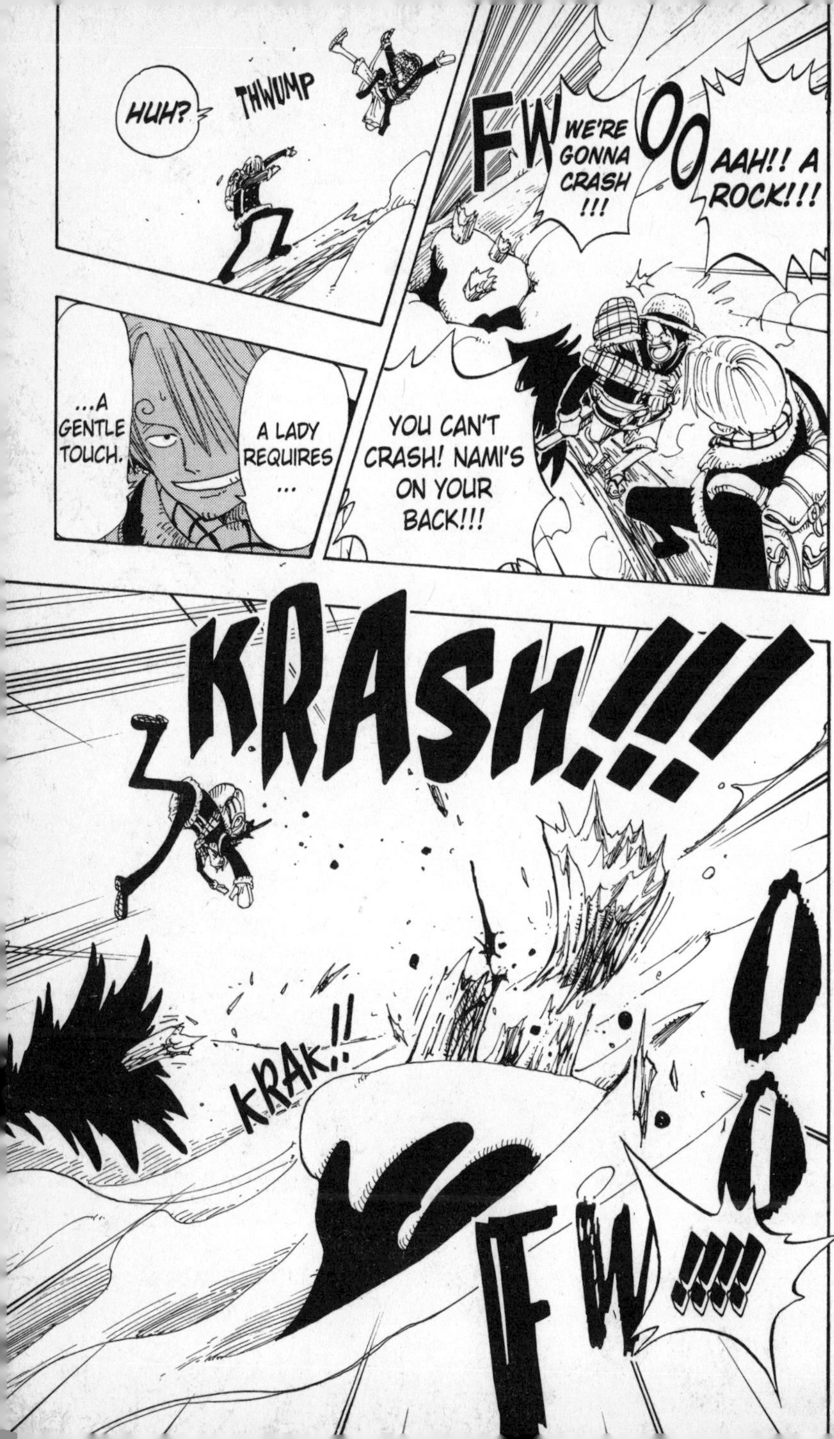
FWOO
AAH!! A ROCK!!!
WE'RE GONNA CRASH!!!
YOU CAN'T CRASH! NAMI'S ON YOUR BACK!!!
HUH?
THWUMP
A LADY REQUIRES...
...A GENTLE TOUCH.
KRASH!!!
KRAK!!
FWOOO!!!!

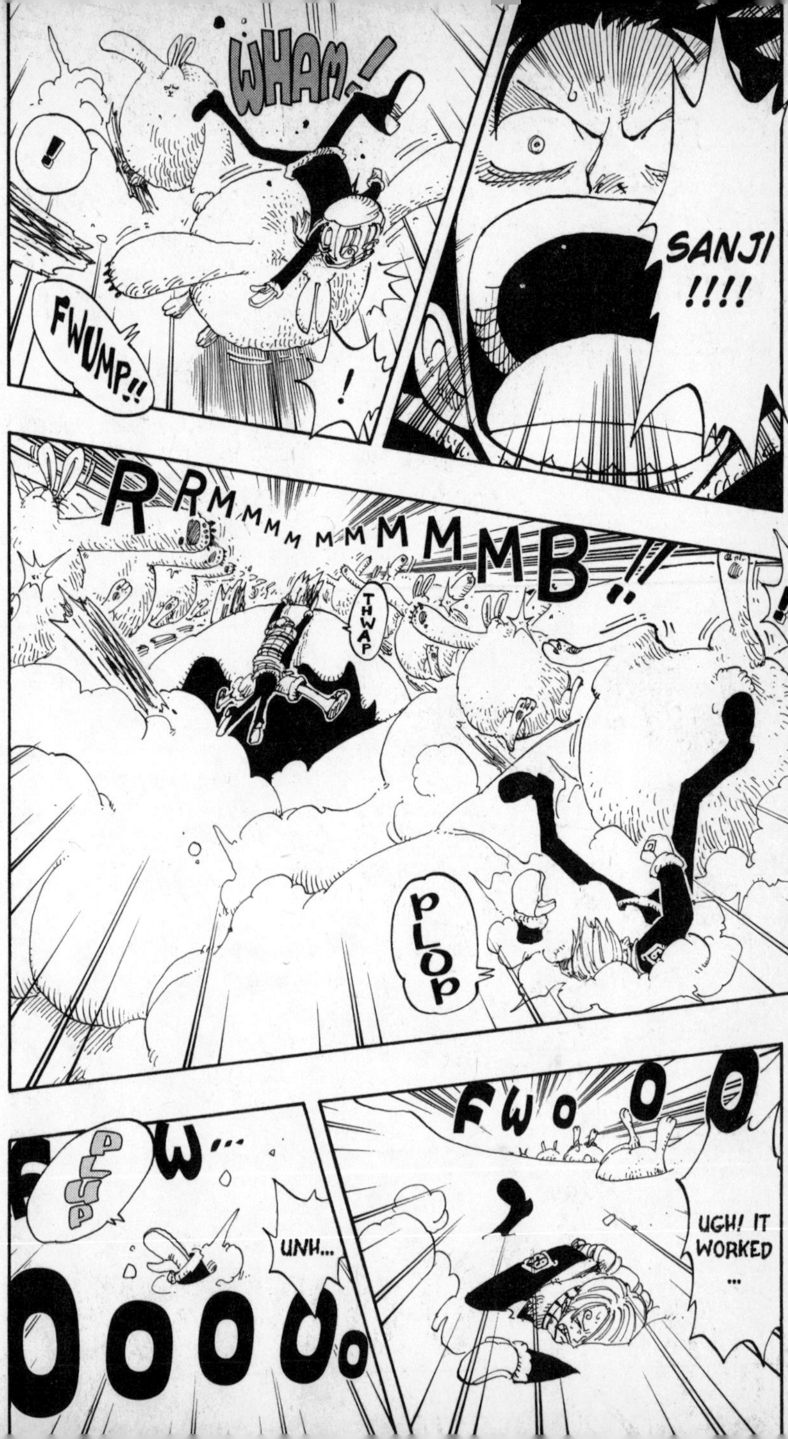
SANJI !!!!
WHAM!
!
!
FWUMP!!
RRMMMMMMMMMMMB!!
!!
THWAP
PLOP
FWOOO
UGH! IT WORKED ...
W...
OOOOo
PLUP
UNH...

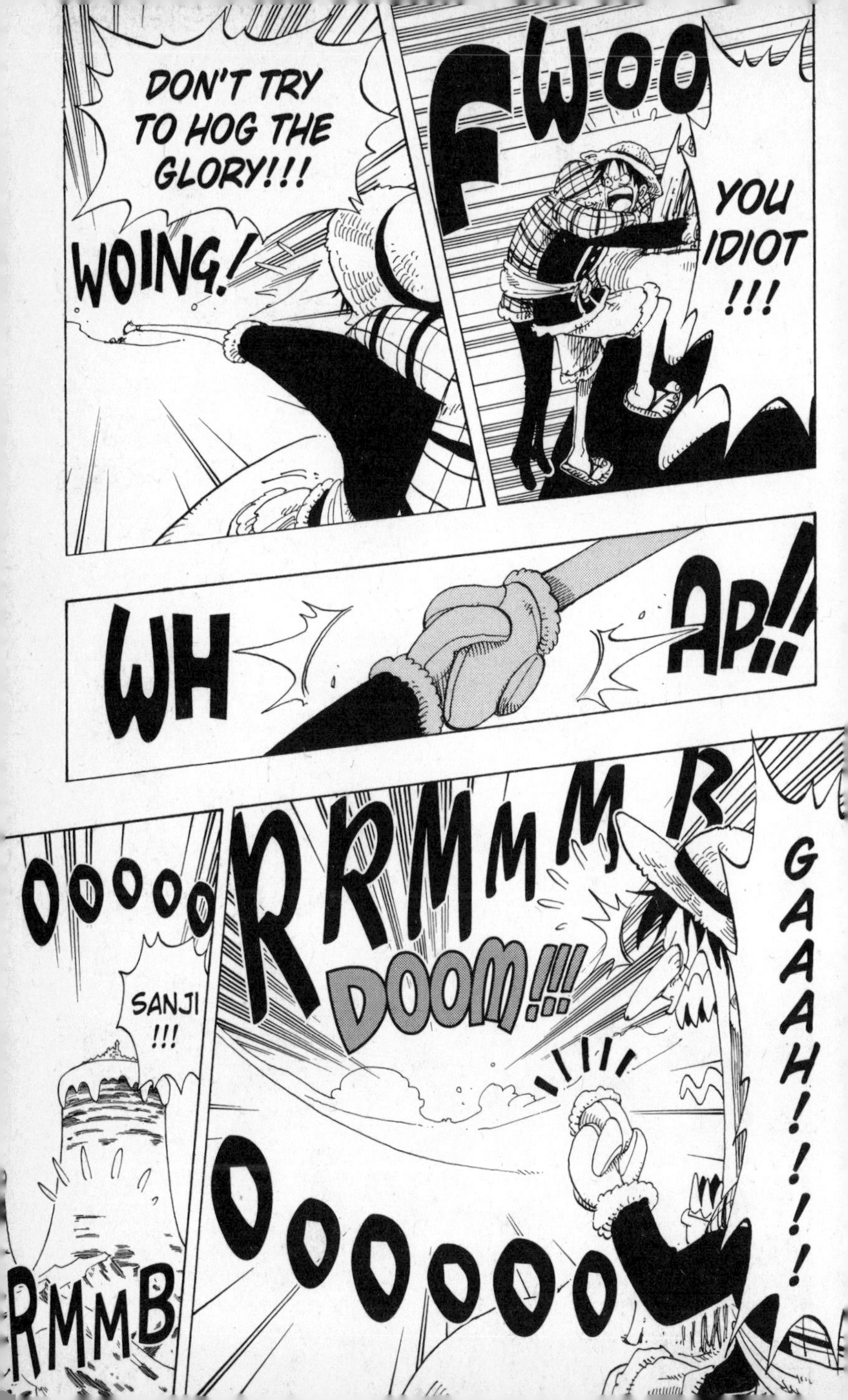
FWOO
YOU IDIOT!!!
DON'T TRY TO HOG THE GLORY!!!
WOING!
WH
AP!!
RRMMMR
DOOM!!!
GAAAH!!!!!!
OOOOOO
OOOOO
SANJI!!!
RMMB

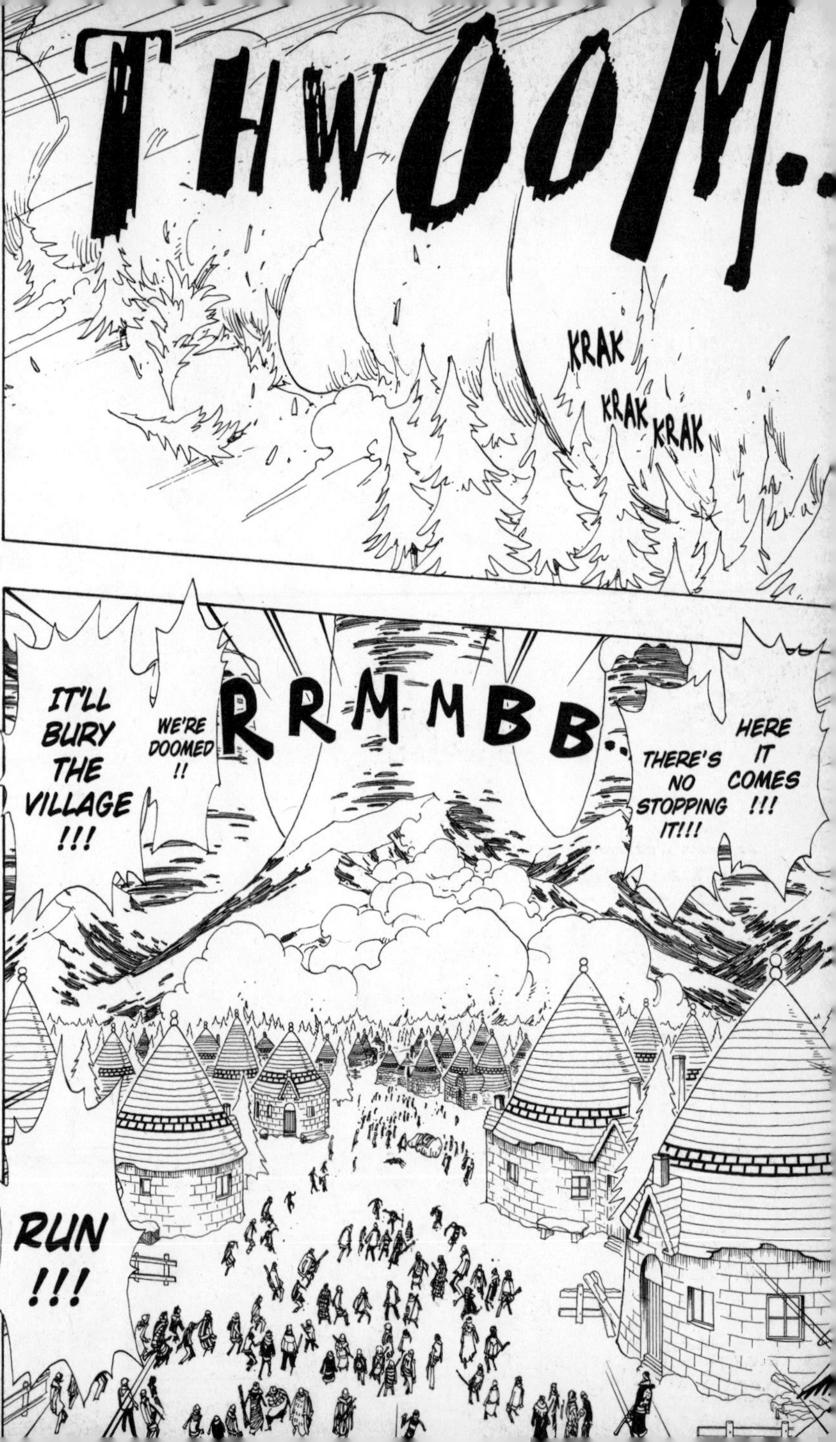
THWOOM..
KRAK
KRAK
KRAK
HERE IT COMES!!!
THERE'S NO STOPPING IT!!!
RRMMBB..
WE'RE DOOMED!!
IT'LL BURY THE VILLAGE!!!
RUN!!!

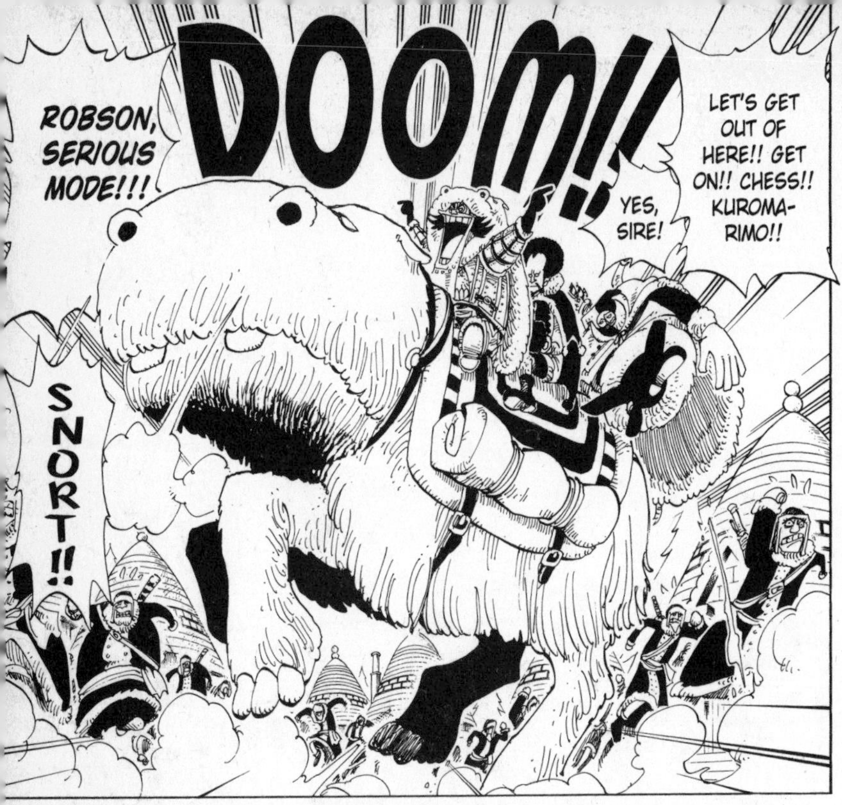
LET'S GET OUT OF HERE!! GET ON!! CHESS!! KUROMA-RIMO!!
YES, SIRE!
DOOM!!
ROBSON, SERIOUS MODE!!!
SNORT!!

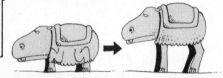

WHITE WALKIE (OR FURRY HIPPO) --FACTOID--

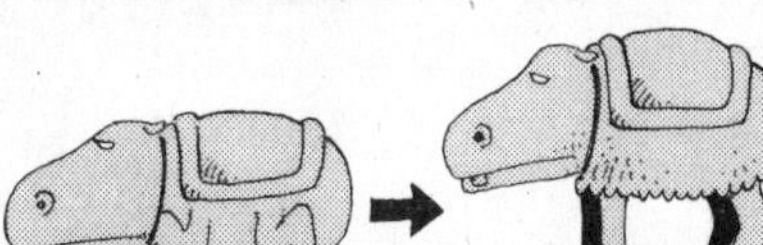

THIS ANIMAL IS WELL ADAPTED TO LIFE IN SNOWY MOUNTAINS. IN FACT, IT'S OVERADAPTED. IT'S SO COMFORTABLE IN THE SNOW THAT IT DOESN'T EVEN BOTHER TO STAND UP MOST OF THE TIME. OMNIVOROUS.

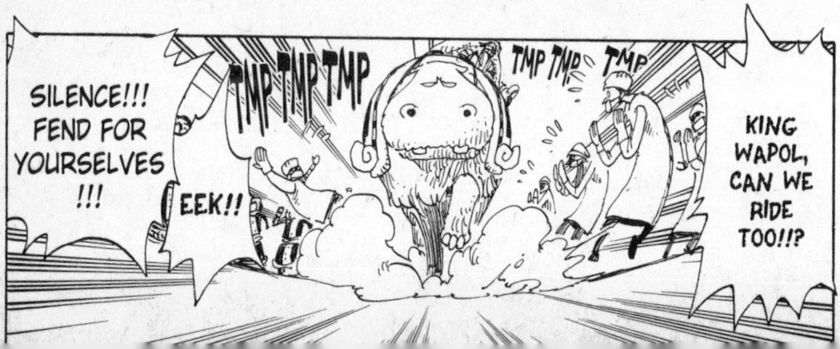
KING WAPOL, CAN WE RIDE TOO!!?
TMP TMP TMP
TMP TMP TMP
EEK!!
SILENCE!!! FEND FOR YOURSELVES!!!

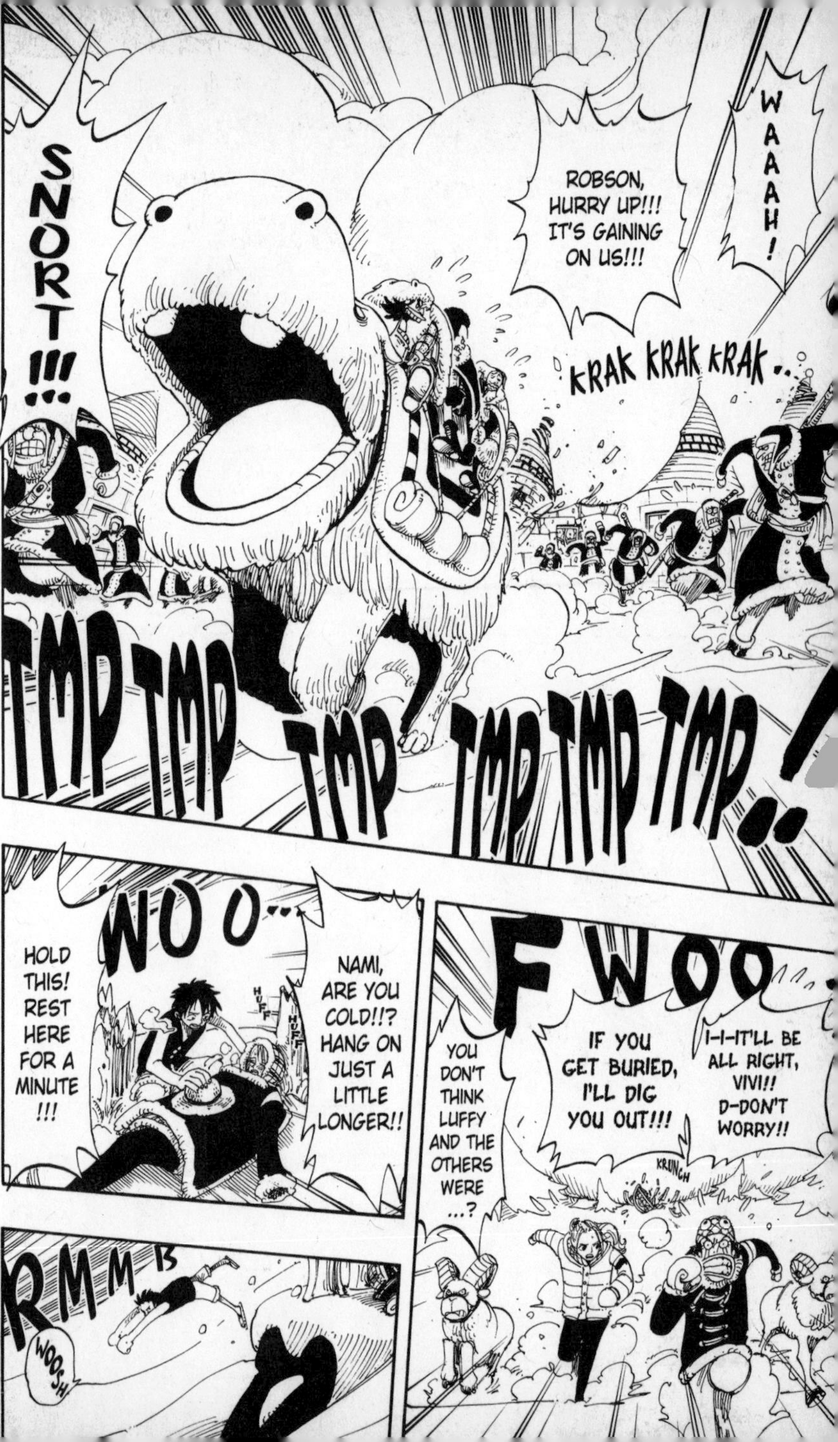
WAAAH!
ROBSON, HURRY UP!!! IT'S GAINING ON US!!!
SNORT!!!
KRAK KRAK KRAK...
TMP TMP TMP TMP TMP TMP..!
FWOO
I-I-IT'LL BE ALL RIGHT, VIVI!! D-DON'T WORRY!!
IF YOU GET BURIED, I'LL DIG YOU OUT!!!
YOU DON'T THINK LUFFY AND THE OTHERS WERE ...?
KRUNCH
WOO...
NAMI, ARE YOU COLD!!? HANG ON JUST A LITTLE LONGER!!
HUFF
HUFF
HOLD THIS! REST HERE FOR A MINUTE!!!
RMMB
WOOSH

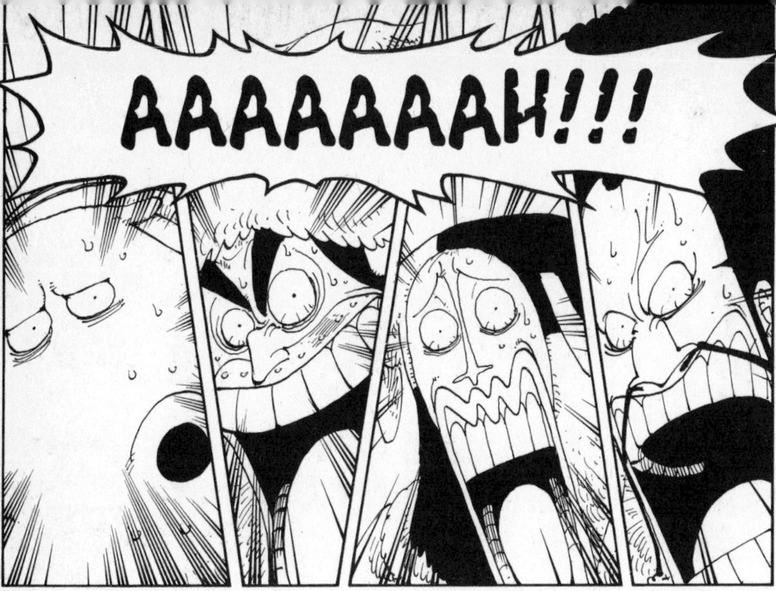
AAAAAAAH!!!

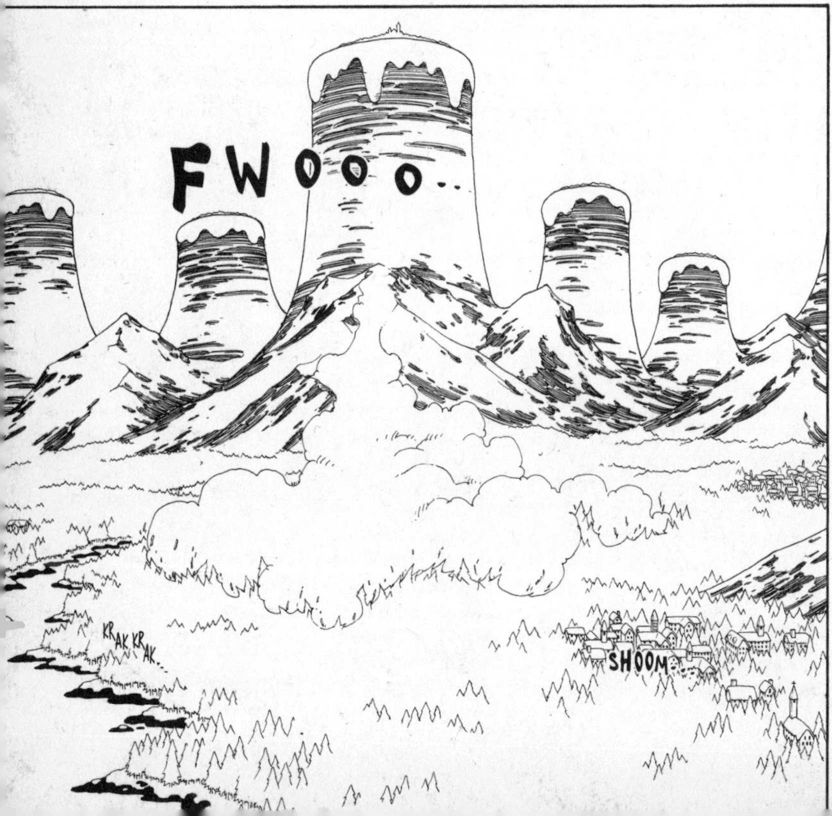
FWOOO...
SHOOM
KRAK KRAK...

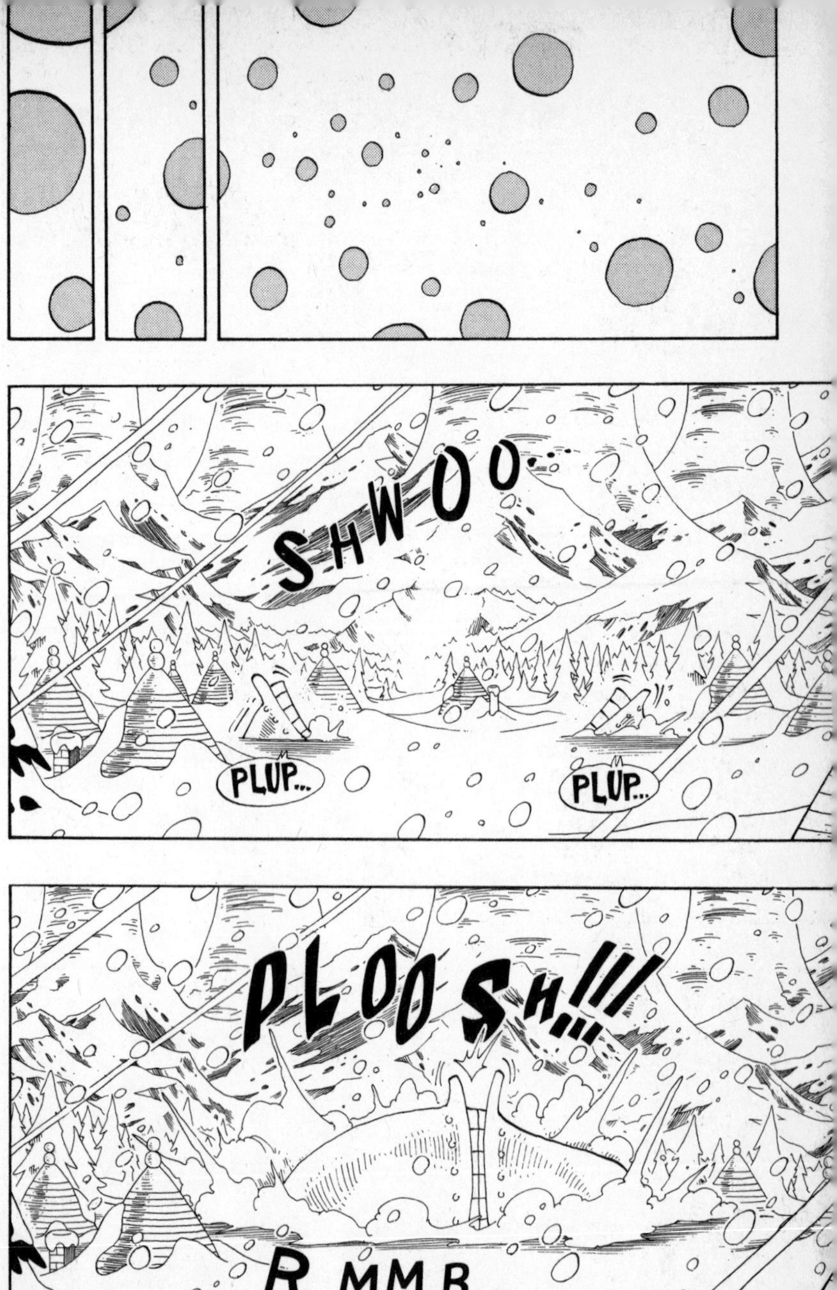
SHWOO
PLUP...
PLUP...
PLOOSH!!!
RMMB....

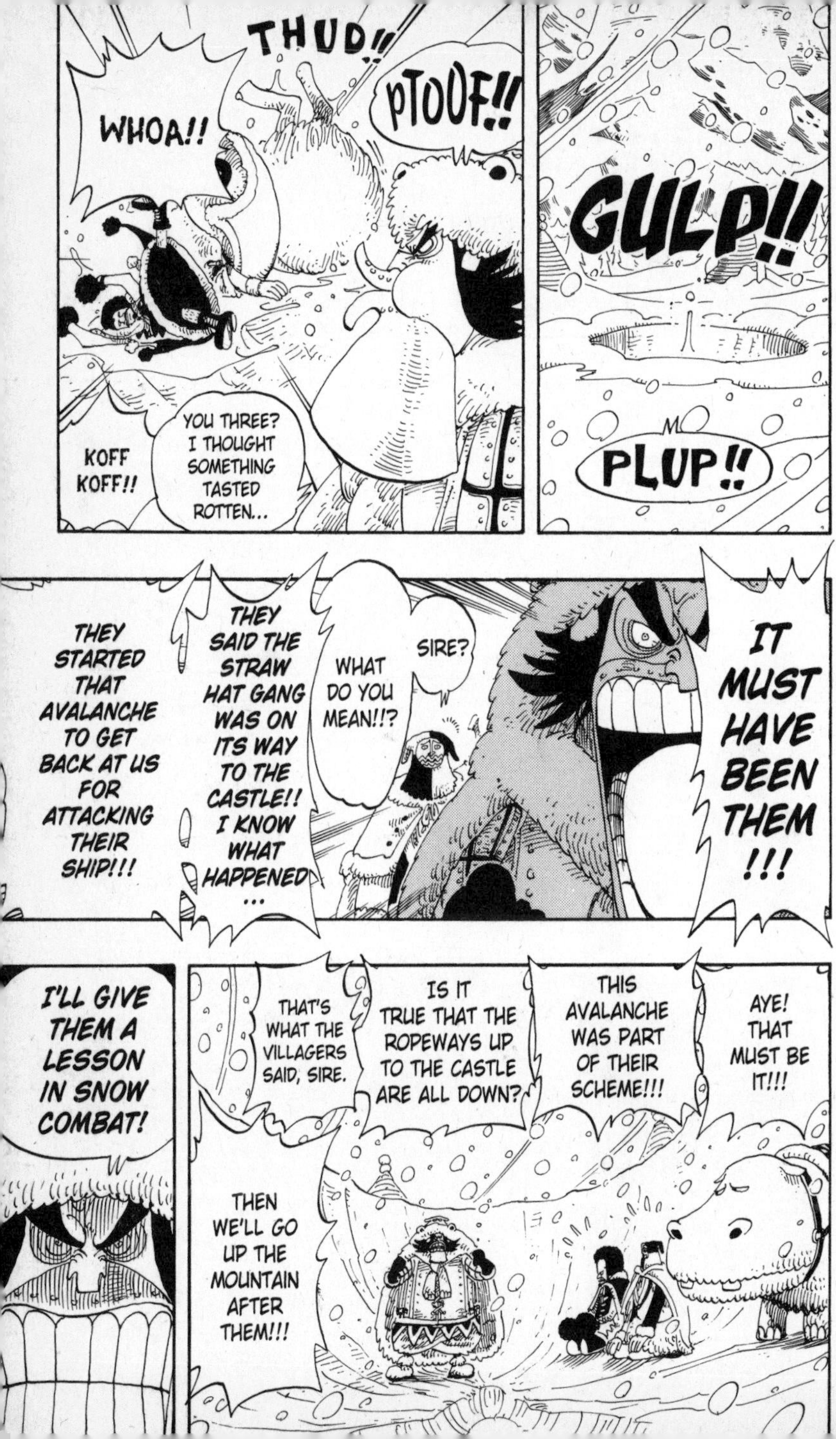
GULP!!
PLUP!!
PTOOF!!
THUD!!
WHOA!!
YOU THREE? I THOUGHT SOMETHING TASTED ROTTEN...
KOFF KOFF!!
IT MUST HAVE BEEN THEM!!!
SIRE?
WHAT DO YOU MEAN!!?
THEY SAID THE STRAW HAT GANG WAS ON ITS WAY TO THE CASTLE!! I KNOW WHAT HAPPENED...
THEY STARTED THAT AVALANCHE TO GET BACK AT US FOR ATTACKING THEIR SHIP!!!
AYE! THAT MUST BE IT!!!
THIS AVALANCHE WAS PART OF THEIR SCHEME!!!
IS IT TRUE THAT THE ROPEWAYS UP TO THE CASTLE ARE ALL DOWN?
THAT'S WHAT THE VILLAGERS SAID, SIRE.
THEN WE'LL GO UP THE MOUNTAIN AFTER THEM!!!
I'LL GIVE THEM A LESSON IN SNOW COMBAT!

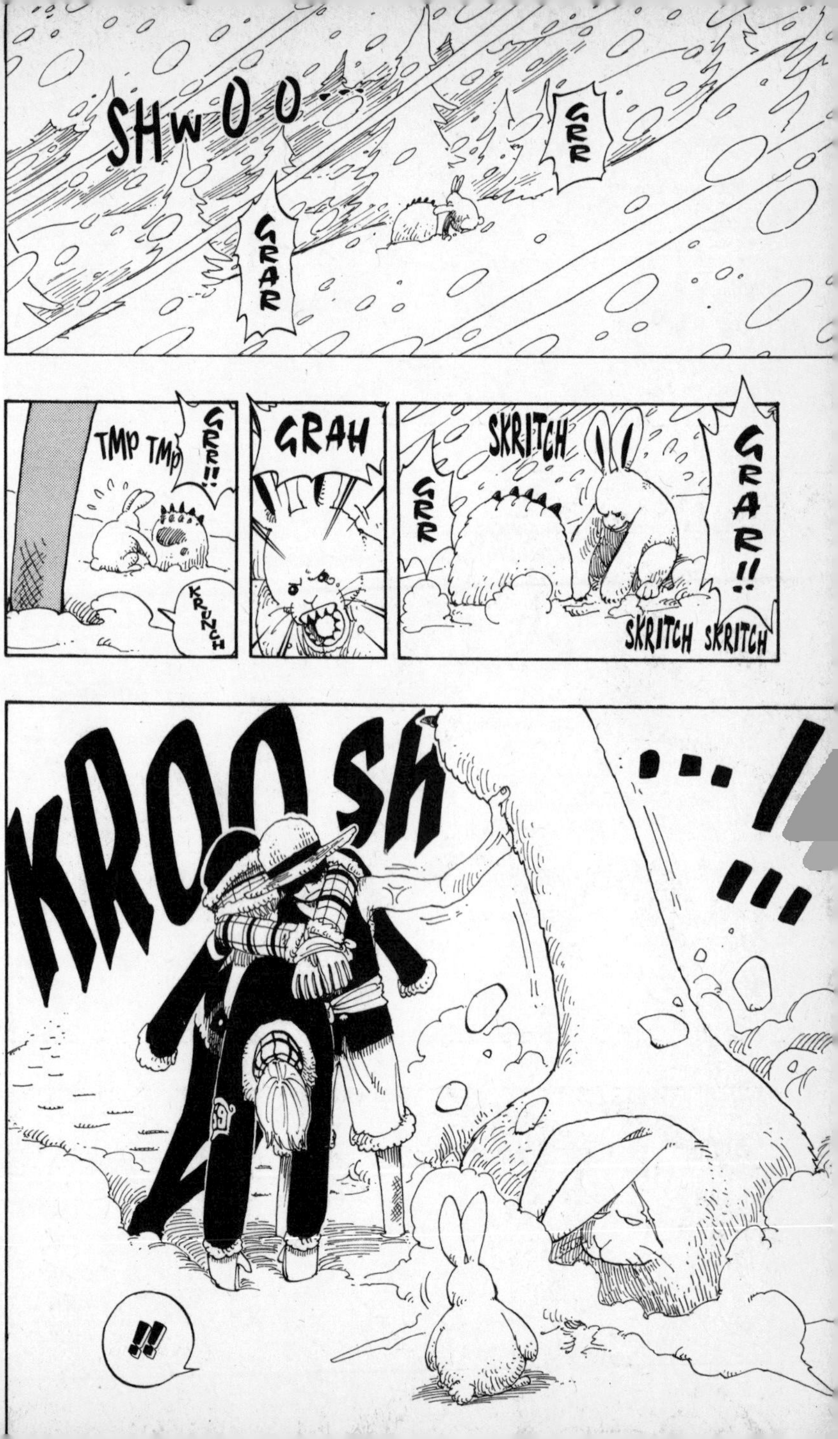
GRR
SHWOO...
GRAR
GRAR!!
SKRITCH
GRR
SKRITCH SKRITCH
GRAH
GRR!!
TMP TMP
KRUNCH
...!!!
KROOSH
!!

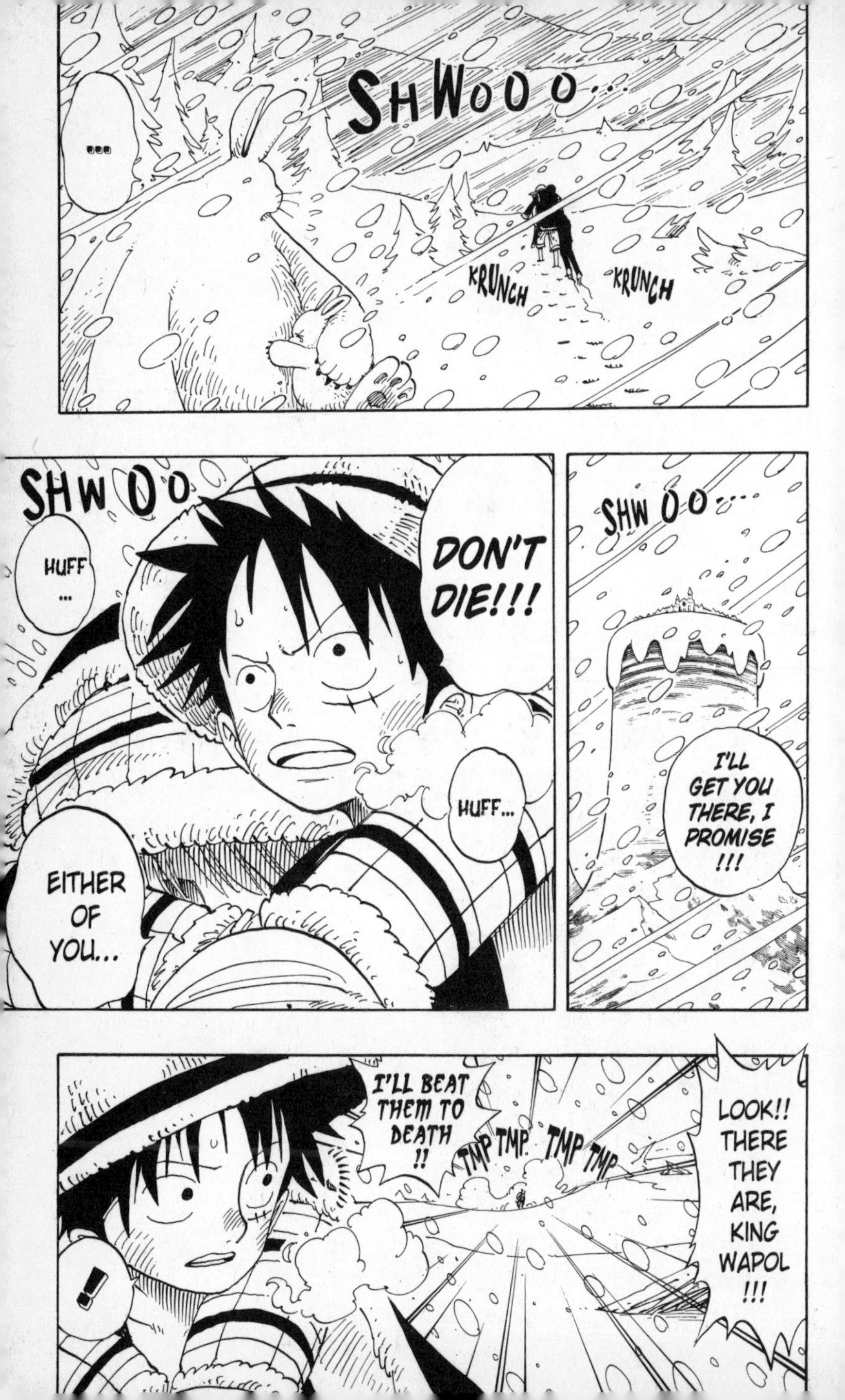
SHWOOO...
...
KRUNCH
KRUNCH
SHWOO...
I'LL GET YOU THERE, I PROMISE!!!
DON'T DIE!!!
SHWOO
HUFF...
HUFF...
EITHER OF YOU...
LOOK!! THERE THEY ARE, KING WAPOL!!!
TMP TMP TMP TMP
I'LL BEAT THEM TO DEATH!!
!

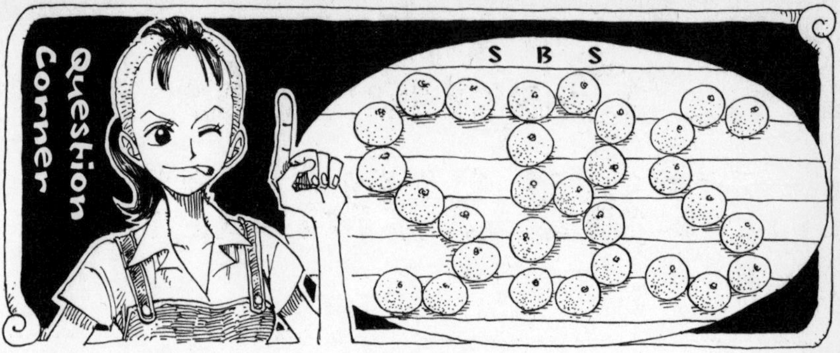
Question Corner
S B S

Reader: Mr. Oda and fellow readers!!!
I'd like today's Question Corner to be started by the hugely popular 20 Doctors!
20 Doctors, go ahead!

M.D.s: "Let's begin the surgery."

Oda: Surgery!!? All right, then I'll respectfully begin the Question Corner.

Q: Oda, old pal! This very day, today of all days, please begin the Question Corner without worries! Are you ready!? Huh? Oda, buddy? Oda, my pal! Oh! There you are, Oda…a…a…atchoo!
Let the Question Corner begin!! Agh!
I accidentally said it!!

A: What a phony sneeze!!

Q: Mr. Oda!! Good afternoon! Are the names Kuina and Tashigi derived from bird names? Please tell me.
--A peruser of picture books about birds

A: I guess so. And the cool thing is that they're both flightless birds. But not all flightless birds can't fly. In the cartoon *The Wonderful Adventures of Nils* that I watched as a kid, there was a big duck that could fly. By the way, Nojiko is also the name of a bird.

Chapter 138:
THE SUMMIT

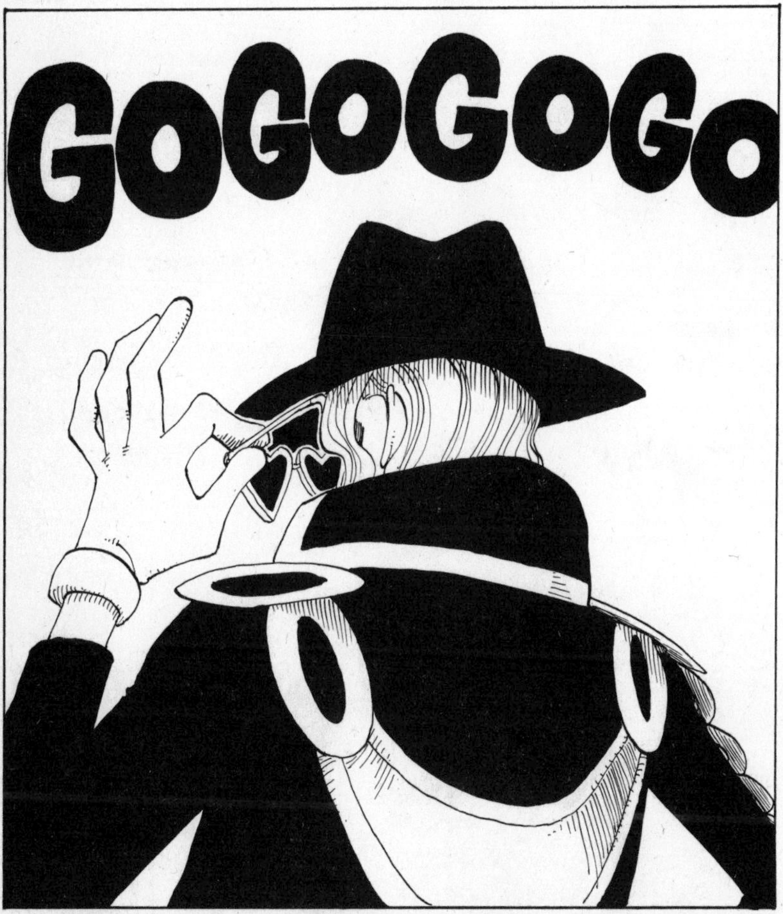
GOGOGOGO

DJANGO'S DANCE PARADISE, VOL. 10: "A DISGUISE IS NECESSARY--FIVE SECONDS UNTIL DJANGO'S TRUE FACE IS REVEALED"

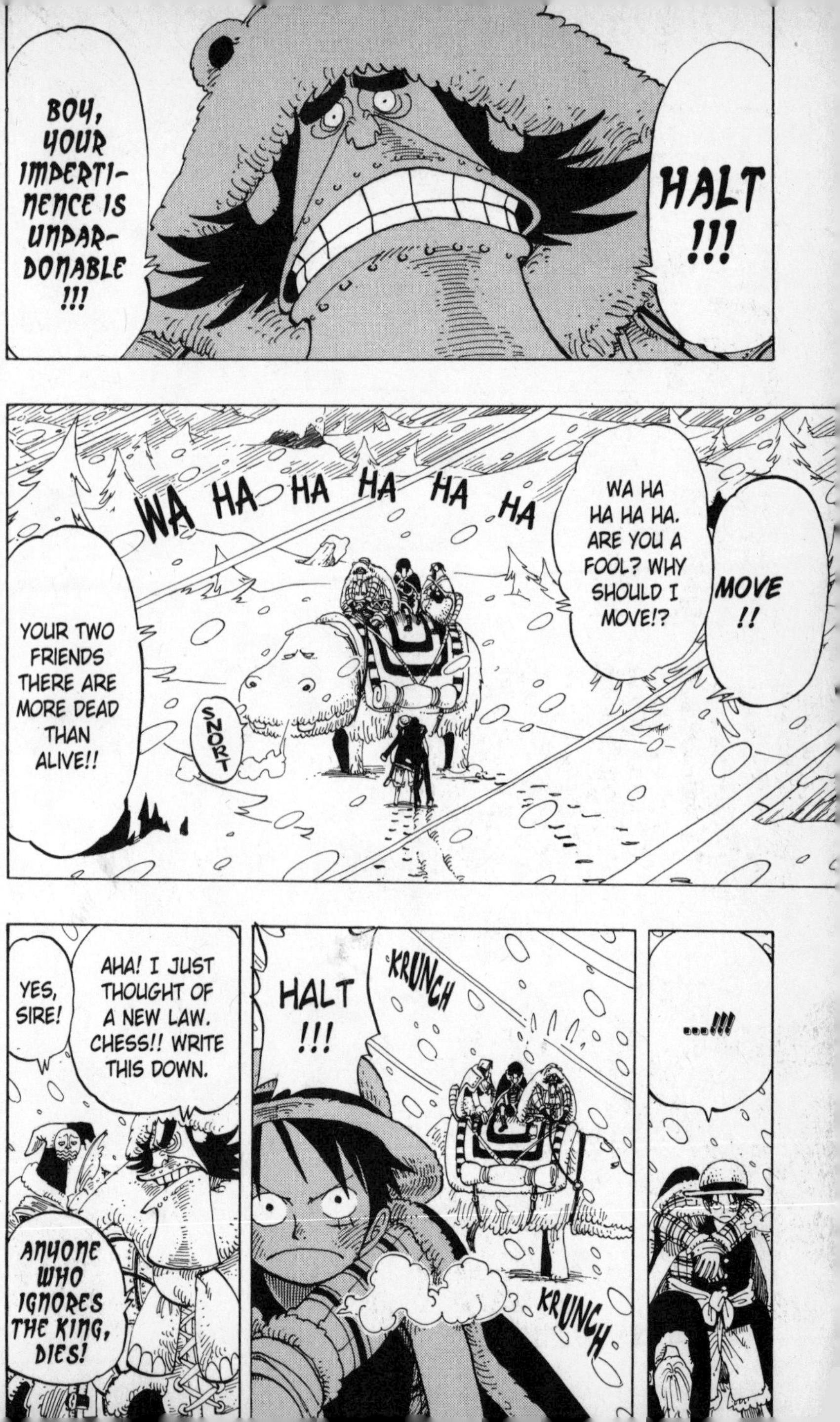
HALT !!!
BOY, YOUR IMPERTINENCE IS UNPARDONABLE !!!
MOVE !!
WA HA HA HA HA. ARE YOU A FOOL? WHY SHOULD I MOVE!?
WA HA HA HA HA HA
SNORT
YOUR TWO FRIENDS THERE ARE MORE DEAD THAN ALIVE!!
...!!!
KRUNCH
HALT !!!
KRUNCH
AHA! I JUST THOUGHT OF A NEW LAW. CHESS!! WRITE THIS DOWN.
YES, SIRE!
ANYONE WHO IGNORES THE KING, DIES!

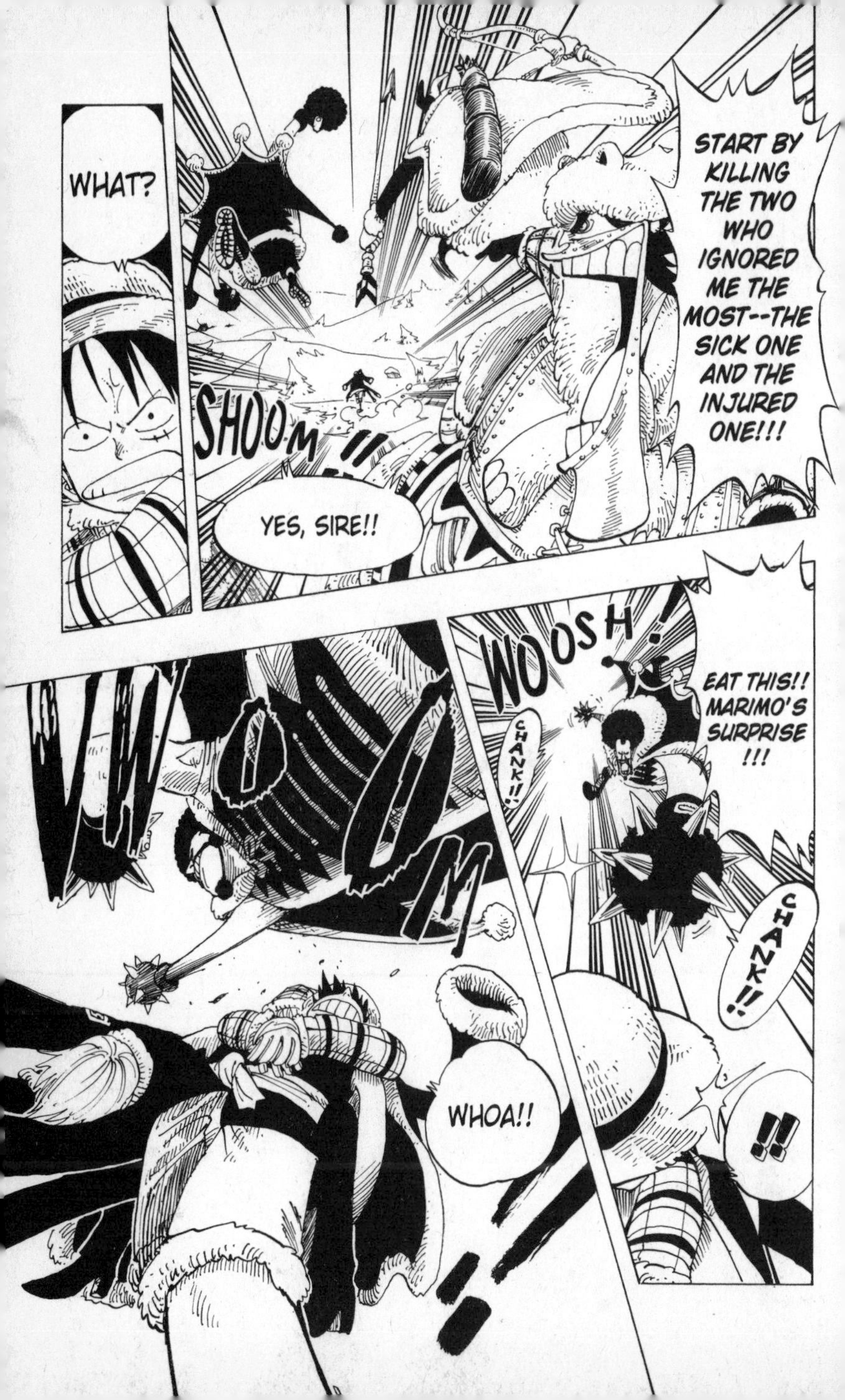
START BY KILLING THE TWO WHO IGNORED ME THE MOST--THE SICK ONE AND THE INJURED ONE!!!
SHOOM!!
YES, SIRE!!
WHAT?
WOOSH!
EAT THIS!! MARIMO'S SURPRISE!!!
CHANK!!
CHANK!!
!!
WHOA!!

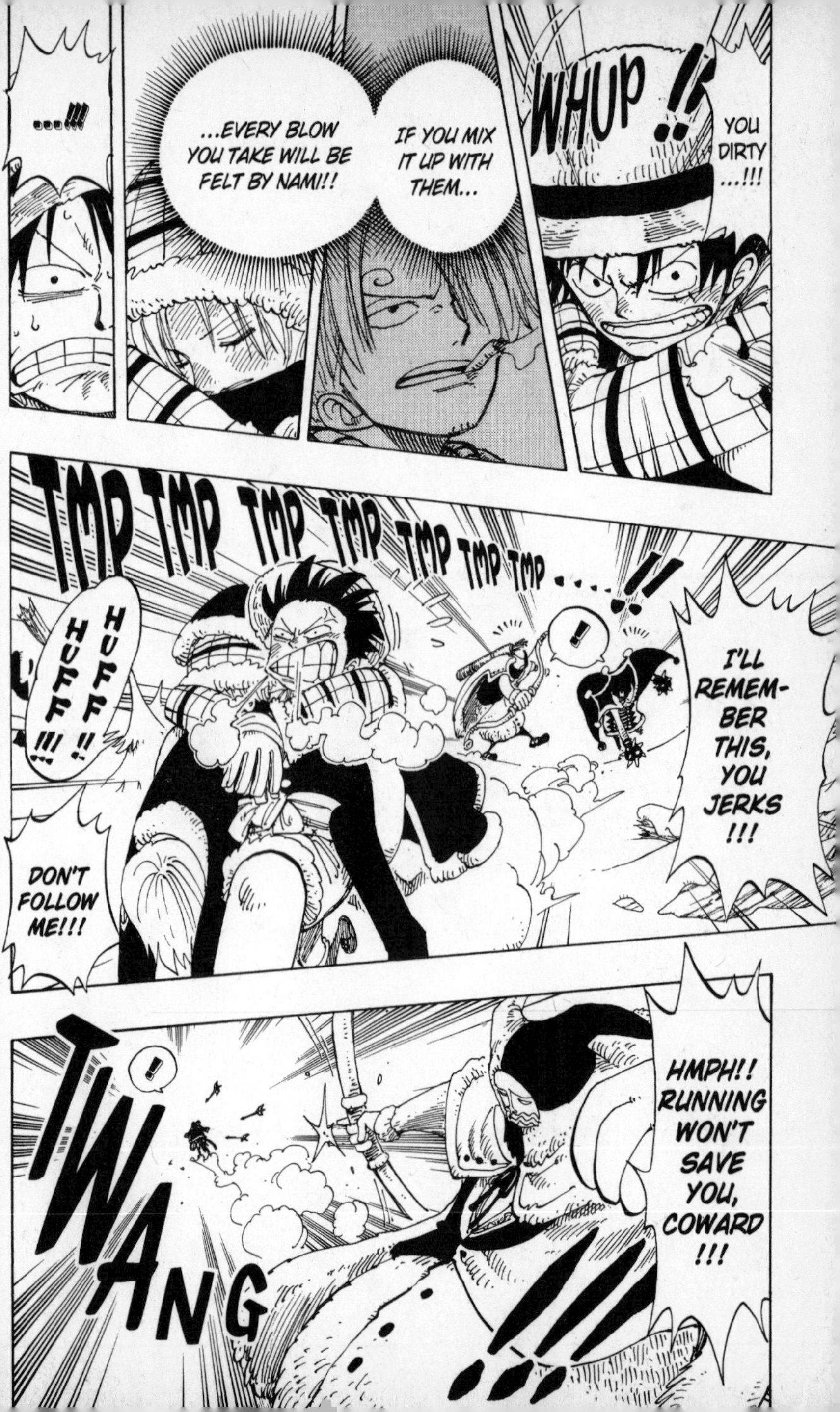
WHUP!!
YOU DIRTY ...!!!
IF YOU MIX IT UP WITH THEM...
...EVERY BLOW YOU TAKE WILL BE FELT BY NAMI!!
...!!!
I'LL REMEMBER THIS, YOU JERKS!!!
TMP TMP TMP TMP TMP TMP TMP TMP ....!!
!
HUFF HUFF!! HUFF!!!
DON'T FOLLOW ME!!!
HMPH!! RUNNING WON'T SAVE YOU, COWARD!!!
!
TWANG

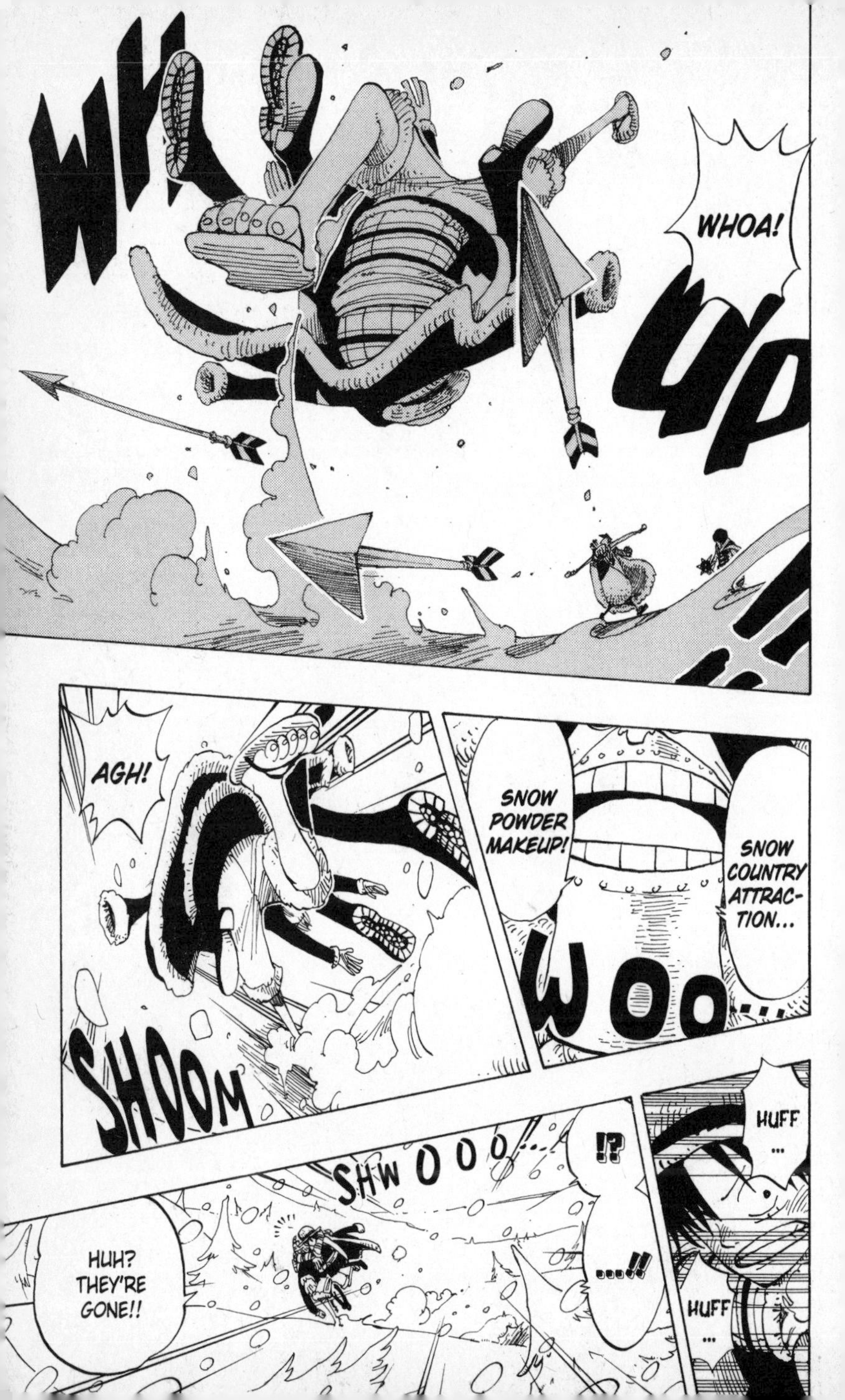

WHOA!
SNOW COUNTRY ATTRACTION...
SNOW POWDER MAKEUP!
WOO...
AGH!
SHOOM
HUFF ...
HUFF ...
!?
...!!
SHWOOO...
HUH? THEY'RE GONE!!

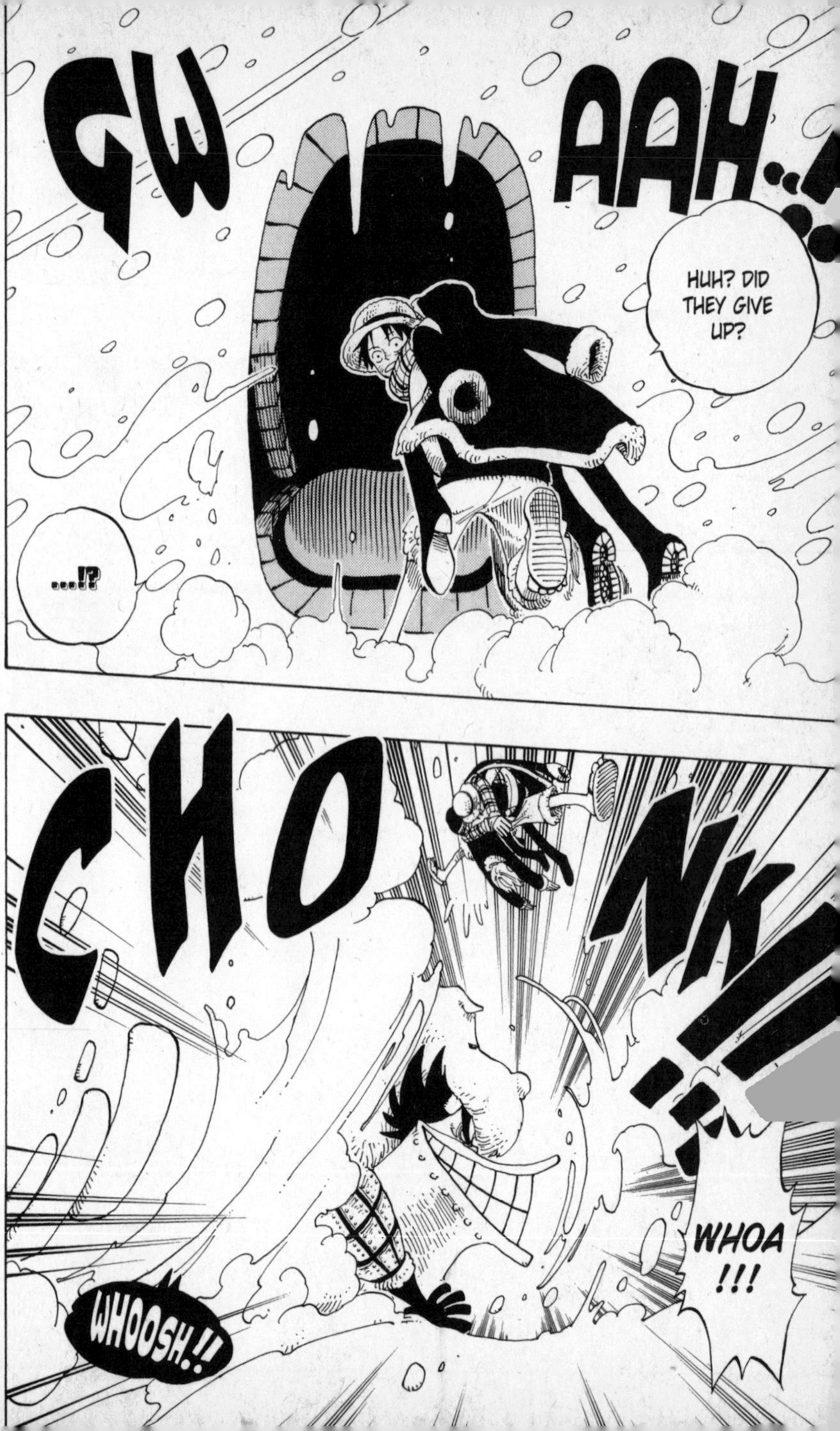
GWAAH..!!
HUH? DID THEY GIVE UP?
...!?
CHONK!!!
WHOA !!!
WHOOSH!!

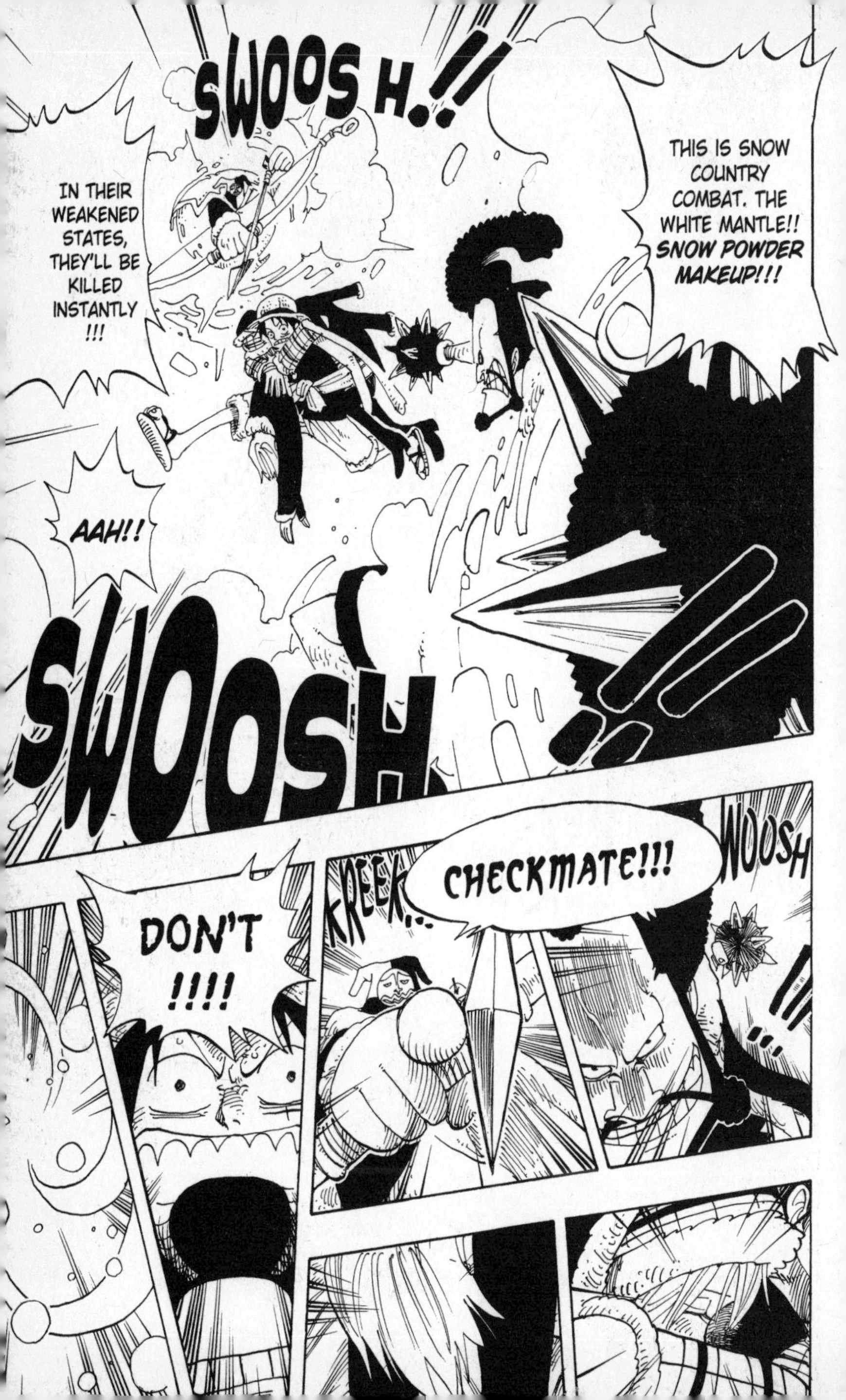
THIS IS SNOW COUNTRY COMBAT. THE WHITE MANTLE!! SNOW POWDER MAKEUP!!!
SWOOS H..!!
IN THEIR WEAKENED STATES, THEY'LL BE KILLED INSTANTLY !!!
AAH!!
SWOOSH
WOOSH
CHECKMATE!!!
KREEK...
DON'T !!!!

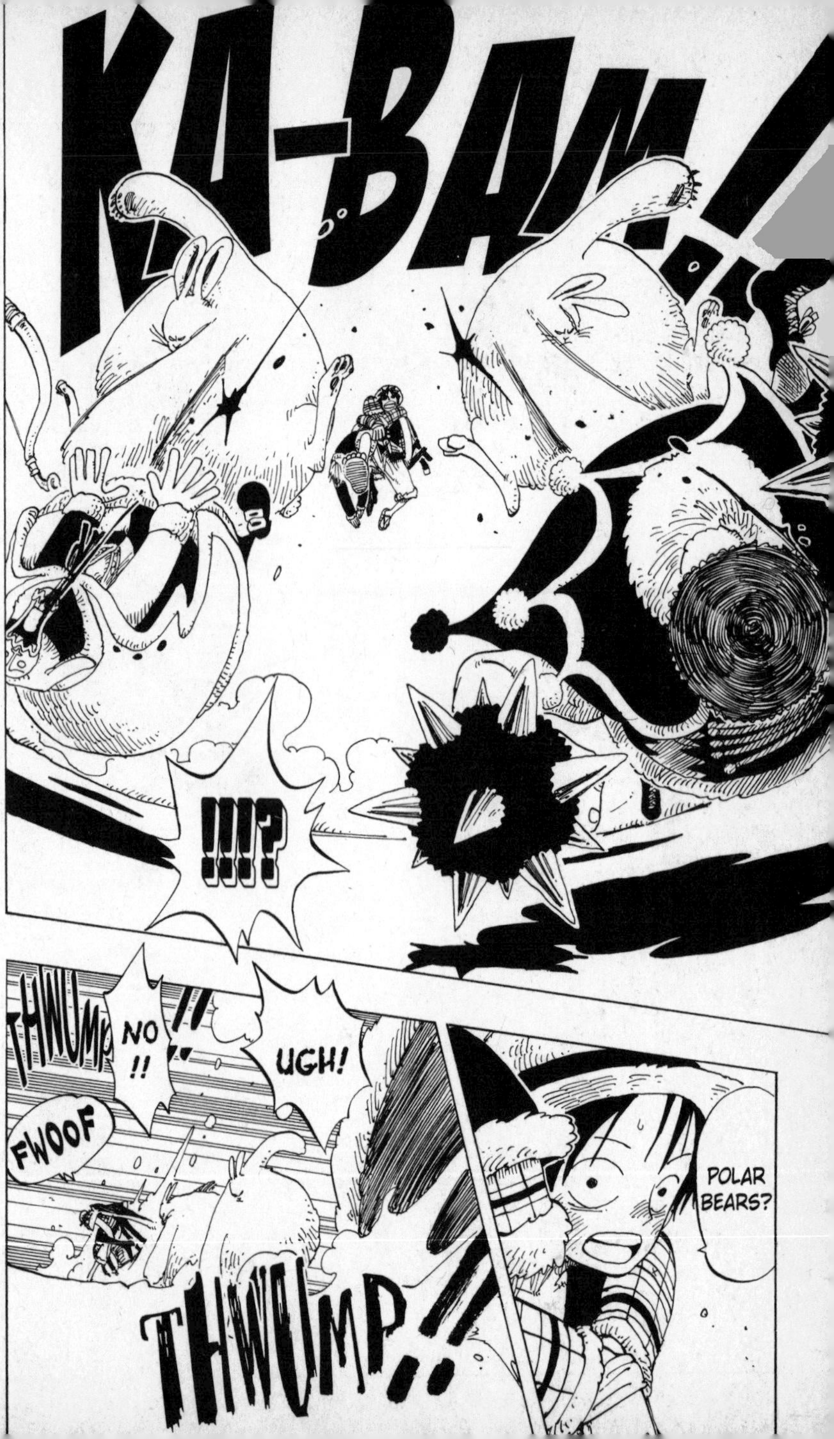
KA-BAM!!
!!!?
POLAR BEARS?
UGH!
NO !!
THWUMP
FWOOF
THWUMP!!

READ THIS WAY

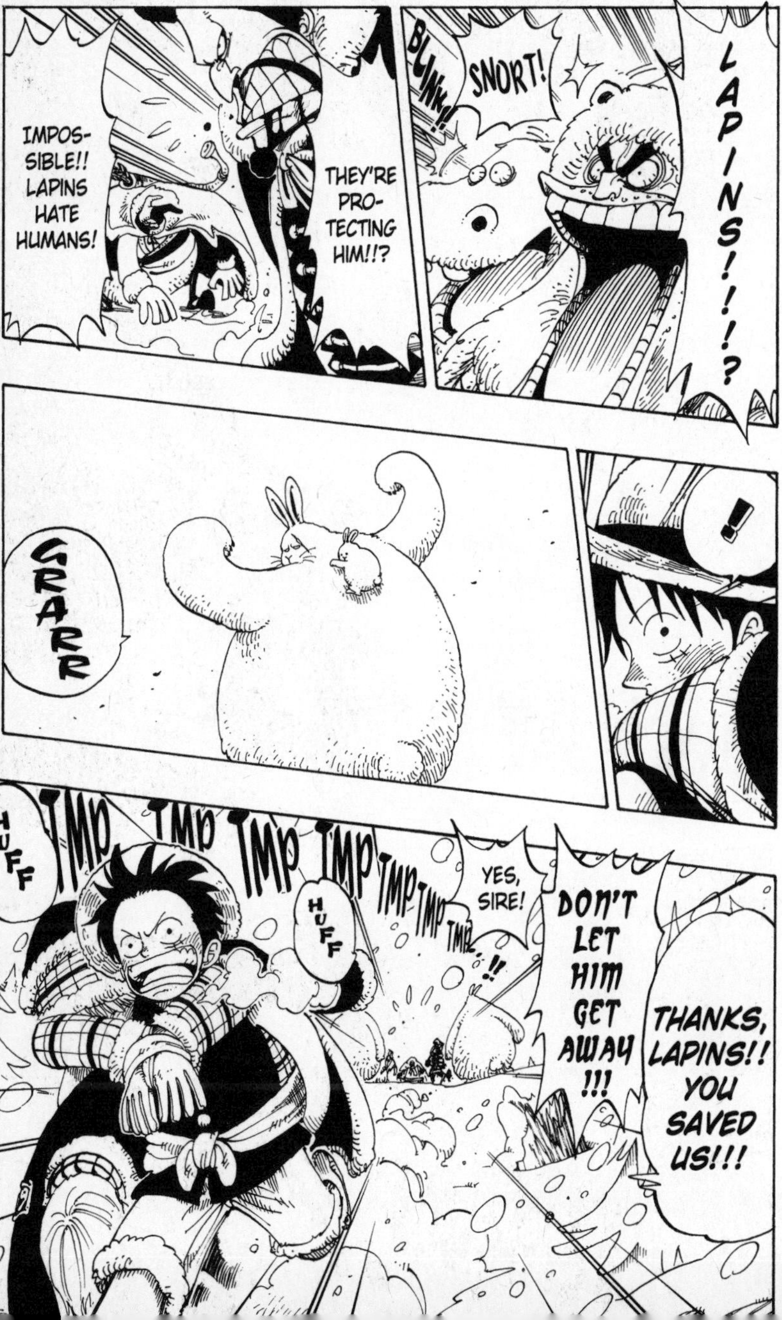
LAPINS!!!?
SNORT!
BLINK!!
THEY'RE PRO-TECTING HIM!!?
IMPOS-SIBLE!! LAPINS HATE HUMANS!
!
GRARR
THANKS, LAPINS!! YOU SAVED US!!!
DON'T LET HIM GET AWAY!!!
YES, SIRE!
TMP TMP TMP TMP TMP TMP TMP!!
HUFF
HUFF

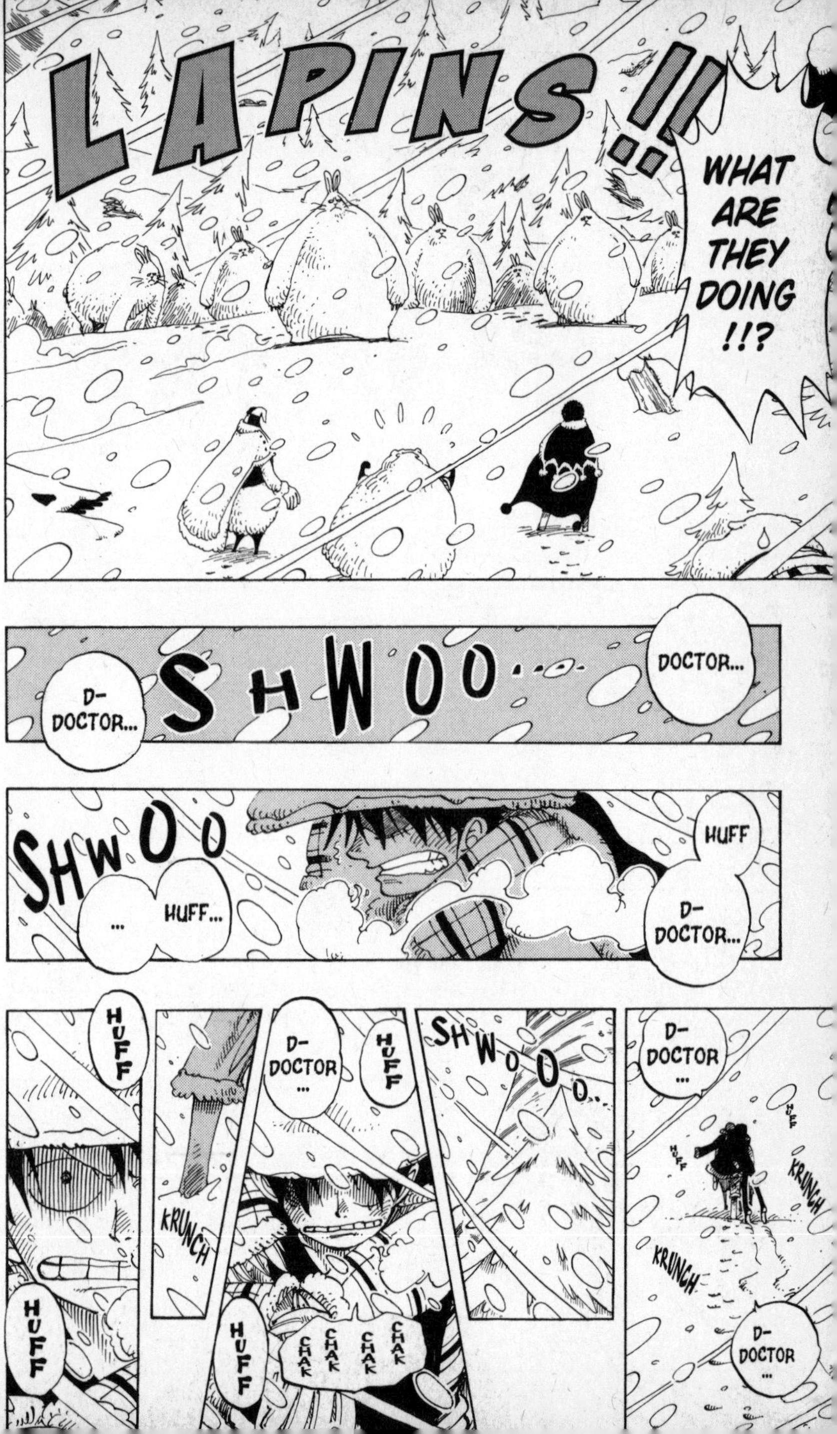
LAPINS!!
WHAT ARE THEY DOING !!?
DOCTOR...
SHWOO...
D-DOCTOR...
HUFF
D-DOCTOR...
SHWOO
HUFF...
...
D-DOCTOR ...
HUFF
HUFF
KRUNCH
KRUNCH
D-DOCTOR ...
SHWOOO...
HUFF
D-DOCTOR ...
HUFF
CHAK CHAK CHAK CHAK
KRUNCH
HUFF
HUFF

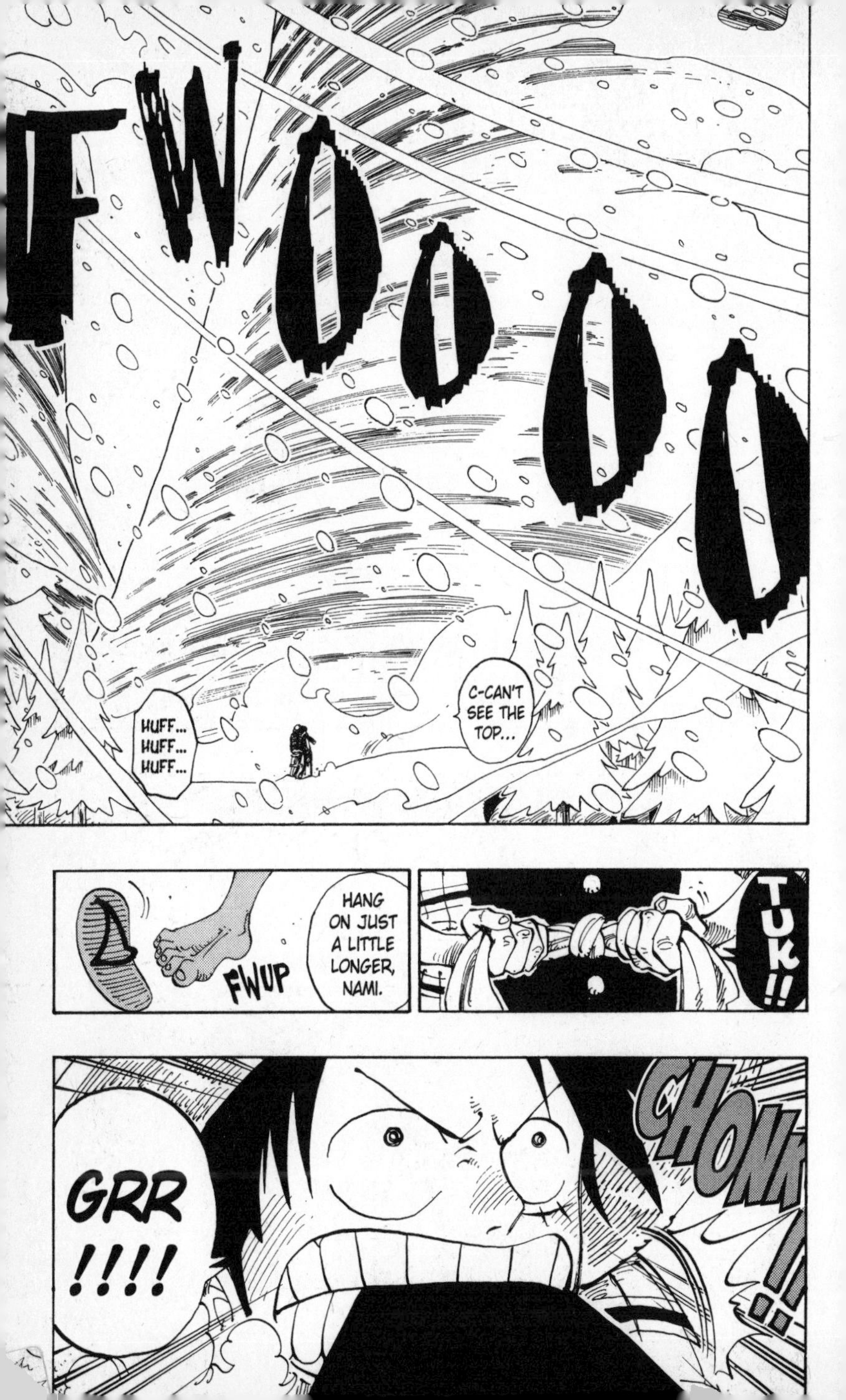
FWOOOO
C-CAN'T SEE THE TOP...
HUFF... HUFF... HUFF...
TUK!!
HANG ON JUST A LITTLE LONGER, NAMI.
FWUP
CHONK!!
GRR !!!!

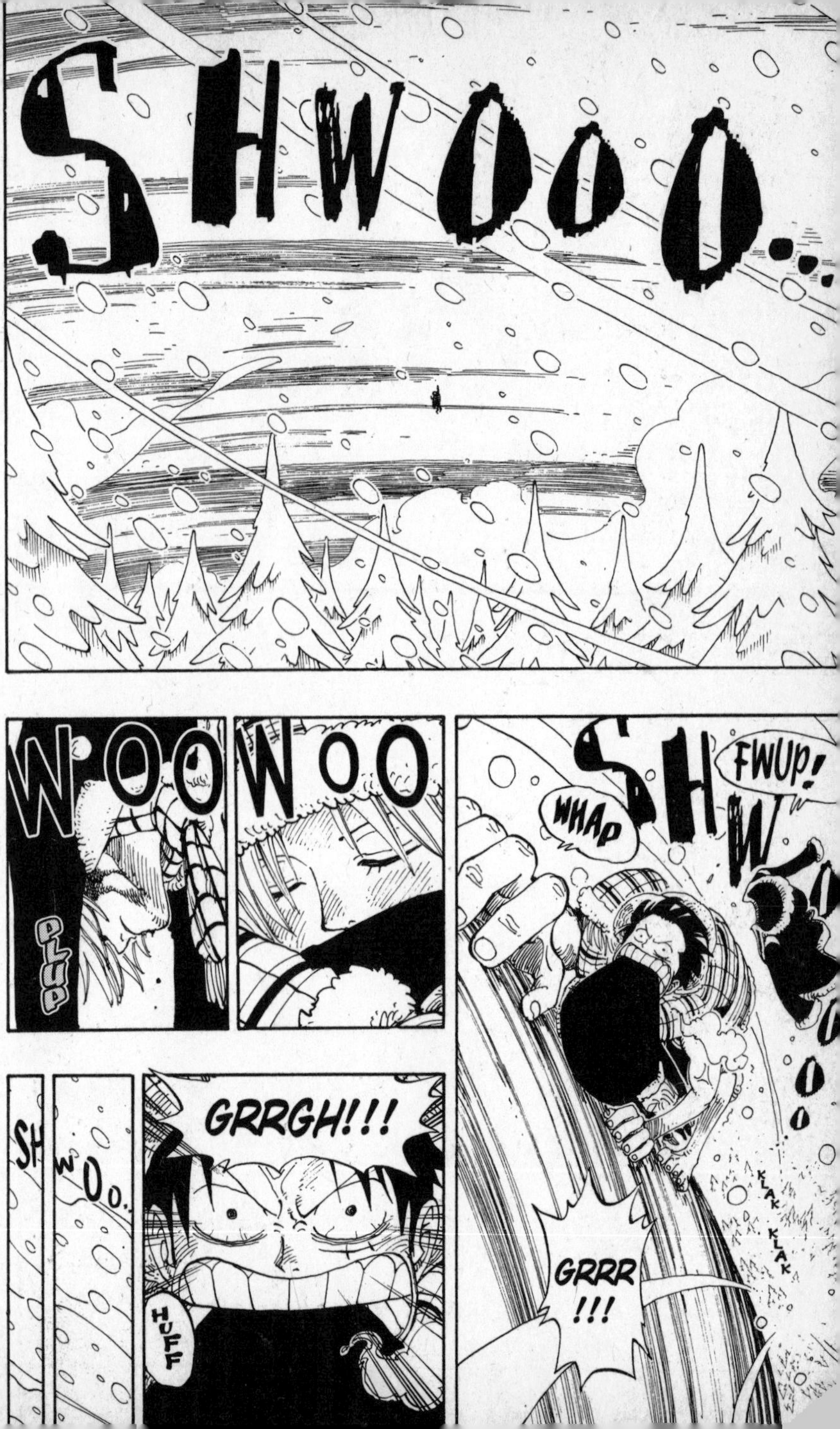
SHWOOO...
SHWOOOO
WHAP
FWUP!
KLAK KLAK
GRRR!!!
WOO
WOO
PLUP
GRRGH!!!
HUFF
SHWOO..

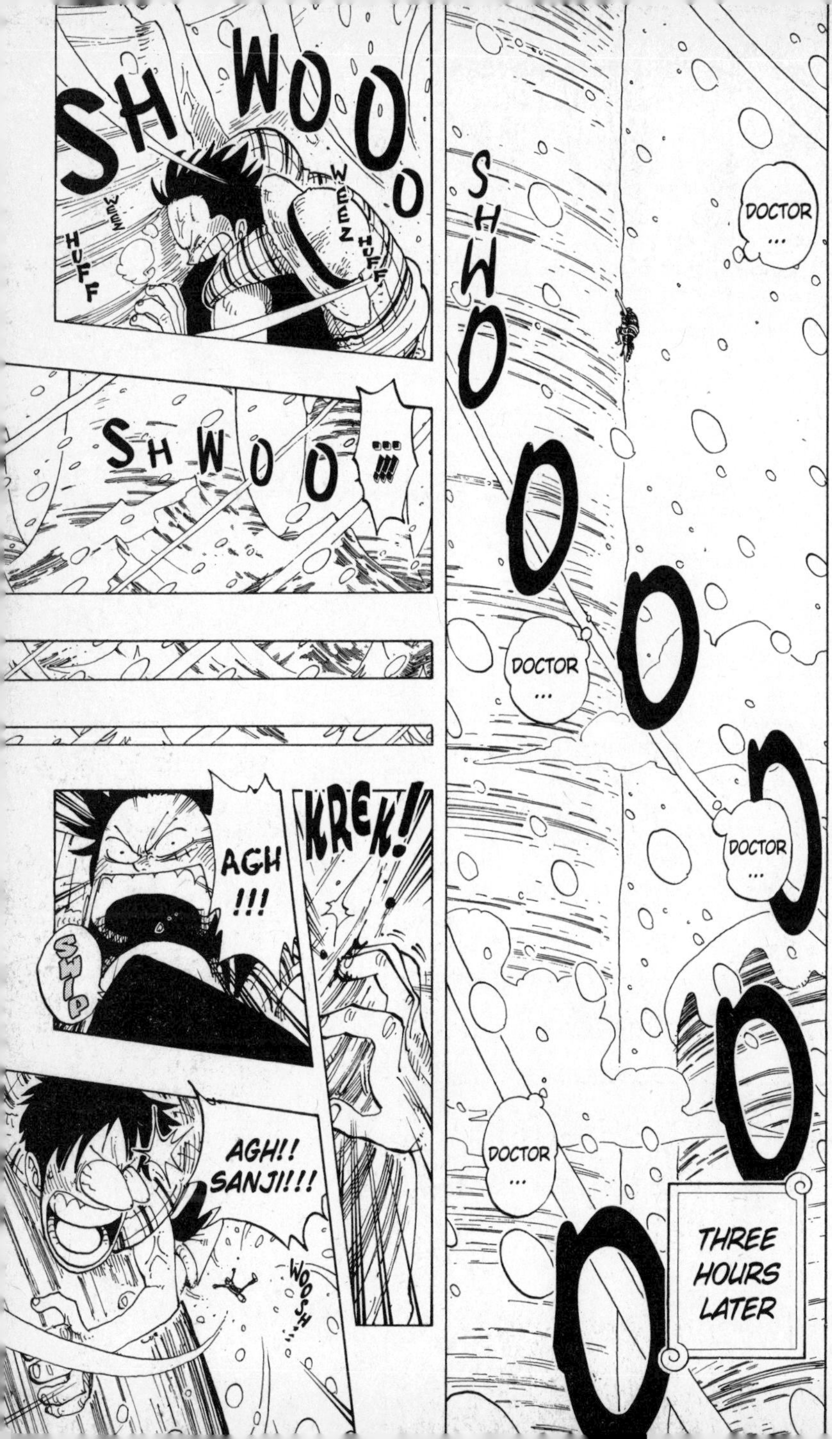

DOCTOR ...
SHWOOOOOOO
DOCTOR ...
DOCTOR ...
DOCTOR ...
THREE HOURS LATER
SHWOOOO
WEEZ HUFF
WEEZ HUFF
SHWOO...!!!
KREK!
AGH !!!
SHIP
AGH!! SANJI!!!
WOOSH...

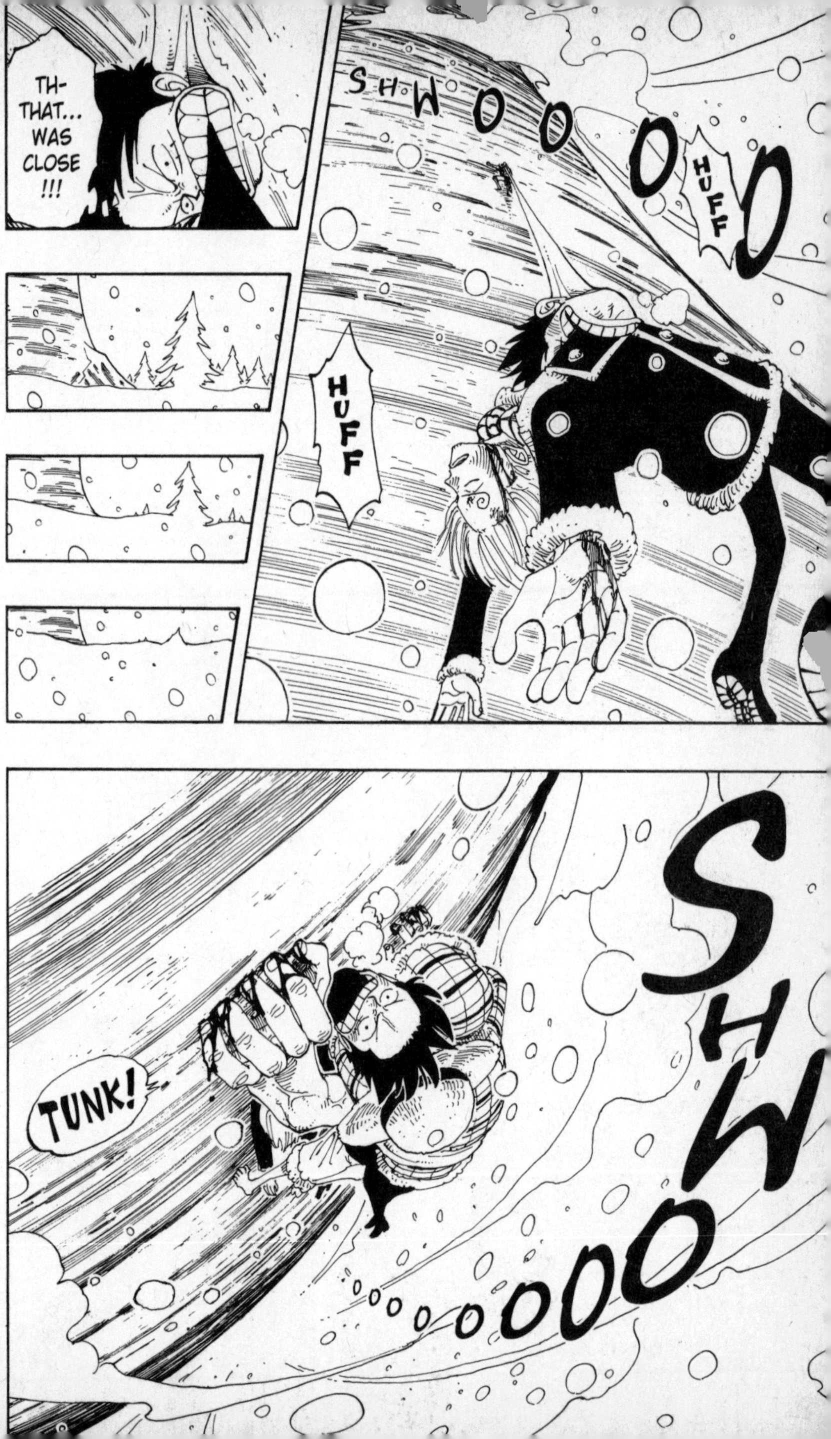
SHWOOOOO
HUFF
HUFF
TH-THAT... WAS CLOSE!!!
SHWOOOOOOOOOO
TUNK!

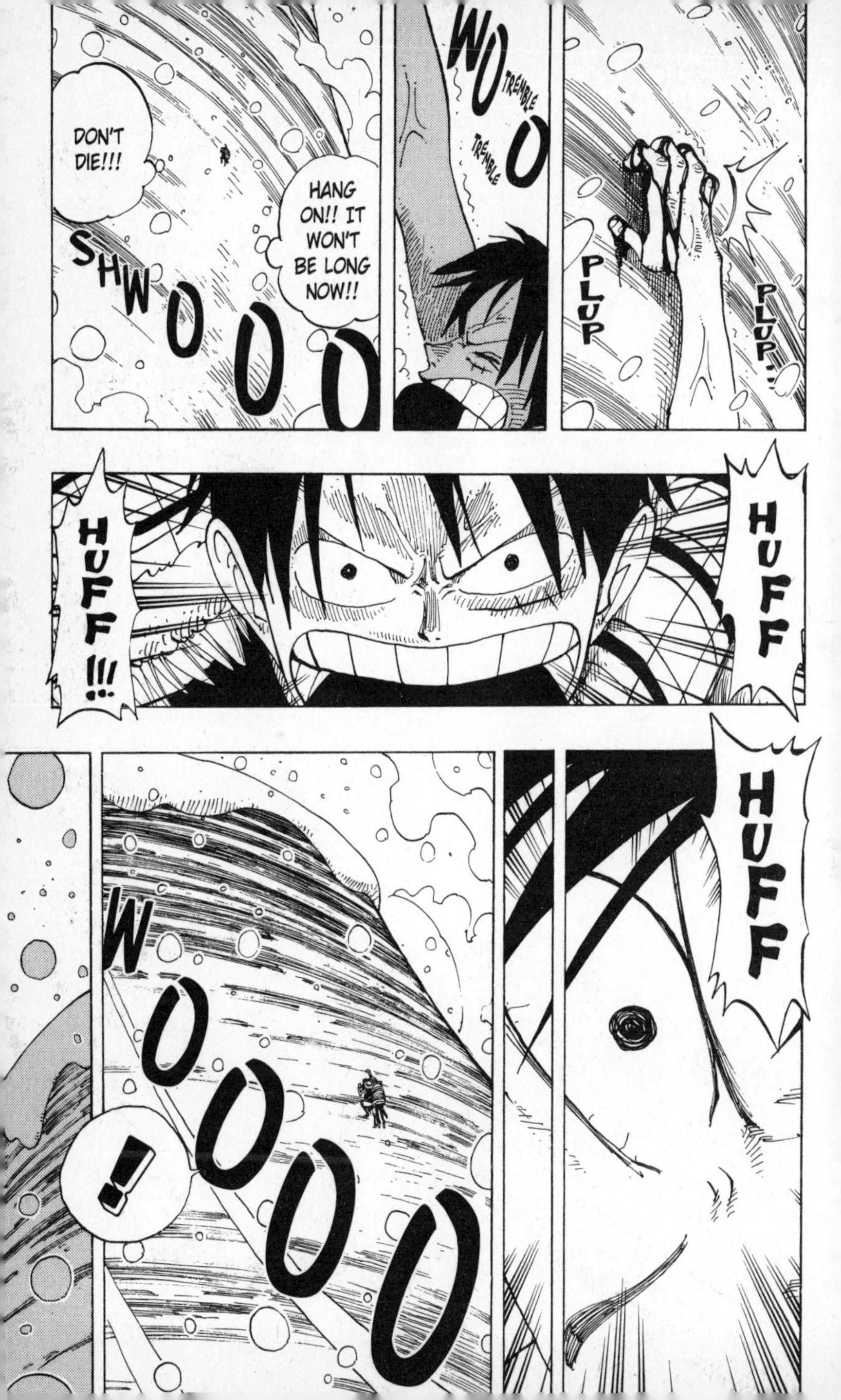
PLUP...
PLUP
WOOO
TREMBLE
TREMBLE
DON'T DIE!!!
HANG ON!! IT WON'T BE LONG NOW!!
SHWOOOO
HUFF
HUFF!!!
HUFF
WOOOOOO
!

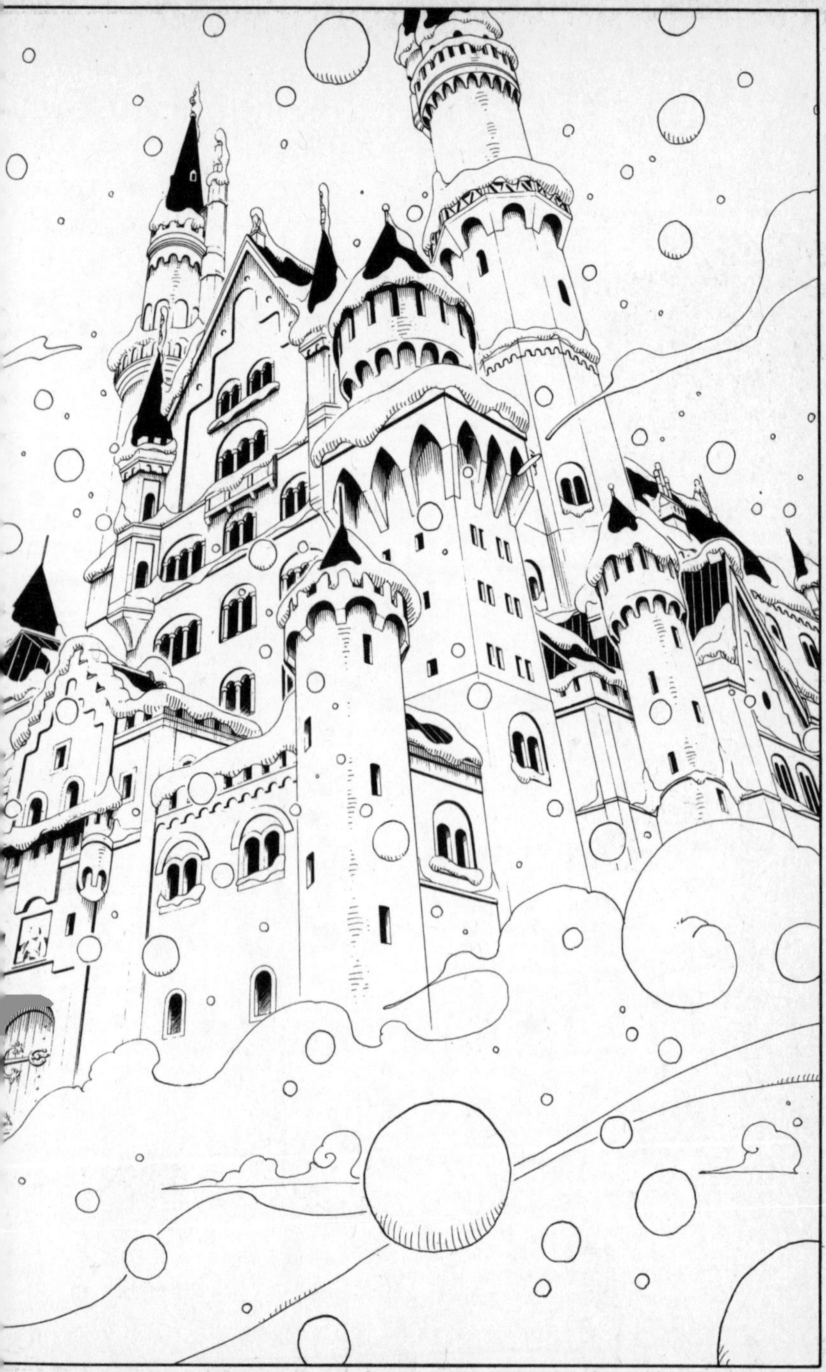

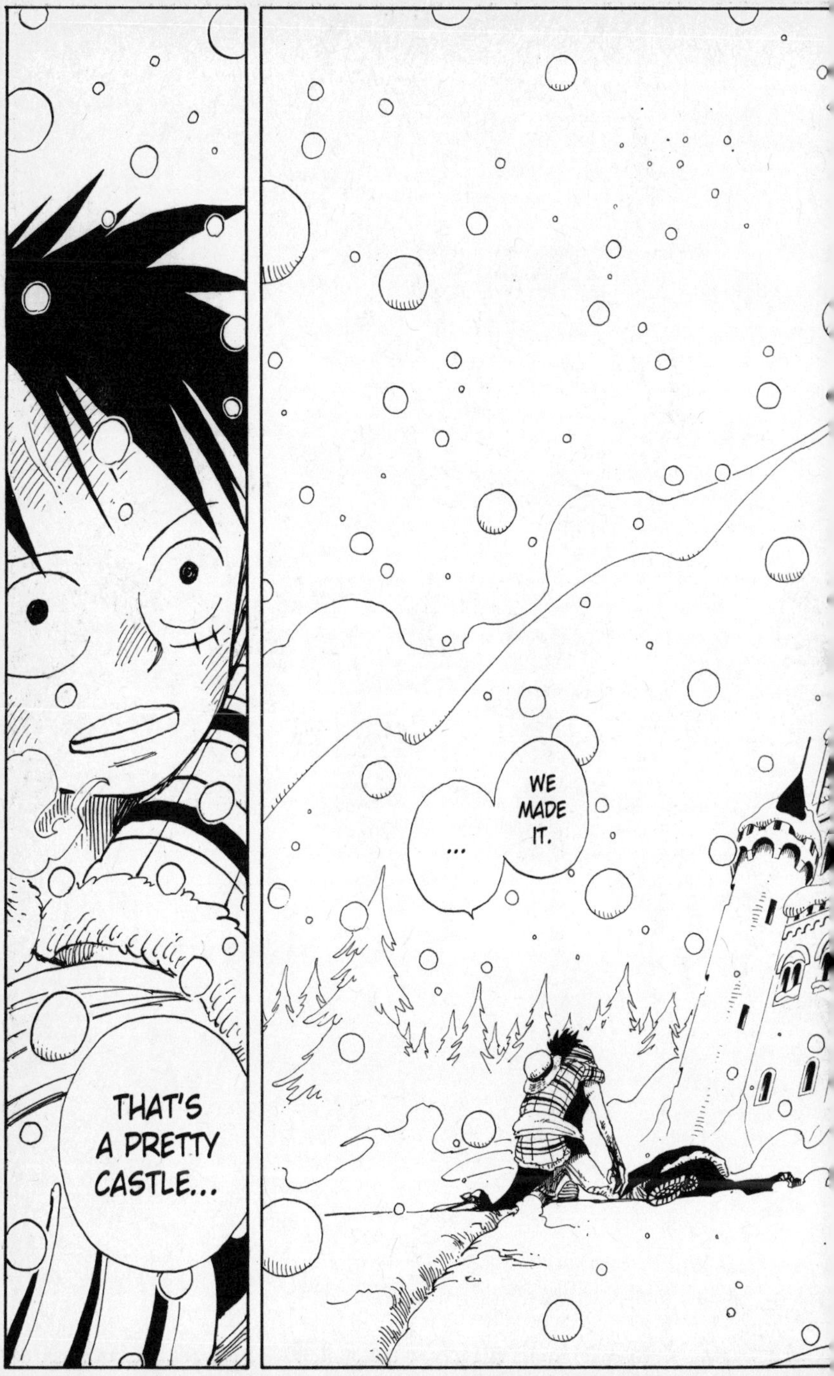
WE MADE IT.
...
THAT'S A PRETTY CASTLE...

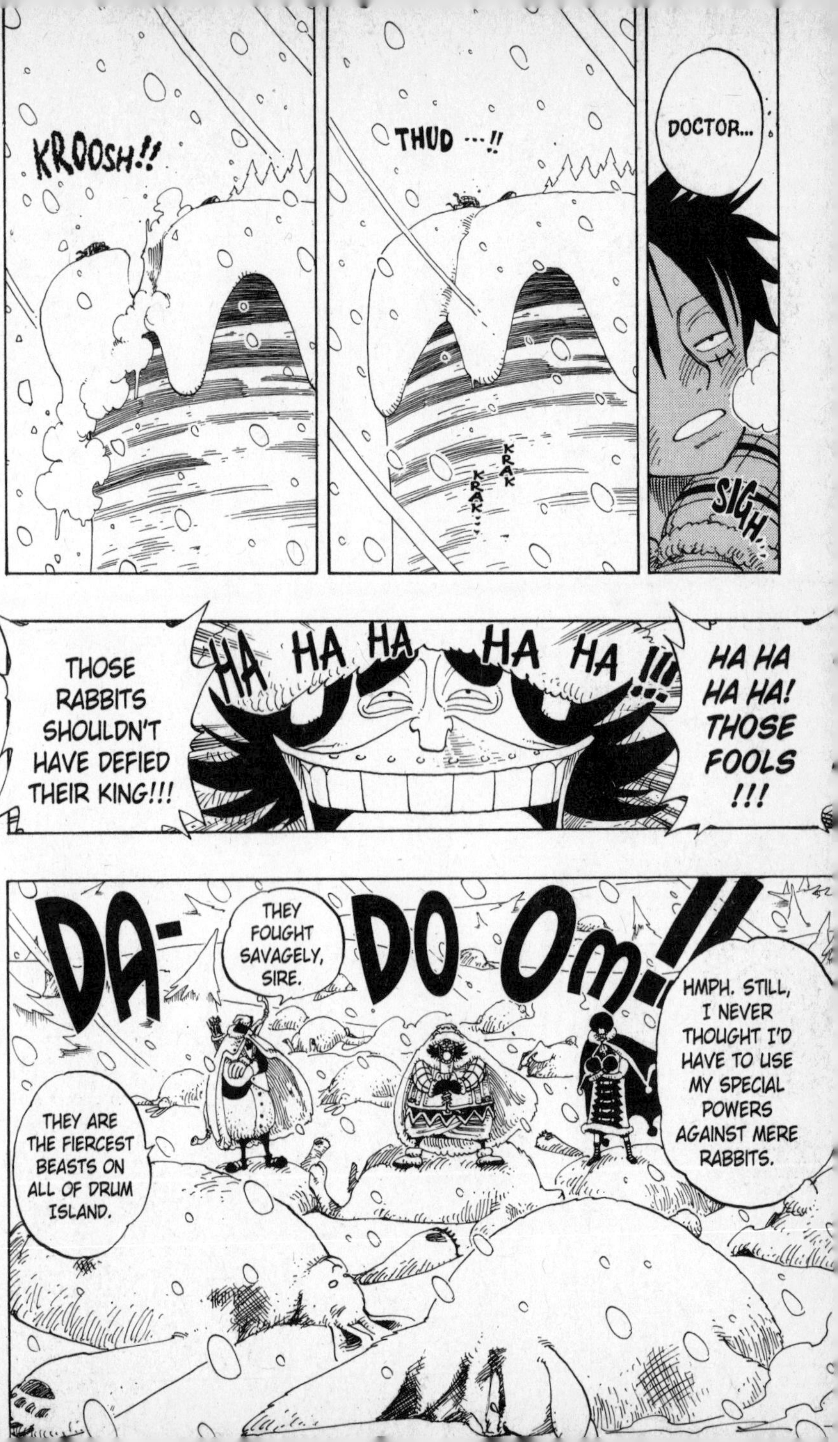
DOCTOR...
SIGH
THUD ...!!
KRAK KRAK...
KROOSH!!
HA HA HA HA! THOSE FOOLS !!!
HA HA HA HA HA !!!
THOSE RABBITS SHOULDN'T HAVE DEFIED THEIR KING!!!
HMPH. STILL, I NEVER THOUGHT I'D HAVE TO USE MY SPECIAL POWERS AGAINST MERE RABBITS.
DA-DO OM!!
THEY FOUGHT SAVAGELY, SIRE.
THEY ARE THE FIERCEST BEASTS ON ALL OF DRUM ISLAND.

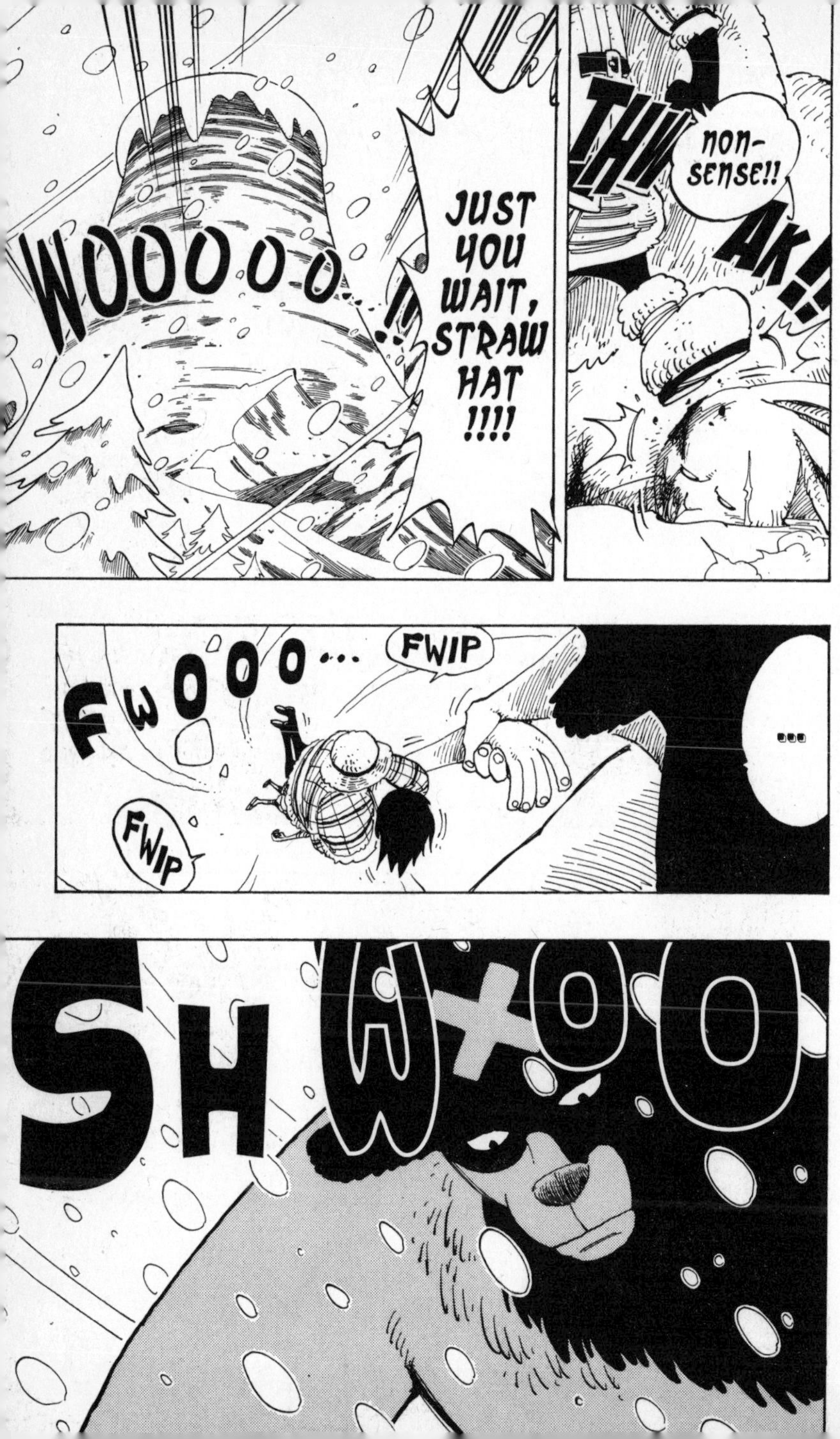
THWAK!!
NON-SENSE!!
WOOOOOO...!!
JUST YOU WAIT, STRAW HAT!!!!
...
FWIP
FWOOO...
FWIP
SHWOO

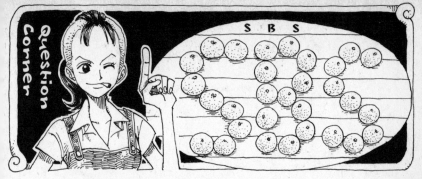

Question Corner
S B S

Q: This is driving me crazy! On page 137 of volume 15, there's something that looks like green onions in the lady's basket! There are three stalks, right!? But look at the same lady's basket on page 162! Look at all those onions! Is she going to make an onion stir-fry or what? An onion hot pot? What was that lady going to have for dinner!? I gotta know!!

A: What!? That shook me up. That postcard actually made me jump out of my seat. And yours wasn't the only one. When I was drawing that scene, someone said, "Look, there are more onions than there were before." My staff and I laughed. "Nobody'll notice," we said. But we should know better than to ever underestimate our readers.

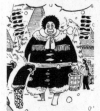

When she first appeared.

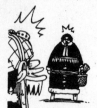

The next time she appeared.

The lady's name is Maria Onion Bear (housewife, age 46). It was her second son's birthday that day. She wanted to bake a delicious onion cake for him, so she went all over town looking for the best onions. So the answer is--an onion cake. Doesn't sound very appetizing, does it?

Q: Reader: In volume 15, page 171, Dr. Kureha tells the child to remember what she did. But why? Shouldn't he try to forget it? It must've been excruciatingly painful!! (sob)

A:

WHAT I DID JUST NOW!!!
DA-DOOM!!
DON'T EVER FORGET IT!!!

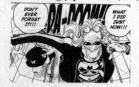

You've got it all wrong. The doctor wants the boy to remember that sometimes you have to endure a little pain to feel a lot better. Isn't that obvious?

Chapter 139:
ENTER TONY TONY CHOPPER

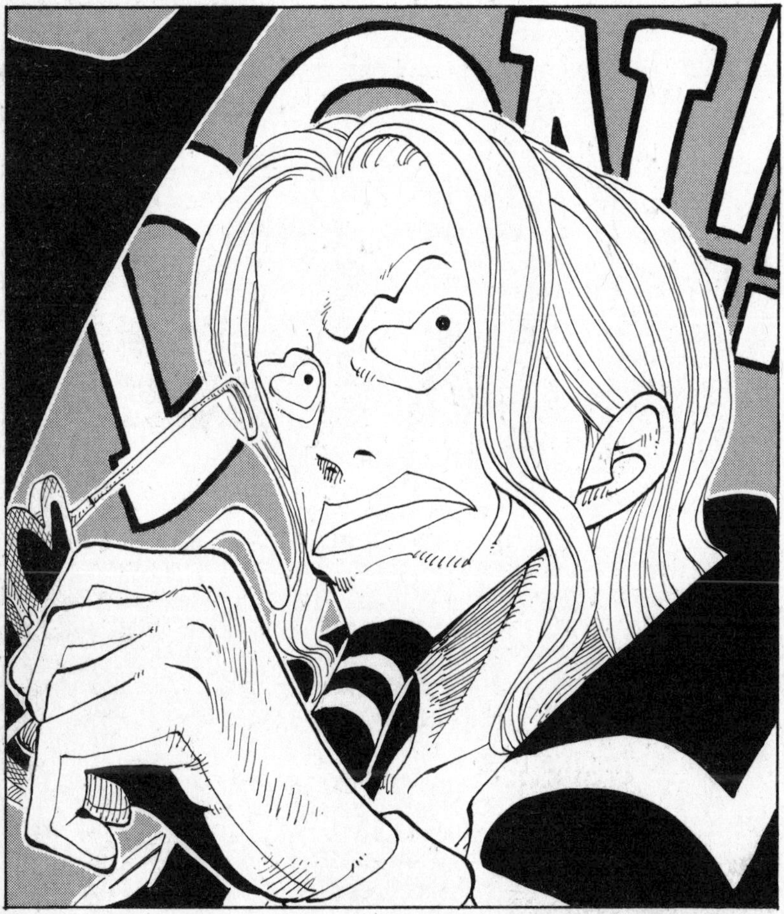

DJANGO'S DANCE PARADISE, VOL. 11: "EYES WITH HEART"

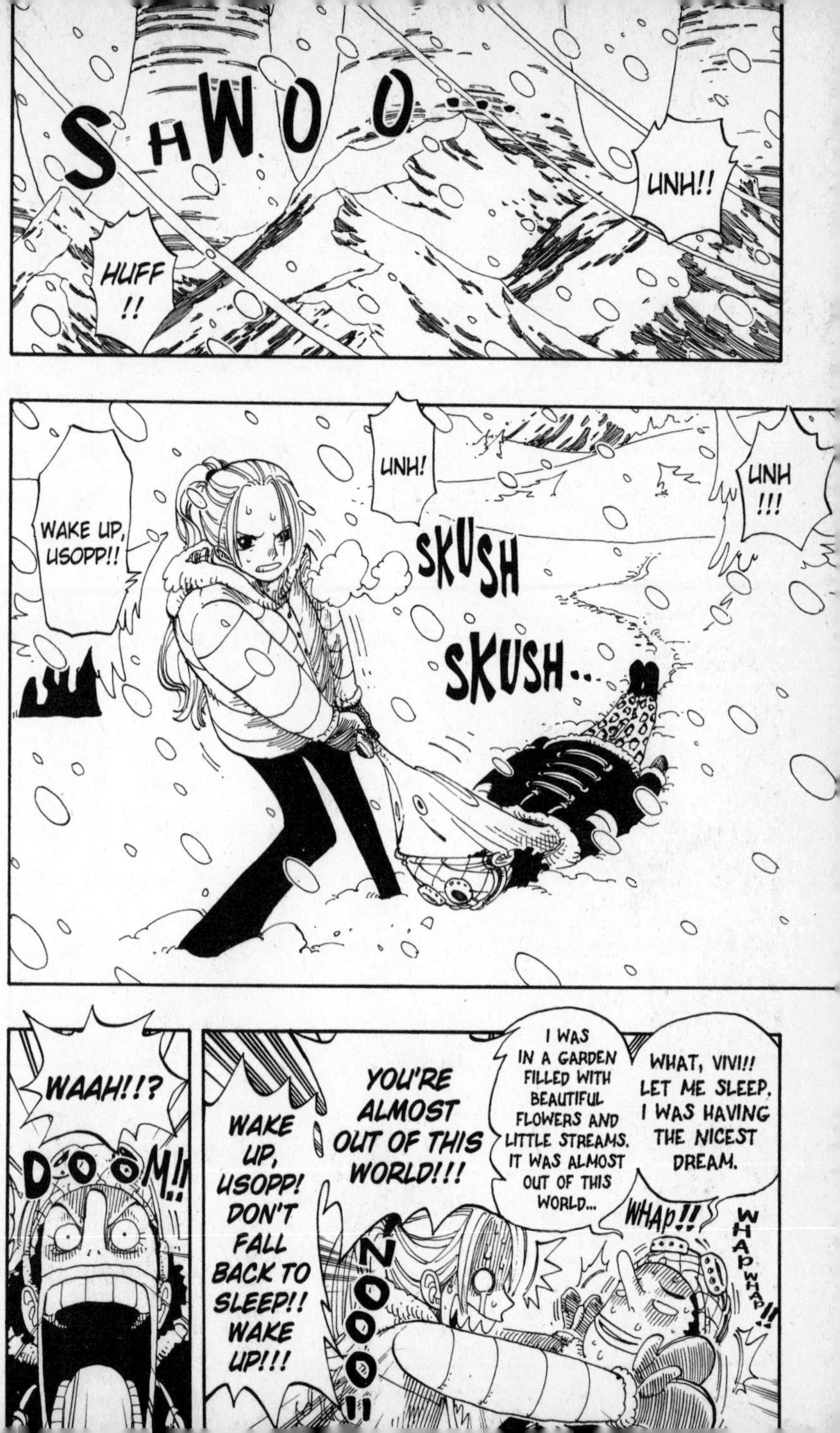
UNH!!
SHWOO
HUFF!!
UNH!!!
UNH!
SKUSH
SKUSH...
WAKE UP, USOPP!!
WHAT, VIVI!! LET ME SLEEP. I WAS HAVING THE NICEST DREAM.
I WAS IN A GARDEN FILLED WITH BEAUTIFUL FLOWERS AND LITTLE STREAMS. IT WAS ALMOST OUT OF THIS WORLD...
WHAP!!
WHAPWHAP!!
YOU'RE ALMOST OUT OF THIS WORLD!!!
WAKE UP, USOPP! DON'T FALL BACK TO SLEEP!! WAKE UP!!!
NOOOO!!
WAAH!!?
DOOM!!

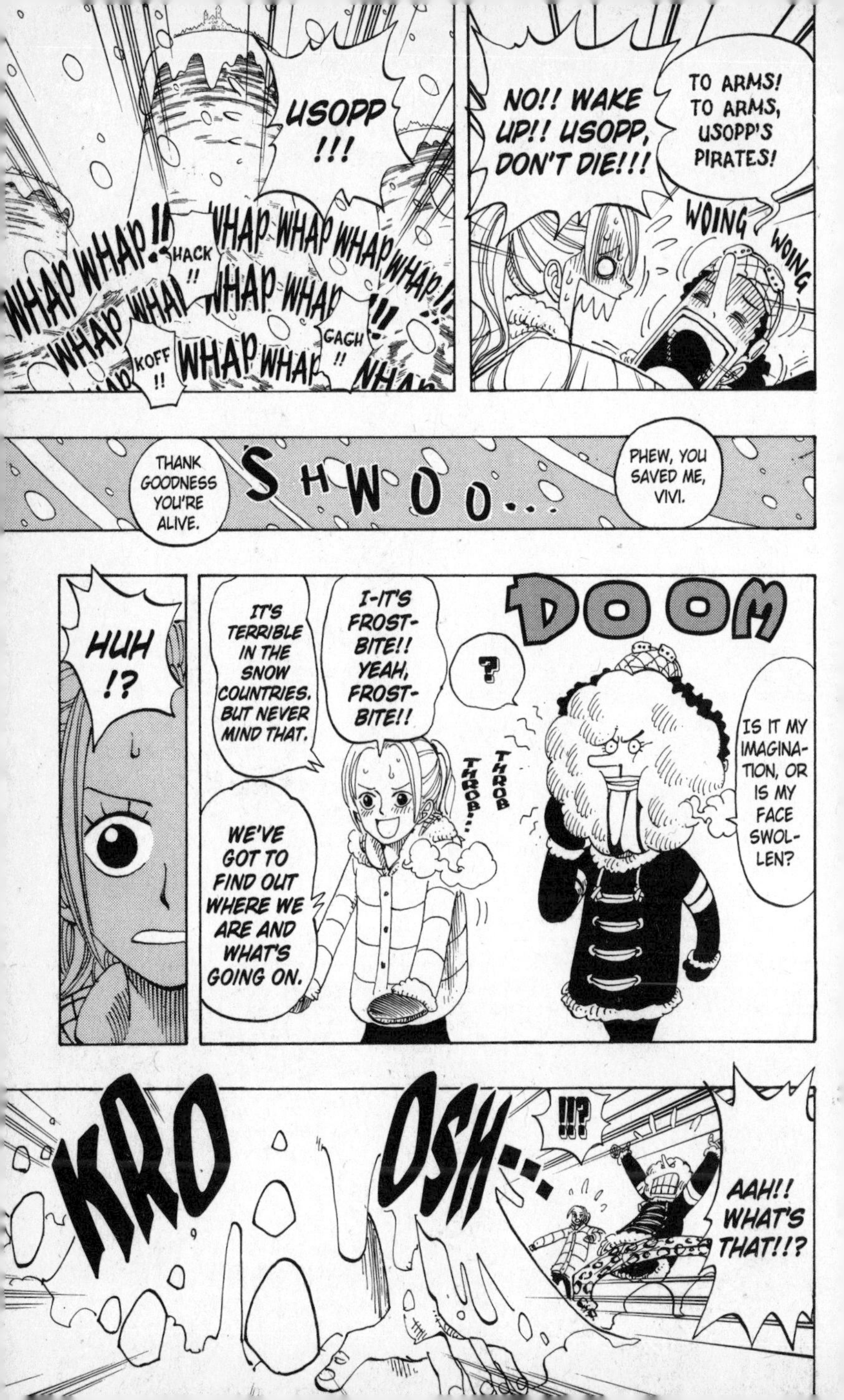
TO ARMS! TO ARMS, USOPP'S PIRATES!
NO!! WAKE UP!! USOPP, DON'T DIE!!!
WOING WOING
USOPP!!!
WHAP WHAP WHAP WHAP!!
WHAP WHAP WHAP WHAP!!
WHAP WHAP WHAP WHAP
HACK!!
GAGH!!
KOFF!!
PHEW, YOU SAVED ME, VIVI.
SHWOO...
THANK GOODNESS YOU'RE ALIVE.
DOOM
IS IT MY IMAGINATION, OR IS MY FACE SWOLLEN?
?
THROB THROB!!
I-IT'S FROSTBITE!! YEAH, FROSTBITE!!
IT'S TERRIBLE IN THE SNOW COUNTRIES. BUT NEVER MIND THAT.
WE'VE GOT TO FIND OUT WHERE WE ARE AND WHAT'S GOING ON.
HUH!?
AAH!! WHAT'S THAT!!?
!!?
KROOSH...

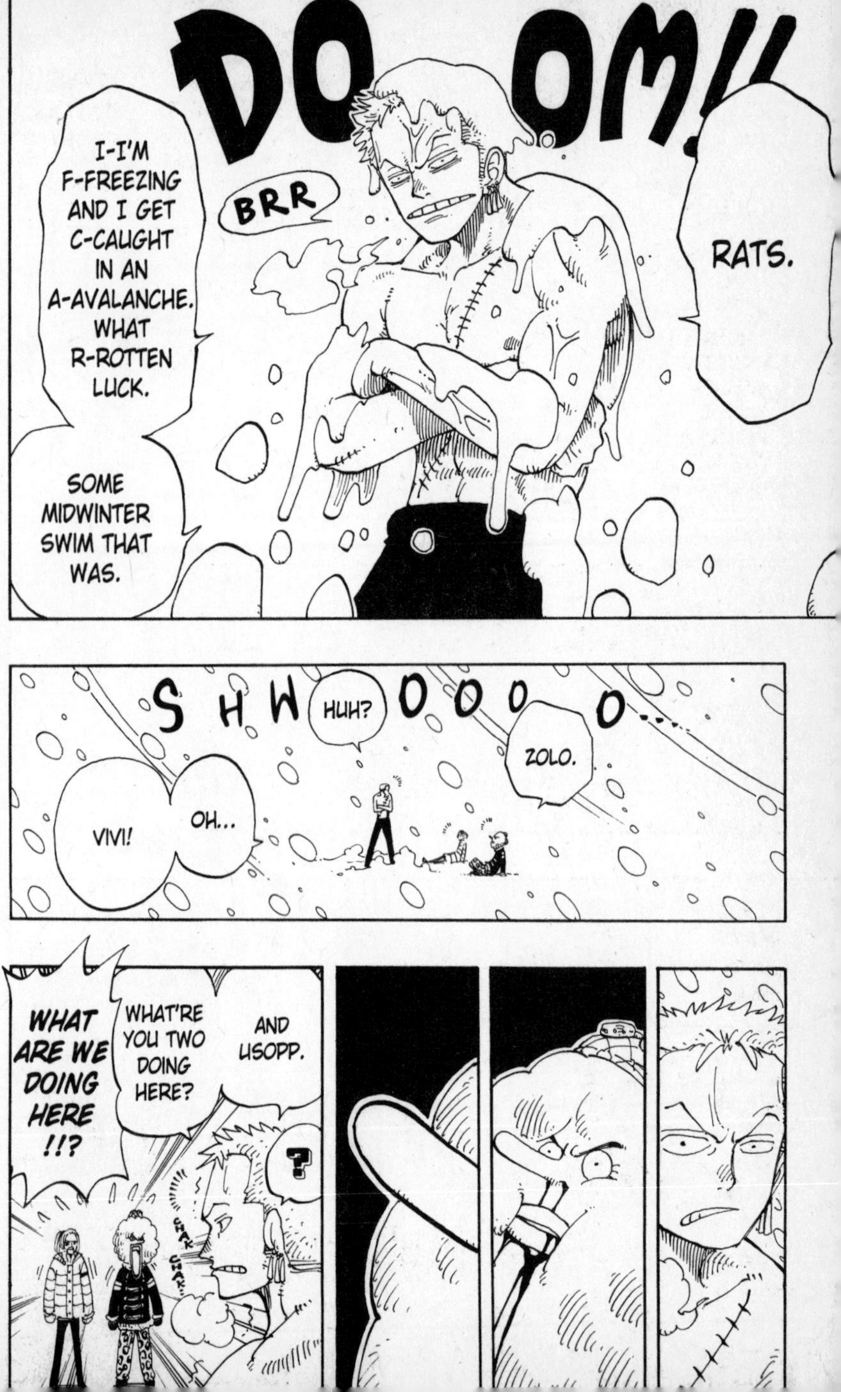
DO OM!!
RATS.
BRR
I-I'M F-FREEZING AND I GET C-CAUGHT IN AN A-AVALANCHE. WHAT R-ROTTEN LUCK.
SOME MIDWINTER SWIM THAT WAS.
SHWOOOOO
ZOLO.
HUH?
OH...
VIVI!
AND USOPP.
WHAT'RE YOU TWO DOING HERE?
?
CHAK CHAK
WHAT ARE WE DOING HERE!!?

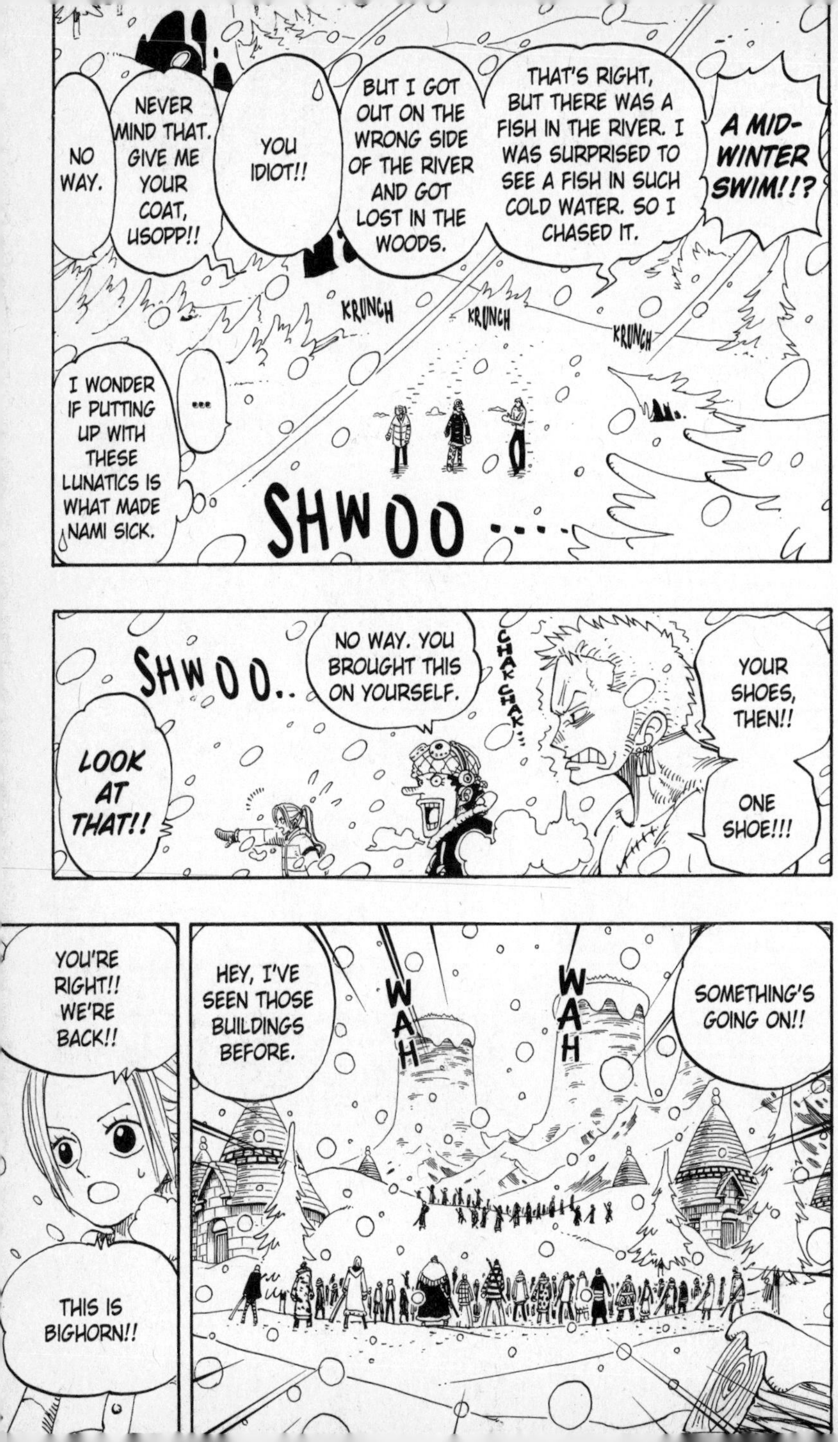
A MID-WINTER SWIM!!?
THAT'S RIGHT, BUT THERE WAS A FISH IN THE RIVER. I WAS SURPRISED TO SEE A FISH IN SUCH COLD WATER. SO I CHASED IT.
BUT I GOT OUT ON THE WRONG SIDE OF THE RIVER AND GOT LOST IN THE WOODS.
YOU IDIOT!!
NEVER MIND THAT. GIVE ME YOUR COAT, USOPP!!
NO WAY.
KRUNCH
KRUNCH
KRUNCH
I WONDER IF PUTTING UP WITH THESE LUNATICS IS WHAT MADE NAMI SICK.
...
SHWOO....
YOUR SHOES, THEN!!
ONE SHOE!!!
CHAK CHAK...
NO WAY. YOU BROUGHT THIS ON YOURSELF.
SHWOO..
LOOK AT THAT!!
SOMETHING'S GOING ON!!
WAH
WAH
HEY, I'VE SEEN THOSE BUILDINGS BEFORE.
YOU'RE RIGHT!! WE'RE BACK!!
THIS IS BIGHORN!!

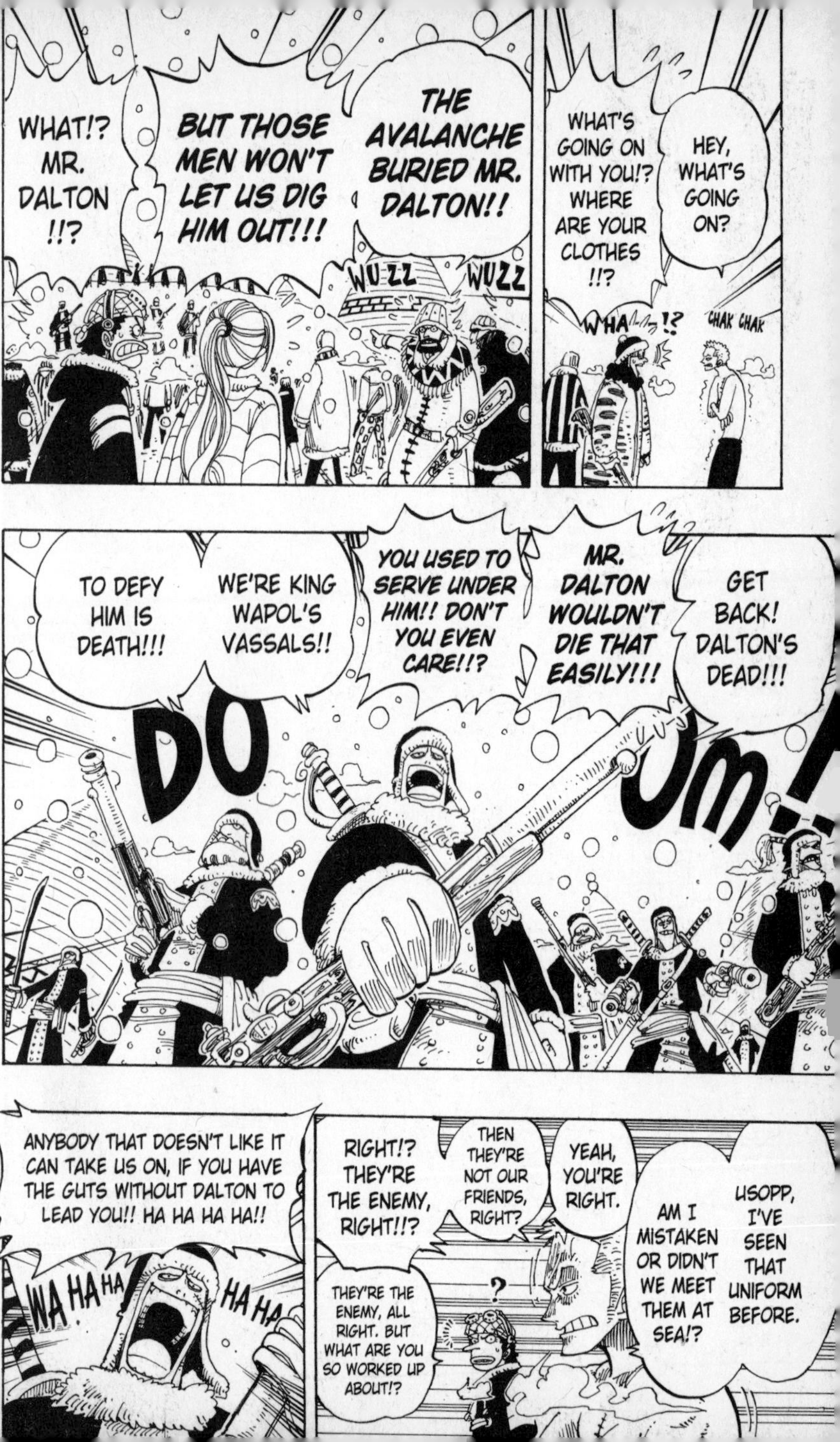
HEY, WHAT'S GOING ON?
WHAT'S GOING ON WITH YOU!? WHERE ARE YOUR CLOTHES!!?
CHAK CHAK
WHA!?
THE AVALANCHE BURIED MR. DALTON!!
BUT THOSE MEN WON'T LET US DIG HIM OUT!!!
WHAT!? MR. DALTON!!?
WUZZ
WUZZ
GET BACK! DALTON'S DEAD!!!
MR. DALTON WOULDN'T DIE THAT EASILY!!!
YOU USED TO SERVE UNDER HIM!! DON'T YOU EVEN CARE!!?
WE'RE KING WAPOL'S VASSALS!!
TO DEFY HIM IS DEATH!!!
DOOM!!
USOPP, I'VE SEEN THAT UNIFORM BEFORE.
AM I MISTAKEN OR DIDN'T WE MEET THEM AT SEA!?
YEAH, YOU'RE RIGHT.
THEN THEY'RE NOT OUR FRIENDS, RIGHT?
RIGHT!? THEY'RE THE ENEMY, RIGHT!!?
?
THEY'RE THE ENEMY, ALL RIGHT. BUT WHAT ARE YOU SO WORKED UP ABOUT!?
ANYBODY THAT DOESN'T LIKE IT CAN TAKE US ON, IF YOU HAVE THE GUTS WITHOUT DALTON TO LEAD YOU!! HA HA HA HA!!
HA HA
WA HA HA

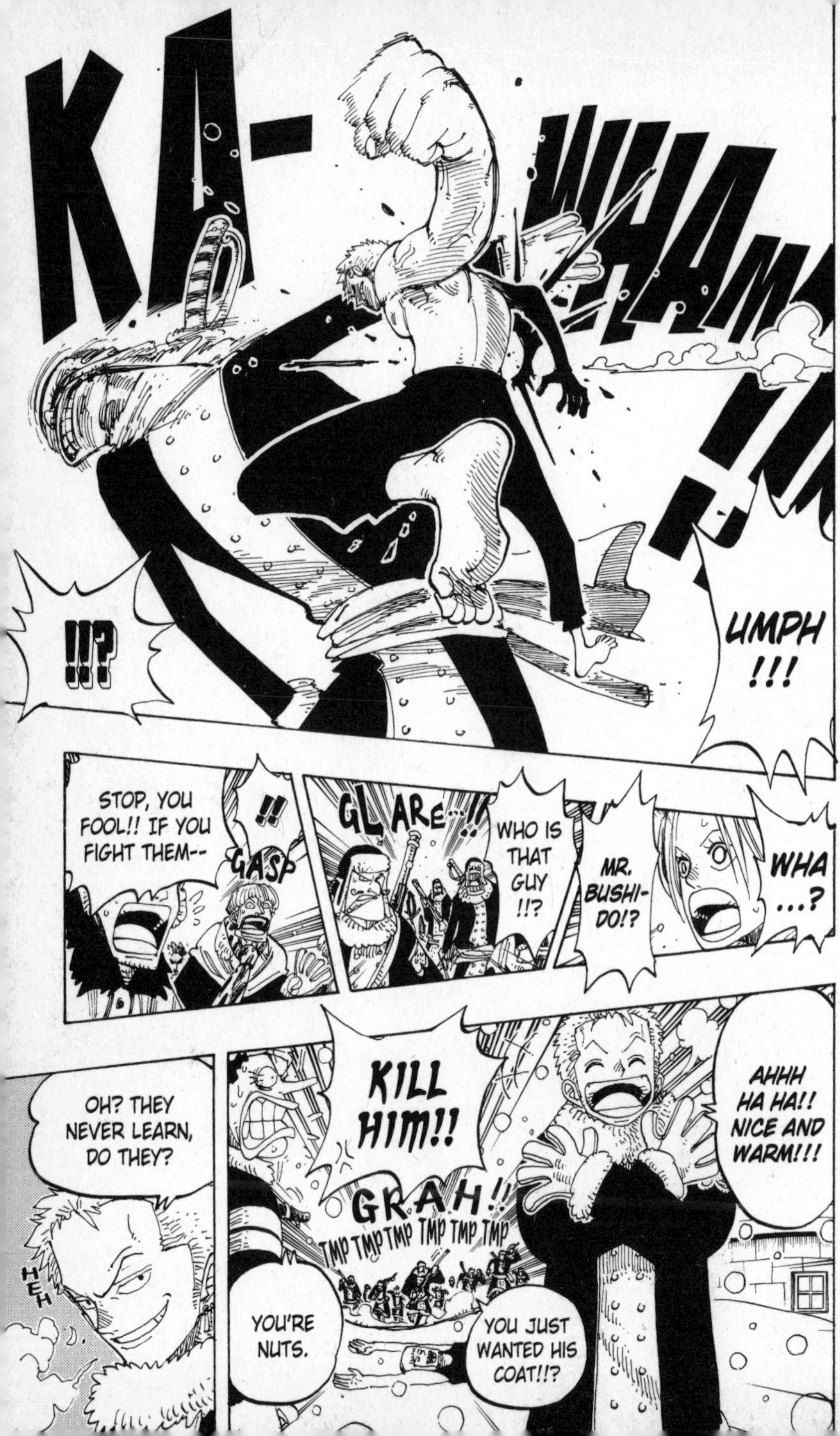
KA-WHAM!!!
UMPH!!!
!!?
WHA...?
MR. BUSHIDO!?
WHO IS THAT GUY!!?
GLARE...!!
!!
GASP
STOP, YOU FOOL!! IF YOU FIGHT THEM--
AHHH HA HA!! NICE AND WARM!!!
KILL HIM!!
GRAH!!
TMP TMP TMP TMP TMP TMP
YOU JUST WANTED HIS COAT!!?
YOU'RE NUTS.
OH? THEY NEVER LEARN, DO THEY?
HEH

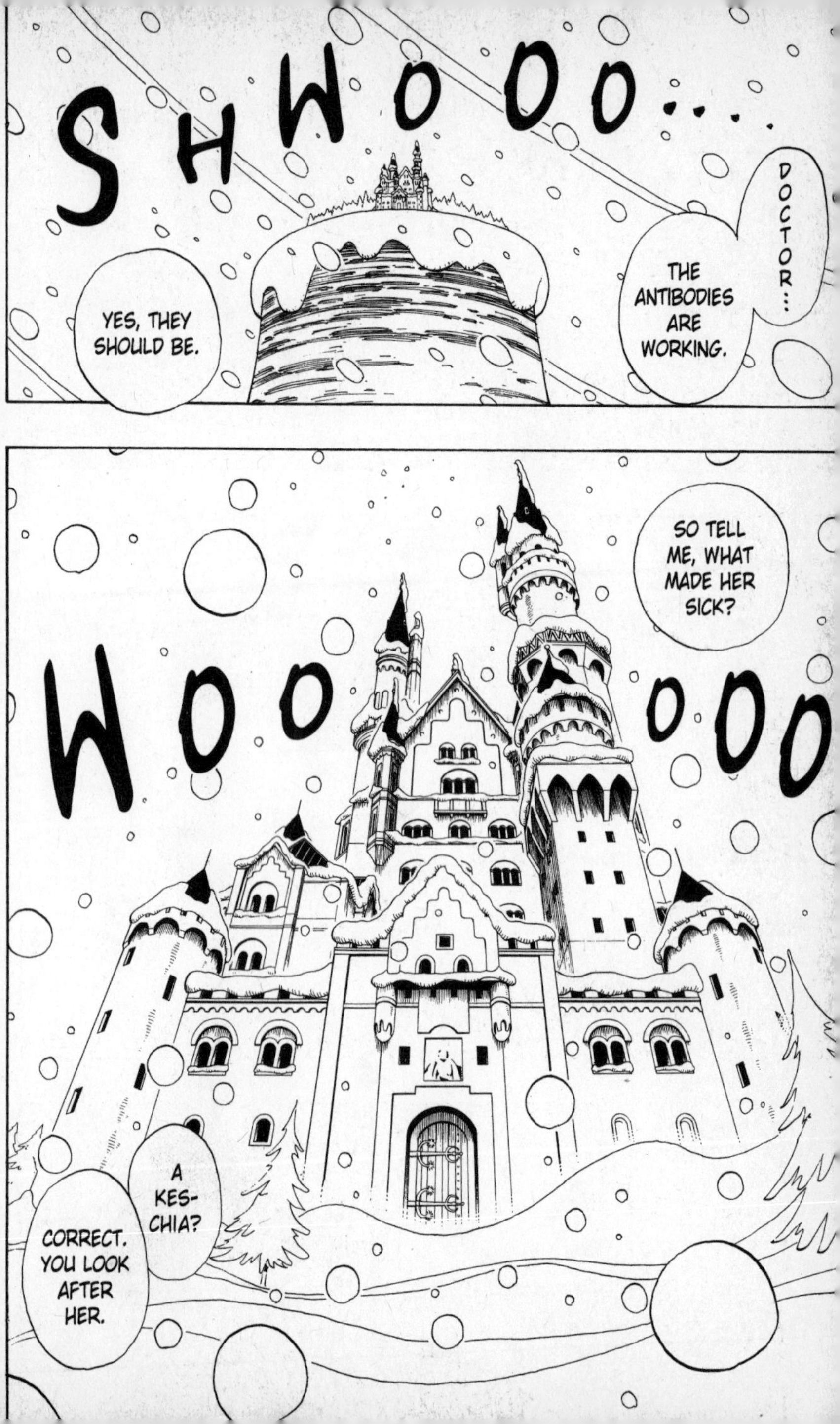
DOCTOR...
THE ANTIBODIES ARE WORKING.
SHWOOO...
YES, THEY SHOULD BE.
SO TELL ME, WHAT MADE HER SICK?
WOOOOOO
A KES-CHIA?
CORRECT. YOU LOOK AFTER HER.

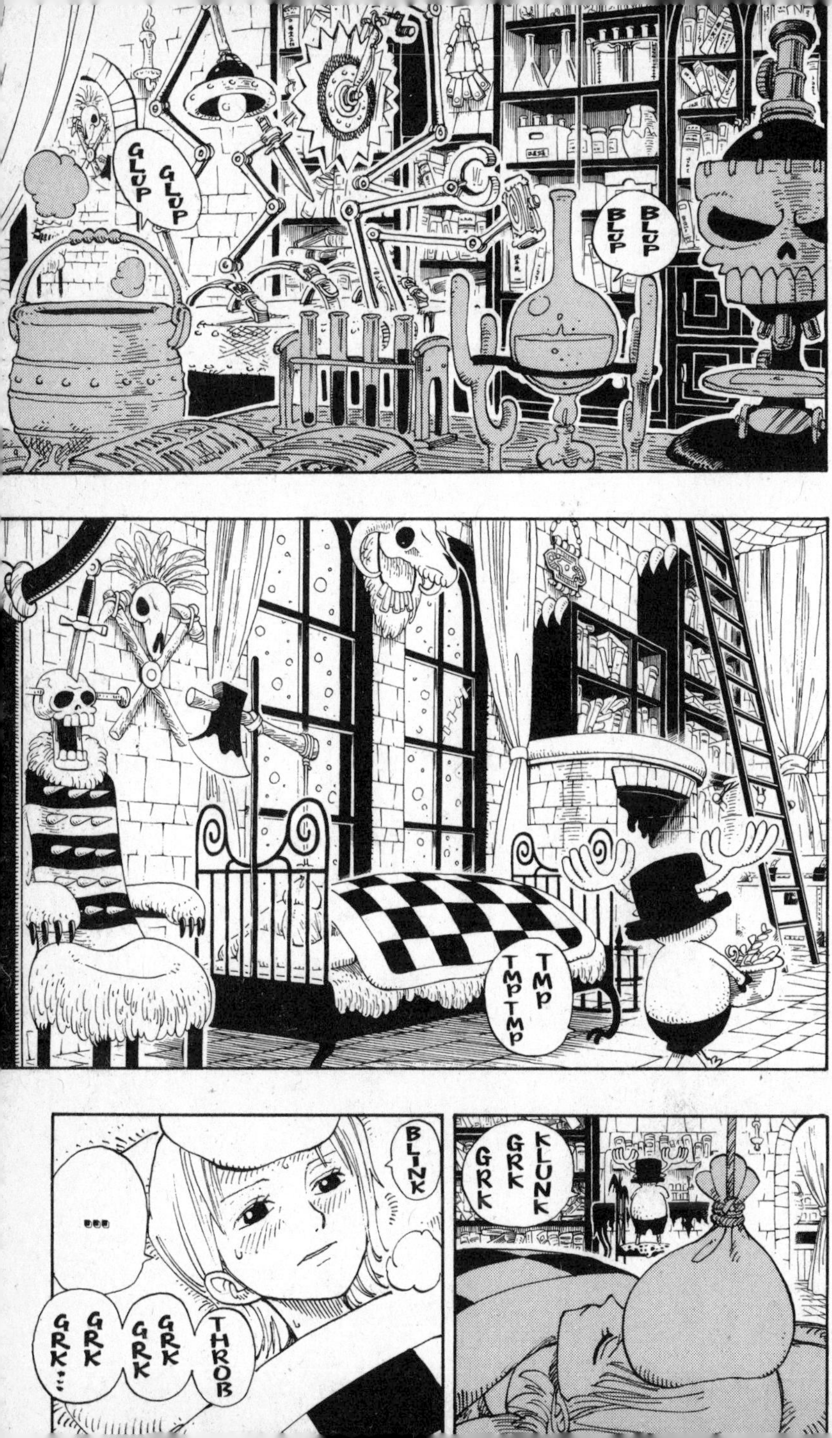
BLUP BLUP
GLUP GLUP
TMP TMPTMP
KLUNK GRK GRK
BLINK
...
THROB
GRK GRK
GRK GRK...

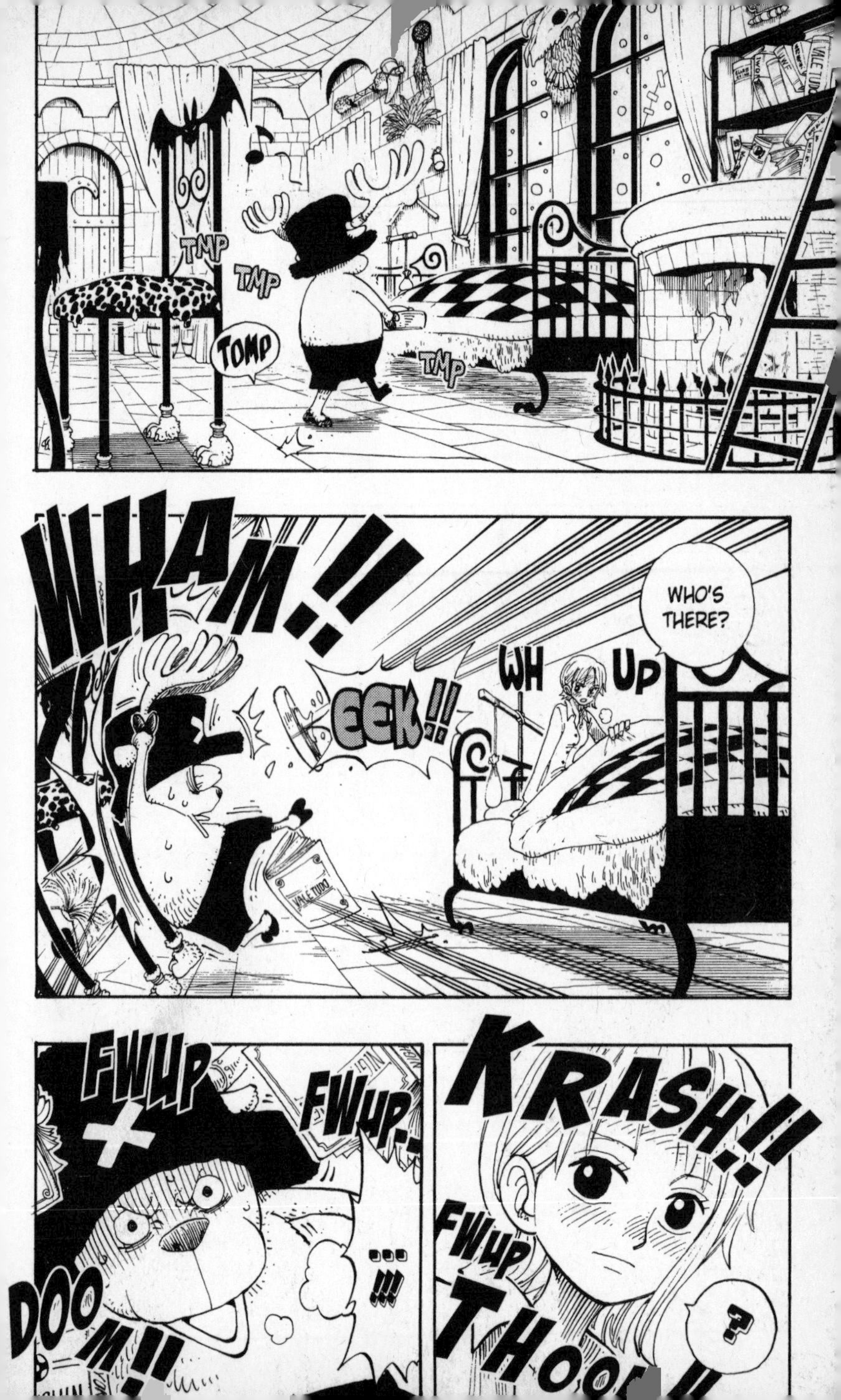
TMP
TMP
TOMP
TMP
WHO'S THERE?
WH
UP
EEK!!
VALE TUDO
WHAM!!
KRASH!!
FWUP
THOO
?
FWUP
FWUP..
...!!!
DOOM!!

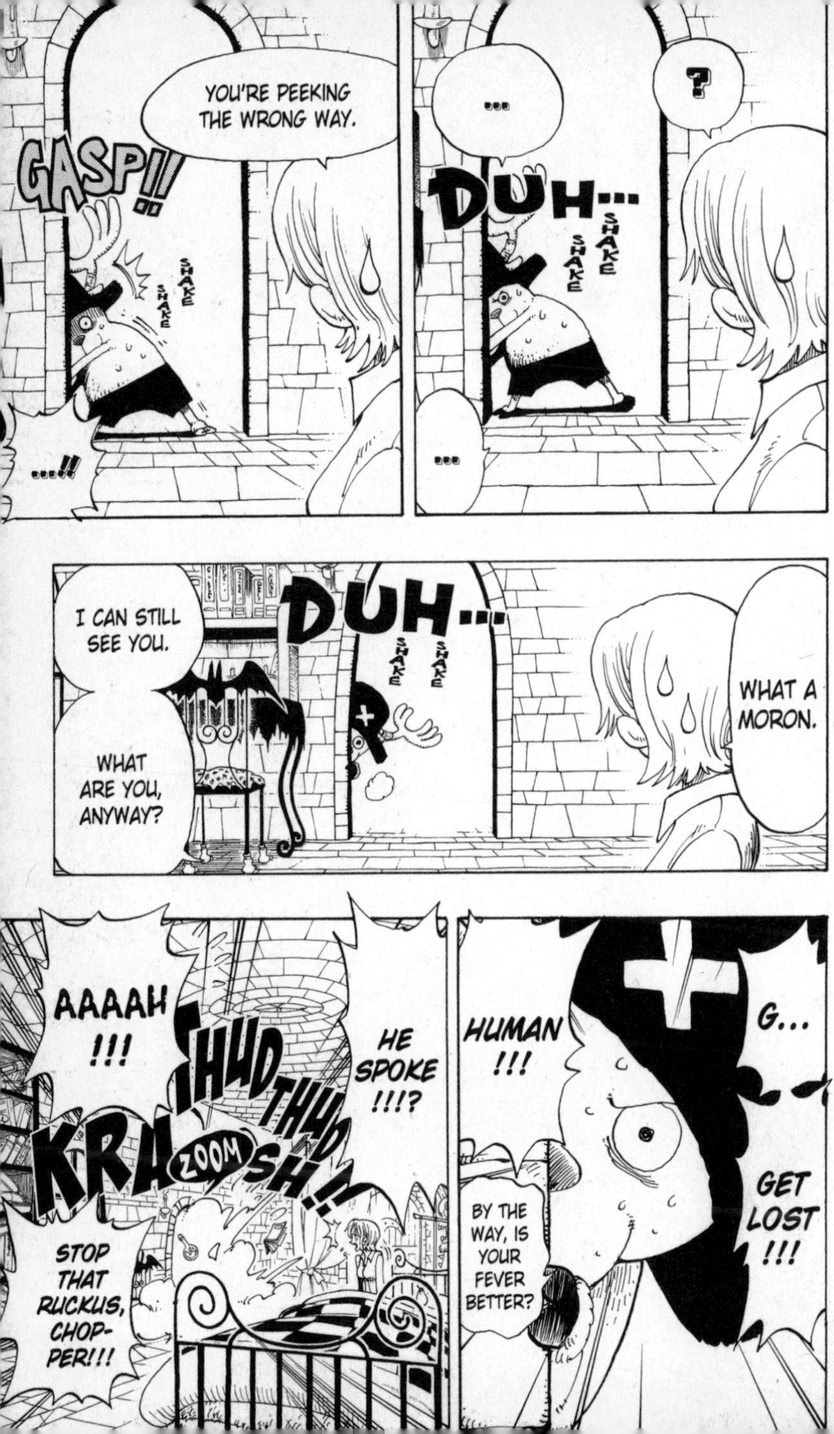
?
...
DUH...
SHAKE
SHAKE
...
YOU'RE PEEKING THE WRONG WAY.
GASP!!
SHAKE
SHAKE
...!!
WHAT A MORON.
DUH...
SHAKE
SHAKE
I CAN STILL SEE YOU.
WHAT ARE YOU, ANYWAY?
G...
HUMAN !!!
GET LOST !!!
BY THE WAY, IS YOUR FEVER BETTER?
HE SPOKE !!!?
AAAAH !!!
THUD THUD
KRA ZOOM SH!!
STOP THAT RUCKUS, CHOPPER!!!

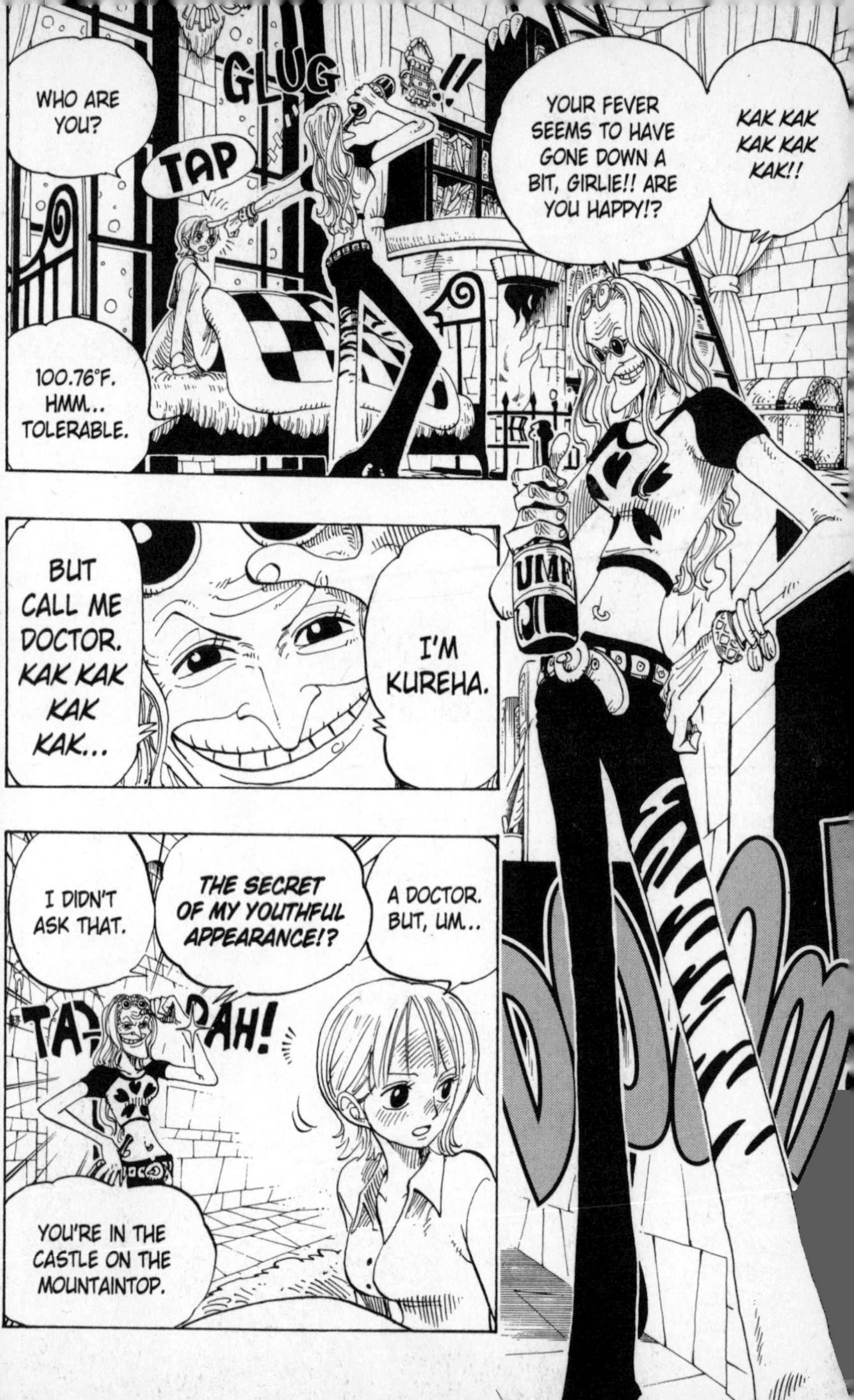
YOUR FEVER SEEMS TO HAVE GONE DOWN A BIT, GIRLIE!! ARE YOU HAPPY!?
KAK KAK KAK KAK KAK!!
UME
GLUG
!!
TAP
WHO ARE YOU?
100.76°F. HMM... TOLERABLE.
I'M KUREHA.
BUT CALL ME DOCTOR. KAK KAK KAK KAK...
A DOCTOR. BUT, UM...
THE SECRET OF MY YOUTHFUL APPEARANCE!?
I DIDN'T ASK THAT.
TA-DAH!
YOU'RE IN THE CASTLE ON THE MOUNTAINTOP.

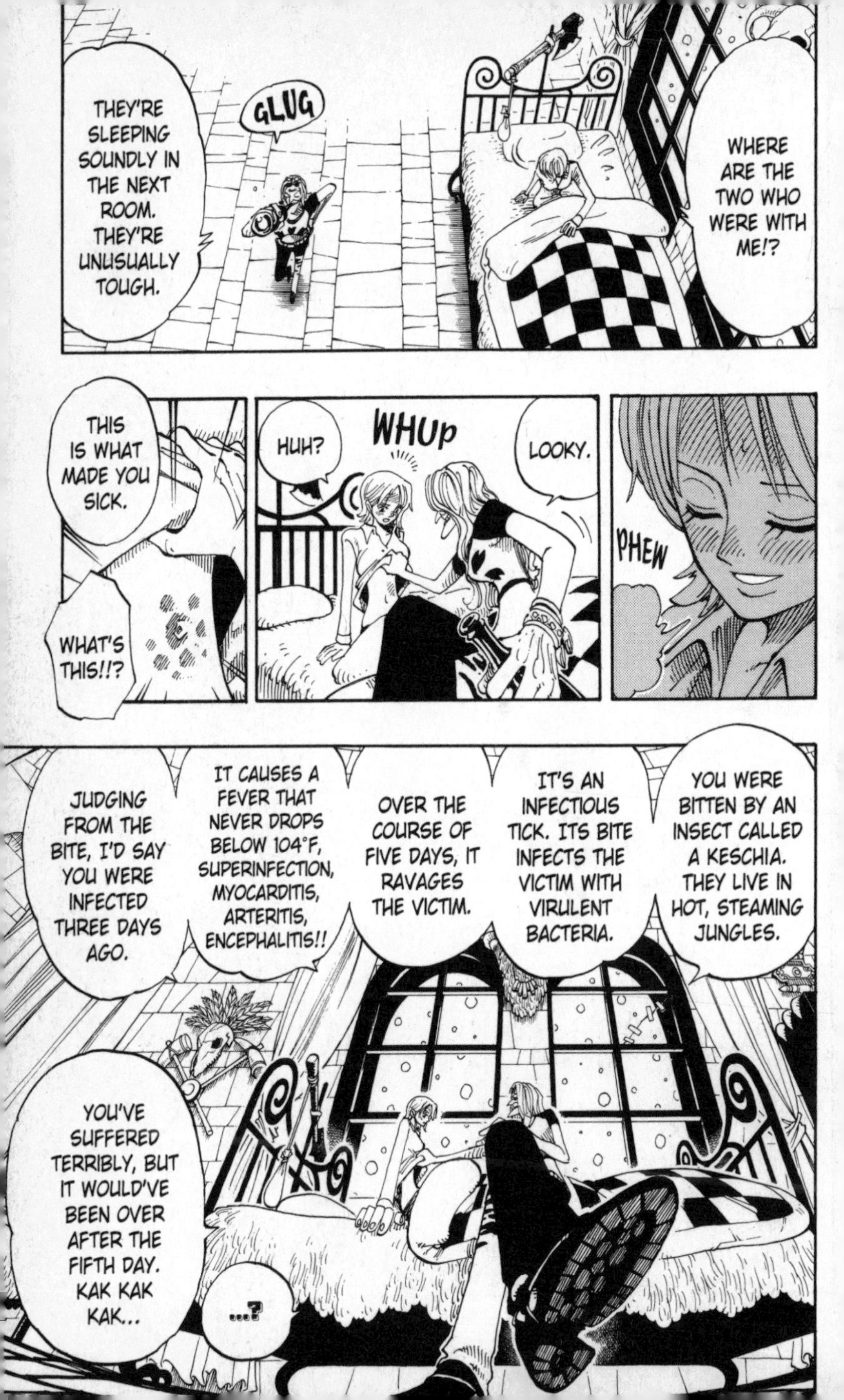
WHERE ARE THE TWO WHO WERE WITH ME!?
GLUG
THEY'RE SLEEPING SOUNDLY IN THE NEXT ROOM. THEY'RE UNUSUALLY TOUGH.
PHEW
LOOKY.
WHUp
HUH?
THIS IS WHAT MADE YOU SICK.
WHAT'S THIS!!?
YOU WERE BITTEN BY AN INSECT CALLED A KESCHIA. THEY LIVE IN HOT, STEAMING JUNGLES.
IT'S AN INFECTIOUS TICK. ITS BITE INFECTS THE VICTIM WITH VIRULENT BACTERIA.
OVER THE COURSE OF FIVE DAYS, IT RAVAGES THE VICTIM.
IT CAUSES A FEVER THAT NEVER DROPS BELOW 104°F, SUPERINFECTION, MYOCARDITIS, ARTERITIS, ENCEPHALITIS!!
JUDGING FROM THE BITE, I'D SAY YOU WERE INFECTED THREE DAYS AGO.
YOU'VE SUFFERED TERRIBLY, BUT IT WOULD'VE BEEN OVER AFTER THE FIFTH DAY. KAK KAK KAK...
...?

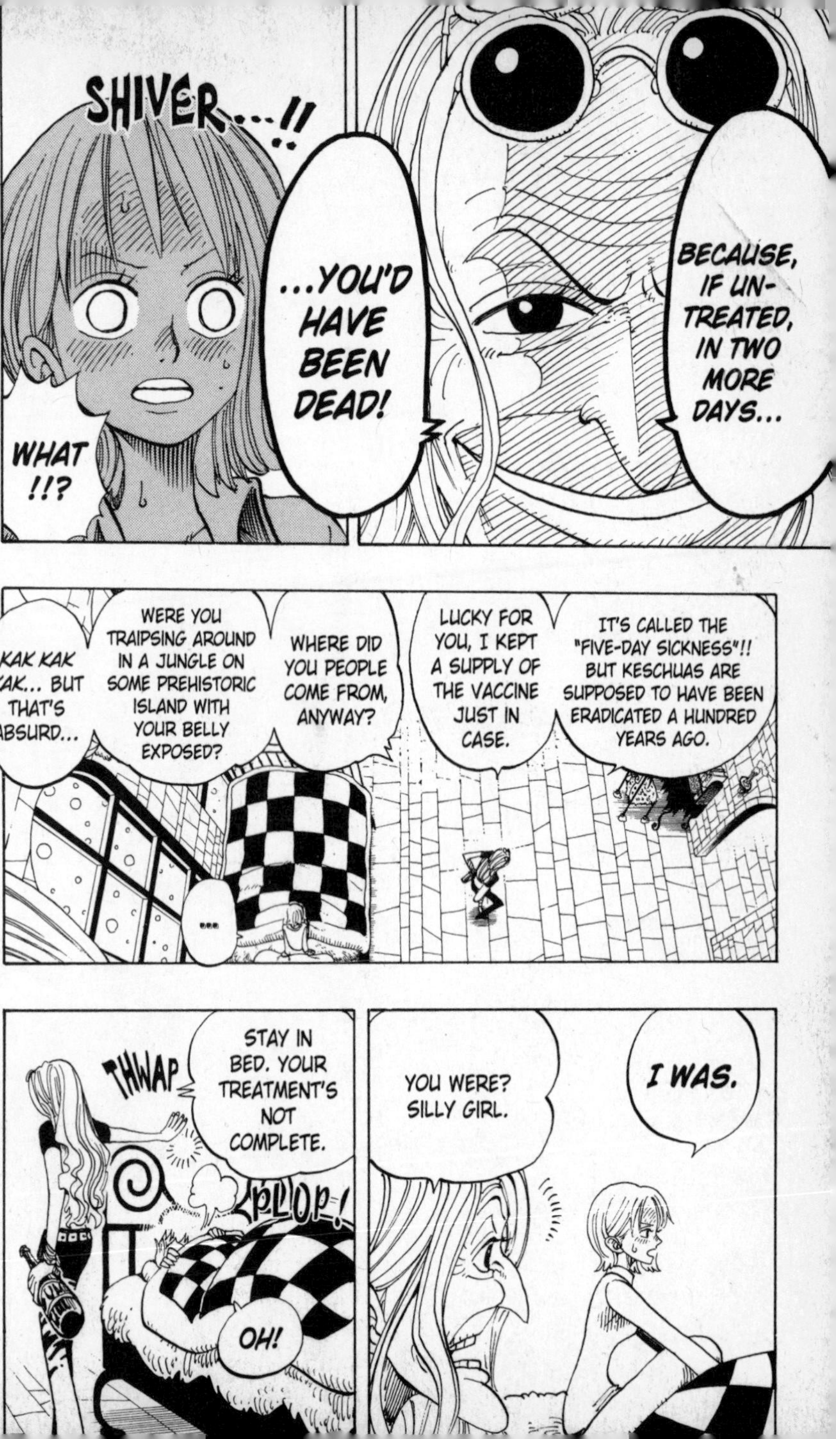
BECAUSE, IF UN-TREATED, IN TWO MORE DAYS...
...YOU'D HAVE BEEN DEAD!
SHIVER...!!
WHAT !!?
IT'S CALLED THE "FIVE-DAY SICKNESS"!! BUT KESCHUAS ARE SUPPOSED TO HAVE BEEN ERADICATED A HUNDRED YEARS AGO.
LUCKY FOR YOU, I KEPT A SUPPLY OF THE VACCINE JUST IN CASE.
WHERE DID YOU PEOPLE COME FROM, ANYWAY?
WERE YOU TRAIPSING AROUND IN A JUNGLE ON SOME PREHISTORIC ISLAND WITH YOUR BELLY EXPOSED?
KAK KAK KAK... BUT THAT'S ABSURD...
...
I WAS.
YOU WERE? SILLY GIRL.
STAY IN BED. YOUR TREATMENT'S NOT COMPLETE.
THWAP
PLOP!
OH!

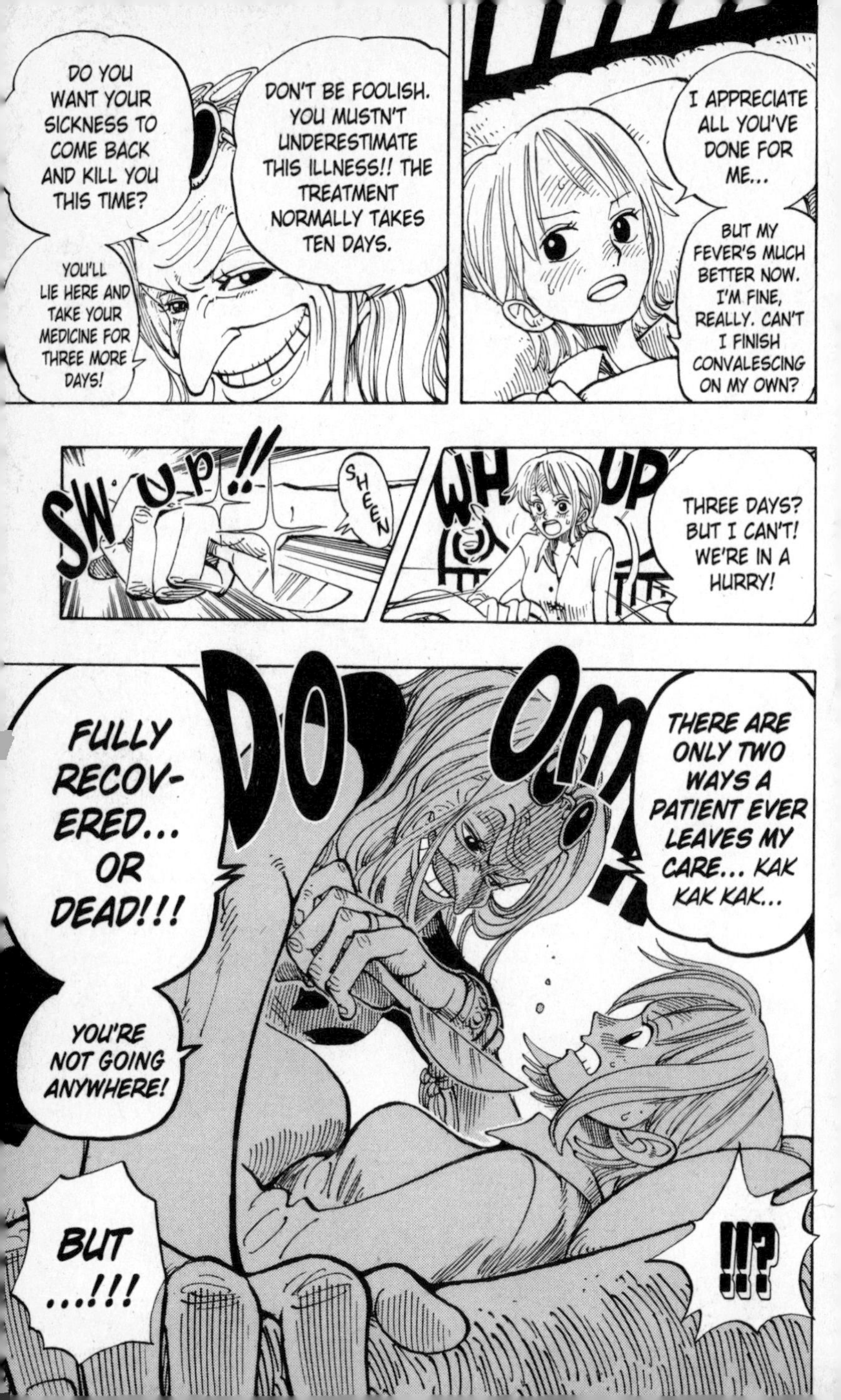
I APPRECIATE ALL YOU'VE DONE FOR ME...
BUT MY FEVER'S MUCH BETTER NOW. I'M FINE, REALLY. CAN'T I FINISH CONVALESCING ON MY OWN?
DON'T BE FOOLISH. YOU MUSTN'T UNDERESTIMATE THIS ILLNESS!! THE TREATMENT NORMALLY TAKES TEN DAYS.
DO YOU WANT YOUR SICKNESS TO COME BACK AND KILL YOU THIS TIME?
YOU'LL LIE HERE AND TAKE YOUR MEDICINE FOR THREE MORE DAYS!
THREE DAYS? BUT I CAN'T! WE'RE IN A HURRY!
WHUP
SHEEN
SWUP!!
THERE ARE ONLY TWO WAYS A PATIENT EVER LEAVES MY CARE... KAK KAK KAK...
DOOM
FULLY RECOV-ERED... OR DEAD!!!
YOU'RE NOT GOING ANYWHERE!
!!?
BUT ...!!!

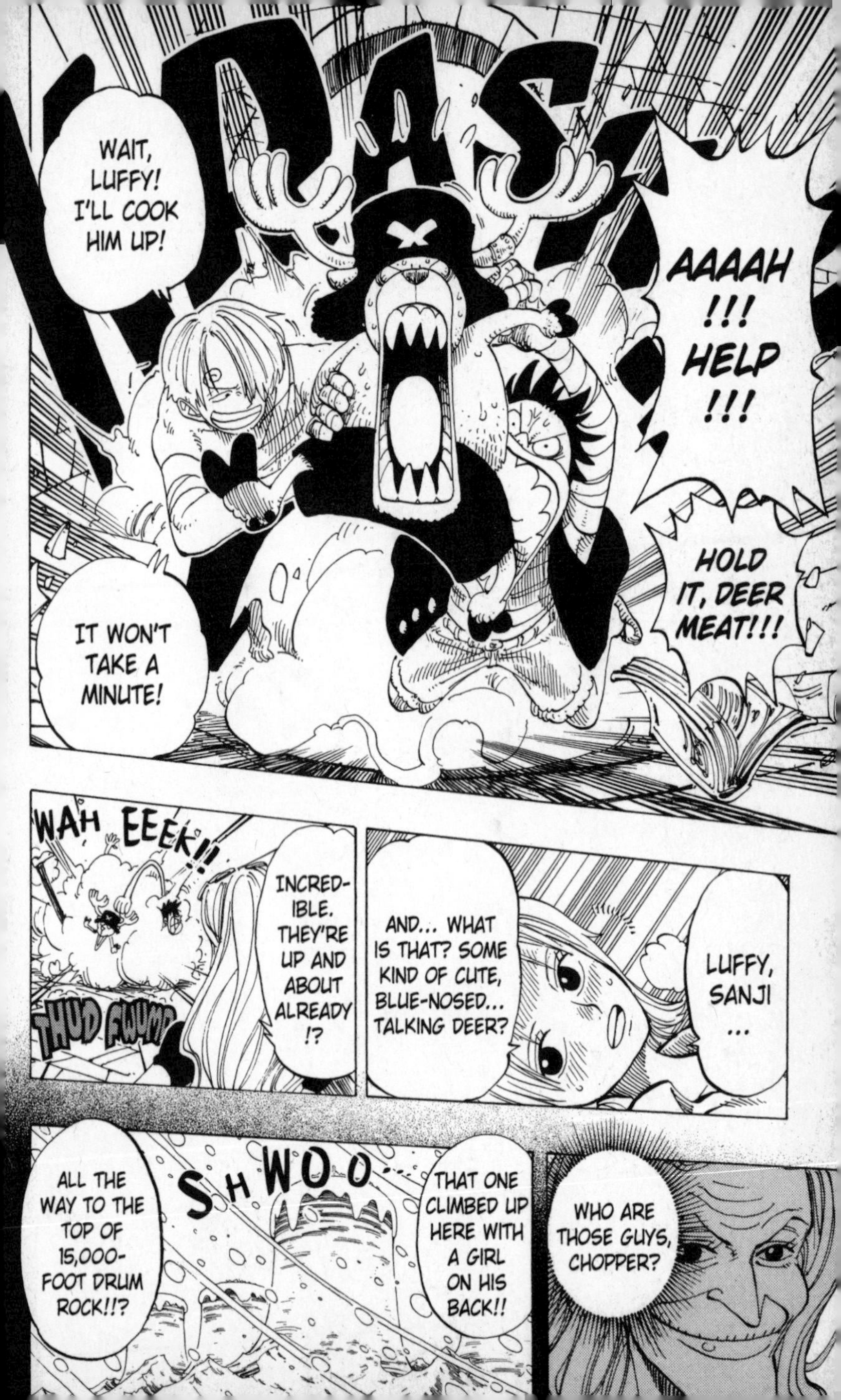
AAAAH !!! HELP !!!
WAIT, LUFFY! I'LL COOK HIM UP!
HOLD IT, DEER MEAT!!!
IT WON'T TAKE A MINUTE!
LUFFY, SANJI ...
AND... WHAT IS THAT? SOME KIND OF CUTE, BLUE-NOSED... TALKING DEER?
INCREDIBLE. THEY'RE UP AND ABOUT ALREADY !?
WAH EEEK!!
THUD FWUMP
WHO ARE THOSE GUYS, CHOPPER?
THAT ONE CLIMBED UP HERE WITH A GIRL ON HIS BACK!!
SHWOO
ALL THE WAY TO THE TOP OF 15,000-FOOT DRUM ROCK!!?

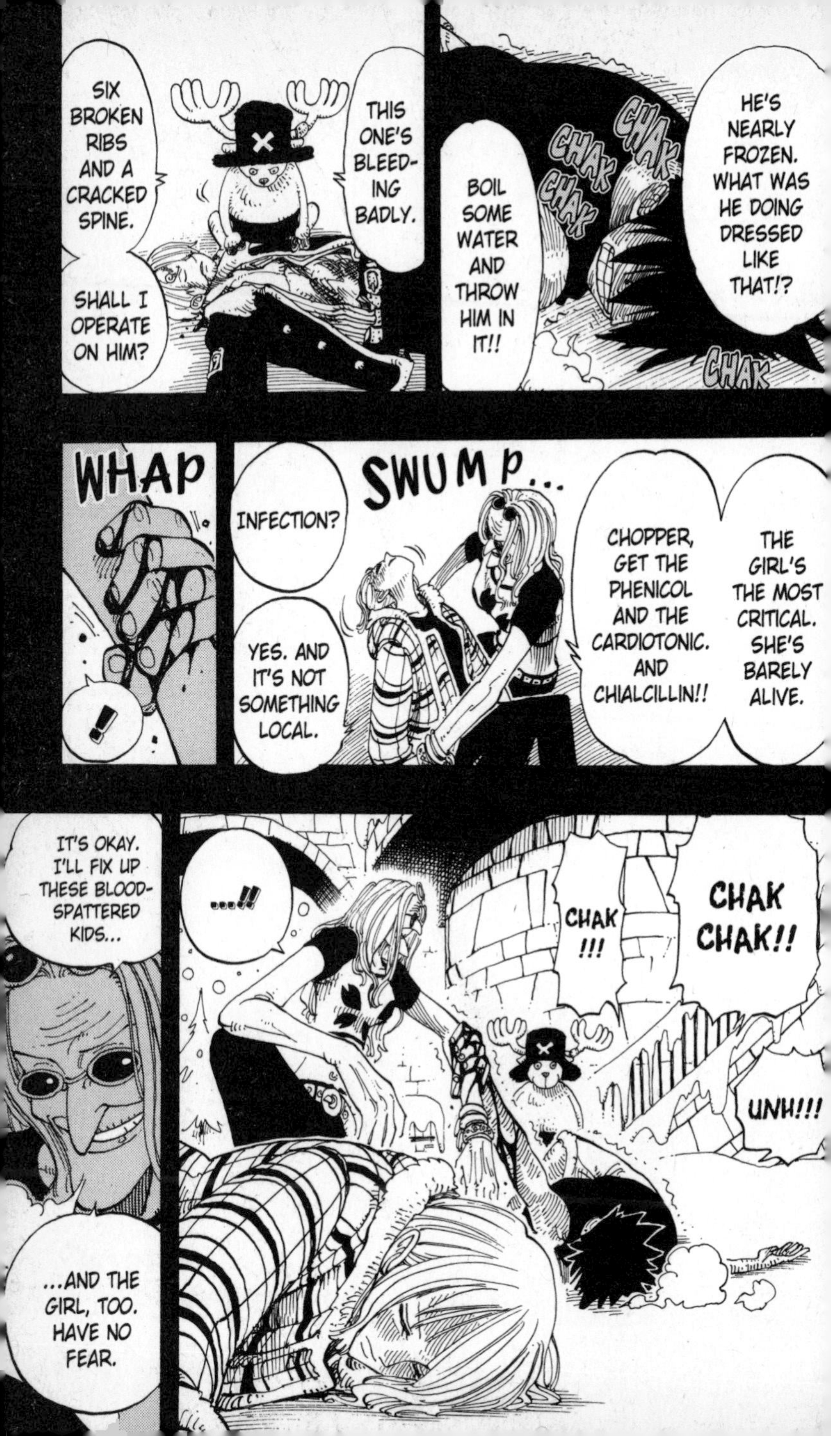
HE'S NEARLY FROZEN. WHAT WAS HE DOING DRESSED LIKE THAT!?
CHAK
CHAK
CHAK
CHAK
BOIL SOME WATER AND THROW HIM IN IT!!
THIS ONE'S BLEED-ING BADLY.
SIX BROKEN RIBS AND A CRACKED SPINE.
SHALL I OPERATE ON HIM?
THE GIRL'S THE MOST CRITICAL. SHE'S BARELY ALIVE.
CHOPPER, GET THE PHENICOL AND THE CARDIOTONIC. AND CHIALCILLIN!!
SWUMP...
INFECTION?
YES. AND IT'S NOT SOMETHING LOCAL.
WHAP
!
CHAK CHAK!!
CHAK !!!
...!!
UNH!!!
IT'S OKAY. I'LL FIX UP THESE BLOOD-SPATTERED KIDS...
...AND THE GIRL, TOO. HAVE NO FEAR.

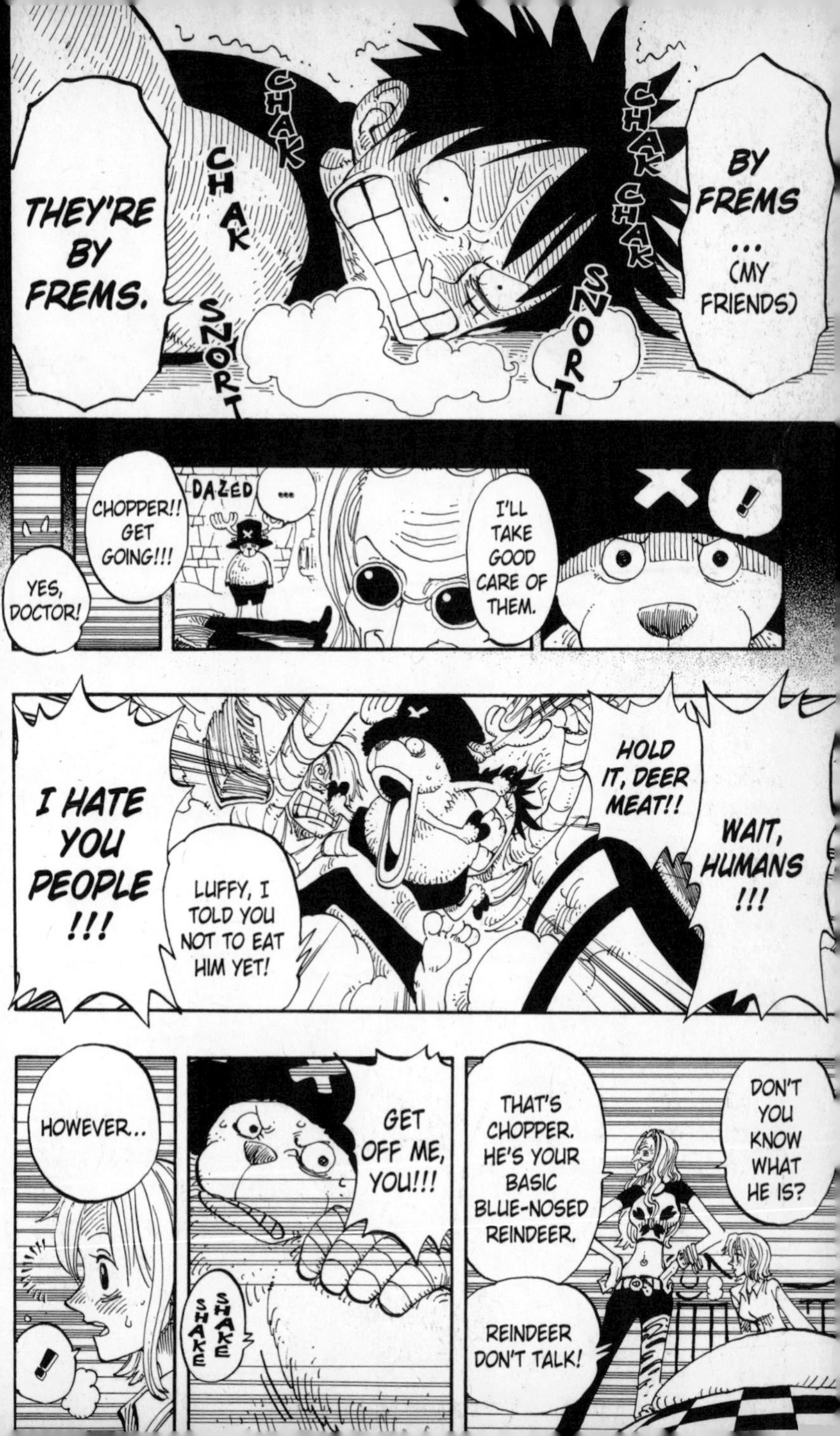
BY FREMS ... (MY FRIENDS)
CHAK CHAK CHAK
SNORT
CHAK
CHAK
SNORT
THEY'RE BY FREMS.
!
I'LL TAKE GOOD CARE OF THEM.
...
DAZED
CHOPPER!! GET GOING!!!
YES, DOCTOR!
WAIT, HUMANS !!!
HOLD IT, DEER MEAT!!
LUFFY, I TOLD YOU NOT TO EAT HIM YET!
I HATE YOU PEOPLE !!!
DON'T YOU KNOW WHAT HE IS?
THAT'S CHOPPER. HE'S YOUR BASIC BLUE-NOSED REINDEER.
REINDEER DON'T TALK!
GET OFF ME, YOU!!!
SHAKE SHAKE
HOWEVER...
!

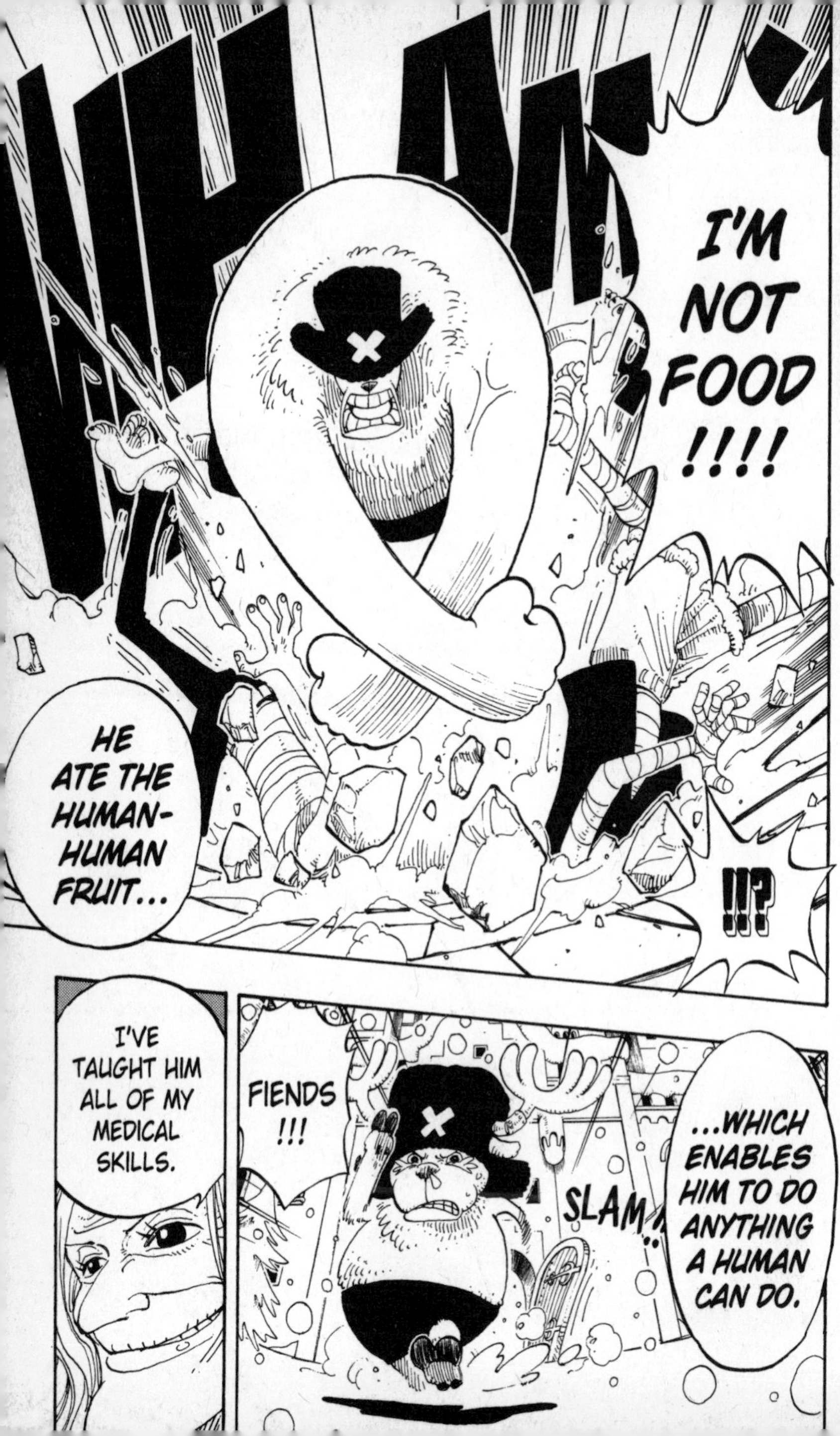
I'M NOT FOOD !!!!
!!?
HE ATE THE HUMAN-HUMAN FRUIT...
...WHICH ENABLES HIM TO DO ANYTHING A HUMAN CAN DO.
SLAM
FIENDS !!!
I'VE TAUGHT HIM ALL OF MY MEDICAL SKILLS.

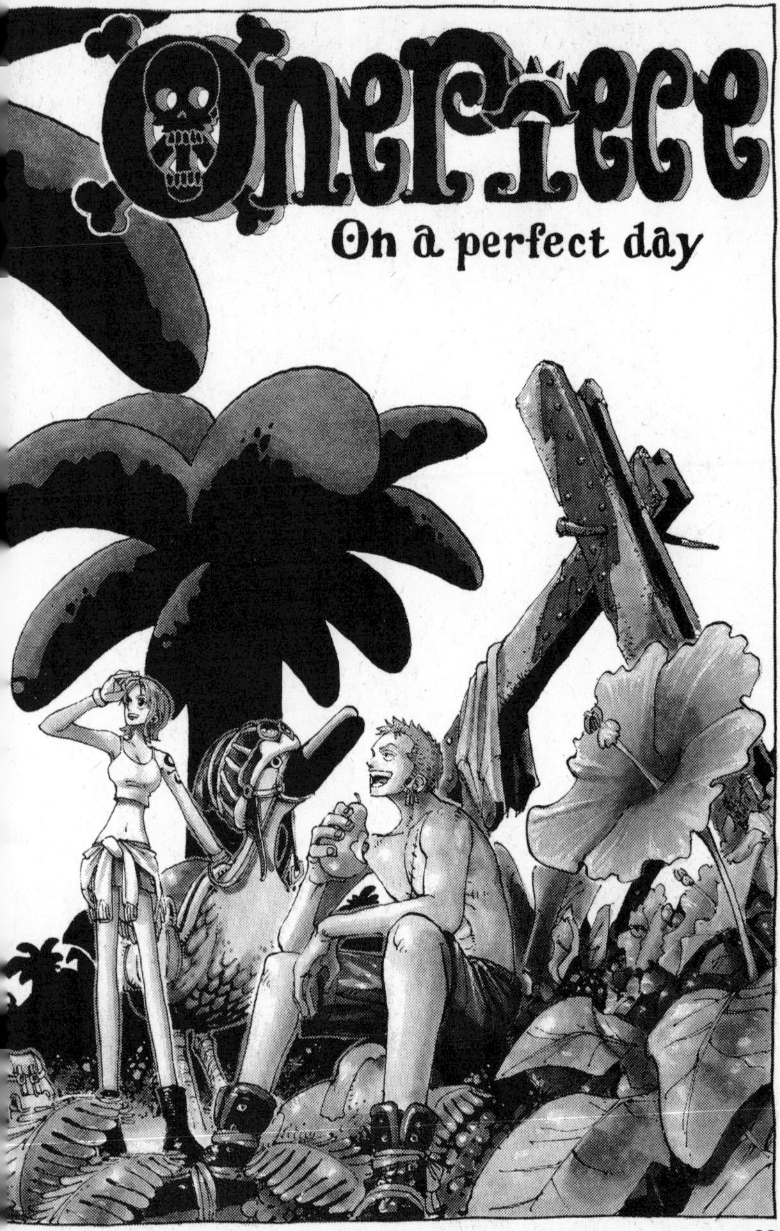
One Piece
On a perfect day

Chapter 140:

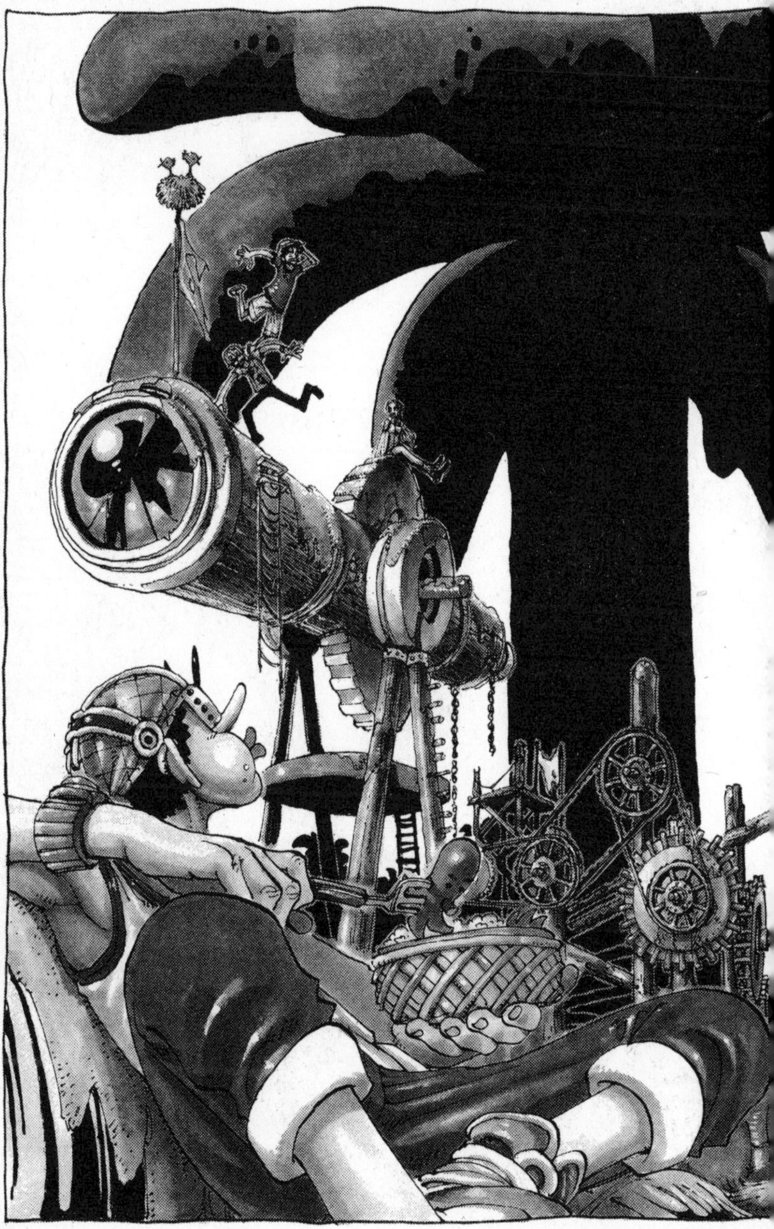

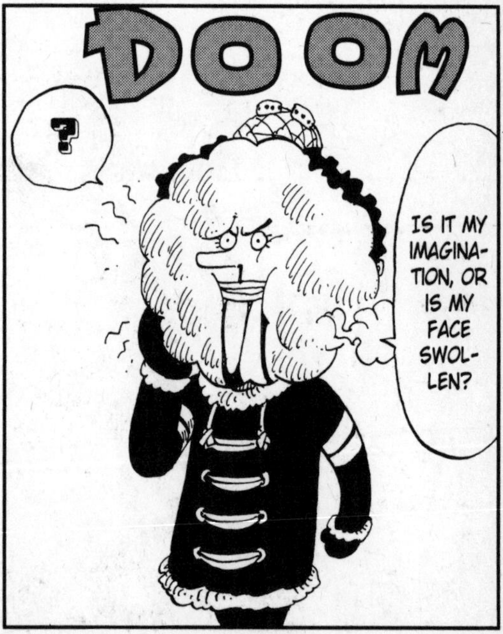
DOOM
IS IT MY IMAGINATION, OR IS MY FACE SWOLLEN?
?

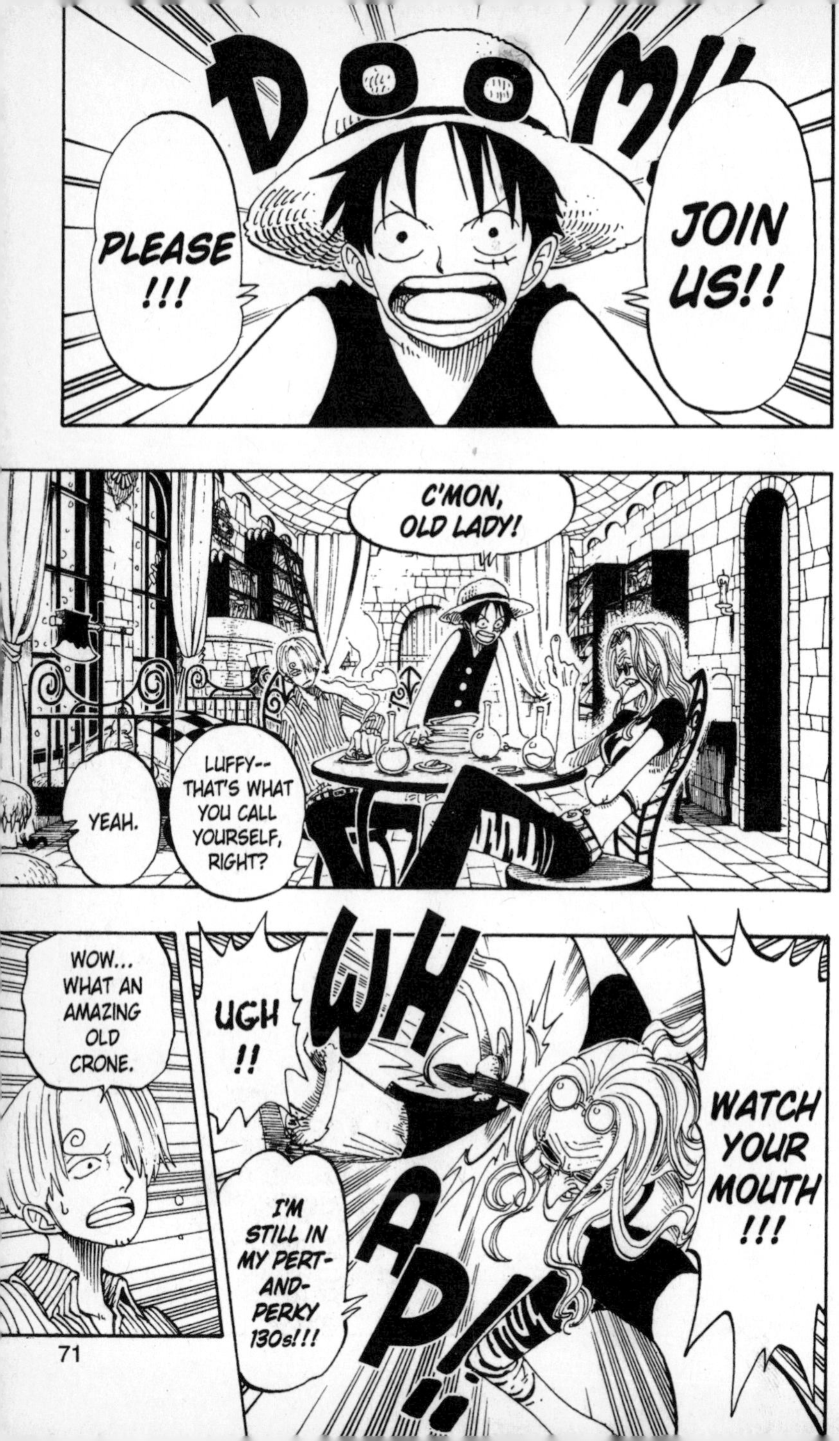
DOOM!!
JOIN US!!
PLEASE!!!
C'MON, OLD LADY!
LUFFY-- THAT'S WHAT YOU CALL YOURSELF, RIGHT?
YEAH.
WATCH YOUR MOUTH!!!
WHAP!!
UGH!!
I'M STILL IN MY PERT-AND-PERKY 130s!!!
WOW... WHAT AN AMAZING OLD CRONE.

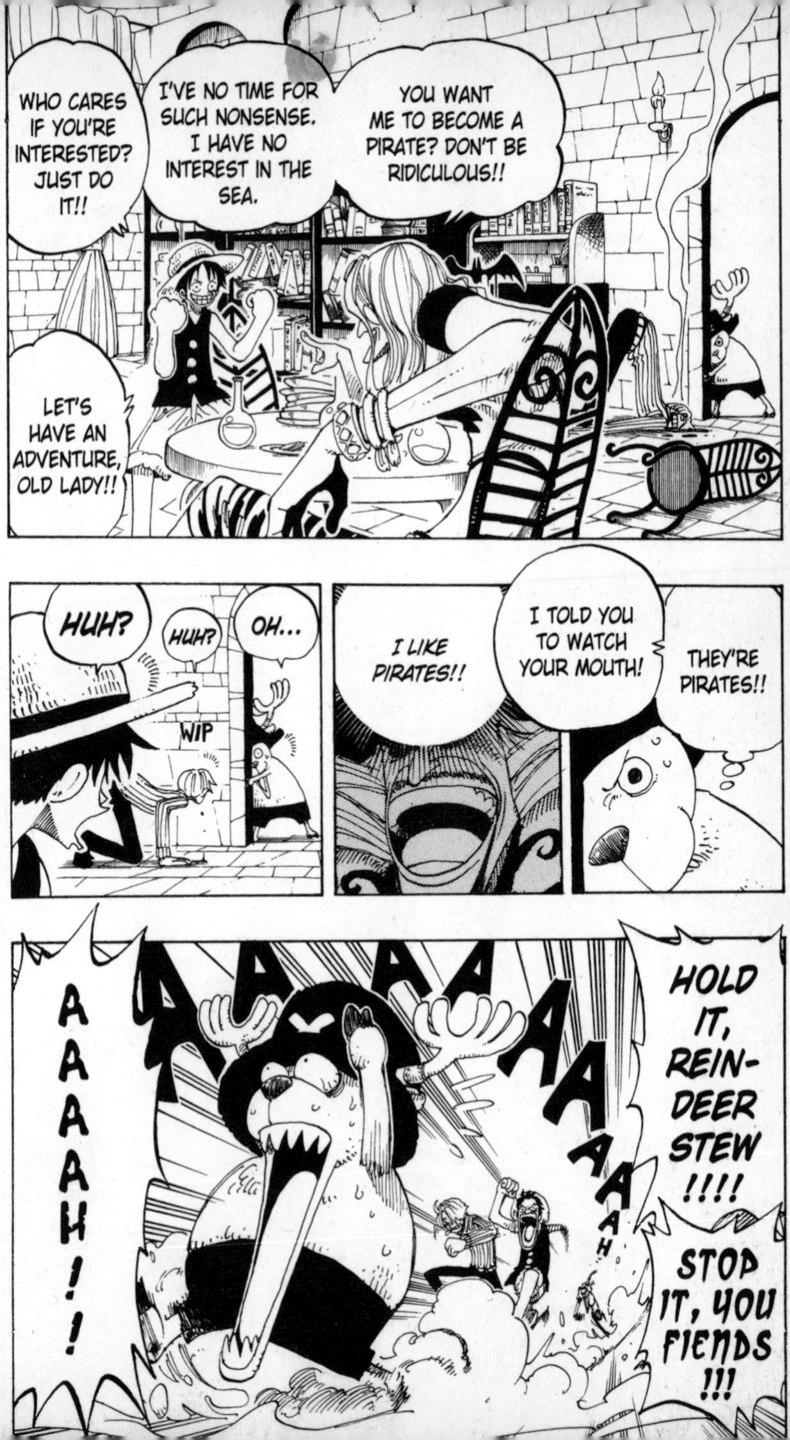
YOU WANT ME TO BECOME A PIRATE? DON'T BE RIDICULOUS!!
I'VE NO TIME FOR SUCH NONSENSE. I HAVE NO INTEREST IN THE SEA.
WHO CARES IF YOU'RE INTERESTED? JUST DO IT!!
LET'S HAVE AN ADVENTURE, OLD LADY!!
THEY'RE PIRATES!!
I TOLD YOU TO WATCH YOUR MOUTH!
I LIKE PIRATES!!
OH...
HUH?
HUH?
WIP
HOLD IT, REIN-DEER STEW!!!!
STOP IT, YOU FIENDS!!!
AAAAAAAAAH
AAAAAH!!

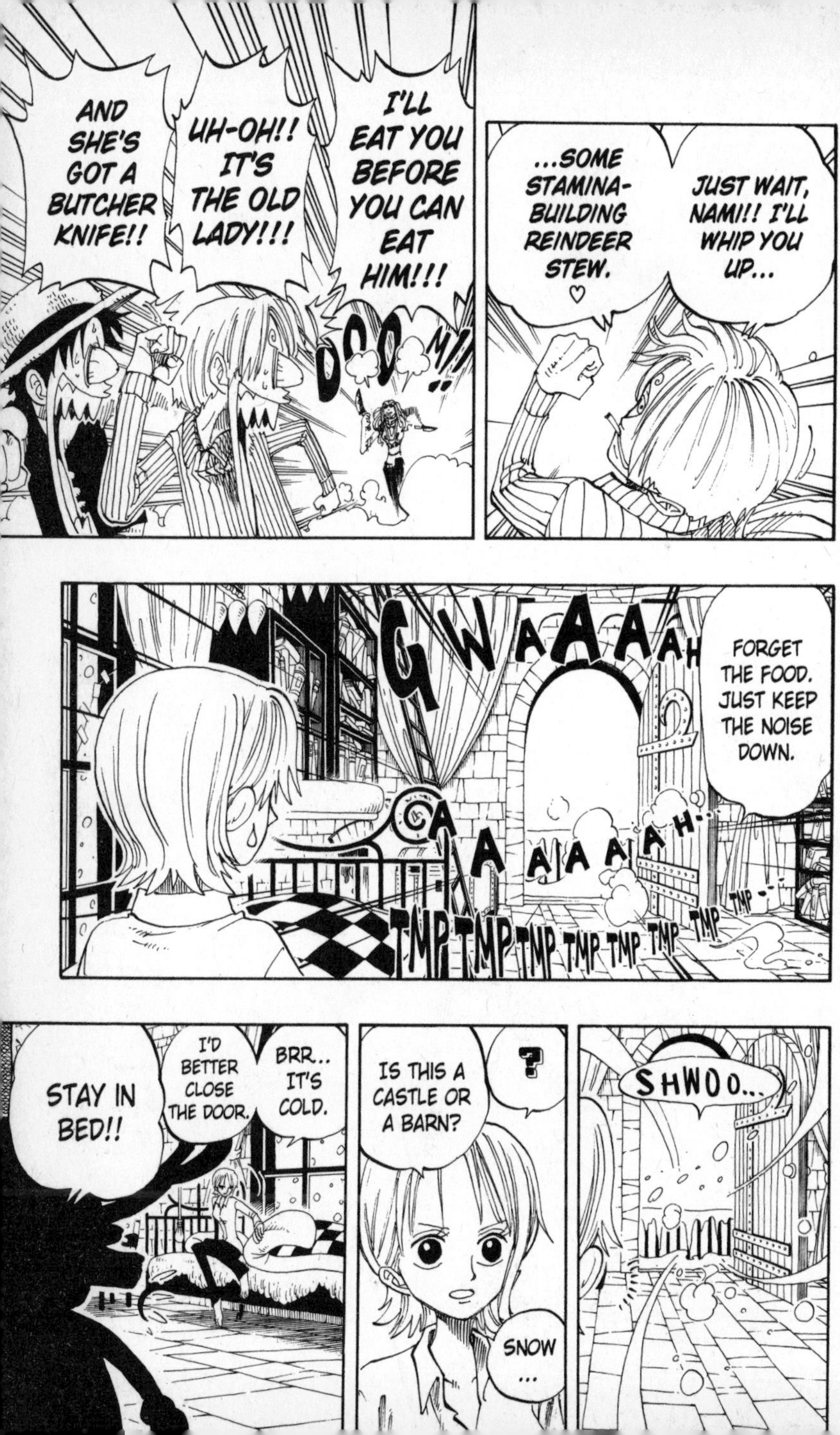
JUST WAIT, NAMI!! I'LL WHIP YOU UP...
...SOME STAMINA-BUILDING REINDEER STEW. ♡
I'LL EAT YOU BEFORE YOU CAN EAT HIM!!!
UH-OH!! IT'S THE OLD LADY!!!
AND SHE'S GOT A BUTCHER KNIFE!!
DOOM!!
FORGET THE FOOD. JUST KEEP THE NOISE DOWN.
GWAAAAAH
AAAAAAH...
TMP TMP TMP TMP TMP TMP TMP TMP
SHWOO...
?
IS THIS A CASTLE OR A BARN?
SNOW ...
BRR... IT'S COLD.
I'D BETTER CLOSE THE DOOR.
STAY IN BED!!

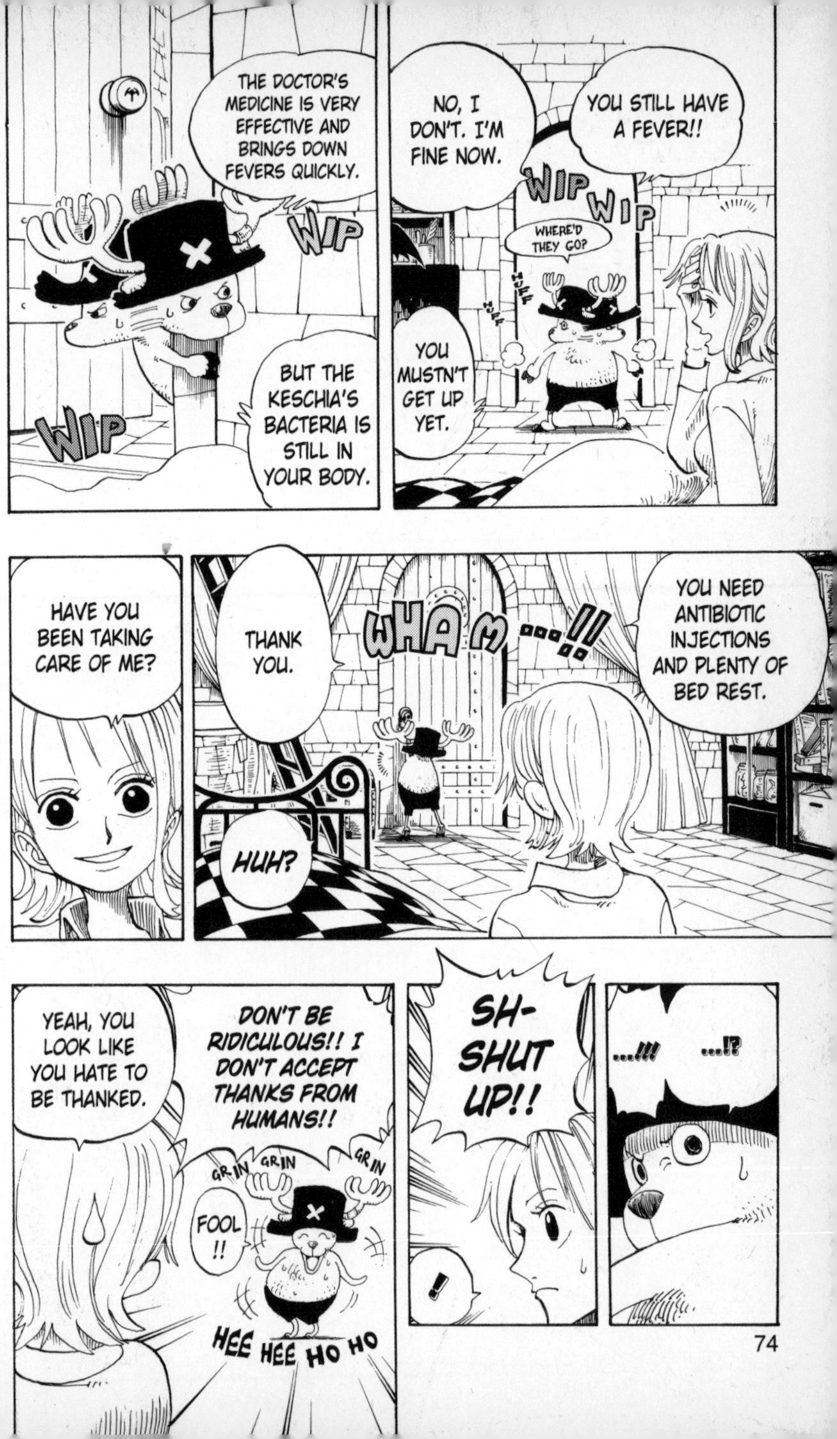
YOU STILL HAVE A FEVER!!
NO, I DON'T. I'M FINE NOW.
WIP WIP
WHERE'D THEY GO?
HUFF
HUFF
YOU MUSTN'T GET UP YET.
THE DOCTOR'S MEDICINE IS VERY EFFECTIVE AND BRINGS DOWN FEVERS QUICKLY.
WIP
BUT THE KESCHIA'S BACTERIA IS STILL IN YOUR BODY.
WIP
YOU NEED ANTIBIOTIC INJECTIONS AND PLENTY OF BED REST.
WHAM...!!
THANK YOU.
HUH?
HAVE YOU BEEN TAKING CARE OF ME?
...!!! ...!?
SH-SHUT UP!!
!
DON'T BE RIDICULOUS!! I DON'T ACCEPT THANKS FROM HUMANS!!
YEAH, YOU LOOK LIKE YOU HATE TO BE THANKED.
GRIN GRIN GRIN
FOOL!!
HEE HEE HO HO

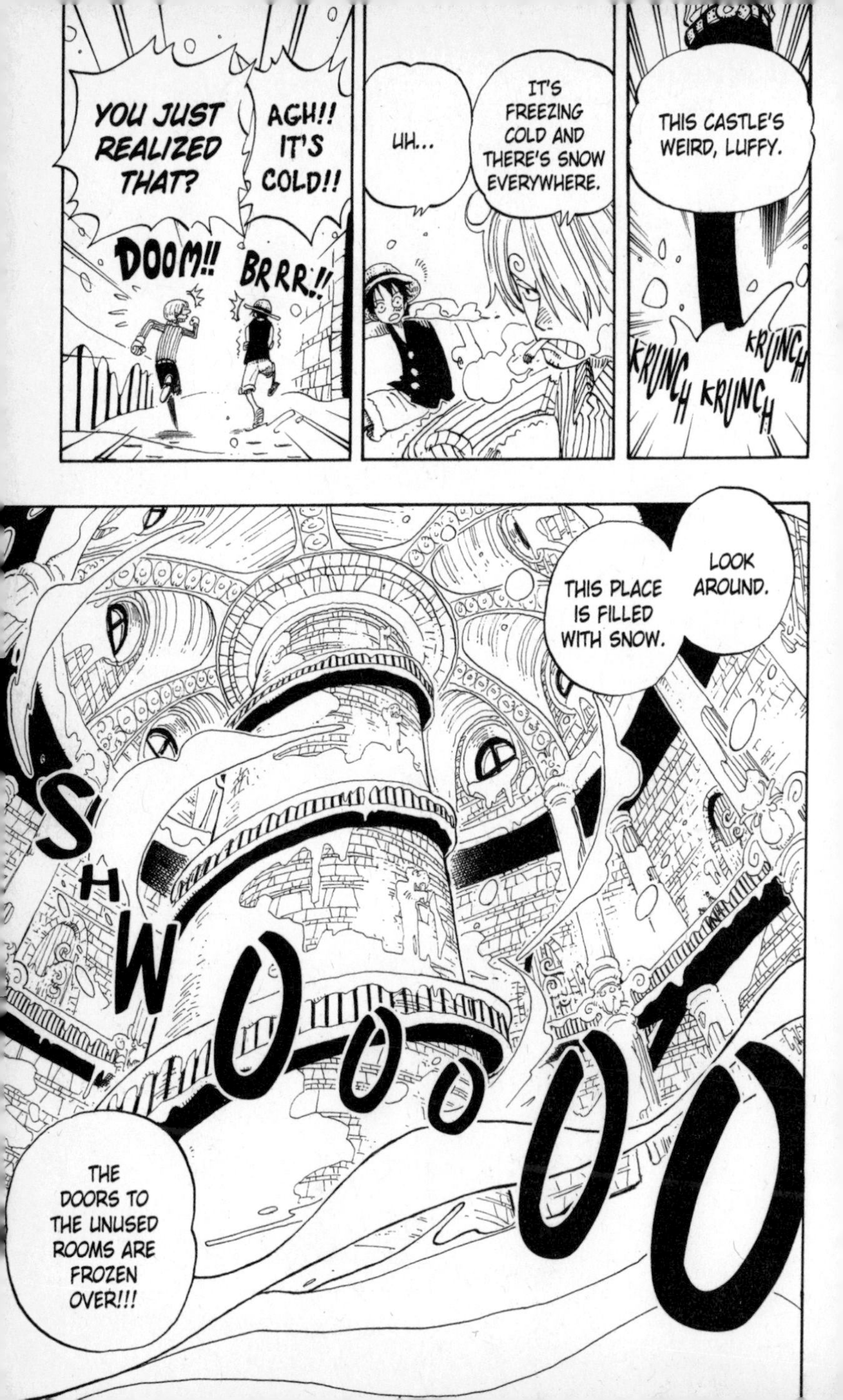
THIS CASTLE'S WEIRD, LUFFY.
KRUNCH KRUNCH KRUNCH
IT'S FREEZING COLD AND THERE'S SNOW EVERYWHERE.
UH...
AGH!! IT'S COLD!!
YOU JUST REALIZED THAT?
BRRR!!
DOOM!!
LOOK AROUND.
THIS PLACE IS FILLED WITH SNOW.
SHWOOOOOOO
THE DOORS TO THE UNUSED ROOMS ARE FROZEN OVER!!!

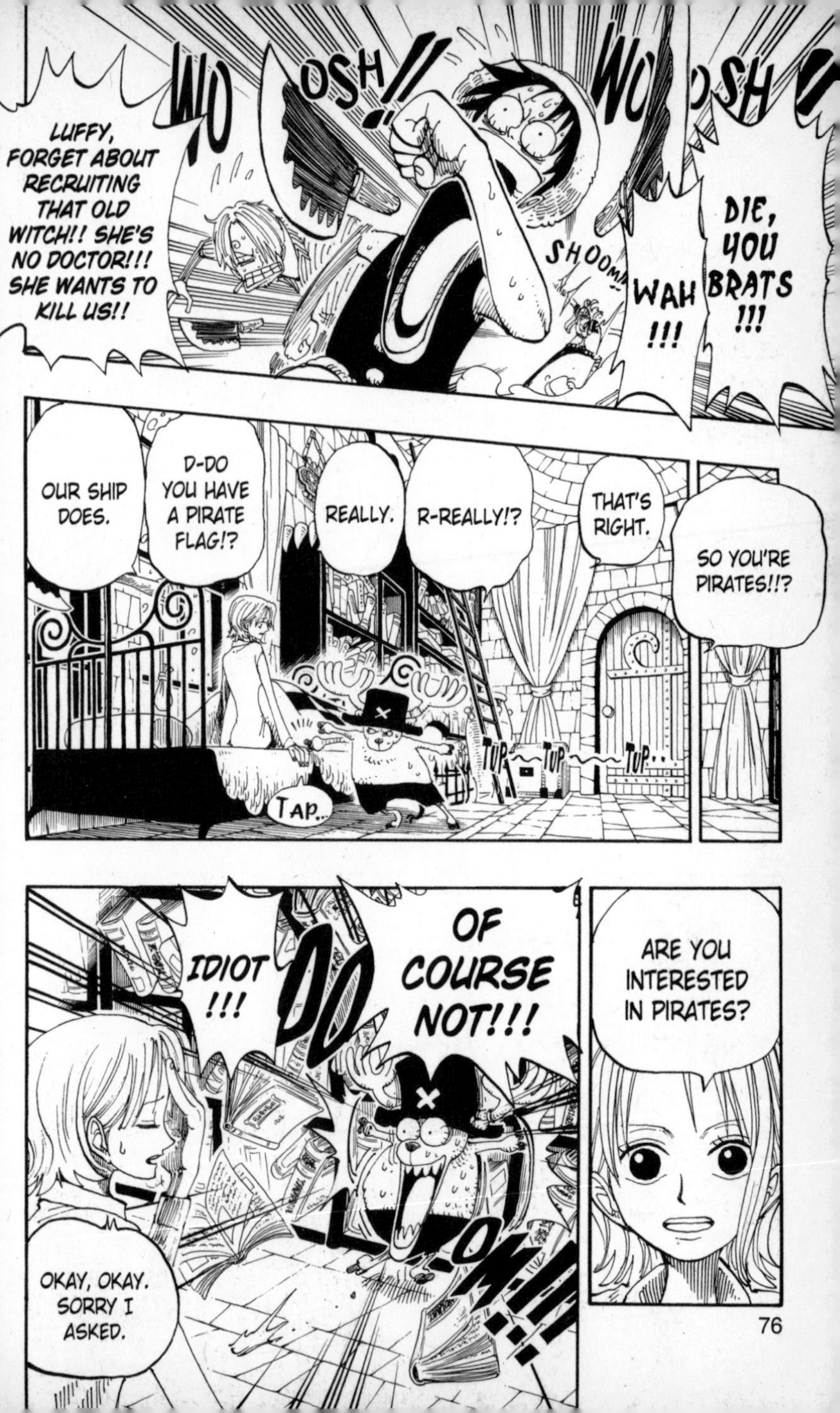
WOOSH
DIE, YOU BRATS!!!
WAH!!!
SHOOM
WOOSH!!
LUFFY, FORGET ABOUT RECRUITING THAT OLD WITCH!! SHE'S NO DOCTOR!!! SHE WANTS TO KILL US!!
SO YOU'RE PIRATES!!?
THAT'S RIGHT.
R-REALLY!?
REALLY.
D-DO YOU HAVE A PIRATE FLAG!?
OUR SHIP DOES.
TUP TUP TUP..
TAP...
ARE YOU INTERESTED IN PIRATES?
OF COURSE NOT!!!
IDIOT!!!
DOOM!!!
OKAY, OKAY. SORRY I ASKED.

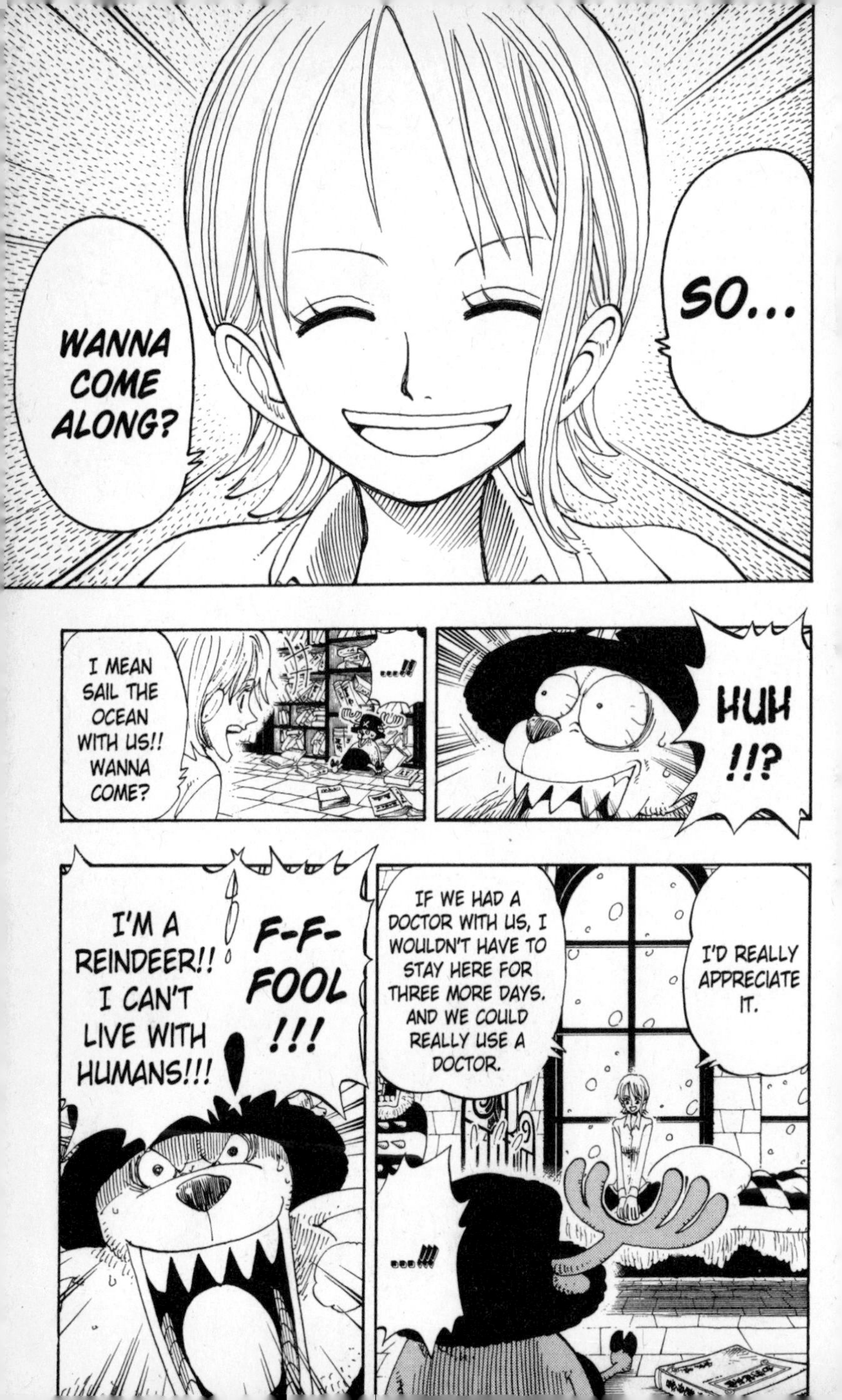
SO...
WANNA COME ALONG?
HUH !!?
...!!
I MEAN SAIL THE OCEAN WITH US!! WANNA COME?
I'D REALLY APPRECIATE IT.
IF WE HAD A DOCTOR WITH US, I WOULDN'T HAVE TO STAY HERE FOR THREE MORE DAYS. AND WE COULD REALLY USE A DOCTOR.
...!!!
F-F-FOOL!!!
I'M A REINDEER!! I CAN'T LIVE WITH HUMANS!!!

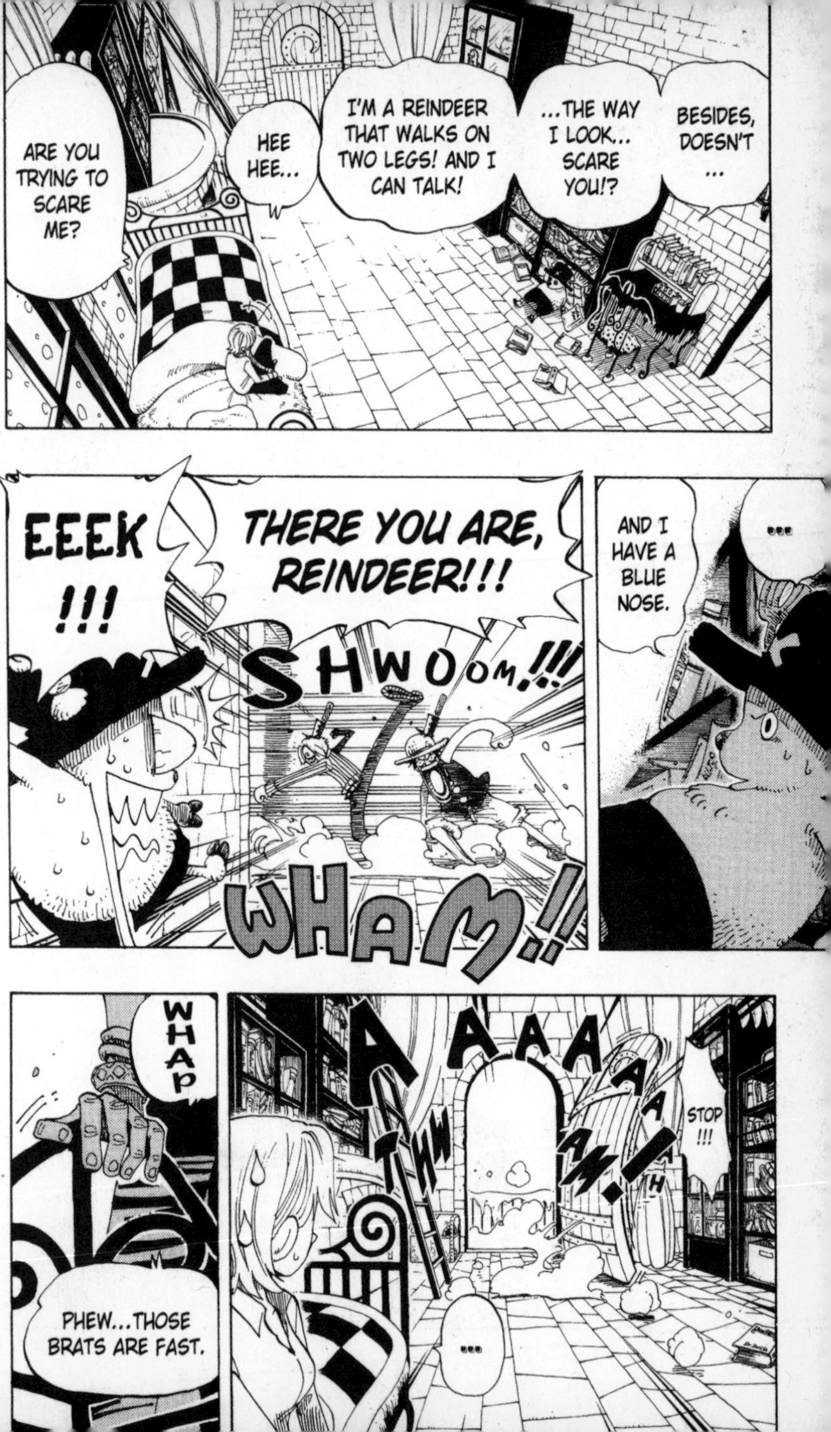
BESIDES, DOESN'T ...
...THE WAY I LOOK... SCARE YOU!?
I'M A REINDEER THAT WALKS ON TWO LEGS! AND I CAN TALK!
HEE HEE...
ARE YOU TRYING TO SCARE ME?
...
AND I HAVE A BLUE NOSE.
THERE YOU ARE, REINDEER!!!
EEEK !!!
SHWOOM!!!
WHAM!!
STOP !!!
AAAAAAAH!
...
WHAP
PHEW...THOSE BRATS ARE FAST.

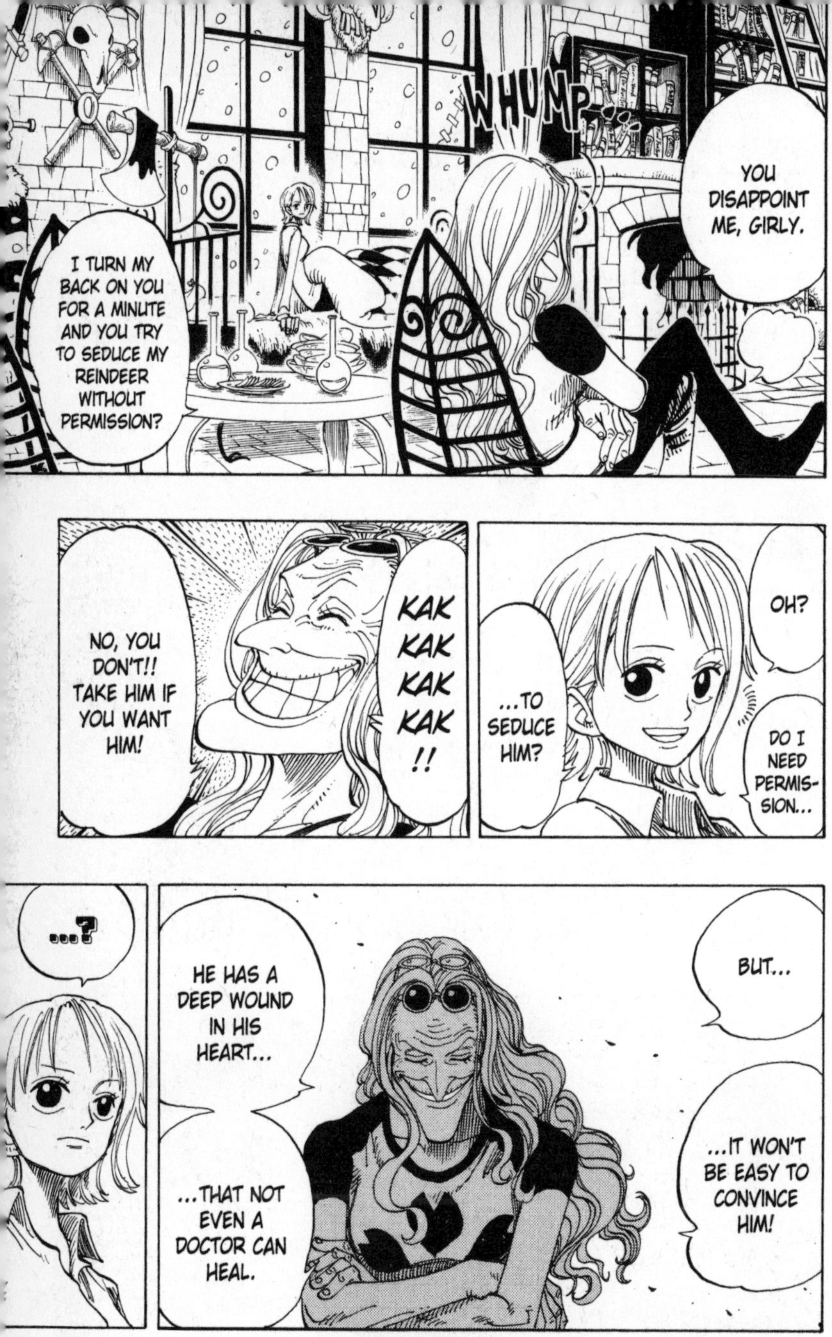
YOU DISAPPOINT ME, GIRLY.
WHUMP
I TURN MY BACK ON YOU FOR A MINUTE AND YOU TRY TO SEDUCE MY REINDEER WITHOUT PERMISSION?
OH?
DO I NEED PERMIS-SION...
...TO SEDUCE HIM?
KAK KAK KAK KAK!!
NO, YOU DON'T!! TAKE HIM IF YOU WANT HIM!
BUT...
...IT WON'T BE EASY TO CONVINCE HIM!
HE HAS A DEEP WOUND IN HIS HEART...
...THAT NOT EVEN A DOCTOR CAN HEAL.
...?

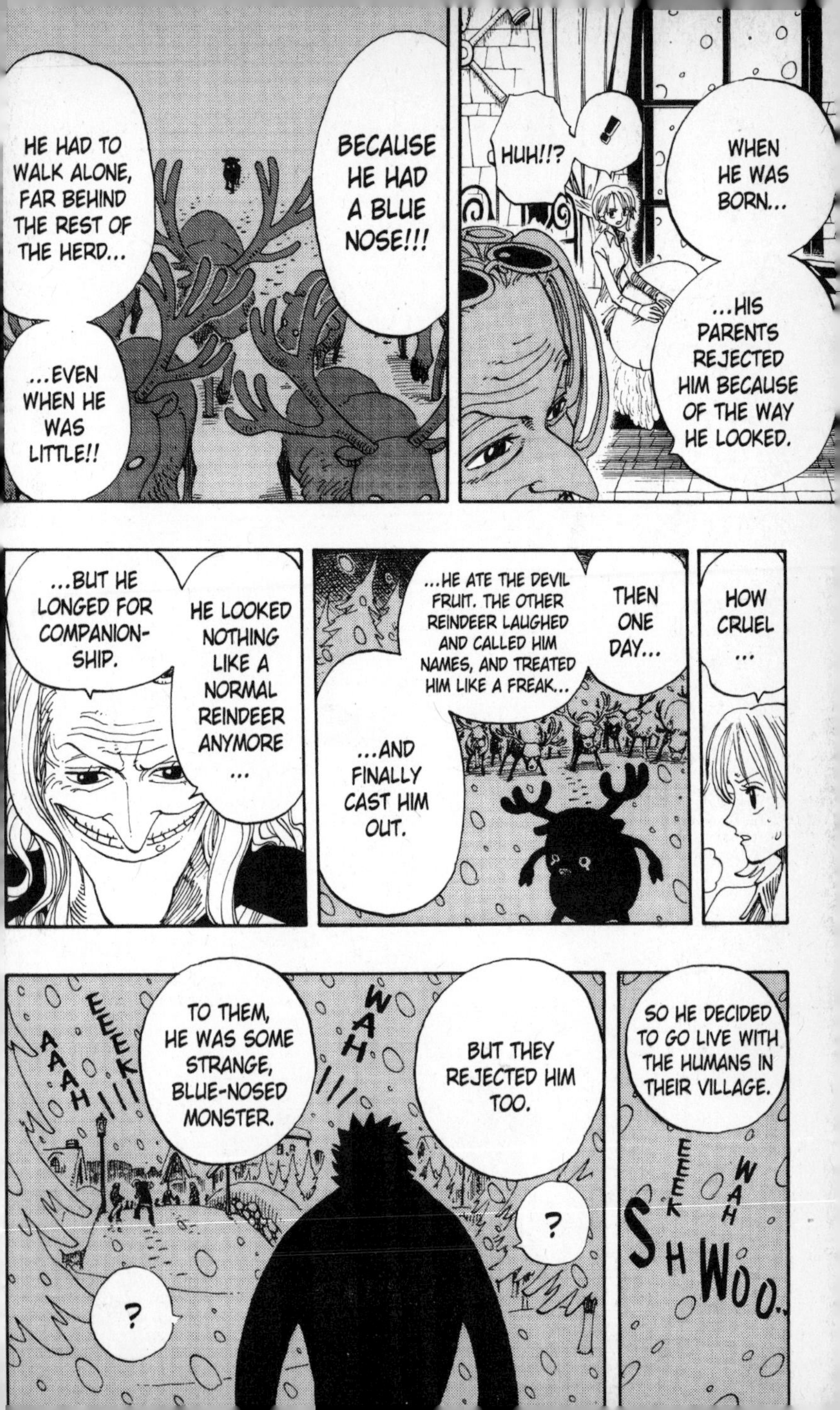
WHEN HE WAS BORN...
!
HUH!!?
...HIS PARENTS REJECTED HIM BECAUSE OF THE WAY HE LOOKED.
BECAUSE HE HAD A BLUE NOSE!!!
HE HAD TO WALK ALONE, FAR BEHIND THE REST OF THE HERD...
...EVEN WHEN HE WAS LITTLE!!
HOW CRUEL...
THEN ONE DAY...
...HE ATE THE DEVIL FRUIT. THE OTHER REINDEER LAUGHED AND CALLED HIM NAMES, AND TREATED HIM LIKE A FREAK...
...AND FINALLY CAST HIM OUT.
HE LOOKED NOTHING LIKE A NORMAL REINDEER ANYMORE...
...BUT HE LONGED FOR COMPANIONSHIP.
SO HE DECIDED TO GO LIVE WITH THE HUMANS IN THEIR VILLAGE.
WAH
EEEK
SHWOO..
BUT THEY REJECTED HIM TOO.
WAH
TO THEM, HE WAS SOME STRANGE, BLUE-NOSED MONSTER.
EEEK
AAAH
?
?

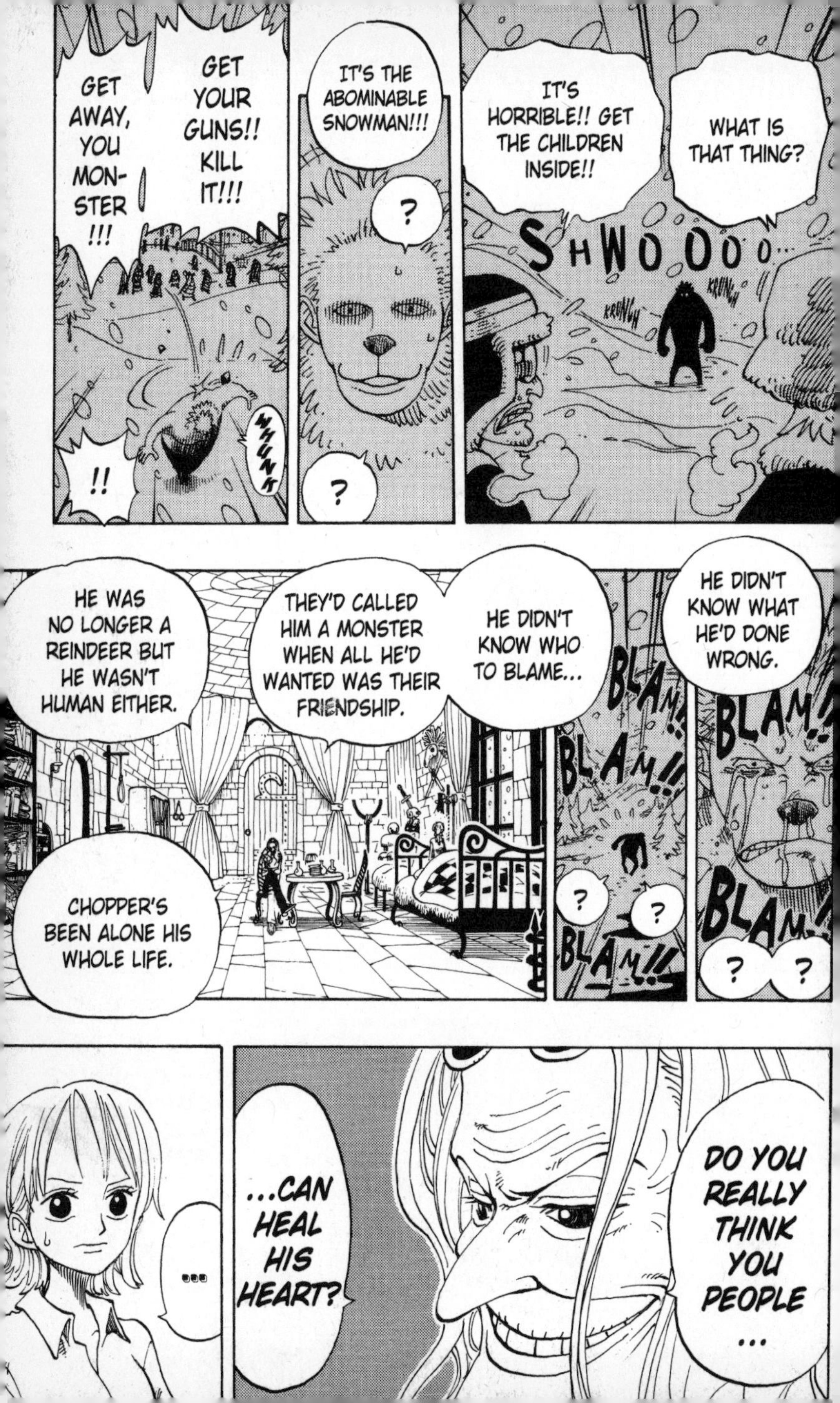

WHAT IS THAT THING?
IT'S HORRIBLE!! GET THE CHILDREN INSIDE!!
SHWOOOO...
KRUNCH
KRUNCH
IT'S THE ABOMINABLE SNOWMAN!!!
?
?
GET YOUR GUNS!! KILL IT!!!
GET AWAY, YOU MONSTER!!!
SHUNK
!!
HE DIDN'T KNOW WHAT HE'D DONE WRONG.
BLAM!!
BLAM!!
?
?
HE DIDN'T KNOW WHO TO BLAME...
BLAM!!
BLAM!!
?
?
BLAM!!
THEY'D CALLED HIM A MONSTER WHEN ALL HE'D WANTED WAS THEIR FRIENDSHIP.
HE WAS NO LONGER A REINDEER BUT HE WASN'T HUMAN EITHER.
CHOPPER'S BEEN ALONE HIS WHOLE LIFE.
DO YOU REALLY THINK YOU PEOPLE...
...CAN HEAL HIS HEART?
...

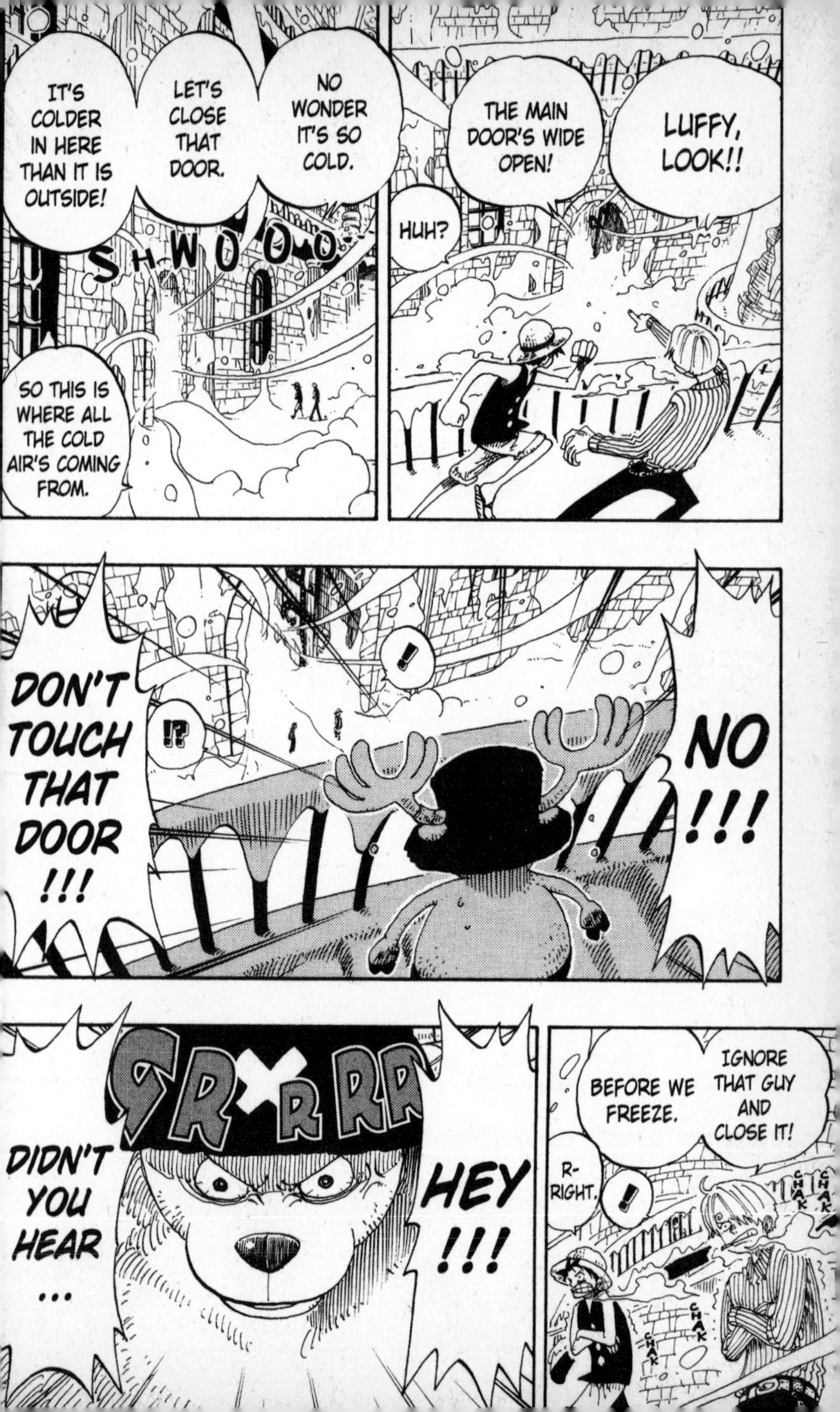
LUFFY, LOOK!!
THE MAIN DOOR'S WIDE OPEN!
HUH?
NO WONDER IT'S SO COLD.
LET'S CLOSE THAT DOOR.
IT'S COLDER IN HERE THAN IT IS OUTSIDE!
SHWOOOO
SO THIS IS WHERE ALL THE COLD AIR'S COMING FROM.
NO!!!
!
!?
DON'T TOUCH THAT DOOR!!!
IGNORE THAT GUY AND CLOSE IT!
BEFORE WE FREEZE.
R-RIGHT.
!
CHAK CHAK
CHAK CHAK
HEY!!!
GRRRR
DIDN'T YOU HEAR...

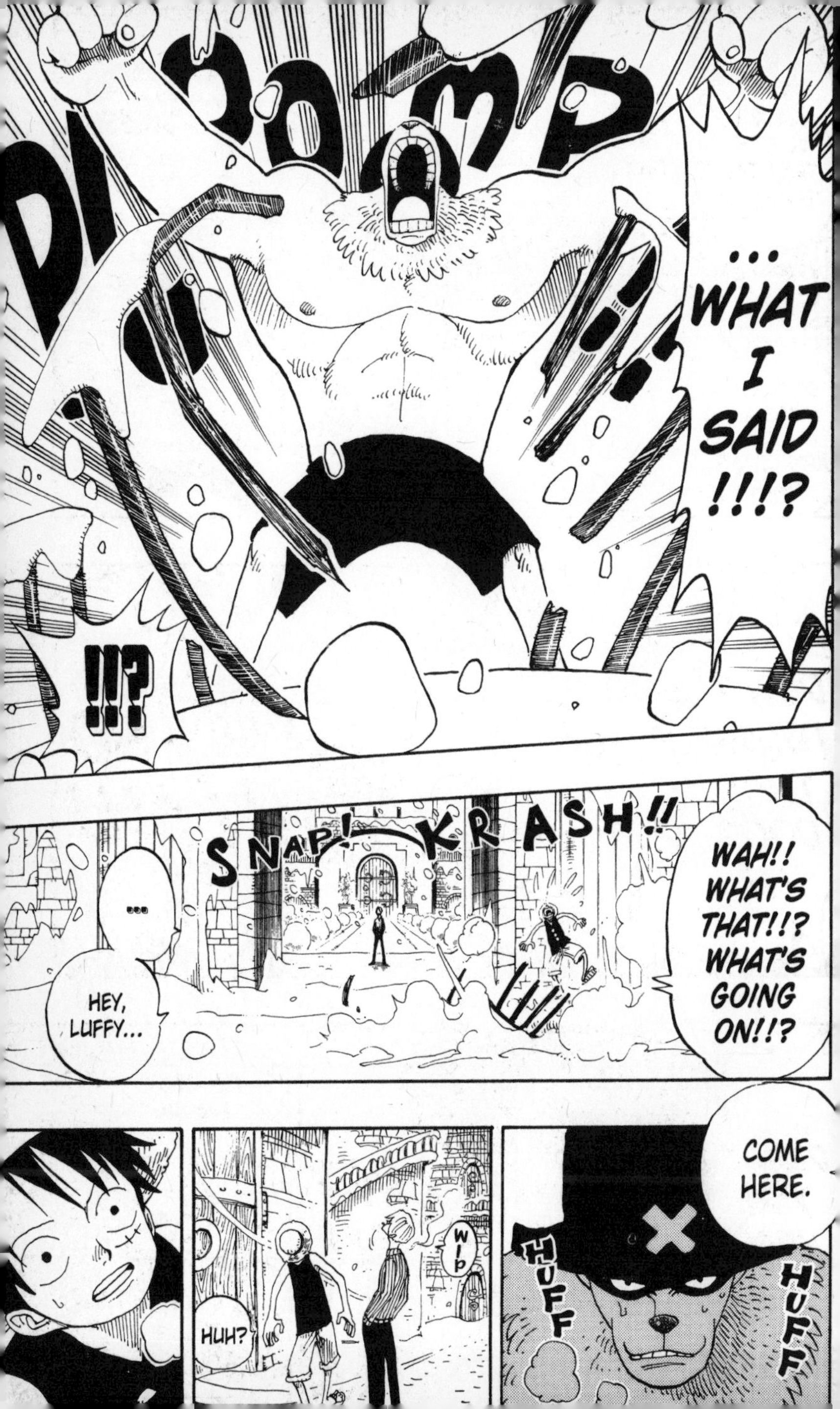
DOOMP
...WHAT I SAID!!!?
!!?
WAH!! WHAT'S THAT!!? WHAT'S GOING ON!!?
SNAP! KRASH!!
...
HEY, LUFFY...
COME HERE.
HUFF
HUFF
WIP
HUH?

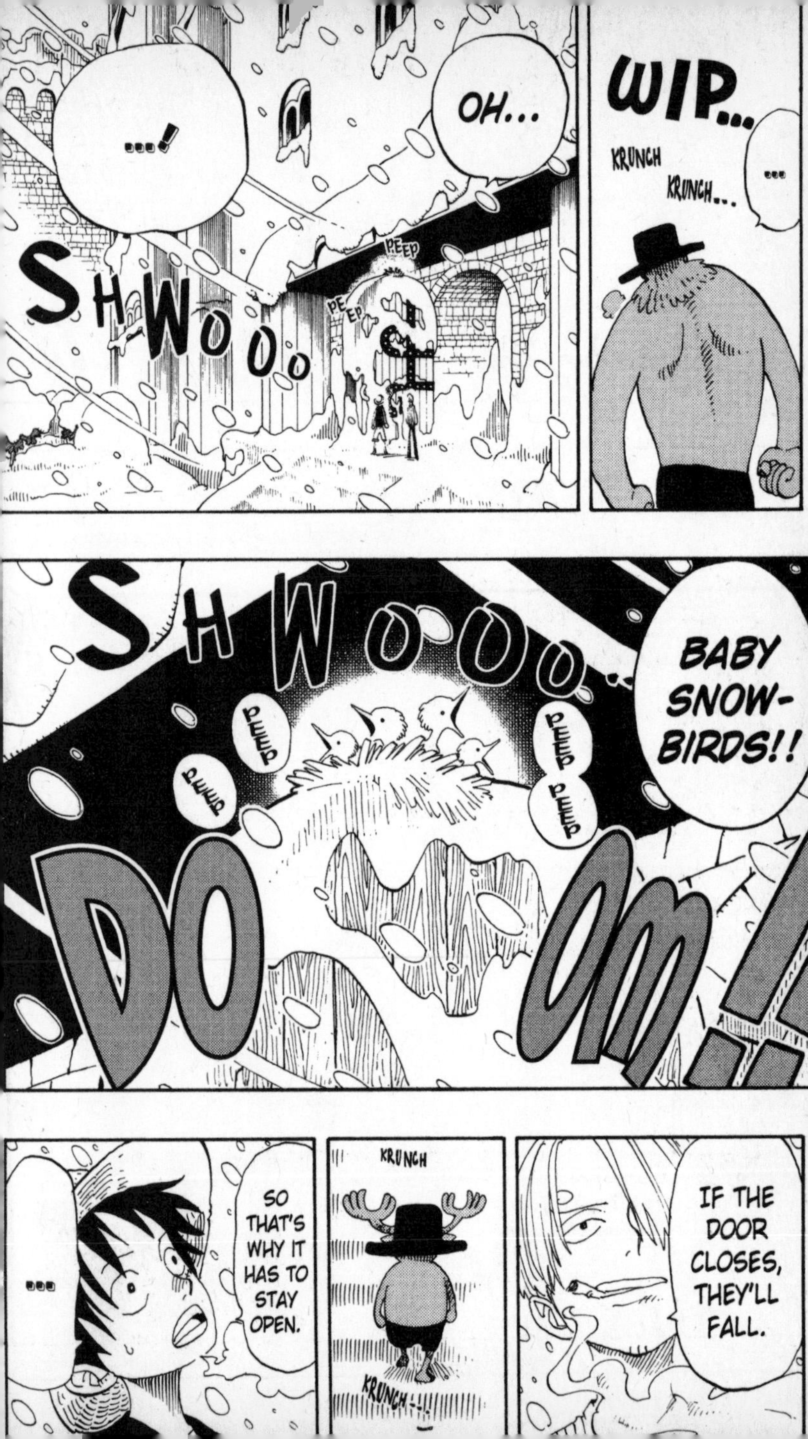
WIP...
KRUNCH
KRUNCH...
...
OH...
...!
PEEP
SHWOOO
PEEP
BABY SNOW-BIRDS!!
SHWOOOO
PEEP
PEEP PEEP
PEEP
PEEP
DOOM!!
IF THE DOOR CLOSES, THEY'LL FALL.
KRUNCH
KRUNCH...!!
SO THAT'S WHY IT HAS TO STAY OPEN.
...

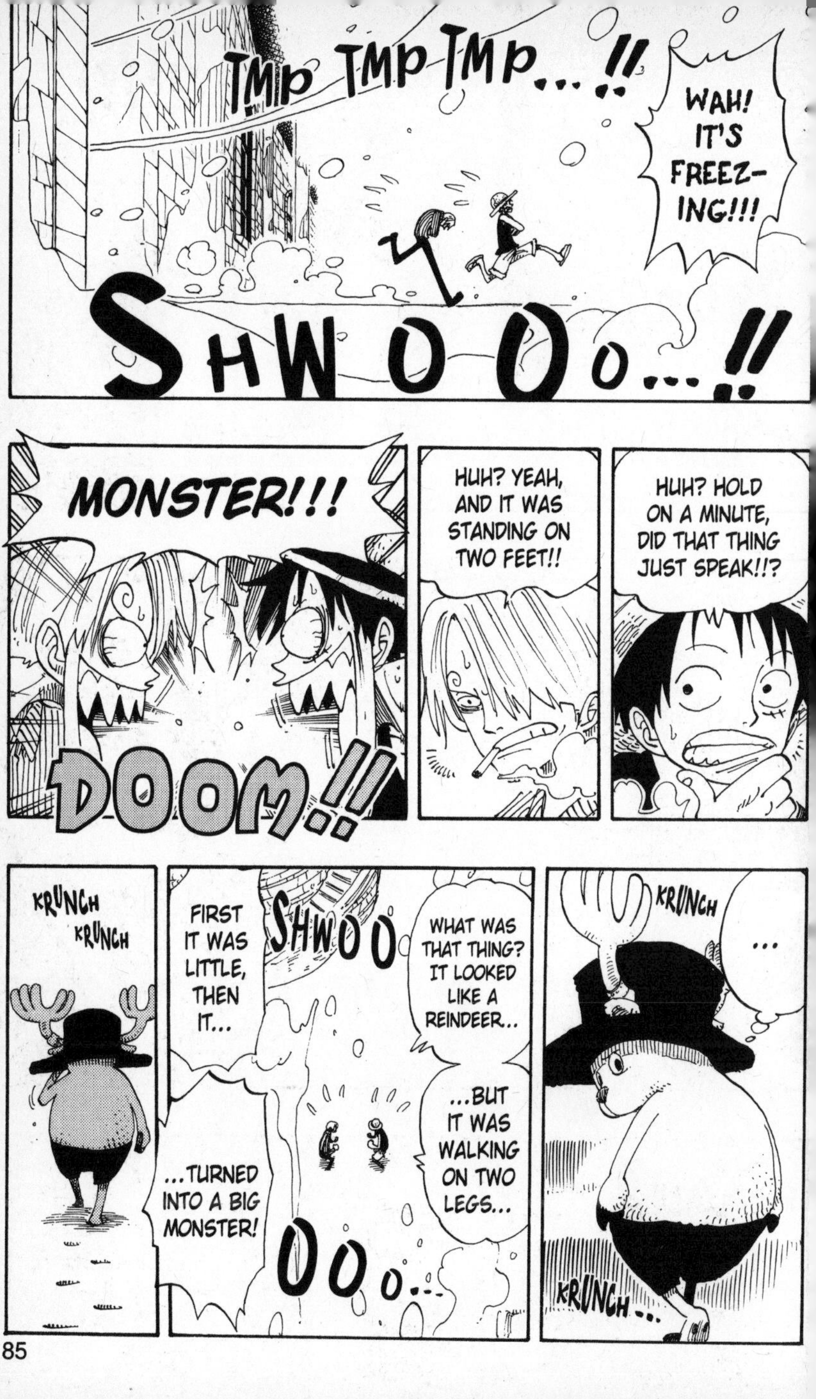
WAH! IT'S FREEZ-ING!!!
TMP TMP TMP...!!
SHWOOo...!!
HUH? HOLD ON A MINUTE, DID THAT THING JUST SPEAK!!?
HUH? YEAH, AND IT WAS STANDING ON TWO FEET!!
MONSTER!!!
DOOM!!
...
KRUNCH
KRUNCH...
WHAT WAS THAT THING? IT LOOKED LIKE A REINDEER...
SHWOOO
FIRST IT WAS LITTLE, THEN IT...
...BUT IT WAS WALKING ON TWO LEGS...
...TURNED INTO A BIG MONSTER!
OOo...
KRUNCH
KRUNCH

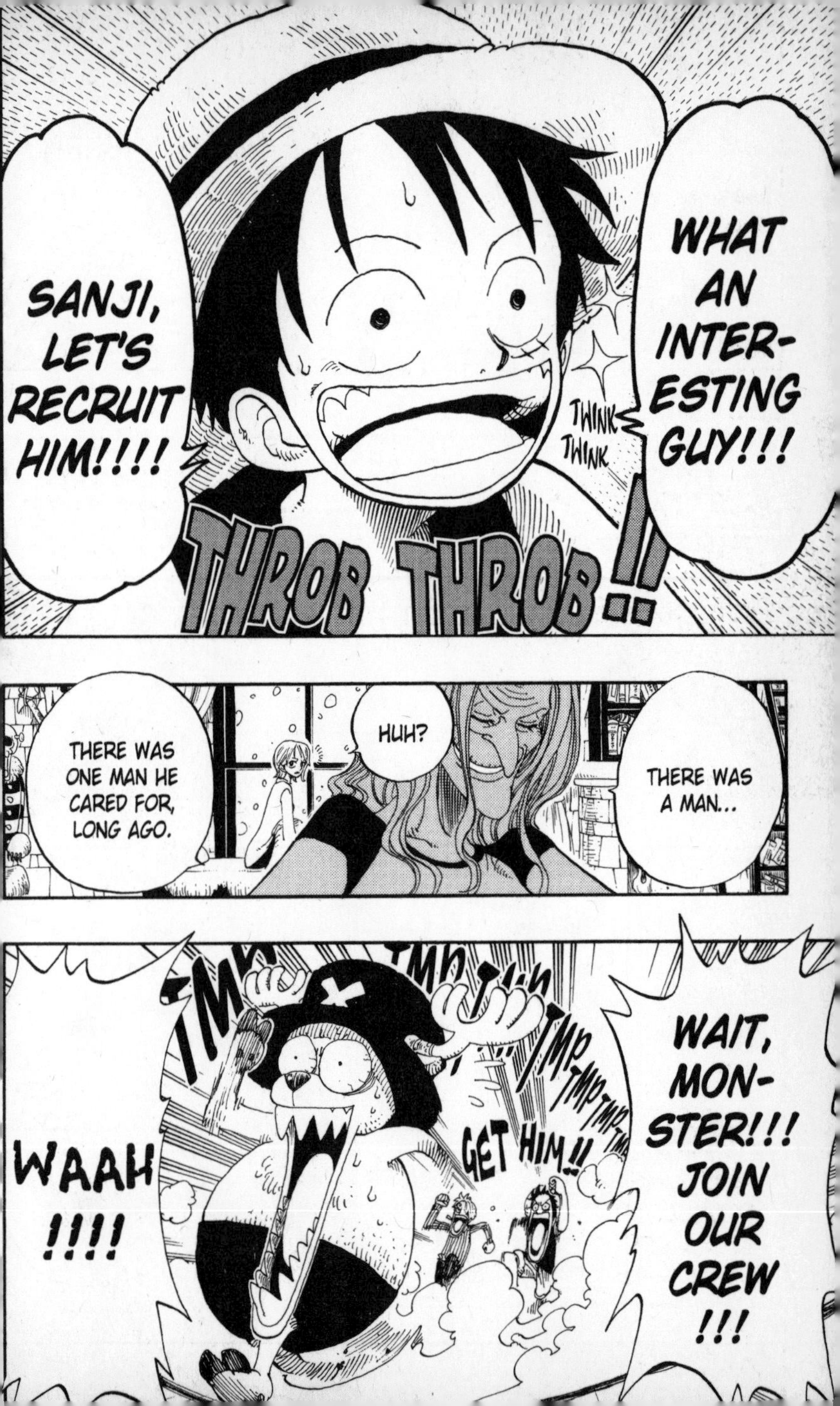
WHAT AN INTER-ESTING GUY!!!
TWINK TWINK
SANJI, LET'S RECRUIT HIM!!!!
THROB THROB!!
THERE WAS A MAN...
HUH?
THERE WAS ONE MAN HE CARED FOR, LONG AGO.
WAIT, MON-STER!!! JOIN OUR CREW!!!
TMP TMP TMP TMP
GET HIM!!
WAAH!!!!

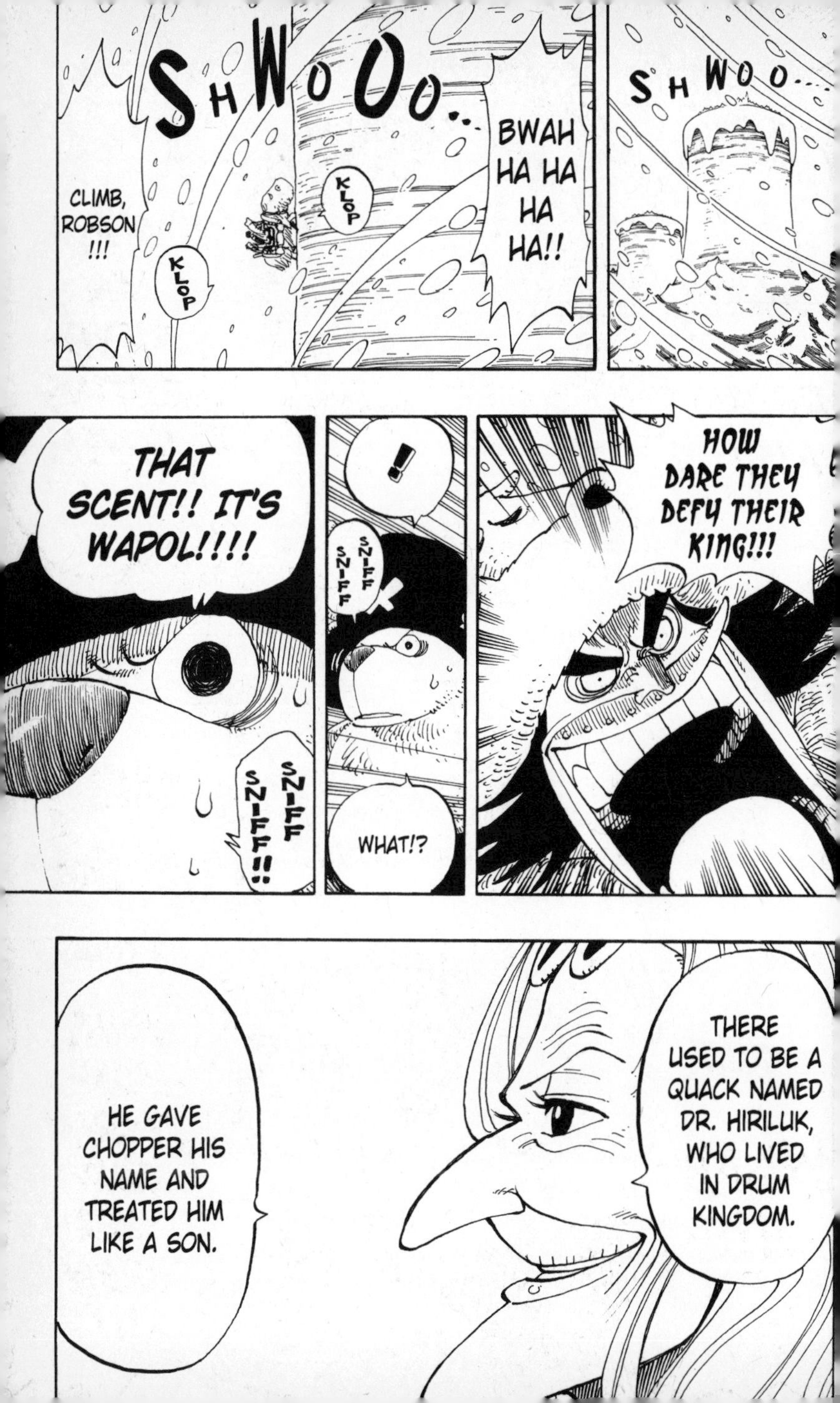
SHWOO...
SHWOOO...
BWAH HA HA HA HA!!
KLOP
CLIMB, ROBSON!!!
KLOP
HOW DARE THEY DEFY THEIR KING!!!
!
SNIFF SNIFF
WHAT!?
THAT SCENT!! IT'S WAPOL!!!!
SNIFF SNIFF!!
THERE USED TO BE A QUACK NAMED DR. HIRILUK, WHO LIVED IN DRUM KINGDOM.
HE GAVE CHOPPER HIS NAME AND TREATED HIM LIKE A SON.

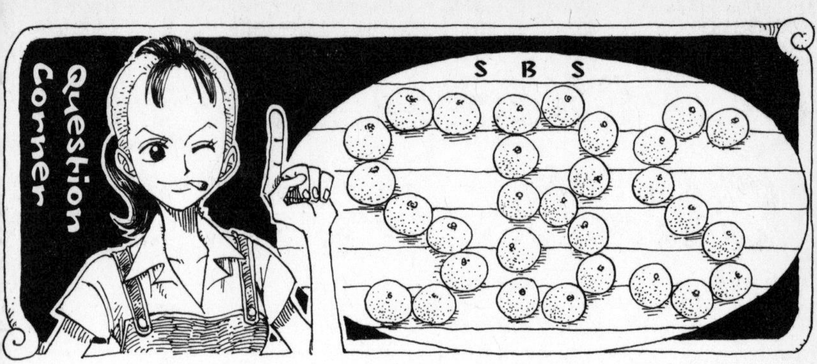
Question Corner
S B S

Reader: Hey, Monkey D. Luffy!! **I'm** gonna be king of the pirates! Got a problem with that, Pirate King?

Oda: Fine, we'll all be pirate kings!! Next question.

Q: This is Jim Jolu Sato!! Here's my question.
If I eat Luffy, will I become a rubber-man!?

A: No, you'll just get food poisoning.

Q: I thought of a catch phrase for *One Piece:*
"Unusual people, friend and foe alike."

A: "Unusual people, reader and author alike."
Nah, the author's totally normal!!

Q: Oda Sensei!! That section on birthdays in volume 15 was way too slapdash!! So I want to discuss this with all of their parents!! But who are Luffy, Zolo, and Sanji's parents?

A: Slapdash? Well, maybe. After all, birthdays determine personality, right? I guess I shouldn't give them birthdays without thinking about it. I think I've learned a valuable lesson.

Q: What are Vivi and Chopper's birthdays? ♡
Could Vivi's be February 2nd, and Chopper's be December 24th?

A: Perfect!! (explosive laugh) Those will work great!!
It's settled! Those are Vivi and Chopper's birthdays!!
Complaints!? I'm not listening to any!! Ha ha ha ha!!

Chapter 141:
QUACK DOCTOR

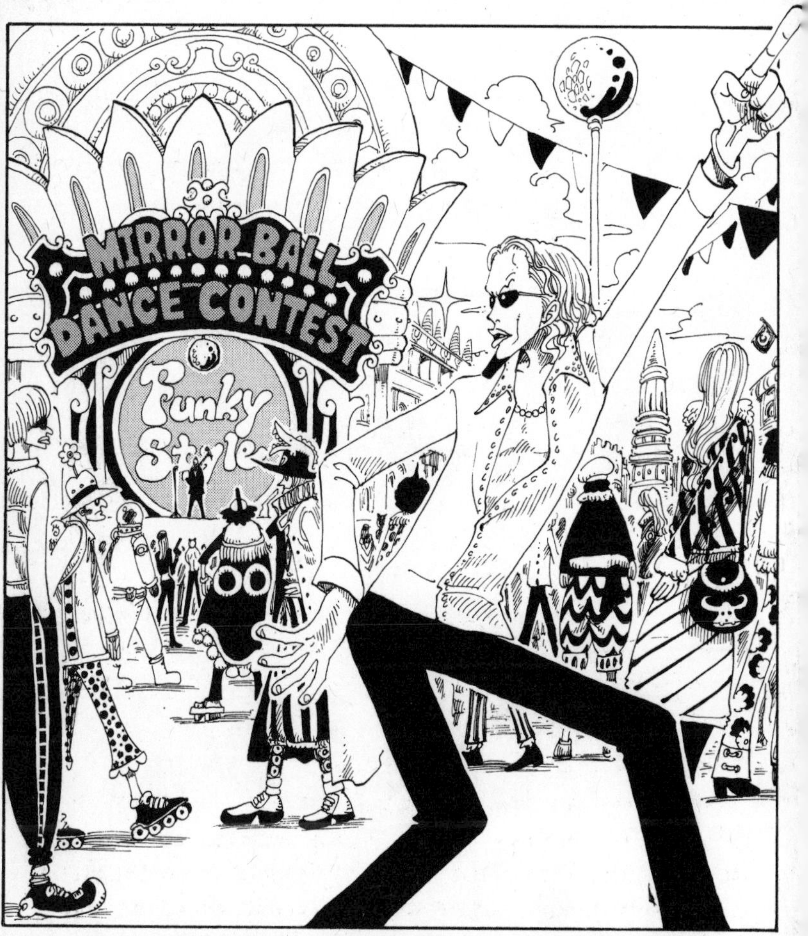
MIRROR-BALL DANCE CONTEST
Funky Style

DJANGO'S DANCE PARADISE, VOL. 12: "DJANGO DISCOVERED IN DISGUISE AT THE DANCE CONTEST"

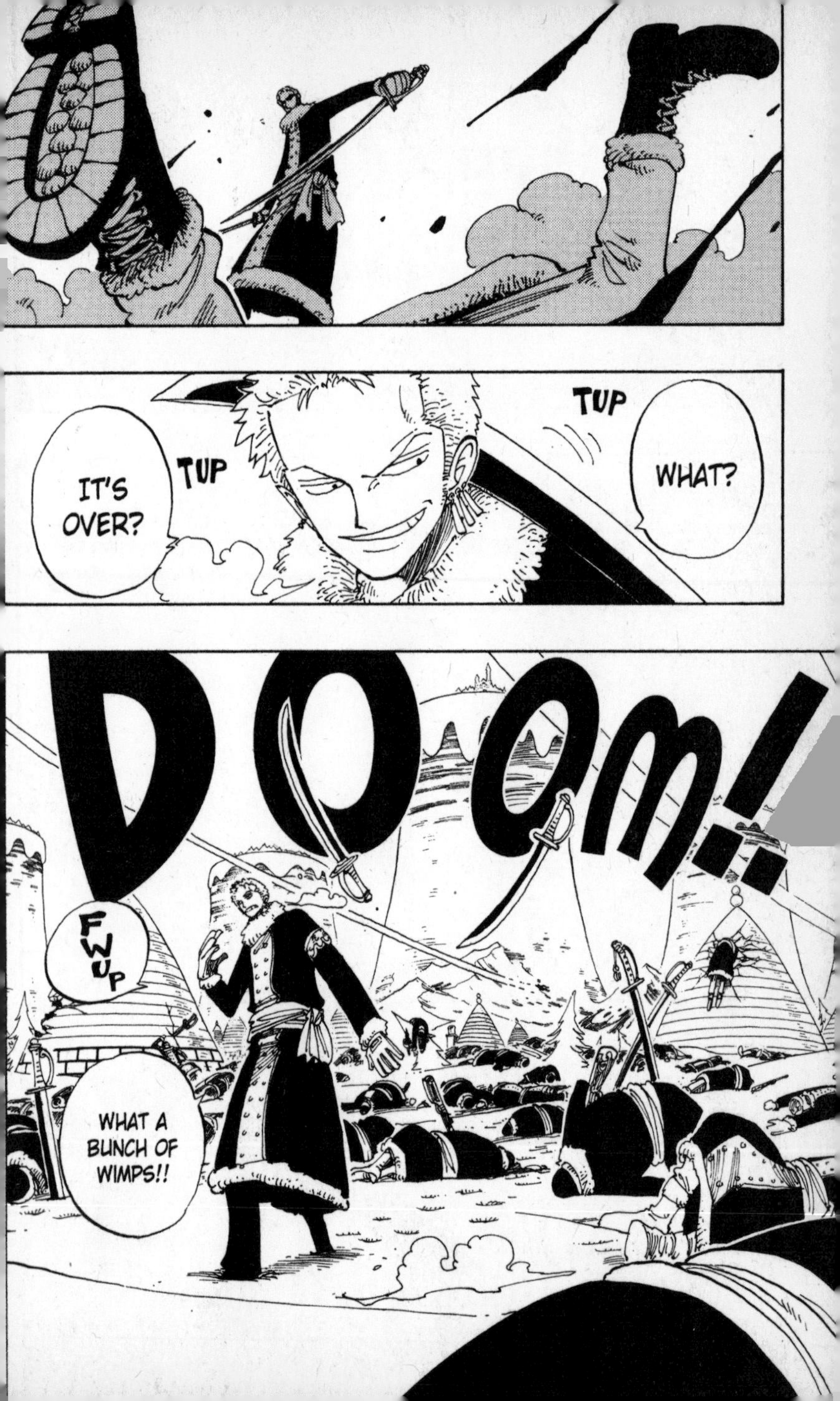
TUP
WHAT?
TUP
IT'S OVER?
DOOM!!
FWUP
WHAT A BUNCH OF WIMPS!!

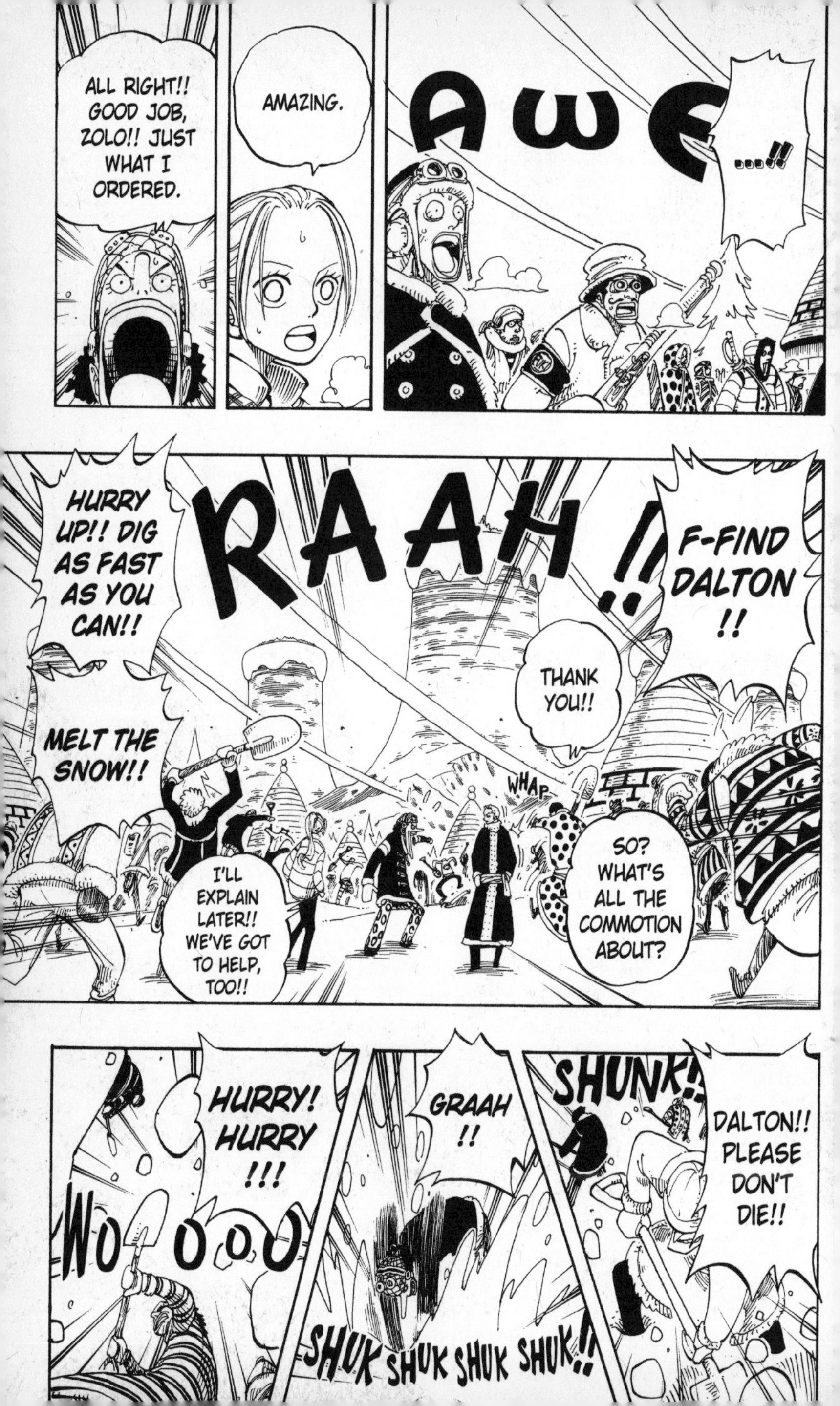

AWE
...!!
AMAZING.
ALL RIGHT!! GOOD JOB, ZOLO!! JUST WHAT I ORDERED.
F-FIND DALTON !!
RAAH !!
HURRY UP!! DIG AS FAST AS YOU CAN!!
THANK YOU!!
MELT THE SNOW!!
WHAP
SO? WHAT'S ALL THE COMMOTION ABOUT?
I'LL EXPLAIN LATER!! WE'VE GOT TO HELP, TOO!!
SHUNK!!
DALTON!! PLEASE DON'T DIE!!
GRAAH !!
SHUK SHUK SHUK SHUK!!
HURRY! HURRY !!!
WOOOOO

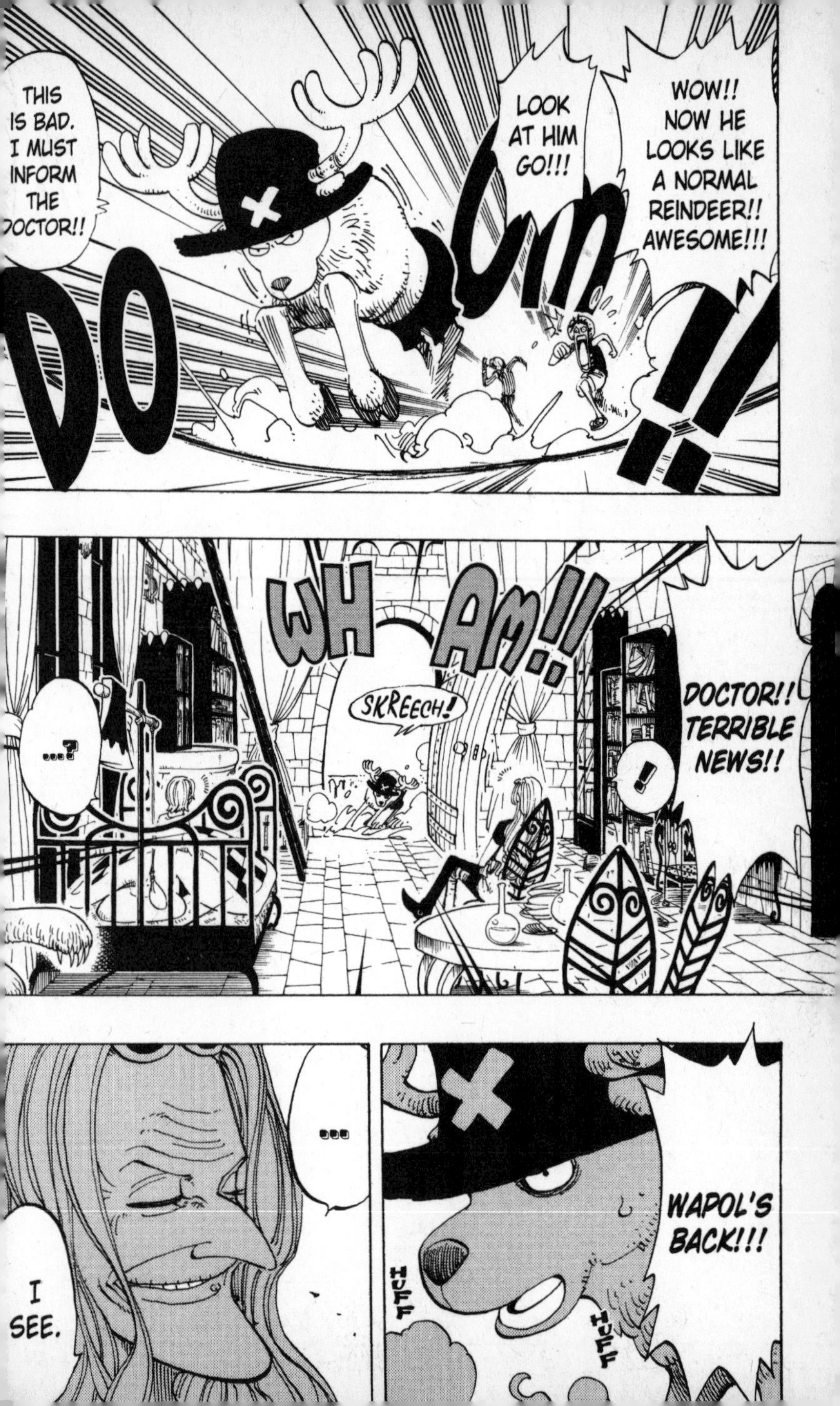

WOW!! NOW HE LOOKS LIKE A NORMAL REINDEER!! AWESOME!!!
LOOK AT HIM GO!!!
DOOM!!
THIS IS BAD. I MUST INFORM THE DOCTOR!!
DOCTOR!! TERRIBLE NEWS!!
!
WHAM!!
SKREECH!
...?
WAPOL'S BACK!!!
HUFF
HUFF
...
I SEE.

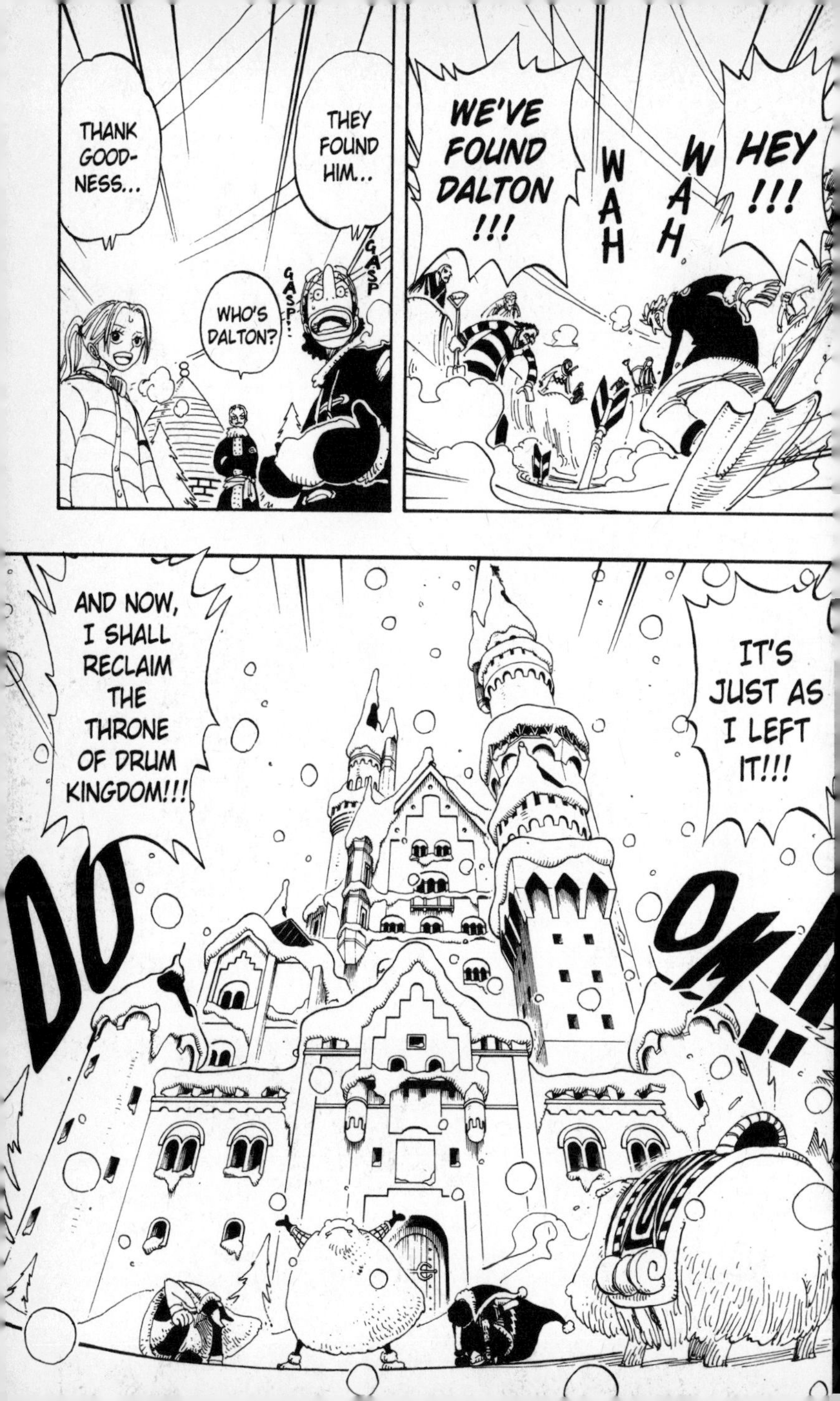
HEY!!!
WAH WAH
WE'VE FOUND DALTON!!!
THEY FOUND HIM...
THANK GOODNESS...
GASP GASP!
WHO'S DALTON?
IT'S JUST AS I LEFT IT!!!
AND NOW, I SHALL RECLAIM THE THRONE OF DRUM KINGDOM!!!
DOOM!!

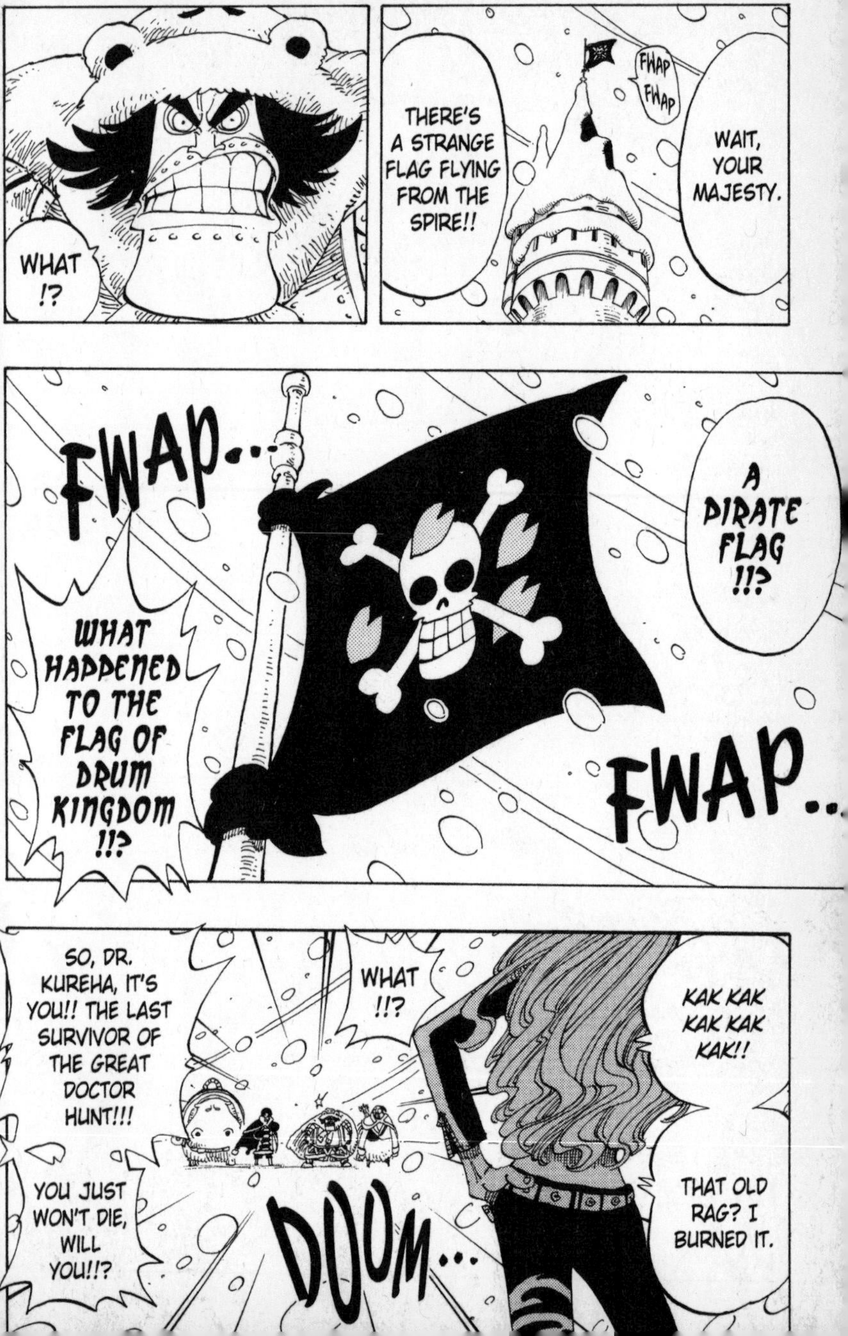
WAIT, YOUR MAJESTY.
FWAP FWAP
THERE'S A STRANGE FLAG FLYING FROM THE SPIRE!!
WHAT !?
A PIRATE FLAG !!?
FWAP...
FWAP...
WHAT HAPPENED TO THE FLAG OF DRUM KINGDOM !!?
KAK KAK KAK KAK KAK!!
THAT OLD RAG? I BURNED IT.
WHAT !!?
SO, DR. KUREHA, IT'S YOU!! THE LAST SURVIVOR OF THE GREAT DOCTOR HUNT!!!
YOU JUST WON'T DIE, WILL YOU!!?
DOOM...

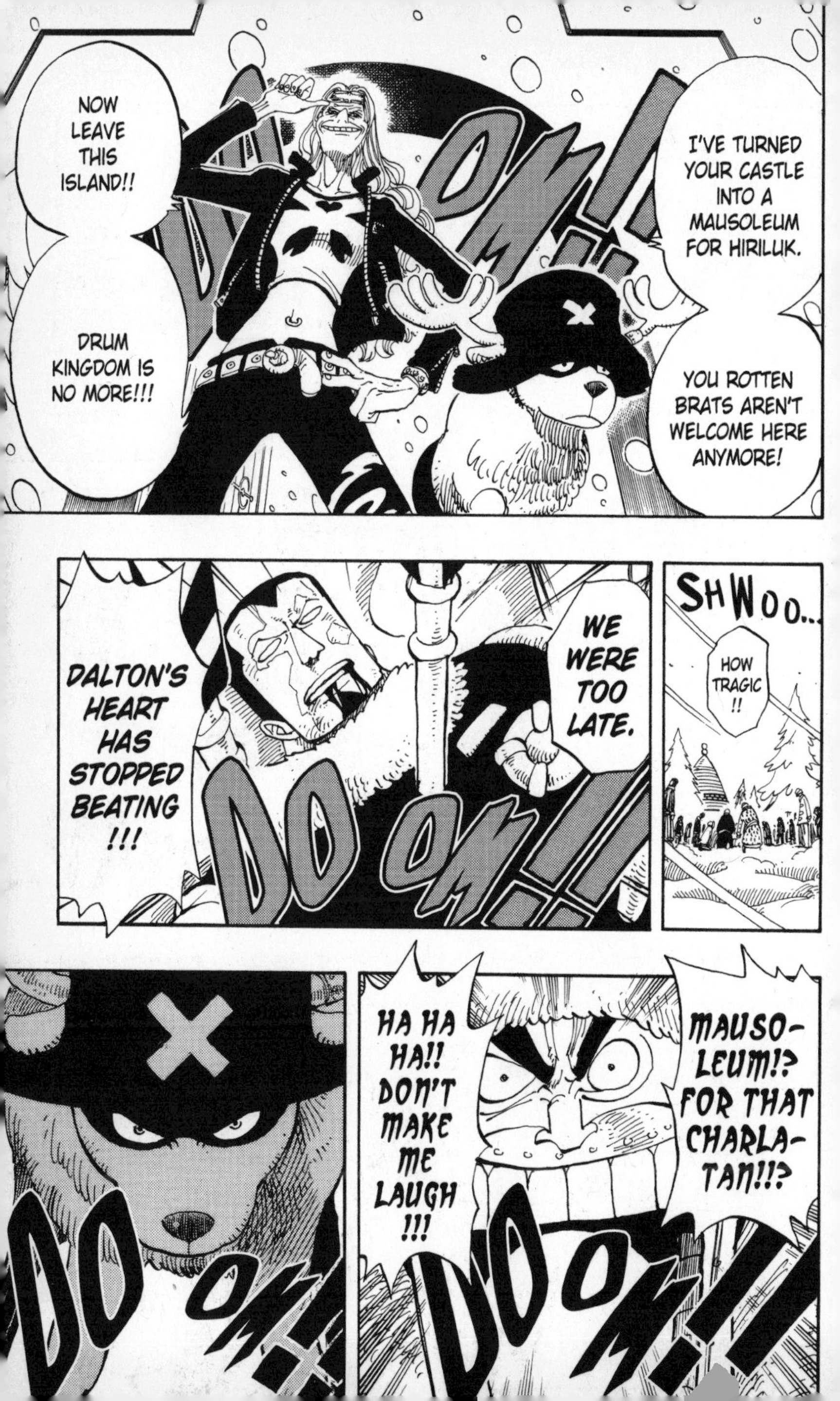
I'VE TURNED YOUR CASTLE INTO A MAUSOLEUM FOR HIRILUK.
YOU ROTTEN BRATS AREN'T WELCOME HERE ANYMORE!
NOW LEAVE THIS ISLAND!!
DRUM KINGDOM IS NO MORE!!!
SHWOO...
HOW TRAGIC!!
WE WERE TOO LATE.
DALTON'S HEART HAS STOPPED BEATING!!!
DOOM!!
MAUSO-LEUM!? FOR THAT CHARLA-TAN!!?
HA HA HA!! DON'T MAKE ME LAUGH!!!
DOOM!!
DOOM!!

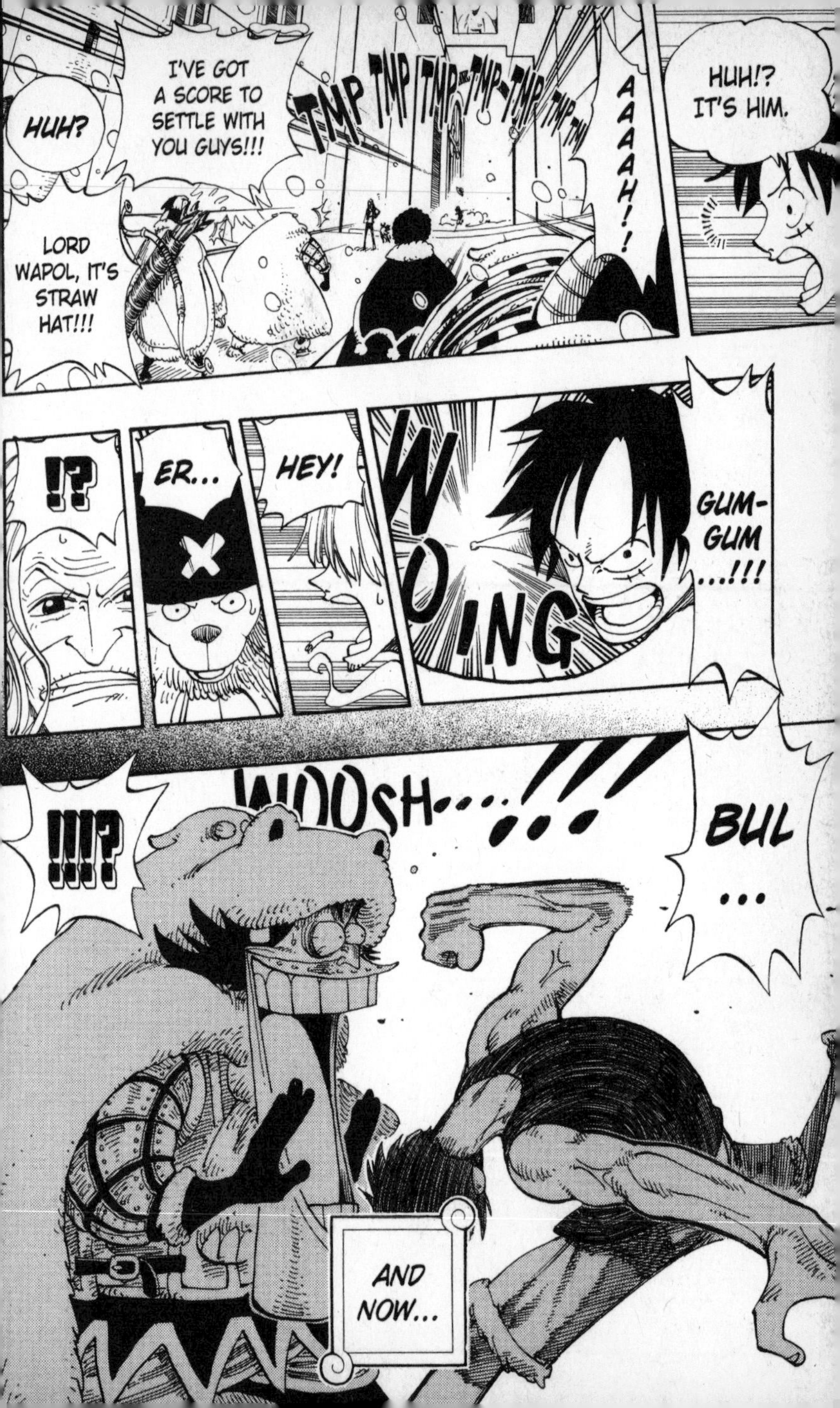
HUH!? IT'S HIM.
AAAAAH!!
TMP TMP TMP TMP TMP TMP TMP
I'VE GOT A SCORE TO SETTLE WITH YOU GUYS!!!
HUH?
LORD WAPOL, IT'S STRAW HAT!!!
GUM-GUM...!!!
WOING
HEY!
ER...
!?
BUL...
WOOSH...!!!
!!!?
AND NOW...

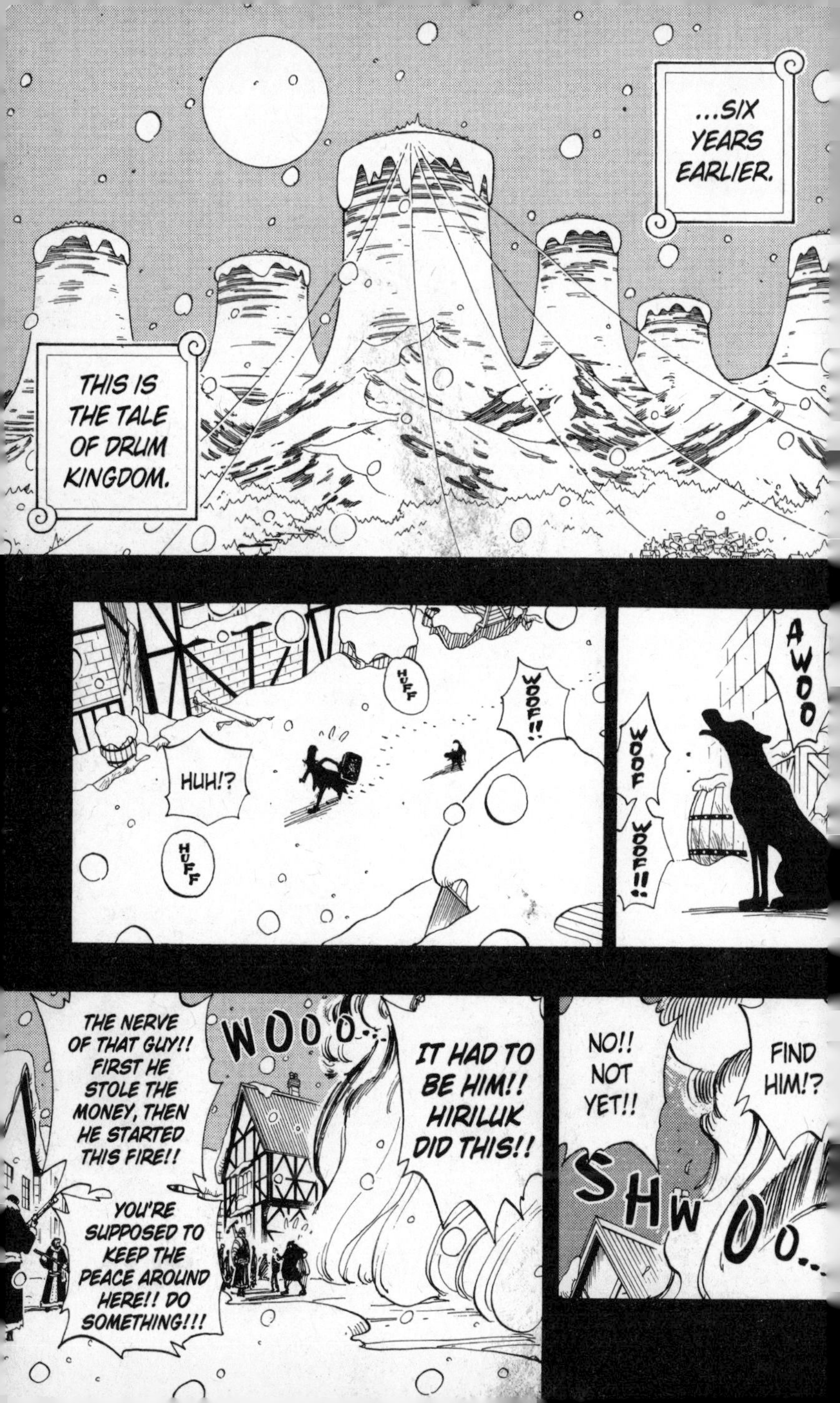
...SIX YEARS EARLIER.
THIS IS THE TALE OF DRUM KINGDOM.
AWOO
WOOF
WOOF!!
WOOF!!
HUFF
HUH!?
HUFF
FIND HIM!?
NO!! NOT YET!!
SHWOO...
WOOO...
IT HAD TO BE HIM!! HIRILUK DID THIS!!
THE NERVE OF THAT GUY!! FIRST HE STOLE THE MONEY, THEN HE STARTED THIS FIRE!!
YOU'RE SUPPOSED TO KEEP THE PEACE AROUND HERE!! DO SOMETHING!!!

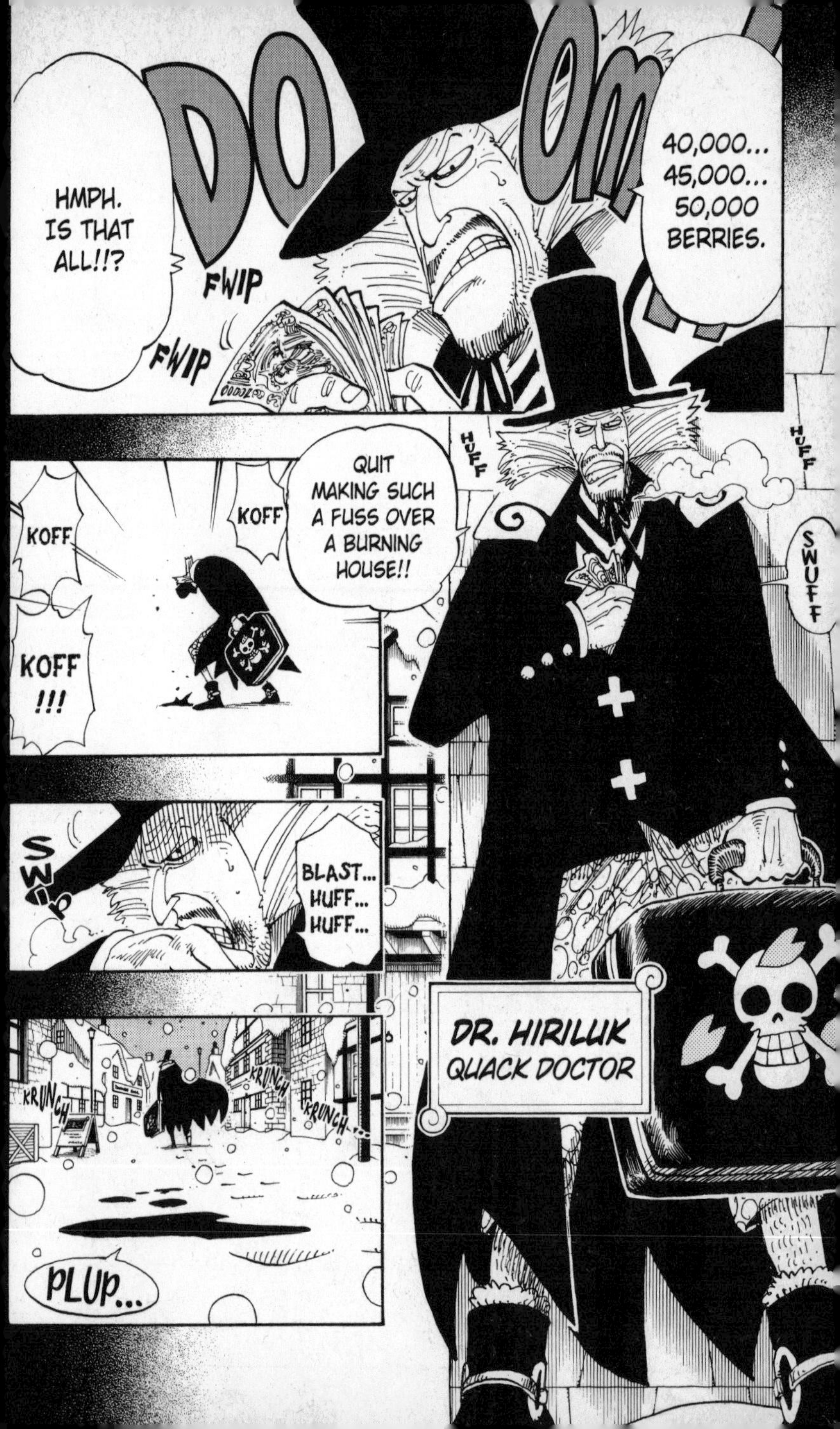
40,000...
45,000...
50,000
BERRIES.
DOOM
FWIP
FWIP
HMPH.
IS THAT
ALL!!?
HUFF
HUFF
SWUFF
DR. HIRILUK
QUACK DOCTOR
QUIT
MAKING SUCH
A FUSS OVER
A BURNING
HOUSE!!
KOFF
KOFF
KOFF
!!!
BLAST...
HUFF...
HUFF...
KRUNCH
KRUNCH
KRUNCH
PLUP...

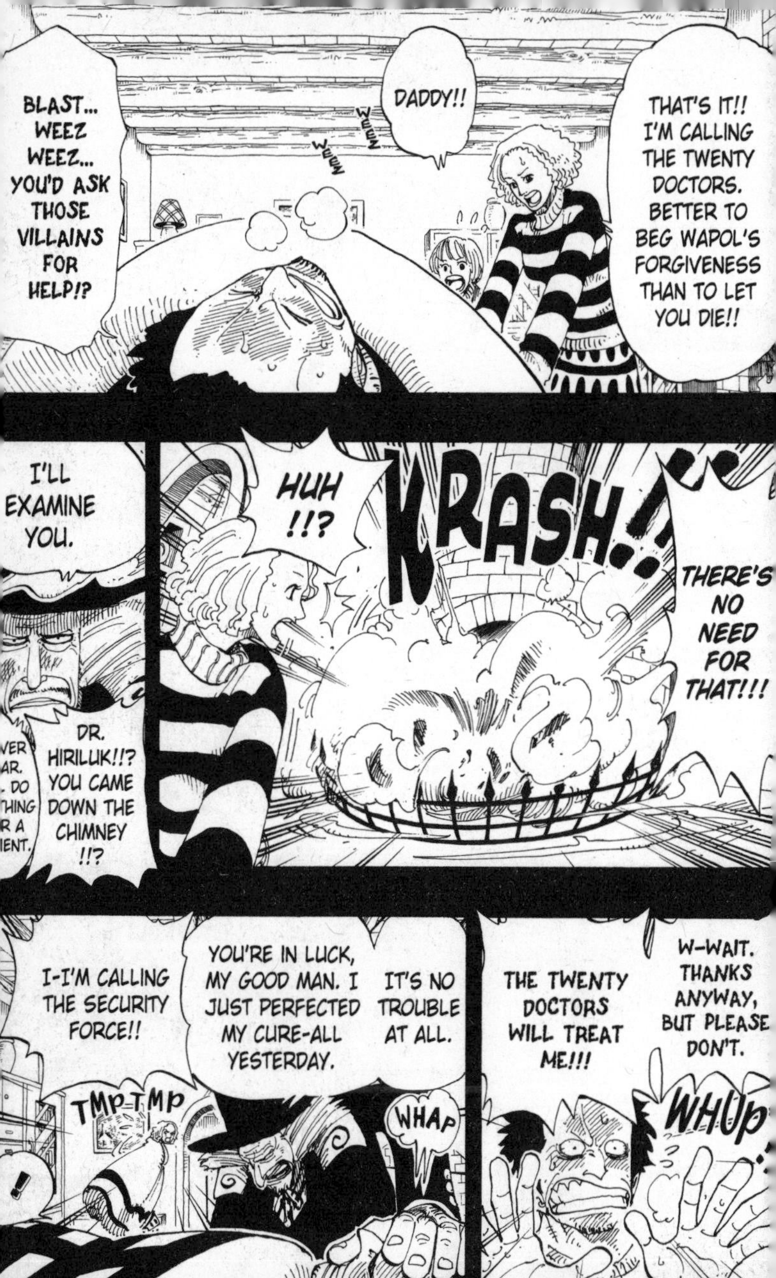
THAT'S IT!! I'M CALLING THE TWENTY DOCTORS. BETTER TO BEG WAPOL'S FORGIVENESS THAN TO LET YOU DIE!!
DADDY!!
WEEZ
WEEZ
BLAST... WEEZ WEEZ... YOU'D ASK THOSE VILLAINS FOR HELP!?
KRASH!!
THERE'S NO NEED FOR THAT!!!
HUH!!?
I'LL EXAMINE YOU.
DR. HIRILUK!!? YOU CAME DOWN THE CHIMNEY!!?
W-WAIT. THANKS ANYWAY, BUT PLEASE DON'T.
THE TWENTY DOCTORS WILL TREAT ME!!!
WHUP
IT'S NO TROUBLE AT ALL.
YOU'RE IN LUCK, MY GOOD MAN. I JUST PERFECTED MY CURE-ALL YESTERDAY.
WHAP
I-I'M CALLING THE SECURITY FORCE!!
TMP TMP
!

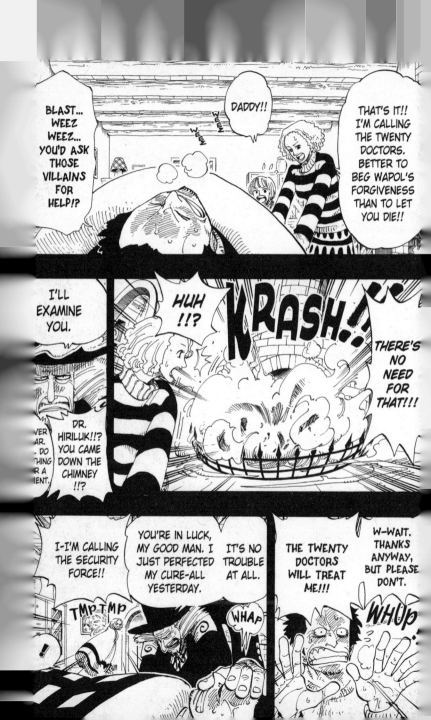

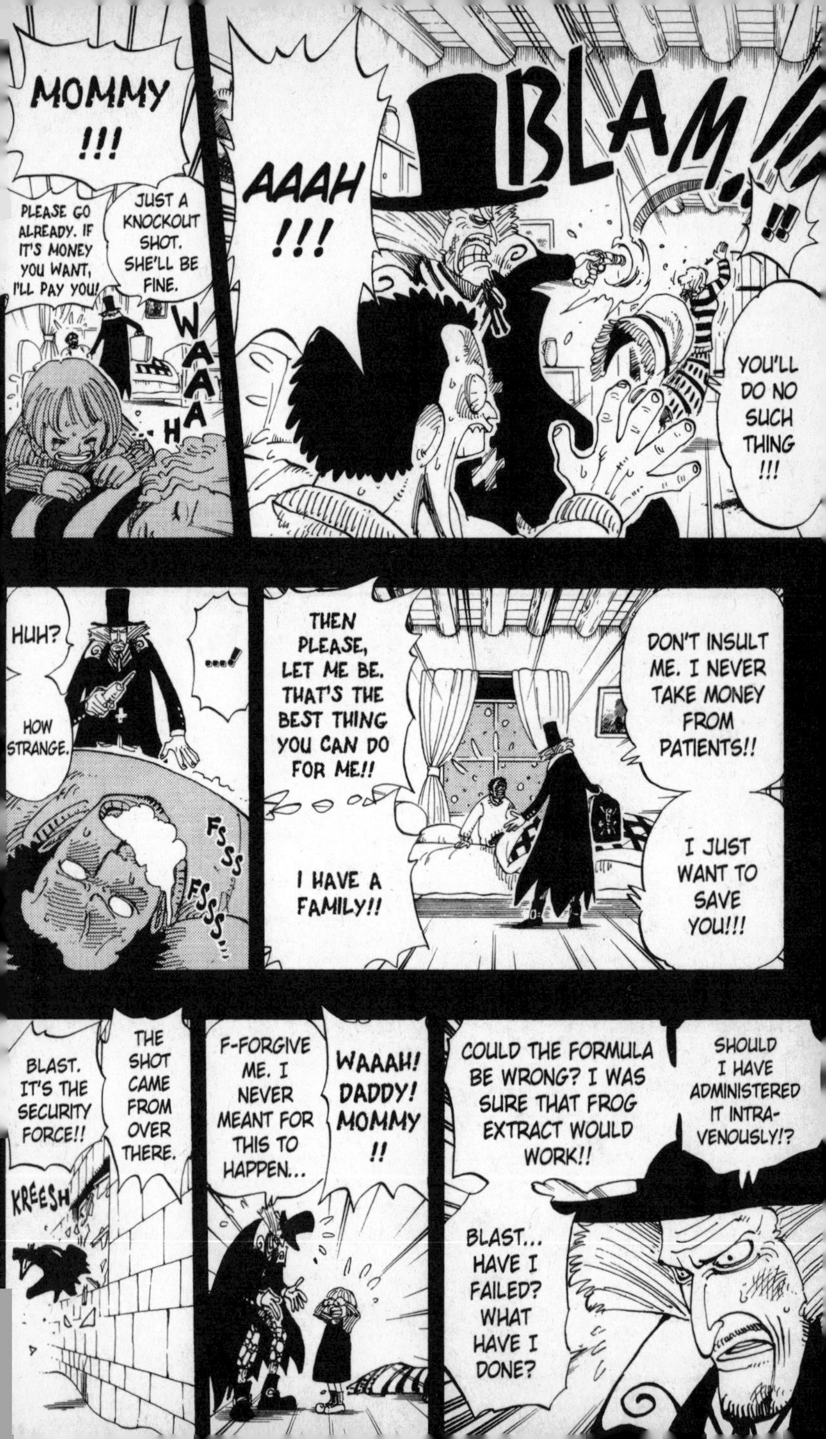

BLAM!!
!!
YOU'LL DO NO SUCH THING!!!
AAAH!!!
MOMMY!!!
JUST A KNOCKOUT SHOT. SHE'LL BE FINE.
PLEASE GO ALREADY. IF IT'S MONEY YOU WANT, I'LL PAY YOU!
WAAAAH
DON'T INSULT ME. I NEVER TAKE MONEY FROM PATIENTS!!
THEN PLEASE, LET ME BE. THAT'S THE BEST THING YOU CAN DO FOR ME!!
I JUST WANT TO SAVE YOU!!!
I HAVE A FAMILY!!
...!
HUH?
HOW STRANGE.
FSSS
FSSS...
SHOULD I HAVE ADMINISTERED IT INTRA-VENOUSLY!?
COULD THE FORMULA BE WRONG? I WAS SURE THAT FROG EXTRACT WOULD WORK!!
BLAST... HAVE I FAILED? WHAT HAVE I DONE?
WAAAH! DADDY! MOMMY!!
F-FORGIVE ME. I NEVER MEANT FOR THIS TO HAPPEN...
THE SHOT CAME FROM OVER THERE.
BLAST. IT'S THE SECURITY FORCE!!
KREESH

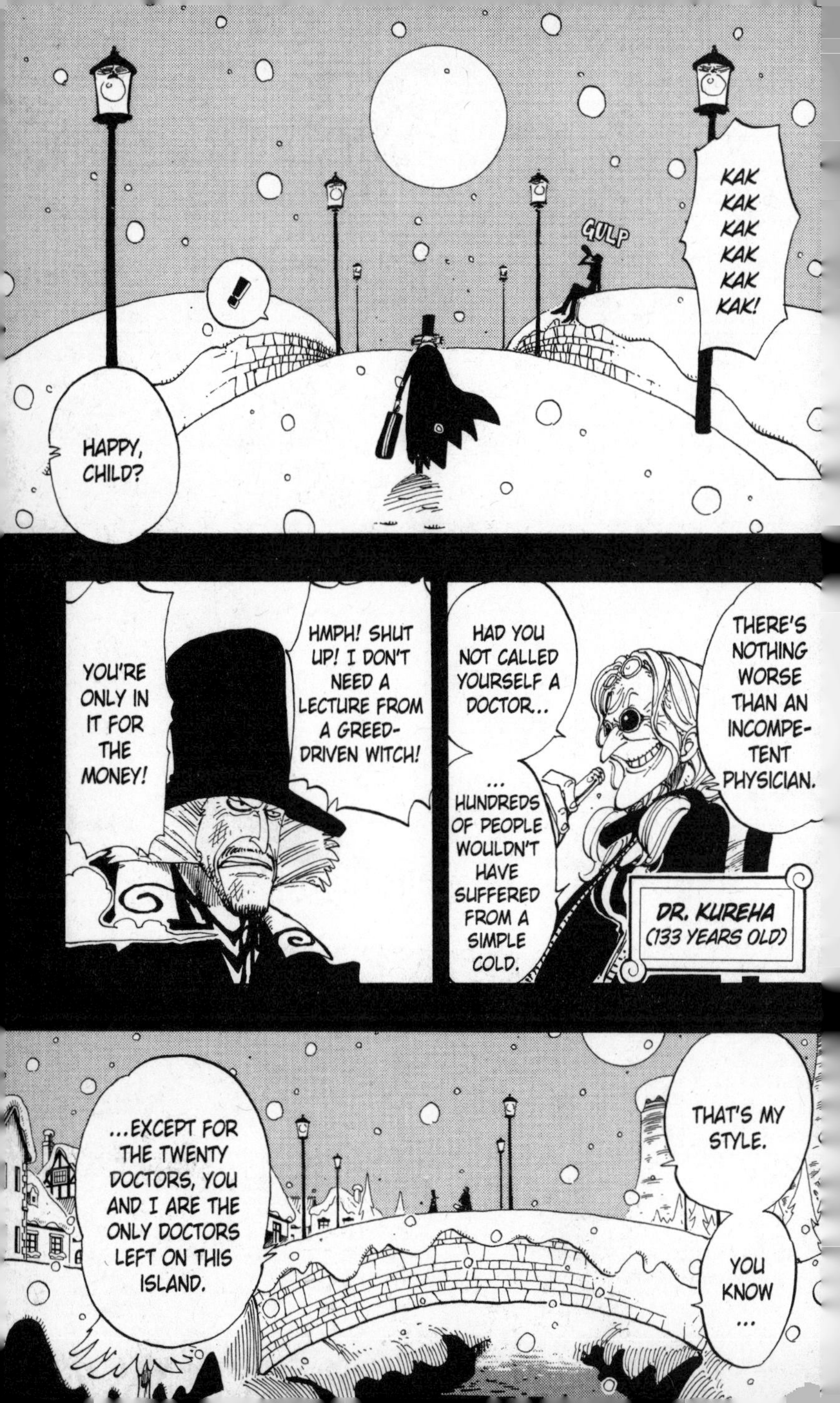
KAK KAK KAK KAK KAK KAK!
GULP
!
HAPPY, CHILD?
THERE'S NOTHING WORSE THAN AN INCOMPETENT PHYSICIAN.
HAD YOU NOT CALLED YOURSELF A DOCTOR...
...HUNDREDS OF PEOPLE WOULDN'T HAVE SUFFERED FROM A SIMPLE COLD.
DR. KUREHA (133 YEARS OLD)
HMPH! SHUT UP! I DON'T NEED A LECTURE FROM A GREED-DRIVEN WITCH!
YOU'RE ONLY IN IT FOR THE MONEY!
THAT'S MY STYLE.
YOU KNOW...
...EXCEPT FOR THE TWENTY DOCTORS, YOU AND I ARE THE ONLY DOCTORS LEFT ON THIS ISLAND.

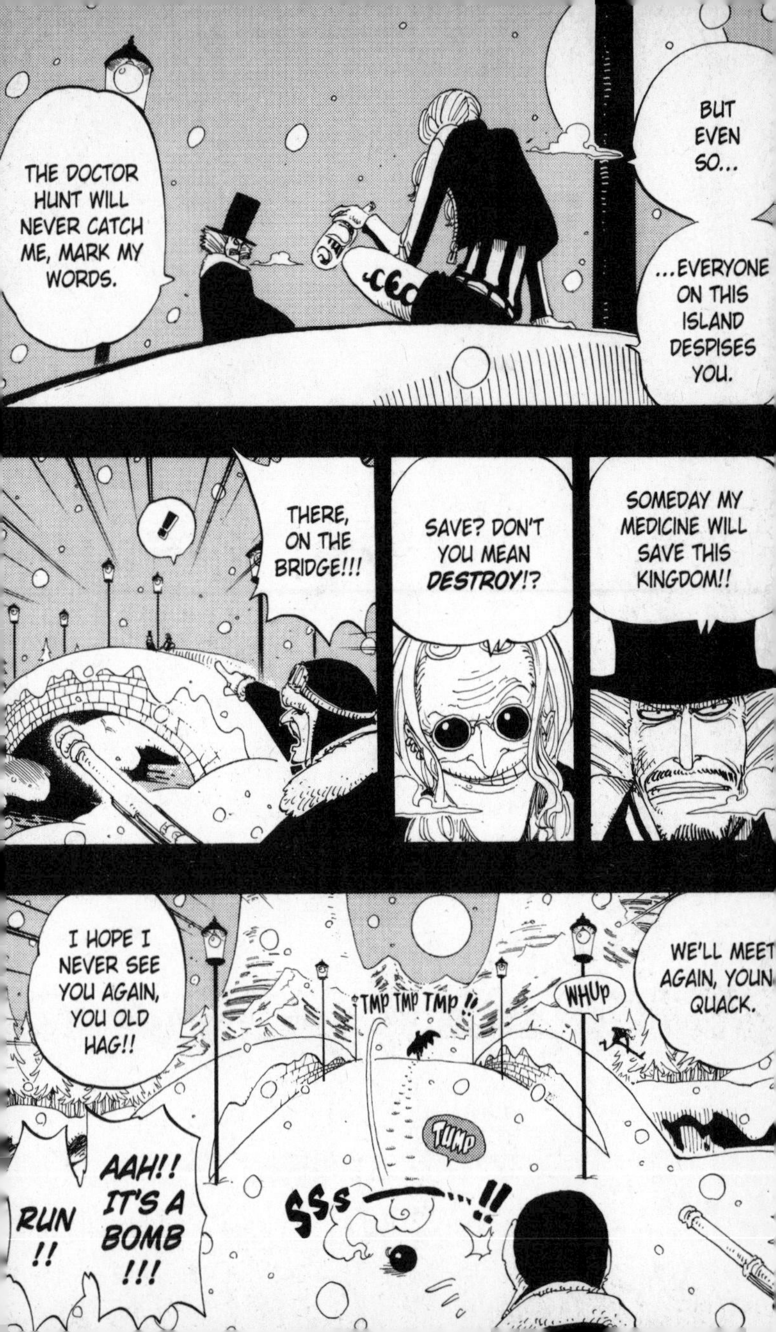
BUT EVEN SO...
...EVERYONE ON THIS ISLAND DESPISES YOU.
THE DOCTOR HUNT WILL NEVER CATCH ME, MARK MY WORDS.
SOMEDAY MY MEDICINE WILL SAVE THIS KINGDOM!!
SAVE? DON'T YOU MEAN DESTROY!?
!
THERE, ON THE BRIDGE!!!
WE'LL MEET AGAIN, YOUN QUACK.
WHUp
TMP TMP TMP!!
I HOPE I NEVER SEE YOU AGAIN, YOU OLD HAG!!
TUMP
SSs—...!!
AAH!! IT'S A BOMB!!!
RUN!!

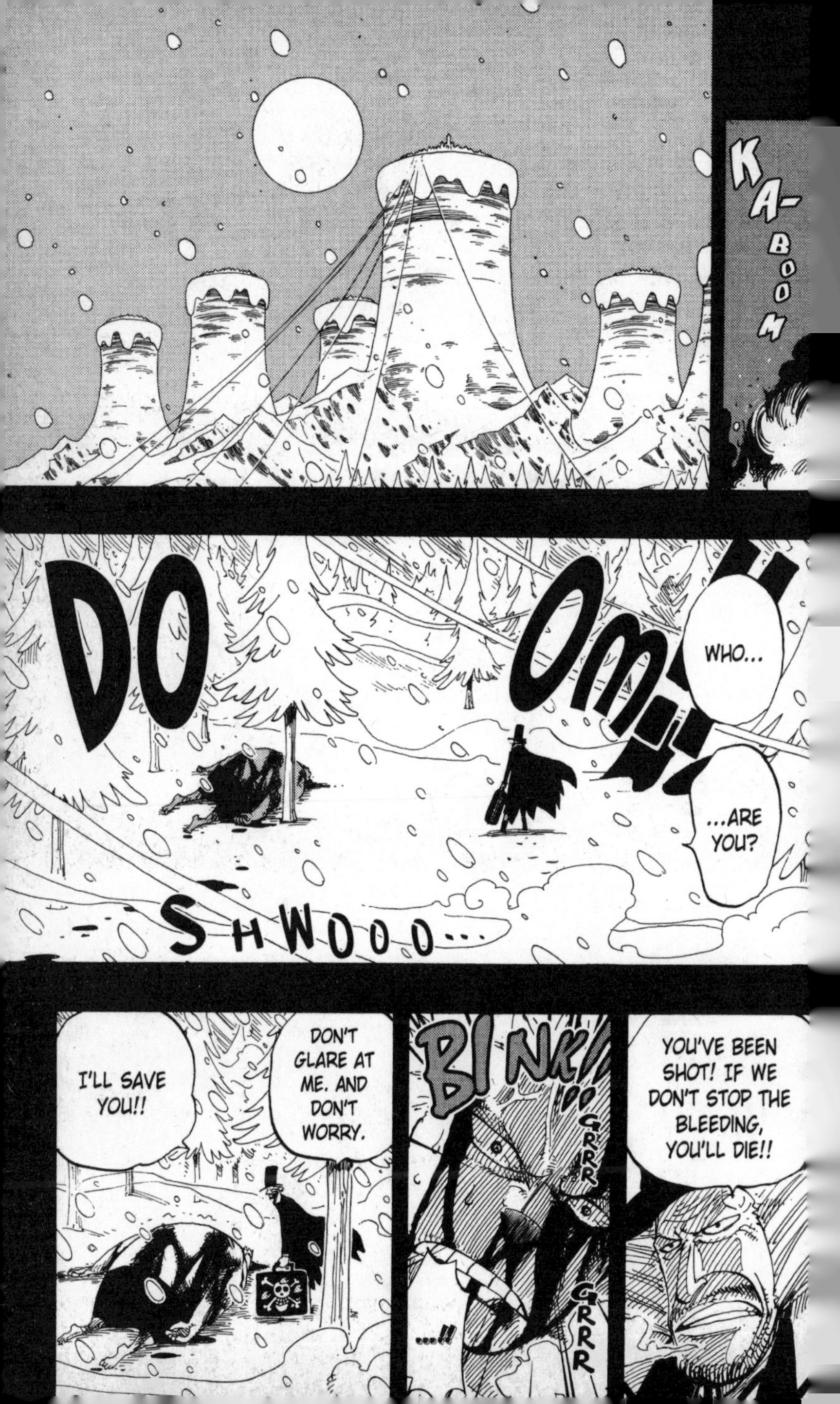
KA-BOOM
DOOM!!
WHO...
...ARE YOU?
SHWOOO...
YOU'VE BEEN SHOT! IF WE DON'T STOP THE BLEEDING, YOU'LL DIE!!
BINK!
GRRR
GRRR
...!!
DON'T GLARE AT ME. AND DON'T WORRY.
I'LL SAVE YOU!!

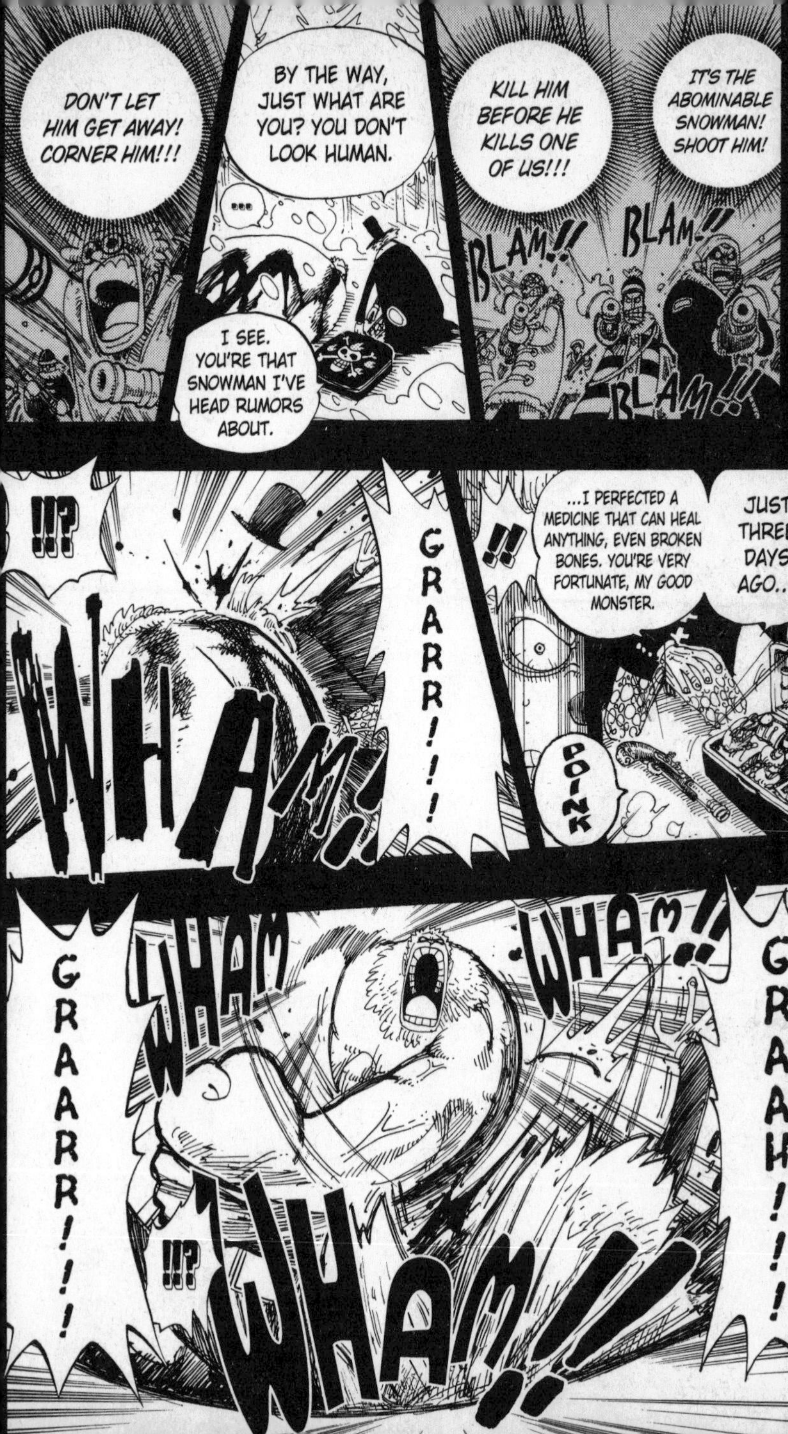
IT'S THE ABOMINABLE SNOWMAN! SHOOT HIM!
BLAM!!
BLAM!!
KILL HIM BEFORE HE KILLS ONE OF US!!!
BLAM!!
BY THE WAY, JUST WHAT ARE YOU? YOU DON'T LOOK HUMAN.
...
I SEE. YOU'RE THAT SNOWMAN I'VE HEAD RUMORS ABOUT.
DON'T LET HIM GET AWAY! CORNER HIM!!!
JUST THREE DAYS AGO...
...I PERFECTED A MEDICINE THAT CAN HEAL ANYTHING, EVEN BROKEN BONES. YOU'RE VERY FORTUNATE, MY GOOD MONSTER.
!!
DOINK
GRARR!!!
!!?
WHAM!!
GRAAH!!!!
WHAM!!
WHAM
GRAARRR!!!!
!!?
WHAM!!

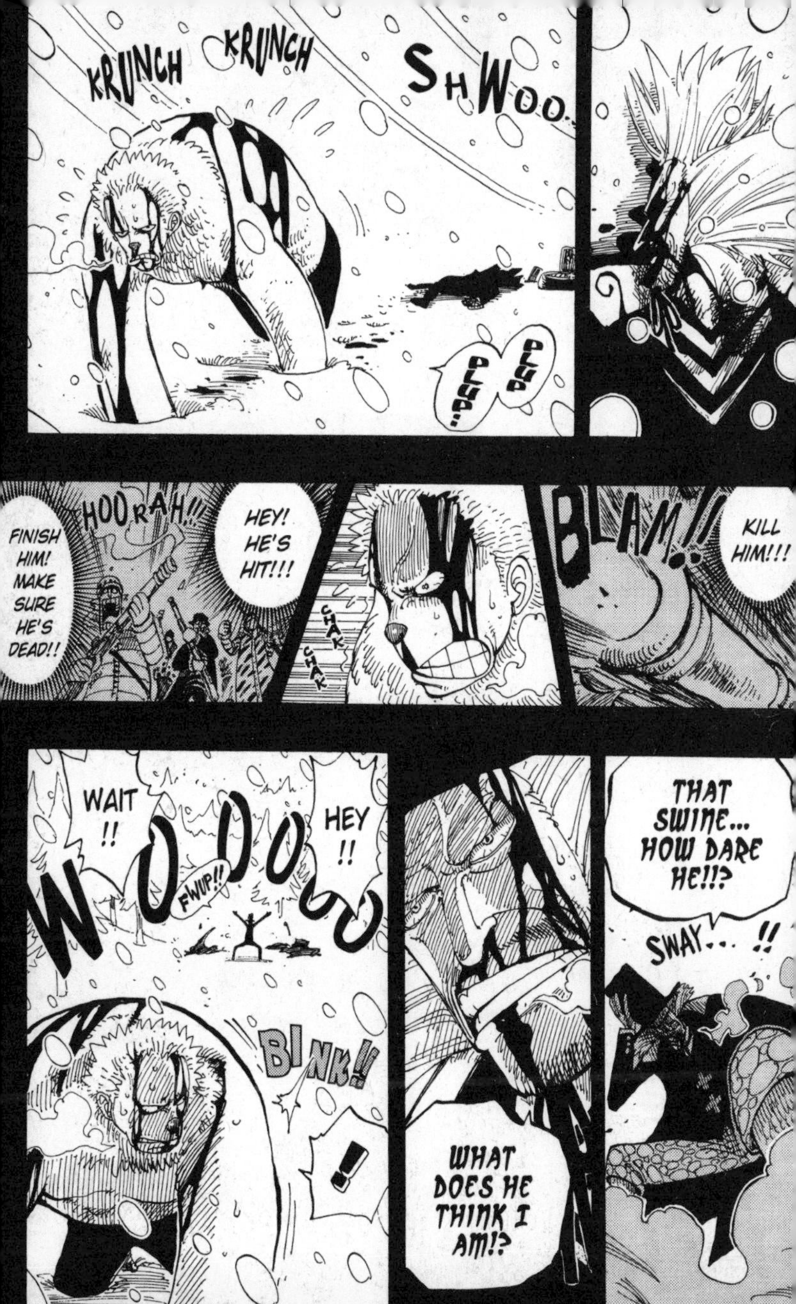

SHWOO...
KRUNCH KRUNCH
PLUP PLUP...
KILL HIM!!!
BLAM!!
CHAK CHAK
HEY! HE'S HIT!!!
HOORAH!!
FINISH HIM! MAKE SURE HE'S DEAD!!
THAT SWINE... HOW DARE HE!!?
SWAY... !!
WHAT DOES HE THINK I AM!?
HEY !!
WAIT !!
WOOOOO
FWUP!!
BINK!!
!

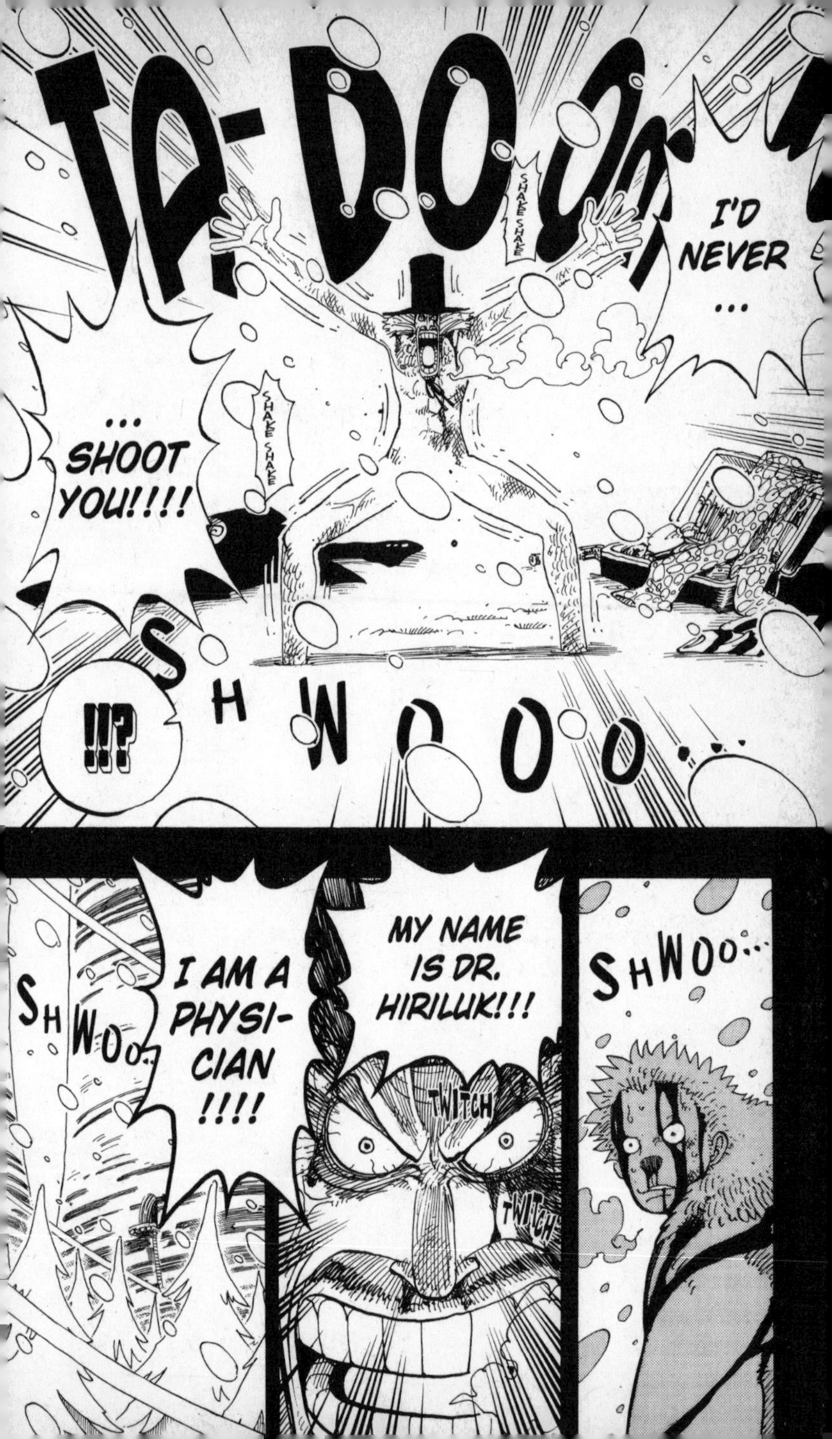
I'D NEVER ...
TA-DOOM
SHAKE SHAKE
SHAKE SHAKE
... SHOOT YOU!!!!
!!?
SHWOOO...
SHWOO...
MY NAME IS DR. HIRILUK!!!
TWITCH
TWITCH
I AM A PHYSI-CIAN!!!!
SHWOO..

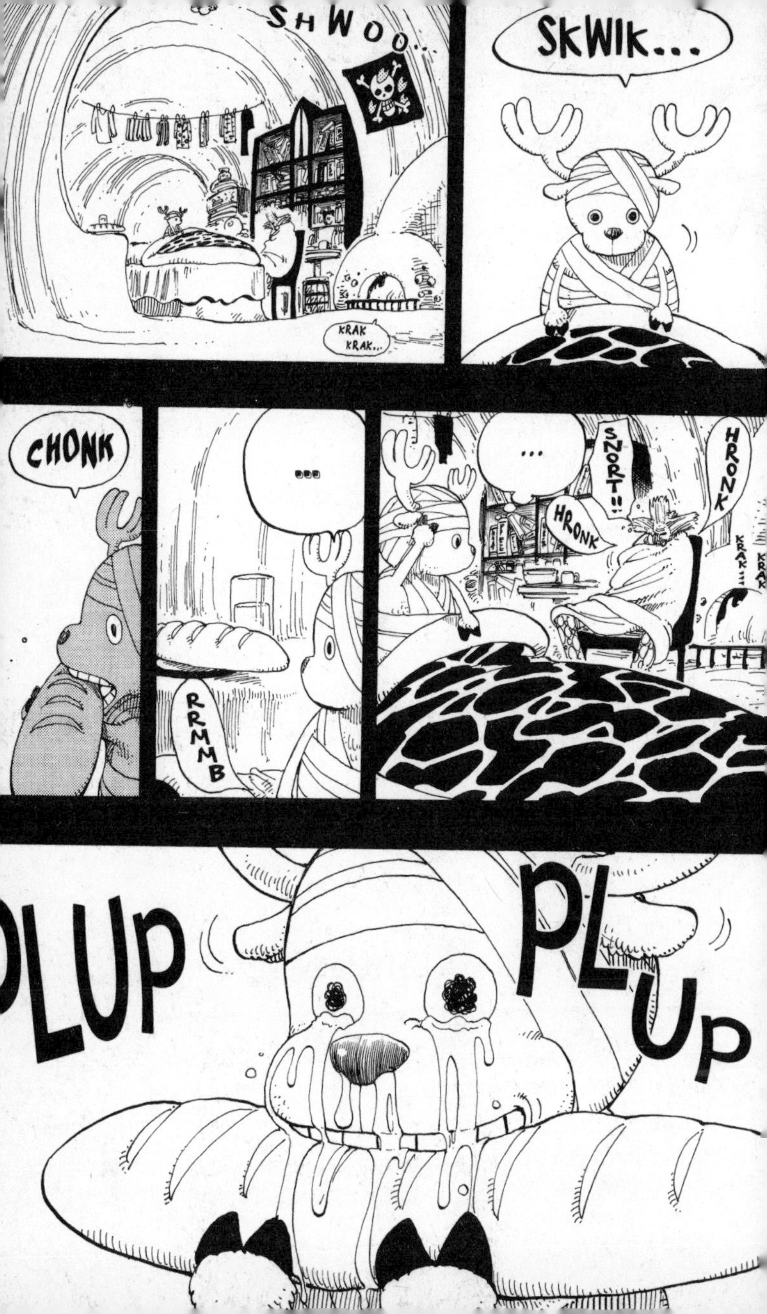
SKWIK...
SHWOO...
KRAK KRAK...
HRONK
SNORT!!
HRONK
...
KRAK...
KRAK
...
RRMMB
CHONK
PLUP
LUP

Question Corner
S B S

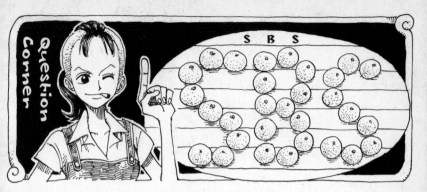

Reader: What's a Super Spotbill?

Oda: You mean Karoo? Well, it's a fantastic spot-billed duck. First of all, it's huge. And it doesn't have webbed feet (it's a land type), and when it feeds, it shows its teeth. Karoo is amazing!!

Q: Hello. I know this is rather sudden, but I have a question for you, Oda Sensei. It's about the Black Snail-o-phone. Can you draw it with its lid closed? How's this? After you explain it, please move on.

Here

A: Well, I-I don't know... I don't remember drawing anything like that. With the lid closed, it kind of looks like...poo. (See volume 15, page 31.)

Q: Hello, how do you do? Oda Sensei, I always read the Question Corner so I wanted to send you a postcard. I thought I'd find some joke or pun that you planted in the manga and join in the fun. But they're so hard to find! You guys are really something.
So anyway, here's my question. What question should I ask?

A: Are you some kind of idiot!!?
See you in the next volume!!!

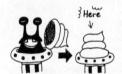

Chapter 142:
SKULL AND CHERRY BLOSSOMS

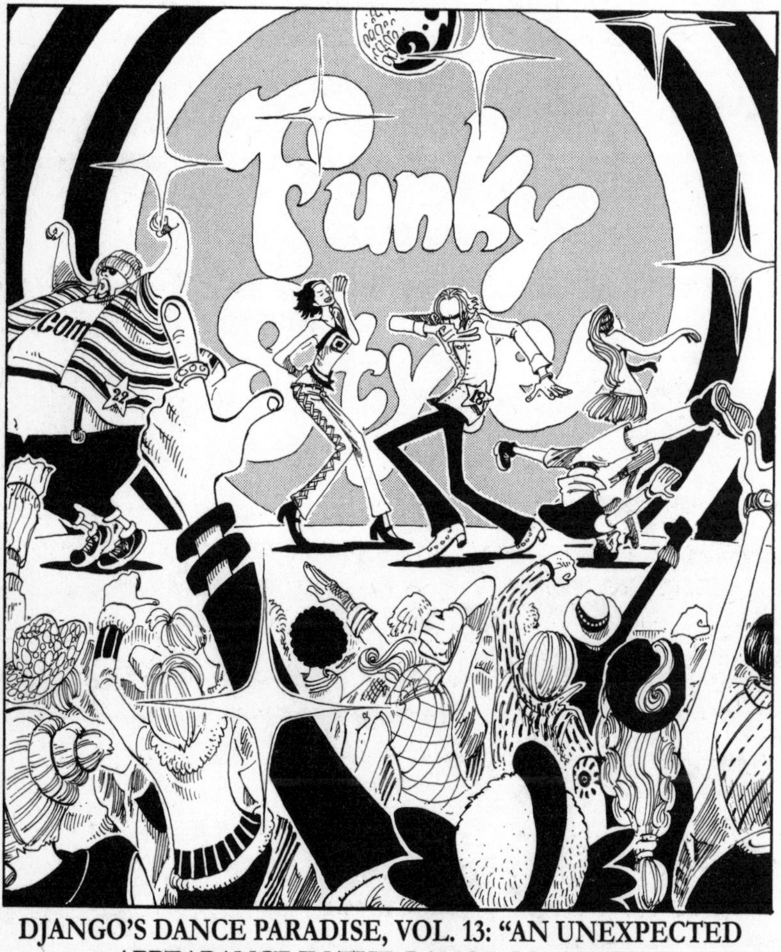
Funky Style
.com
22
13

DJANGO'S DANCE PARADISE, VOL. 13: "AN UNEXPECTED APPEARANCE IN THE DANCE CONTEST"

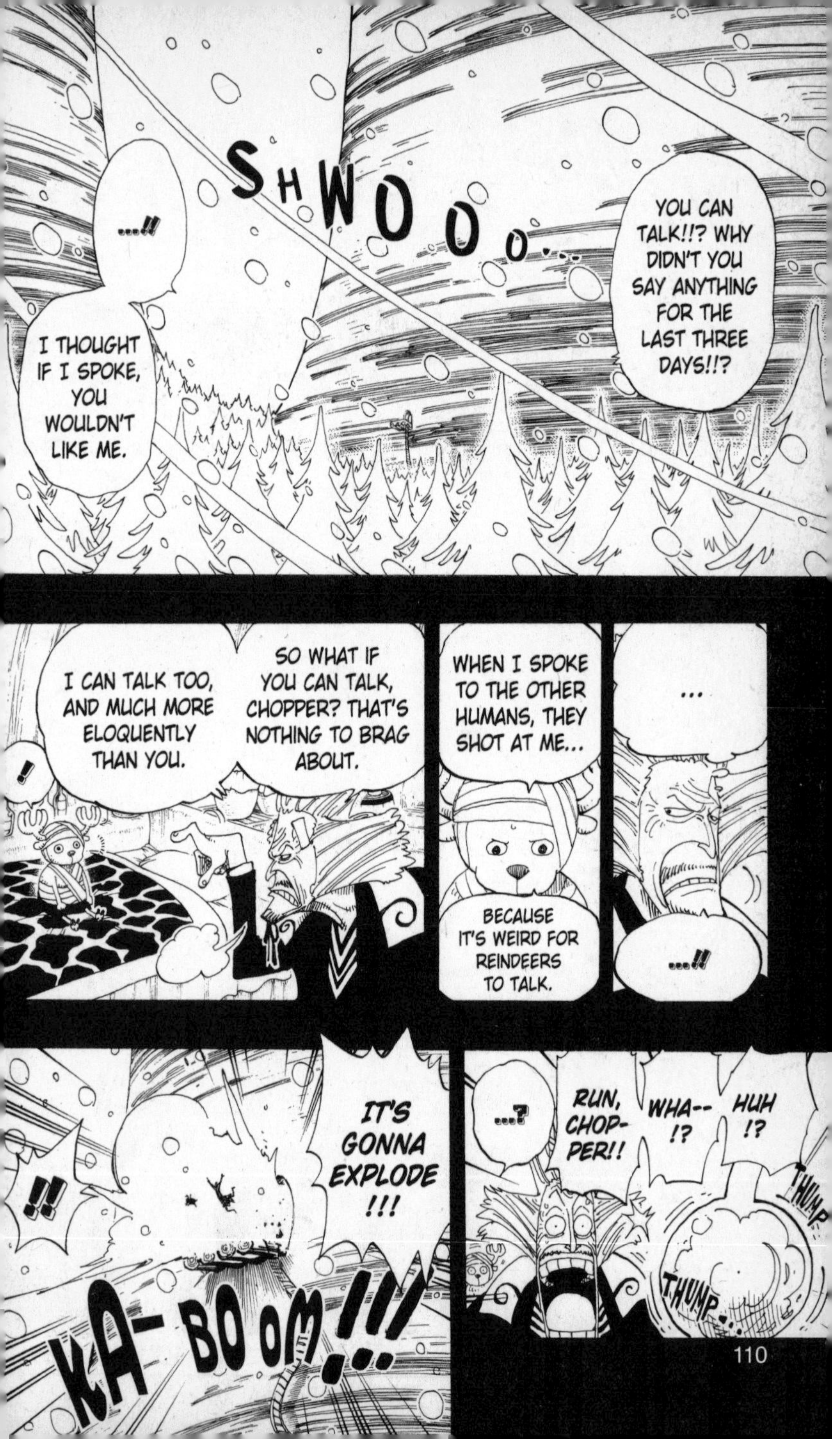

YOU CAN TALK!!? WHY DIDN'T YOU SAY ANYTHING FOR THE LAST THREE DAYS!!?
SHWOOOO...
...!!
I THOUGHT IF I SPOKE, YOU WOULDN'T LIKE ME.
...
...!!
WHEN I SPOKE TO THE OTHER HUMANS, THEY SHOT AT ME...
BECAUSE IT'S WEIRD FOR REINDEERS TO TALK.
SO WHAT IF YOU CAN TALK, CHOPPER? THAT'S NOTHING TO BRAG ABOUT.
I CAN TALK TOO, AND MUCH MORE ELOQUENTLY THAN YOU.
!
HUH !?
WHA-- !?
RUN, CHOPPER!!
...?
THUMP
THUMP...
IT'S GONNA EXPLODE !!!
!!
KA-BOOM!!!

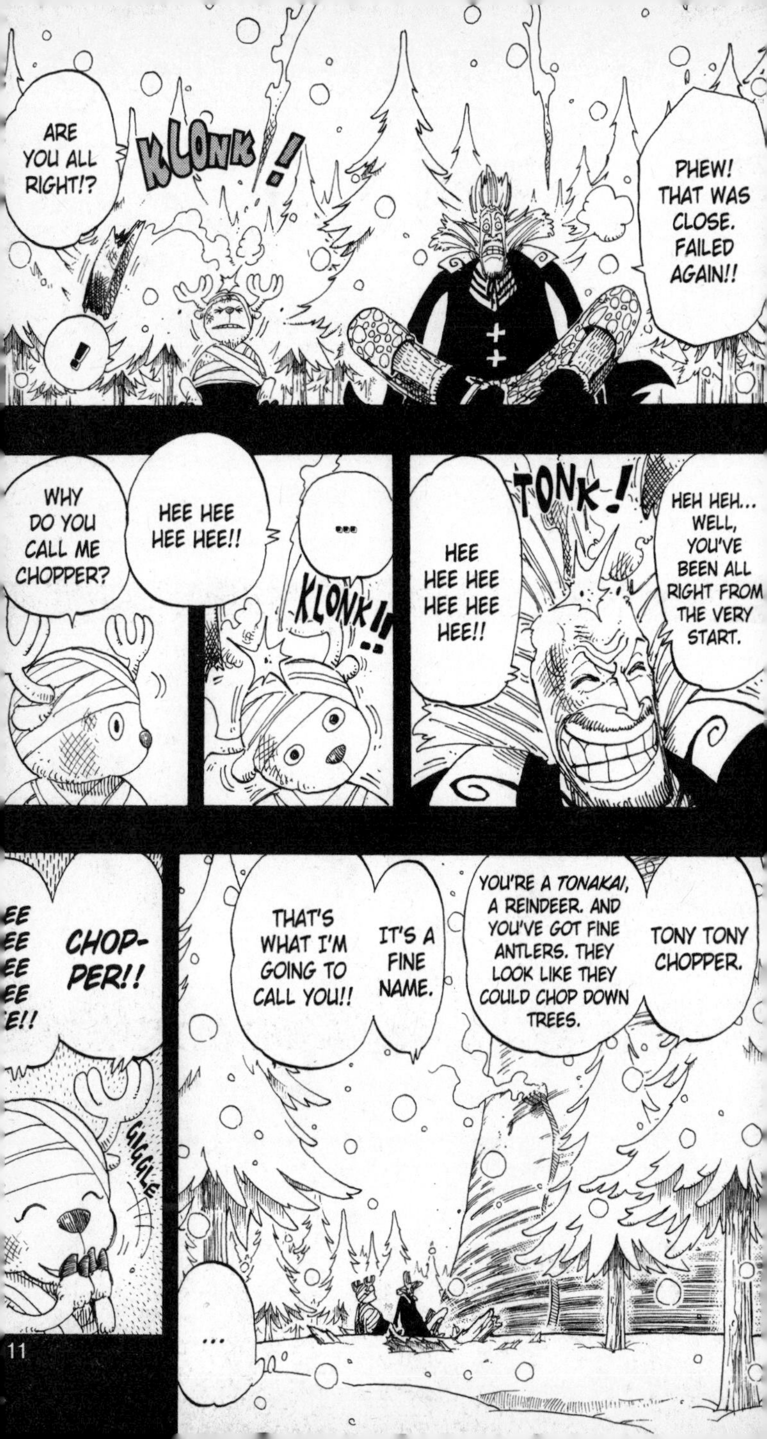
PHEW! THAT WAS CLOSE. FAILED AGAIN!!
KLONK!
ARE YOU ALL RIGHT!?
!
TONK!
HEH HEH... WELL, YOU'VE BEEN ALL RIGHT FROM THE VERY START.
HEE HEE HEE HEE HEE HEE!!
...
KLONK!!
HEE HEE HEE HEE!!
WHY DO YOU CALL ME CHOPPER?
TONY TONY CHOPPER.
YOU'RE A *TONAKAI*, A REINDEER. AND YOU'VE GOT FINE ANTLERS. THEY LOOK LIKE THEY COULD CHOP DOWN TREES.
IT'S A FINE NAME.
THAT'S WHAT I'M GOING TO CALL YOU!!
...
CHOP-PER!!
GIGGLE

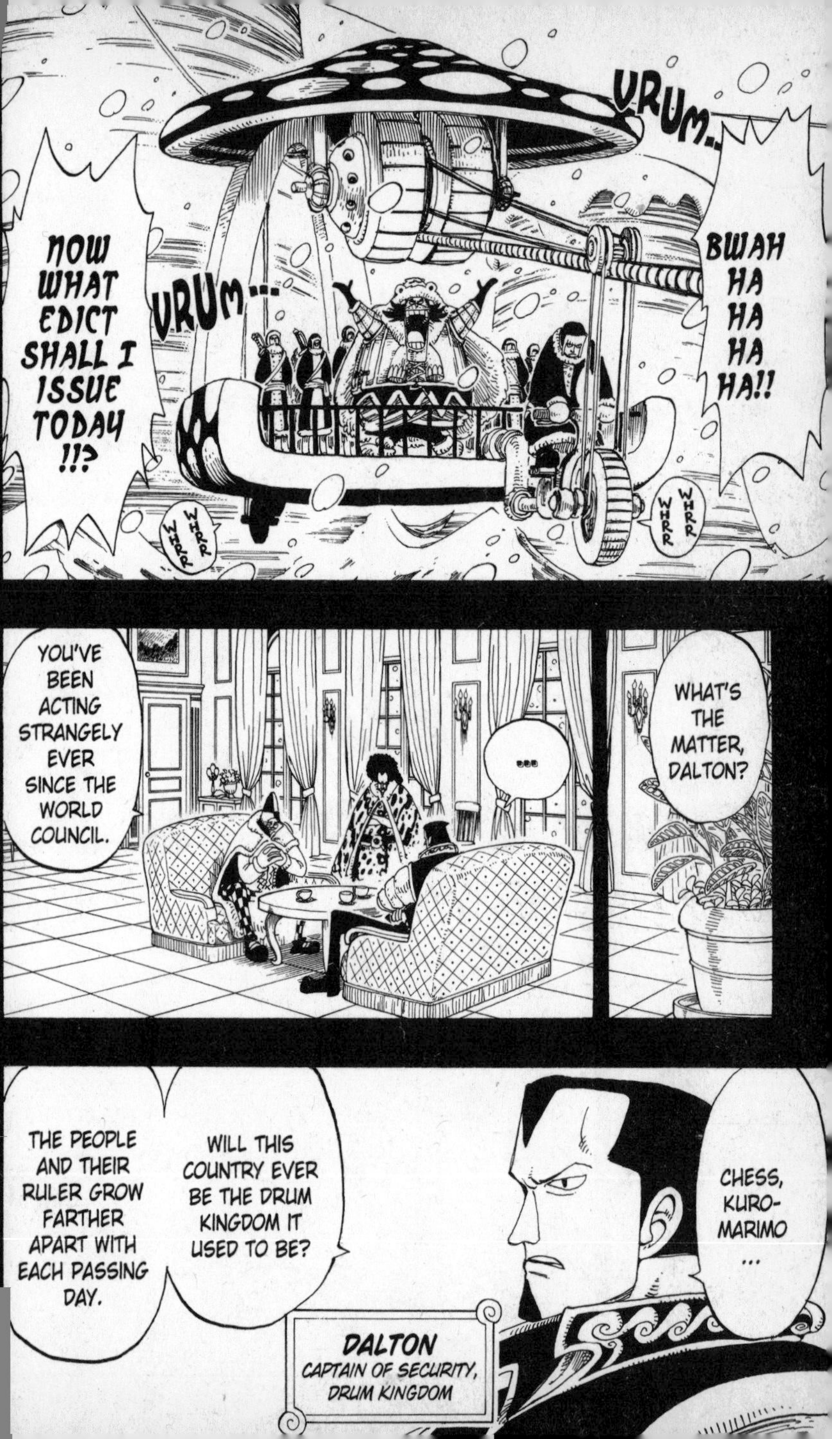
VRUM...
BWAH HA HA HA HA!!
NOW WHAT EDICT SHALL I ISSUE TODAY!!?
VRUM...
WHRR WHRR
WHRR WHRR
WHAT'S THE MATTER, DALTON?
...
YOU'VE BEEN ACTING STRANGELY EVER SINCE THE WORLD COUNCIL.
CHESS, KURO-MARIMO...
WILL THIS COUNTRY EVER BE THE DRUM KINGDOM IT USED TO BE?
THE PEOPLE AND THEIR RULER GROW FARTHER APART WITH EACH PASSING DAY.
DALTON
CAPTAIN OF SECURITY, DRUM KINGDOM

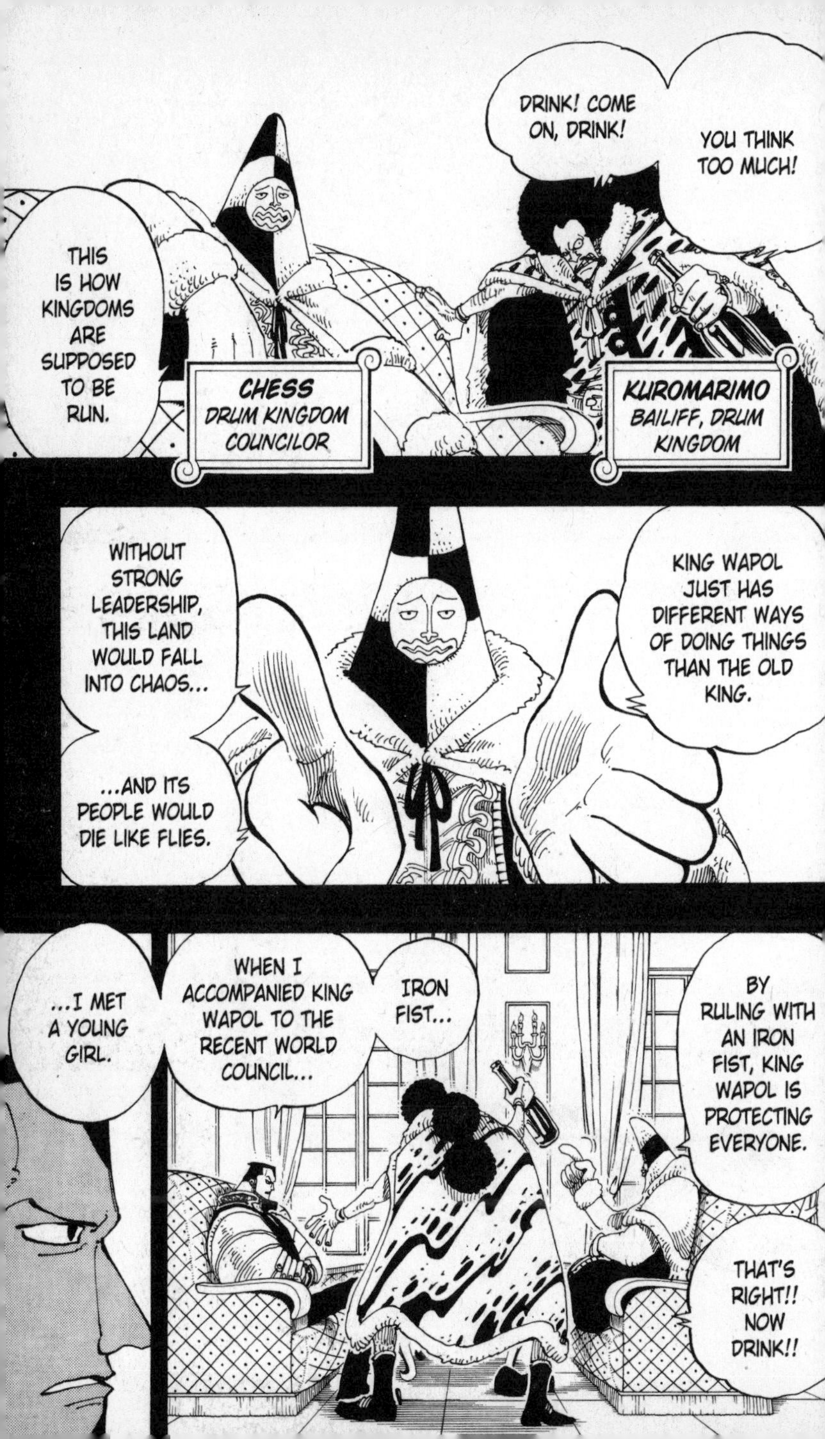
DRINK! COME ON, DRINK!
YOU THINK TOO MUCH!
KUROMARIMO BAILIFF, DRUM KINGDOM
CHESS DRUM KINGDOM COUNCILOR
THIS IS HOW KINGDOMS ARE SUPPOSED TO BE RUN.
KING WAPOL JUST HAS DIFFERENT WAYS OF DOING THINGS THAN THE OLD KING.
WITHOUT STRONG LEADERSHIP, THIS LAND WOULD FALL INTO CHAOS...
...AND ITS PEOPLE WOULD DIE LIKE FLIES.
BY RULING WITH AN IRON FIST, KING WAPOL IS PROTECTING EVERYONE.
THAT'S RIGHT!! NOW DRINK!!
IRON FIST...
WHEN I ACCOMPANIED KING WAPOL TO THE RECENT WORLD COUNCIL...
...I MET A YOUNG GIRL.

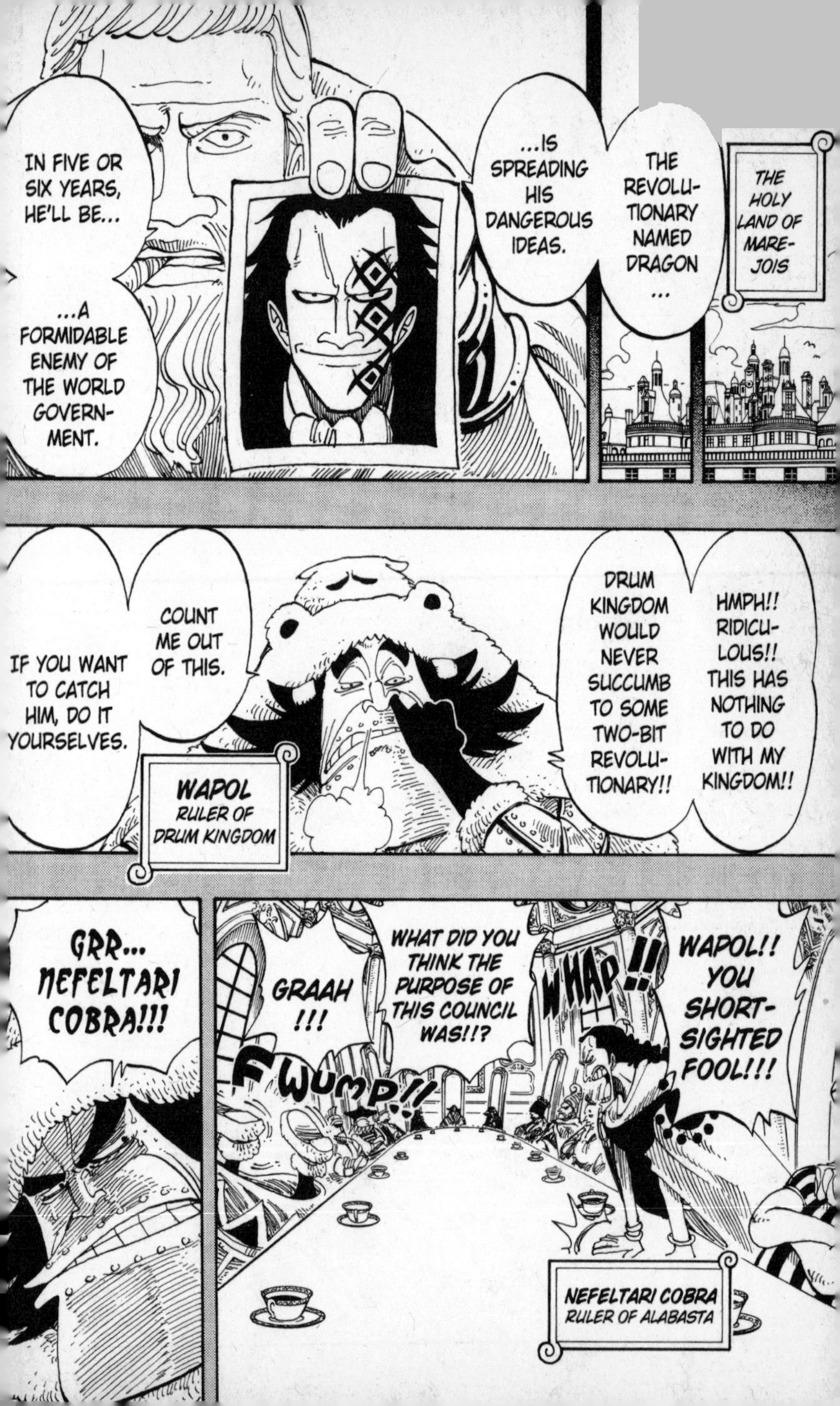
THE HOLY LAND OF MARE-JOIS
THE REVOLUTIONARY NAMED DRAGON...
...IS SPREADING HIS DANGEROUS IDEAS.
IN FIVE OR SIX YEARS, HE'LL BE...
...A FORMIDABLE ENEMY OF THE WORLD GOVERNMENT.
HMPH!! RIDICULOUS!! THIS HAS NOTHING TO DO WITH MY KINGDOM!!
DRUM KINGDOM WOULD NEVER SUCCUMB TO SOME TWO-BIT REVOLUTIONARY!!
COUNT ME OUT OF THIS.
IF YOU WANT TO CATCH HIM, DO IT YOURSELVES.
WAPOL RULER OF DRUM KINGDOM
WAPOL!! YOU SHORT-SIGHTED FOOL!!!
WHAP!!
WHAT DID YOU THINK THE PURPOSE OF THIS COUNCIL WAS!!?
GRAAH!!!
FWUMP!!
NEFELTARI COBRA RULER OF ALABASTA
GRR... NEFELTARI COBRA!!!

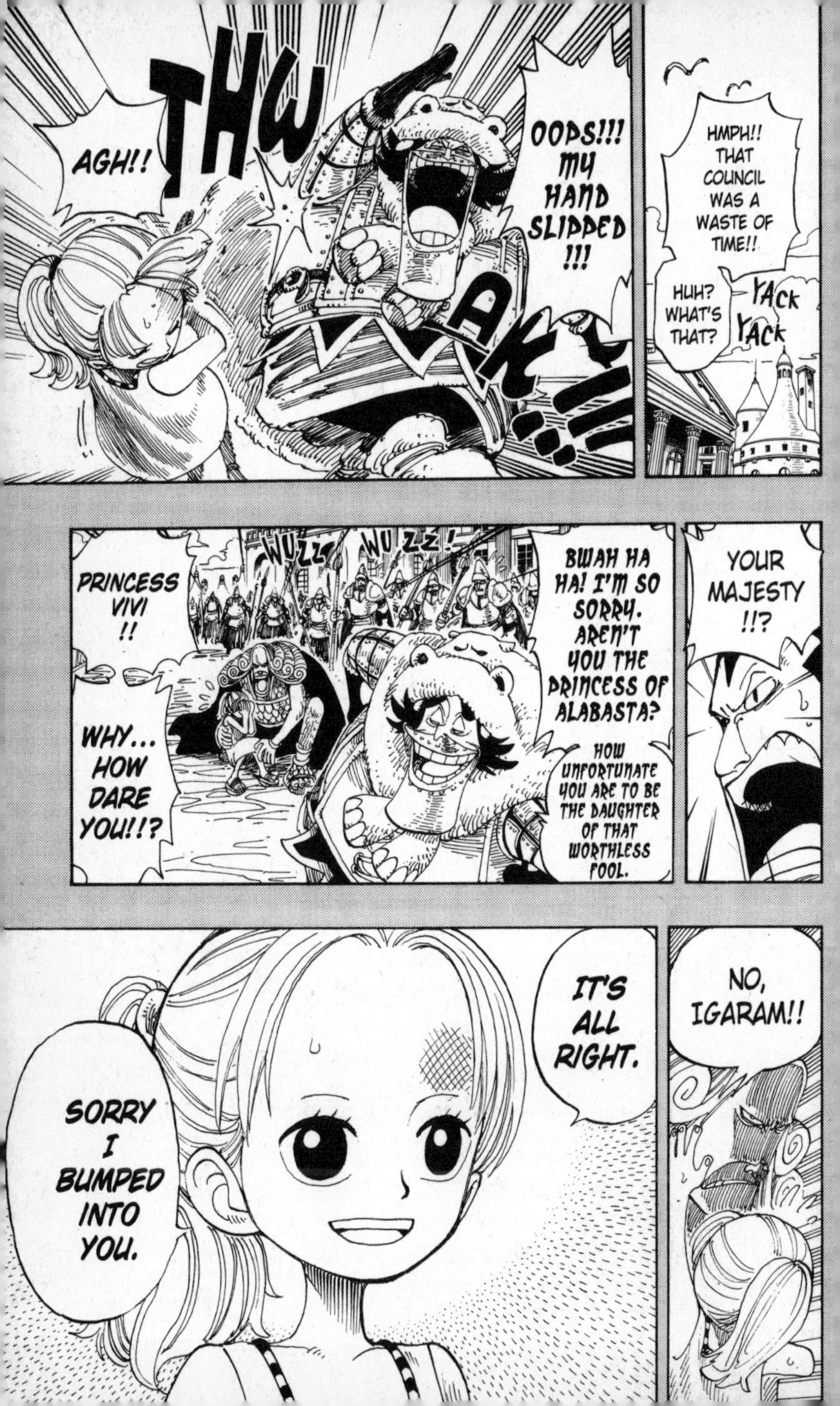
HMPH!! THAT COUNCIL WAS A WASTE OF TIME!!
YACK YACK
HUH? WHAT'S THAT?
OOPS!!! MY HAND SLIPPED!!!
THWAK!!
AGH!!
YOUR MAJESTY!!?
WUZZ WUZZ!
BWAH HA HA! I'M SO SORRY. AREN'T YOU THE PRINCESS OF ALABASTA?
HOW UNFORTUNATE YOU ARE TO BE THE DAUGHTER OF THAT WORTHLESS FOOL.
PRINCESS VIVI!!
WHY... HOW DARE YOU!!?
NO, IGARAM!!
IT'S ALL RIGHT.
SORRY I BUMPED INTO YOU.

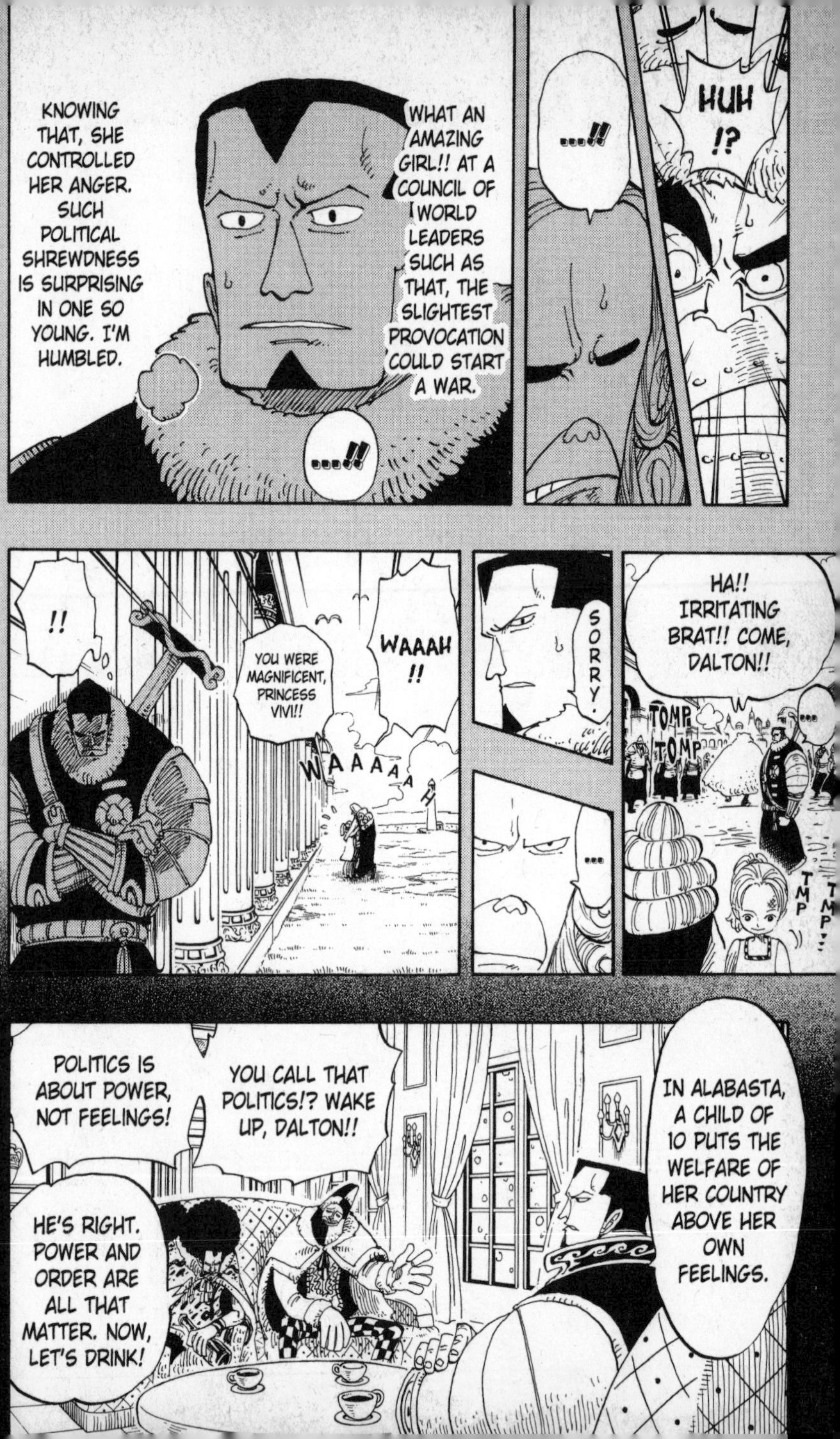
HUH !?
...!!
WHAT AN AMAZING GIRL!! AT A COUNCIL OF WORLD LEADERS SUCH AS THAT, THE SLIGHTEST PROVOCATION COULD START A WAR.
KNOWING THAT, SHE CONTROLLED HER ANGER. SUCH POLITICAL SHREWDNESS IS SURPRISING IN ONE SO YOUNG. I'M HUMBLED.
...!!
HA!! IRRITATING BRAT!! COME, DALTON!!
...
TOMP TOMP
TMP TMP...
SORRY.
...
WAAAH !!
YOU WERE MAGNIFICENT, PRINCESS VIVI!!
WAAAAAAH
!!
IN ALABASTA, A CHILD OF 10 PUTS THE WELFARE OF HER COUNTRY ABOVE HER OWN FEELINGS.
YOU CALL THAT POLITICS!? WAKE UP, DALTON!!
POLITICS IS ABOUT POWER, NOT FEELINGS!
HE'S RIGHT. POWER AND ORDER ARE ALL THAT MATTER. NOW, LET'S DRINK!

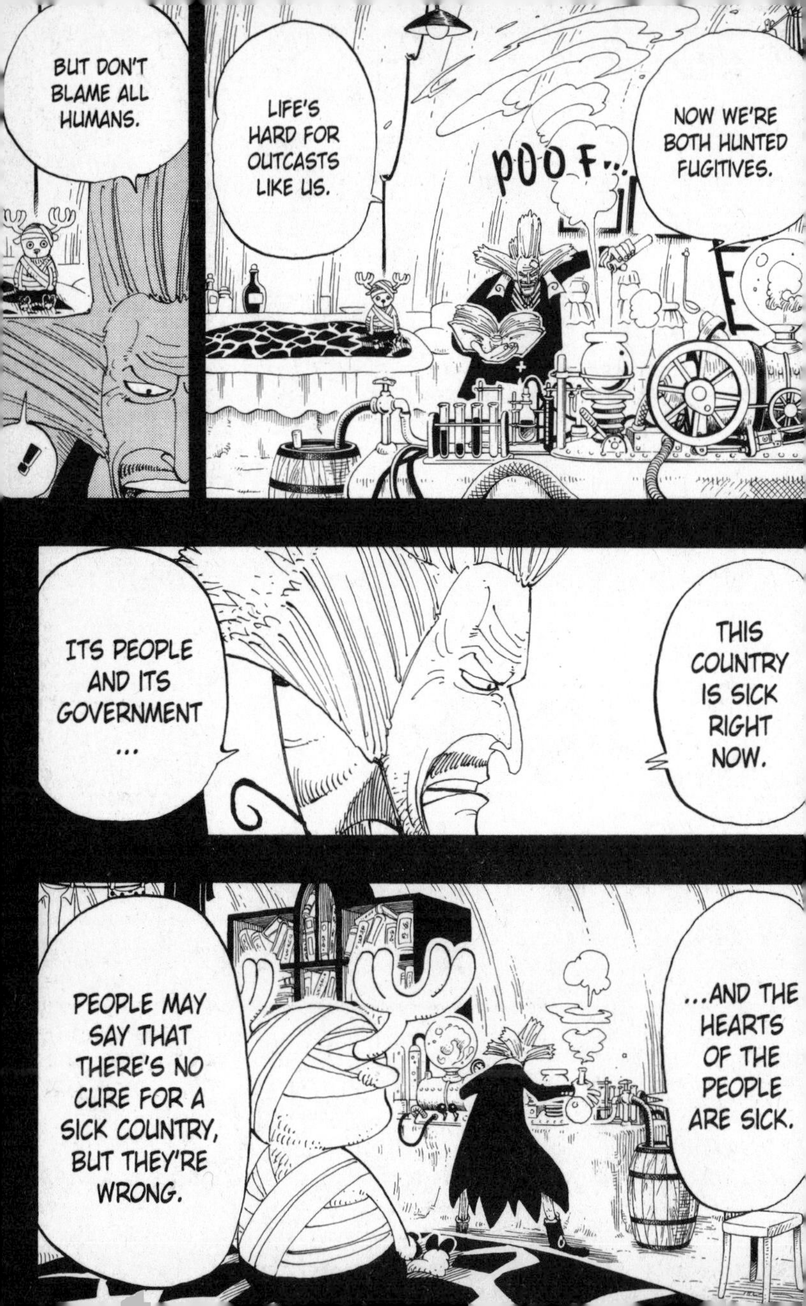
NOW WE'RE BOTH HUNTED FUGITIVES.
POOF...
LIFE'S HARD FOR OUTCASTS LIKE US.
BUT DON'T BLAME ALL HUMANS.
!
THIS COUNTRY IS SICK RIGHT NOW.
ITS PEOPLE AND ITS GOVERNMENT ...
...AND THE HEARTS OF THE PEOPLE ARE SICK.
PEOPLE MAY SAY THAT THERE'S NO CURE FOR A SICK COUNTRY, BUT THEY'RE WRONG.

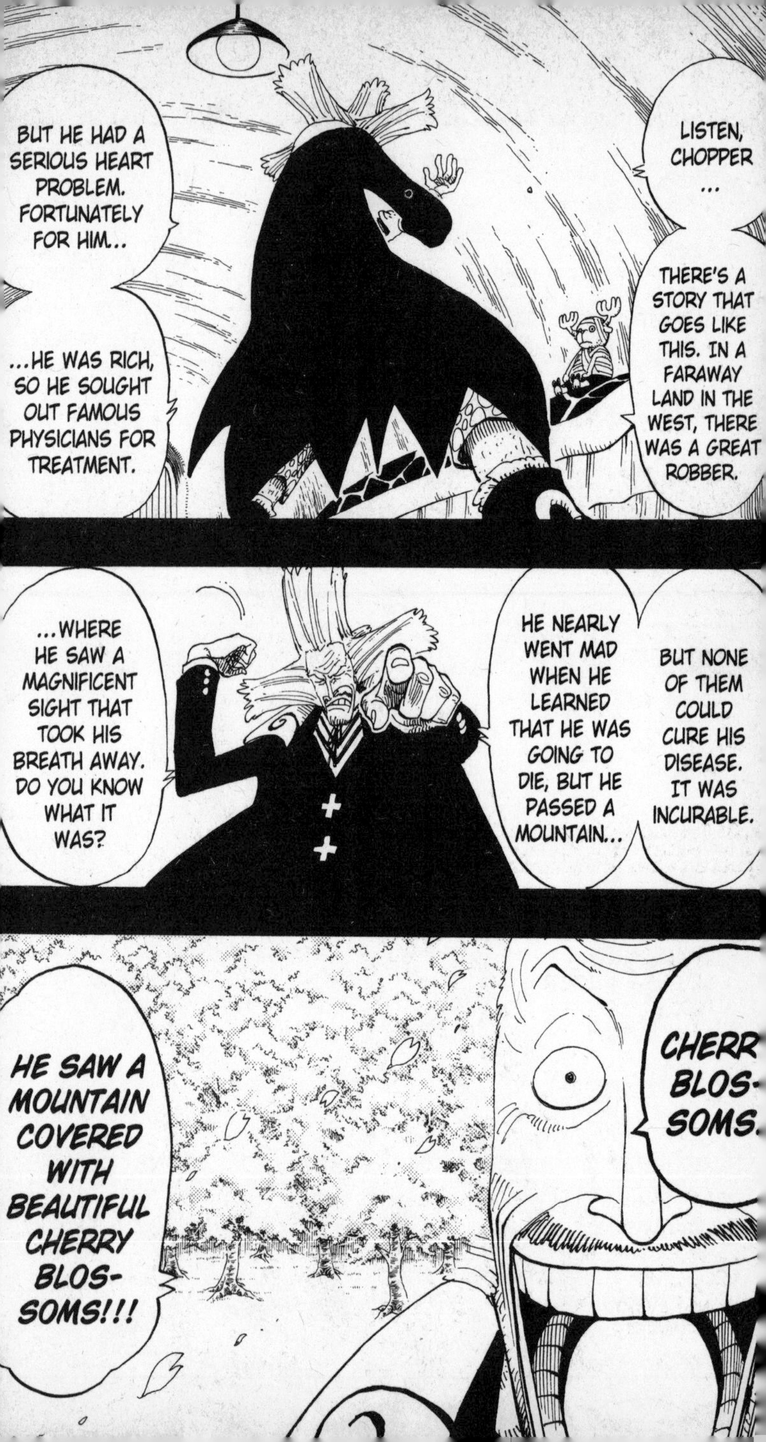
LISTEN, CHOPPER ...
THERE'S A STORY THAT GOES LIKE THIS. IN A FARAWAY LAND IN THE WEST, THERE WAS A GREAT ROBBER.
BUT HE HAD A SERIOUS HEART PROBLEM. FORTUNATELY FOR HIM...
...HE WAS RICH, SO HE SOUGHT OUT FAMOUS PHYSICIANS FOR TREATMENT.
BUT NONE OF THEM COULD CURE HIS DISEASE. IT WAS INCURABLE.
HE NEARLY WENT MAD WHEN HE LEARNED THAT HE WAS GOING TO DIE, BUT HE PASSED A MOUNTAIN...
...WHERE HE SAW A MAGNIFICENT SIGHT THAT TOOK HIS BREATH AWAY. DO YOU KNOW WHAT IT WAS?
CHERR BLOS- SOMS.
HE SAW A MOUNTAIN COVERED WITH BEAUTIFUL CHERRY BLOS- SOMS!!!

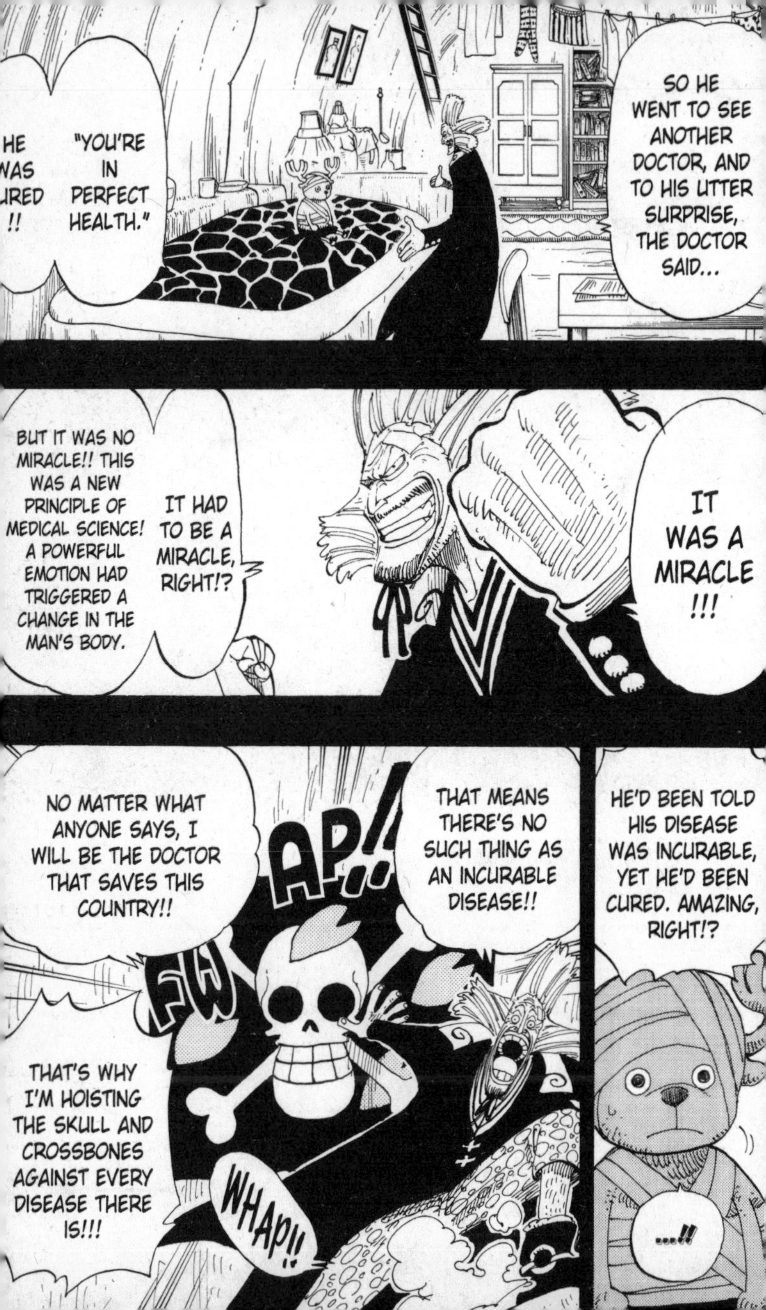
SO HE WENT TO SEE ANOTHER DOCTOR, AND TO HIS UTTER SURPRISE, THE DOCTOR SAID...
"YOU'RE IN PERFECT HEALTH."
HE WAS URED !!
IT WAS A MIRACLE !!!
IT HAD TO BE A MIRACLE, RIGHT!?
BUT IT WAS NO MIRACLE!! THIS WAS A NEW PRINCIPLE OF MEDICAL SCIENCE! A POWERFUL EMOTION HAD TRIGGERED A CHANGE IN THE MAN'S BODY.
HE'D BEEN TOLD HIS DISEASE WAS INCURABLE, YET HE'D BEEN CURED. AMAZING, RIGHT!?
...!!
THAT MEANS THERE'S NO SUCH THING AS AN INCURABLE DISEASE!!
AP!!
NO MATTER WHAT ANYONE SAYS, I WILL BE THE DOCTOR THAT SAVES THIS COUNTRY!!
FW
THAT'S WHY I'M HOISTING THE SKULL AND CROSSBONES AGAINST EVERY DISEASE THERE IS!!!
WHAP!!

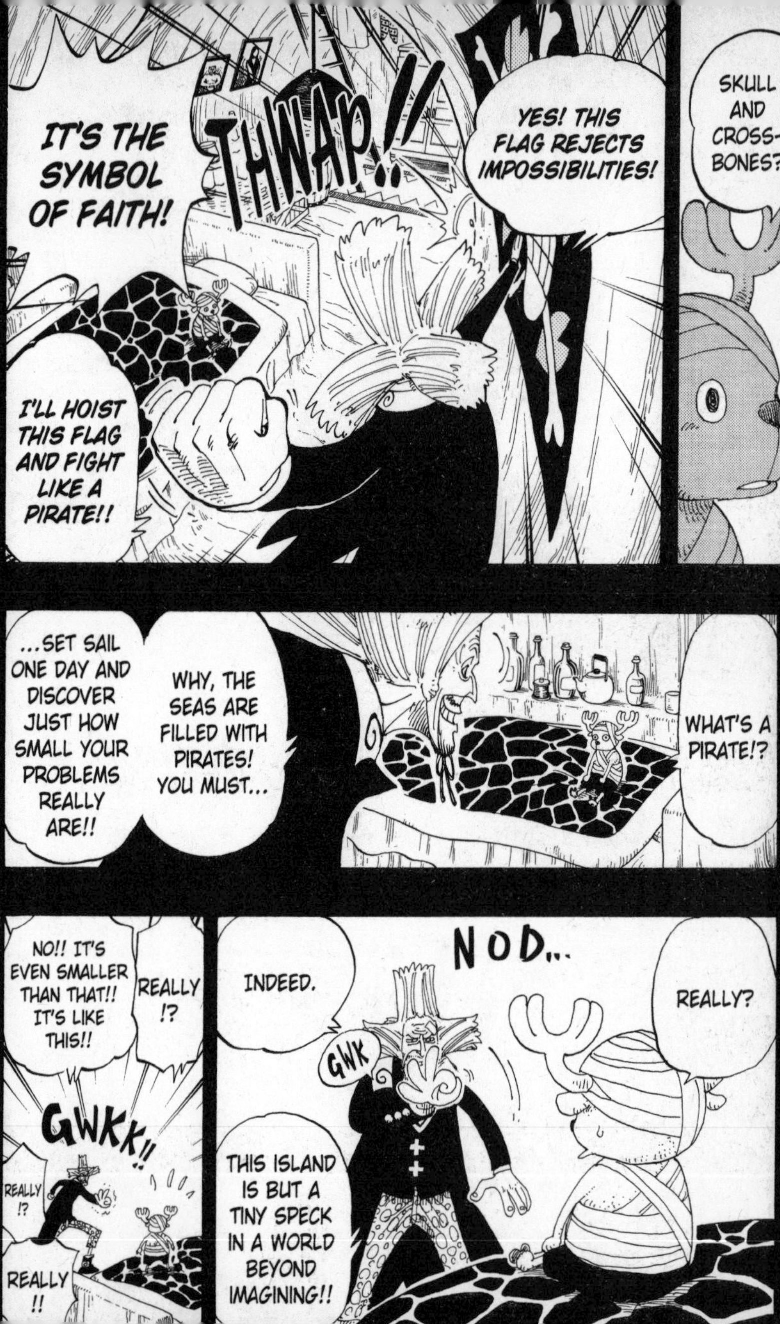
SKULL AND CROSS-BONES?
YES! THIS FLAG REJECTS IMPOSSIBILITIES!
THWAP!!
IT'S THE SYMBOL OF FAITH!
I'LL HOIST THIS FLAG AND FIGHT LIKE A PIRATE!!
WHAT'S A PIRATE!?
WHY, THE SEAS ARE FILLED WITH PIRATES! YOU MUST...
...SET SAIL ONE DAY AND DISCOVER JUST HOW SMALL YOUR PROBLEMS REALLY ARE!!
REALLY?
NOD...
INDEED.
GWK
THIS ISLAND IS BUT A TINY SPECK IN A WORLD BEYOND IMAGINING!!
REALLY !?
NO!! IT'S EVEN SMALLER THAN THAT!! IT'S LIKE THIS!!
GWKK!!
REALLY !?
REALLY !!

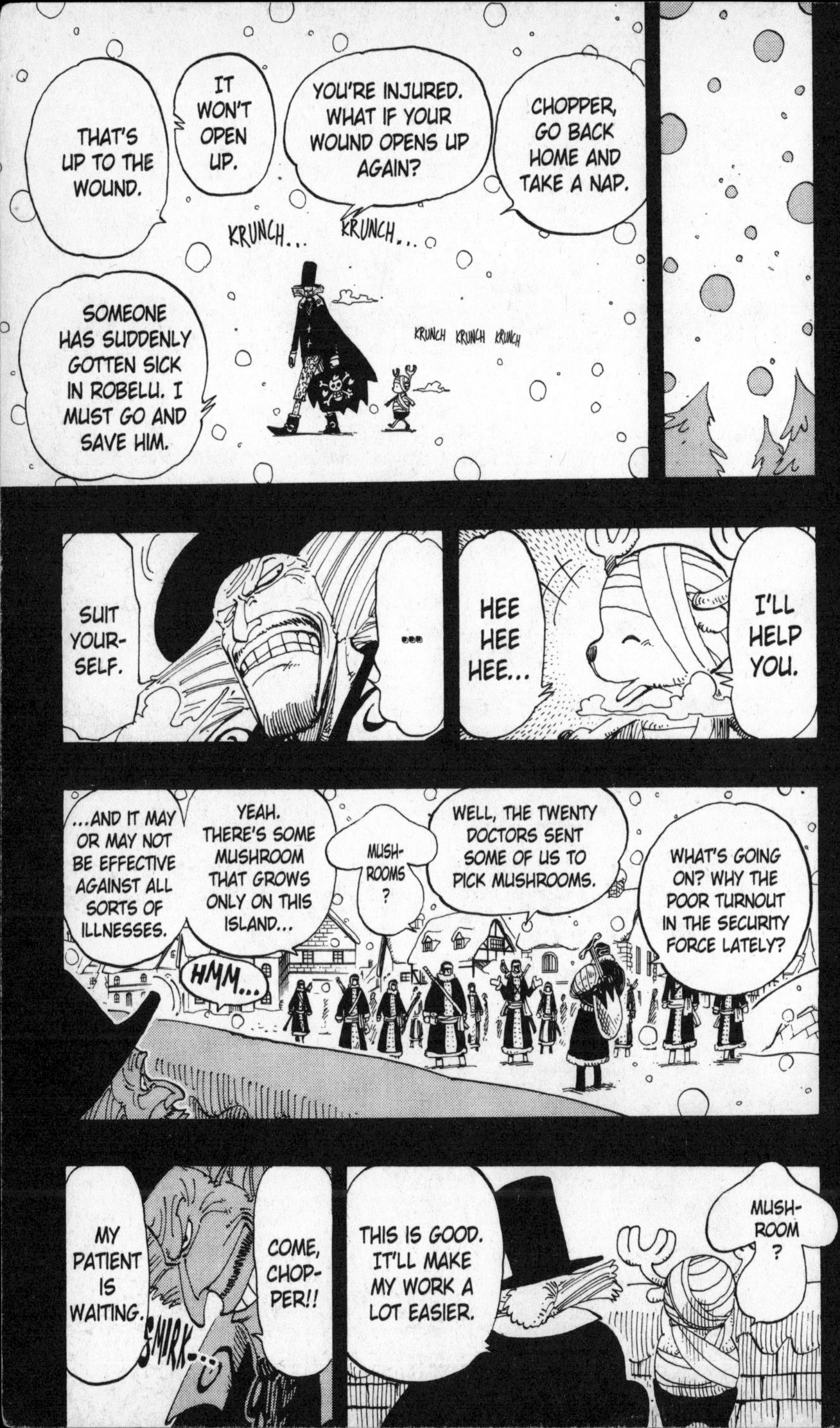

CHOPPER, GO BACK HOME AND TAKE A NAP.
YOU'RE INJURED. WHAT IF YOUR WOUND OPENS UP AGAIN?
IT WON'T OPEN UP.
THAT'S UP TO THE WOUND.
KRUNCH...
KRUNCH...
KRUNCH KRUNCH KRUNCH
SOMEONE HAS SUDDENLY GOTTEN SICK IN ROBELU. I MUST GO AND SAVE HIM.
I'LL HELP YOU.
HEE HEE HEE...
...
SUIT YOURSELF.
WHAT'S GOING ON? WHY THE POOR TURNOUT IN THE SECURITY FORCE LATELY?
WELL, THE TWENTY DOCTORS SENT SOME OF US TO PICK MUSHROOMS.
MUSHROOMS?
YEAH. THERE'S SOME MUSHROOM THAT GROWS ONLY ON THIS ISLAND...
...AND IT MAY OR MAY NOT BE EFFECTIVE AGAINST ALL SORTS OF ILLNESSES.
HMM...
MUSHROOM?
THIS IS GOOD. IT'LL MAKE MY WORK A LOT EASIER.
COME, CHOPPER!!
MY PATIENT IS WAITING.
SMIRK...

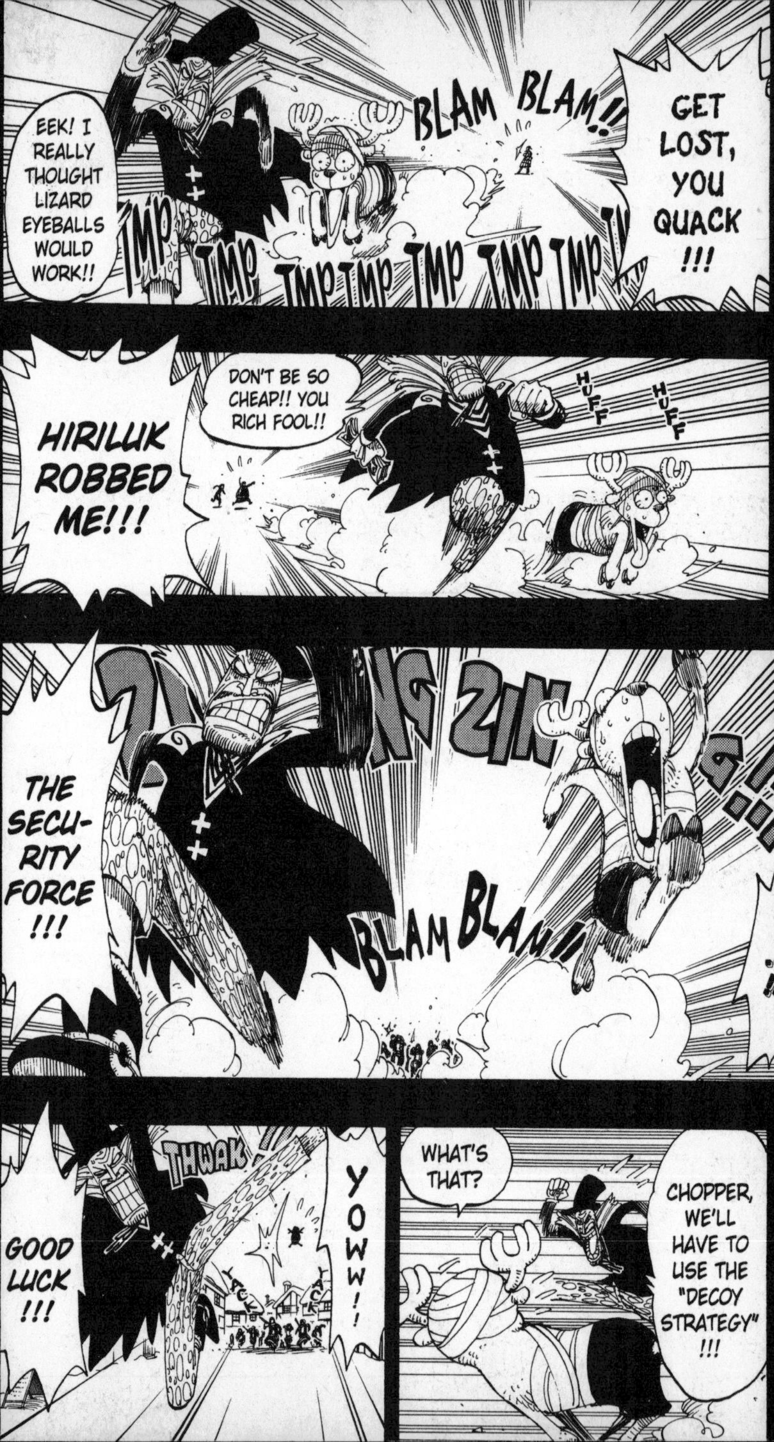
GET LOST, YOU QUACK!!!
BLAM BLAM!!
EEK! I REALLY THOUGHT LIZARD EYEBALLS WOULD WORK!!
TMP TMP TMP TMP TMP TMP TMP
HUFF HUFF
DON'T BE SO CHEAP!! YOU RICH FOOL!!
HIRILUK ROBBED ME!!!
...!!
BLAM BLAM!!
THE SECURITY FORCE!!!
CHOPPER, WE'LL HAVE TO USE THE "DECOY STRATEGY"!!!
WHAT'S THAT?
YOWW!!
THWAK
GOOD LUCK!!!

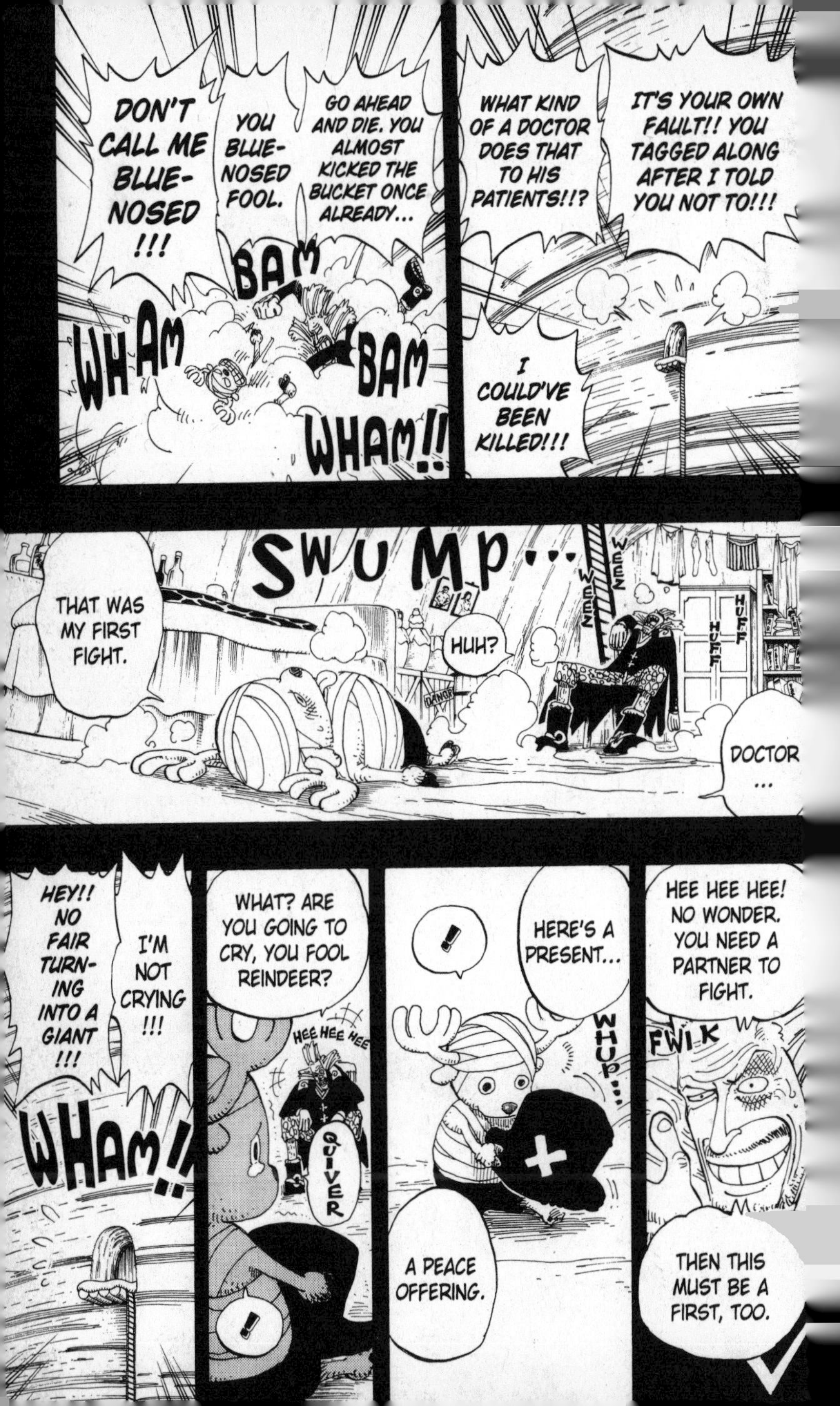

IT'S YOUR OWN FAULT!! YOU TAGGED ALONG AFTER I TOLD YOU NOT TO!!!
WHAT KIND OF A DOCTOR DOES THAT TO HIS PATIENTS!!?
I COULD'VE BEEN KILLED!!!
GO AHEAD AND DIE. YOU ALMOST KICKED THE BUCKET ONCE ALREADY...
YOU BLUE-NOSED FOOL.
DON'T CALL ME BLUE-NOSED!!!
BAM
BAM
WHAM
WHAM!!
DOCTOR...
HUFF
HUFF
WEEZ
WEEZ
HUH?
SWUMP...
THAT WAS MY FIRST FIGHT.
HEE HEE HEE! NO WONDER. YOU NEED A PARTNER TO FIGHT.
FWIK
THEN THIS MUST BE A FIRST, TOO.
HERE'S A PRESENT...
!
WHUP...
A PEACE OFFERING.
WHAT? ARE YOU GOING TO CRY, YOU FOOL REINDEER?
HEE HEE HEE
QUIVER
!
I'M NOT CRYING!!!
HEY!! NO FAIR TURNING INTO A GIANT!!!
WHAM!!

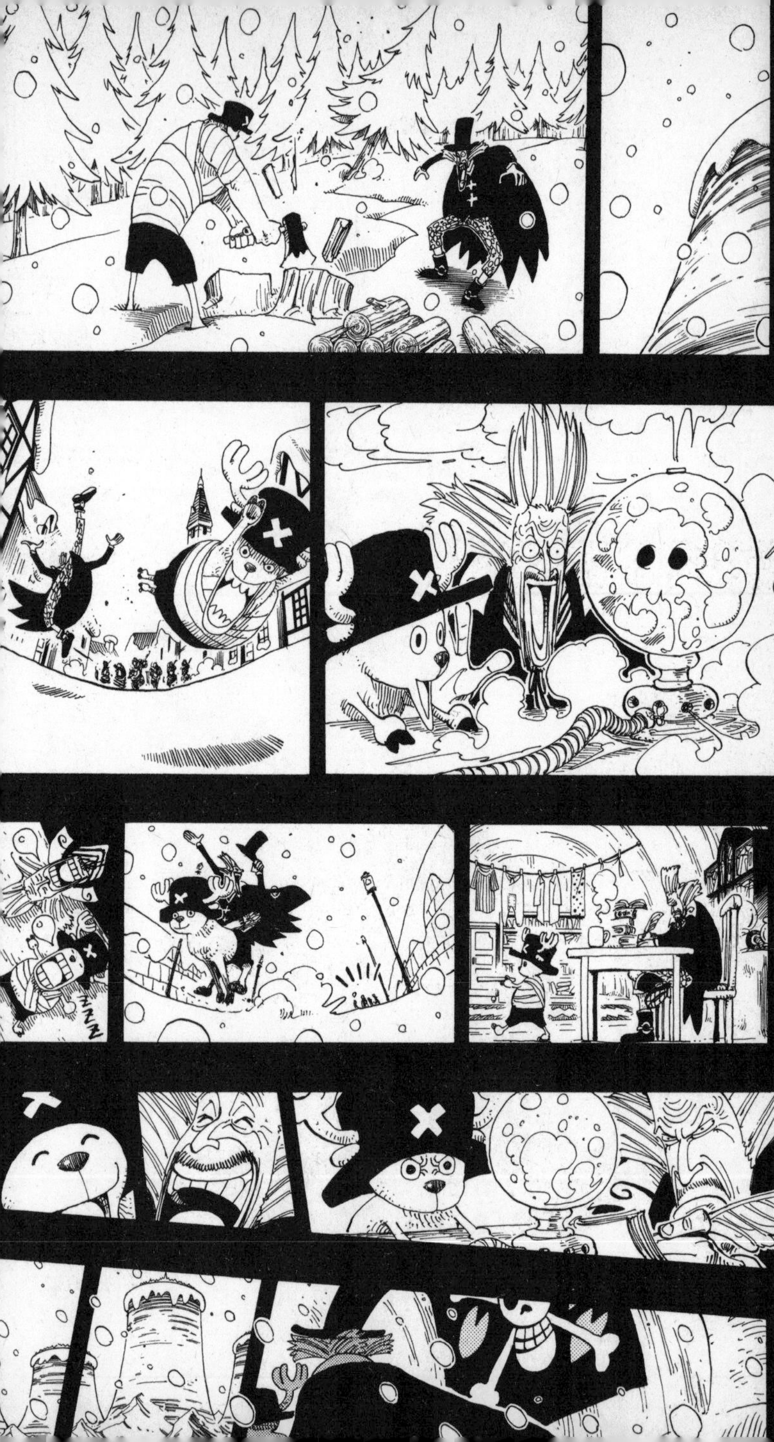
ZZZ

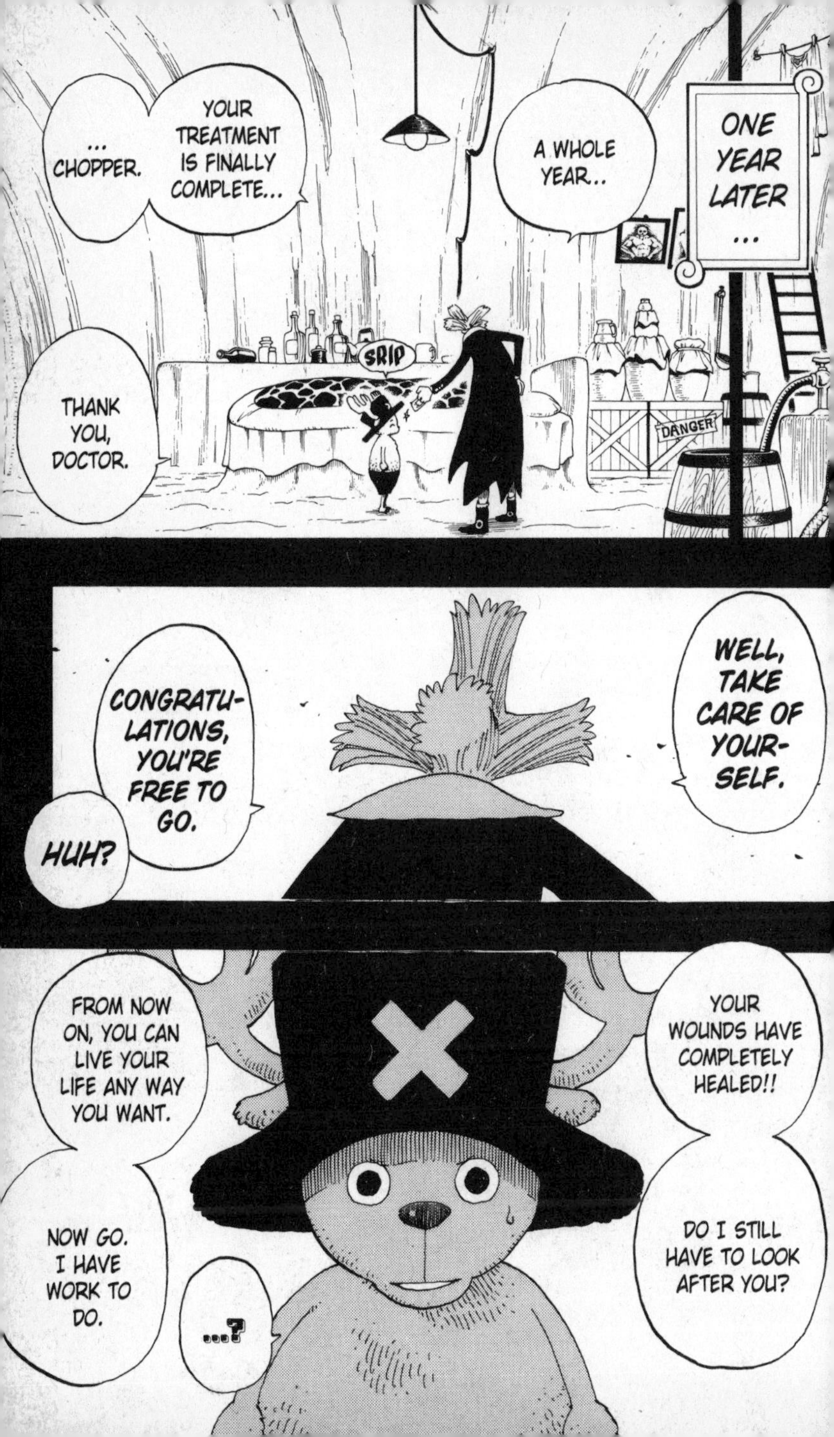
ONE YEAR LATER ...
A WHOLE YEAR...
YOUR TREATMENT IS FINALLY COMPLETE...
... CHOPPER.
DANGER
SRIP
THANK YOU, DOCTOR.
WELL, TAKE CARE OF YOURSELF.
CONGRATULATIONS, YOU'RE FREE TO GO.
HUH?
YOUR WOUNDS HAVE COMPLETELY HEALED!!
FROM NOW ON, YOU CAN LIVE YOUR LIFE ANY WAY YOU WANT.
DO I STILL HAVE TO LOOK AFTER YOU?
NOW GO. I HAVE WORK TO DO.
...?

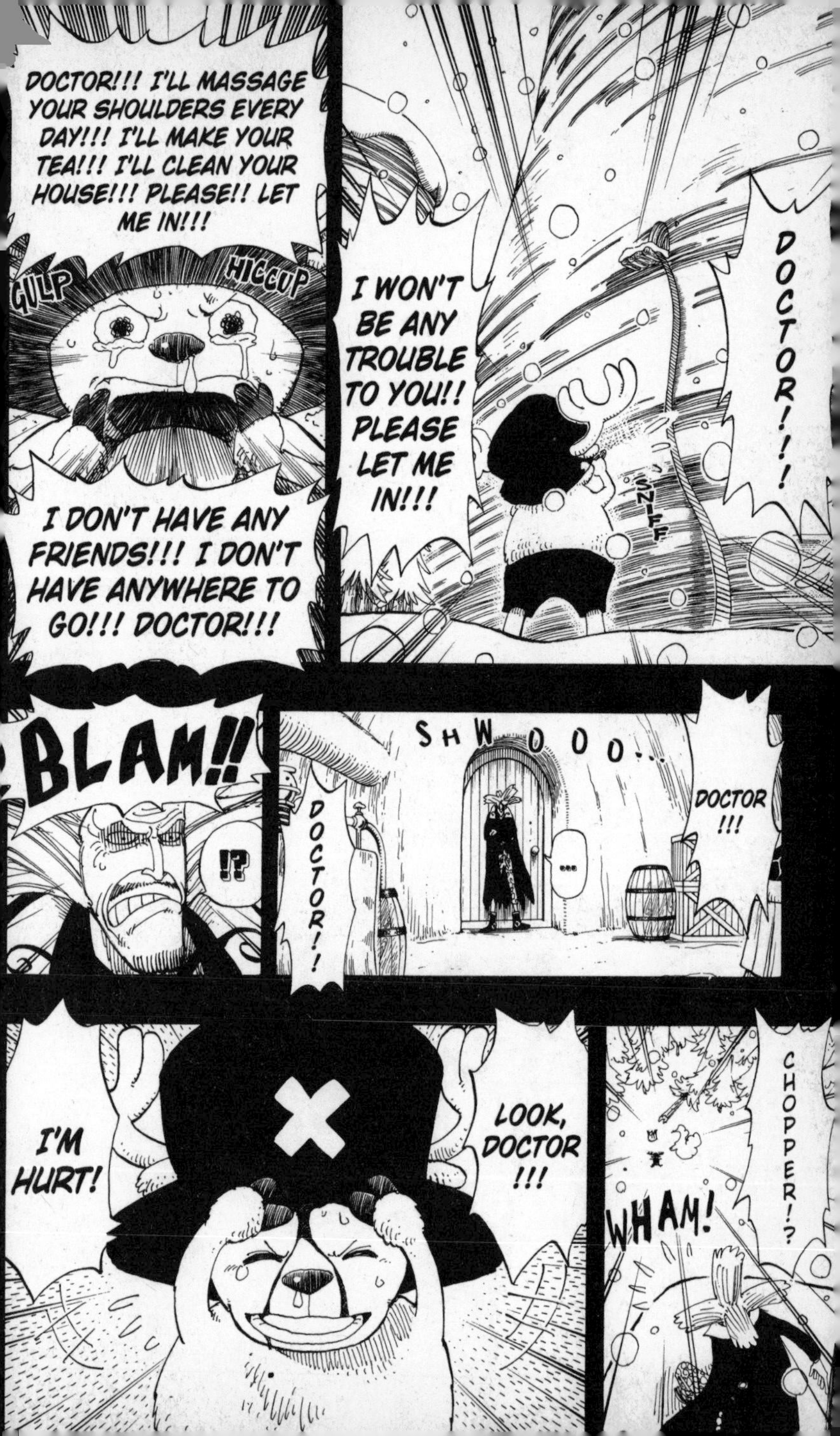
DOCTOR!!!
I WON'T BE ANY TROUBLE TO YOU!! PLEASE LET ME IN!!!
SNIFF
DOCTOR!!! I'LL MASSAGE YOUR SHOULDERS EVERY DAY!!! I'LL MAKE YOUR TEA!!! I'LL CLEAN YOUR HOUSE!!! PLEASE!! LET ME IN!!!
HICCUP
GULP
I DON'T HAVE ANY FRIENDS!!! I DON'T HAVE ANYWHERE TO GO!!! DOCTOR!!!
DOCTOR !!!
SHWOOO...
...
DOCTOR!!
BLAM!!
!?
CHOPPER!?
WHAM!
LOOK, DOCTOR !!!
I'M HURT!

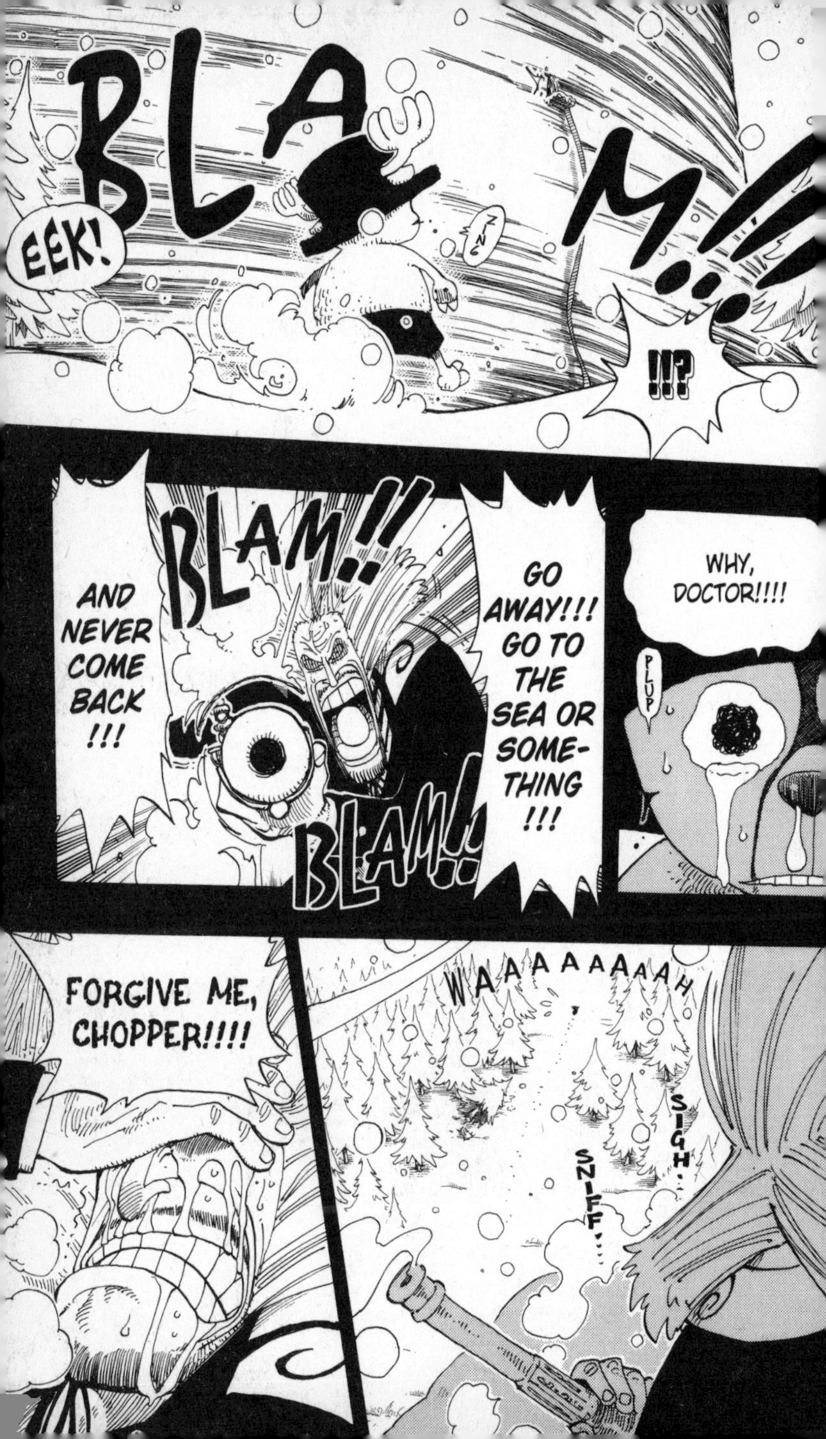
BLAM!!
!!?
ZING
EEK!
WHY, DOCTOR!!!!
PLUP
GO AWAY!!! GO TO THE SEA OR SOME-THING!!!
BLAM!!
AND NEVER COME BACK!!!
BLAM!!
WAAAAAAAH
SIGH..
SNIFF...
FORGIVE ME, CHOPPER!!!!

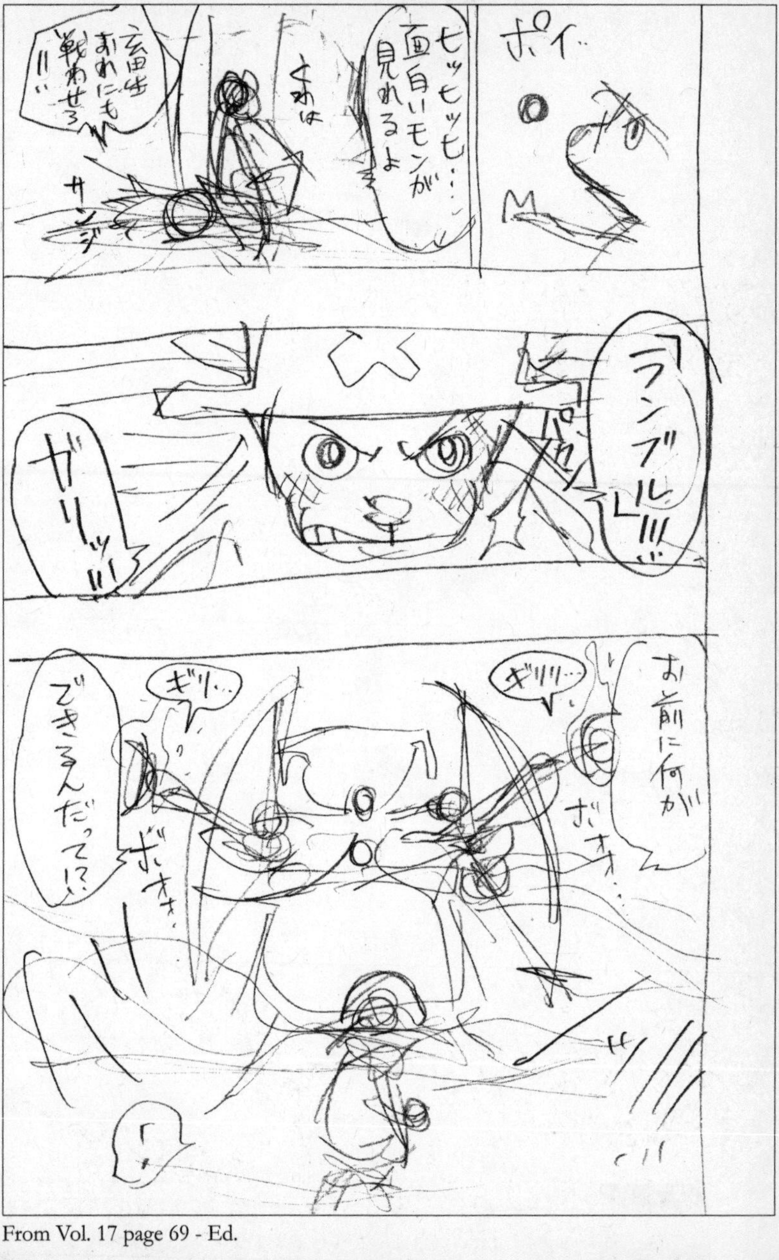
ポイ
ヒッヒッヒ…面白いモンが見れるよ
おれにも戦わせろ!!
「ランブル」!!
ガリッ!!
お前に何が
ギリ…
ギリ…
できるんだって!!

From Vol. 17 page 69 - Ed.

Chapter 143:
CLUMSY

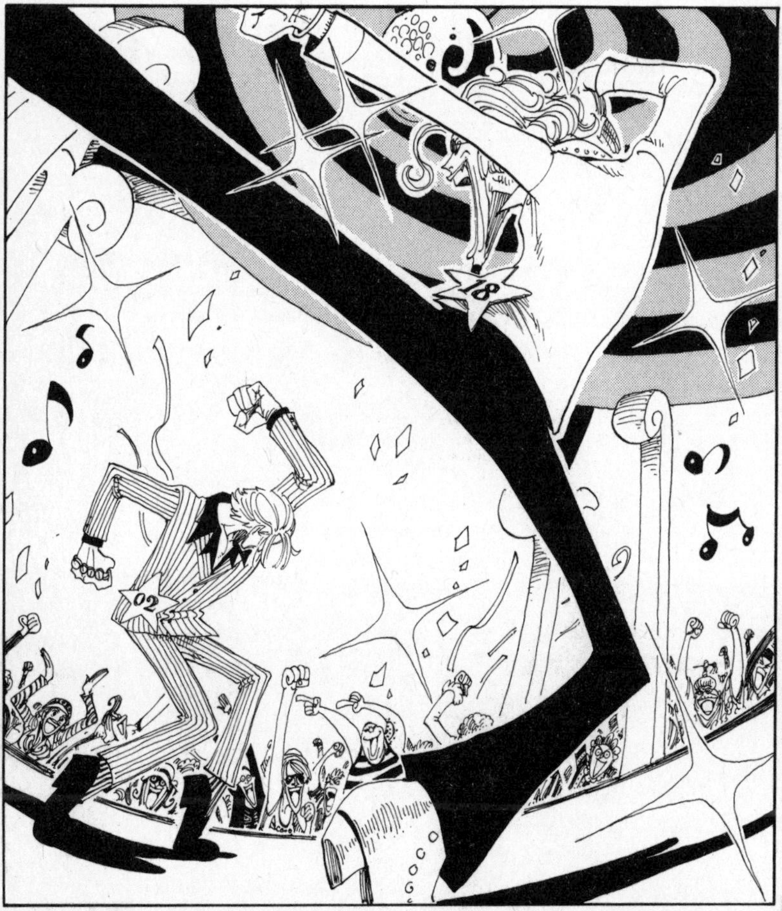
18
02

DJANGO'S DANCE HEAVEN, VOL. 14: "CALCULATING THE OUTCOME OF THE DANCE CONTEST"

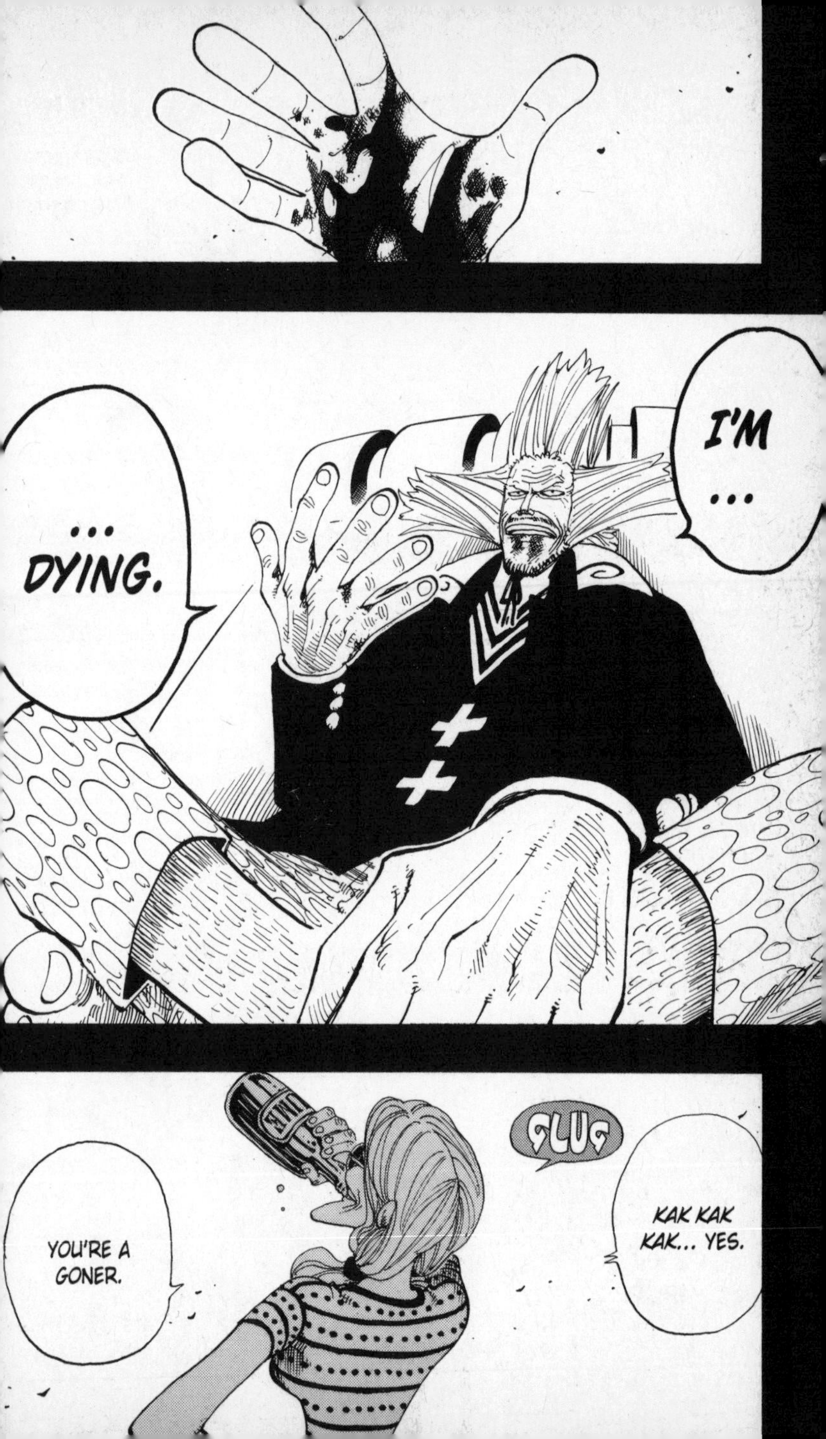
I'M ...
... DYING.
GLUG
KAK KAK KAK... YES.
YOU'RE A GONER.

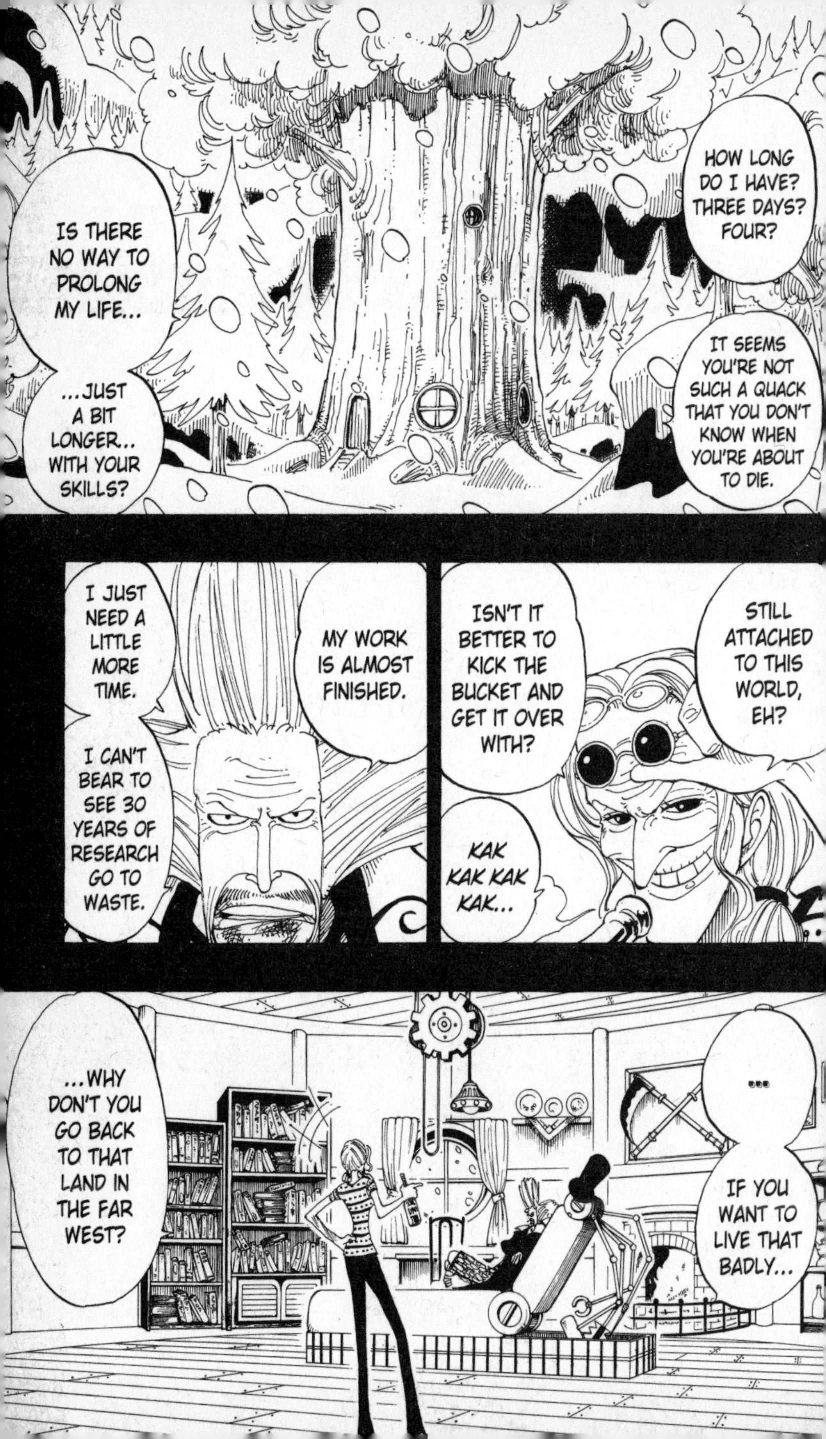
HOW LONG DO I HAVE? THREE DAYS? FOUR?
IT SEEMS YOU'RE NOT SUCH A QUACK THAT YOU DON'T KNOW WHEN YOU'RE ABOUT TO DIE.
IS THERE NO WAY TO PROLONG MY LIFE...
...JUST A BIT LONGER... WITH YOUR SKILLS?
STILL ATTACHED TO THIS WORLD, EH?
ISN'T IT BETTER TO KICK THE BUCKET AND GET IT OVER WITH?
KAK KAK KAK KAK...
MY WORK IS ALMOST FINISHED.
I JUST NEED A LITTLE MORE TIME.
I CAN'T BEAR TO SEE 30 YEARS OF RESEARCH GO TO WASTE.
...
IF YOU WANT TO LIVE THAT BADLY...
...WHY DON'T YOU GO BACK TO THAT LAND IN THE FAR WEST?

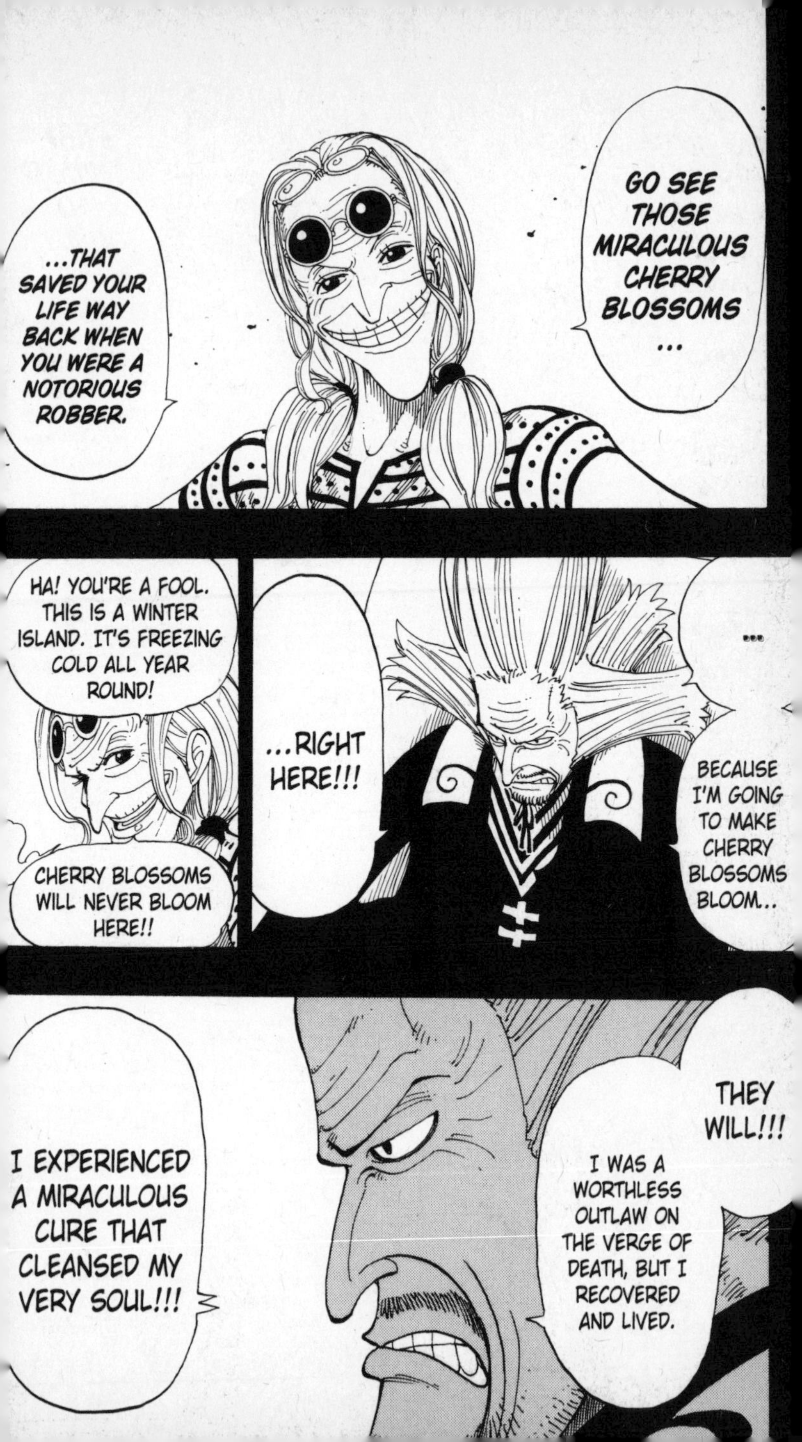
GO SEE THOSE MIRACULOUS CHERRY BLOSSOMS ...
...THAT SAVED YOUR LIFE WAY BACK WHEN YOU WERE A NOTORIOUS ROBBER.
...
BECAUSE I'M GOING TO MAKE CHERRY BLOSSOMS BLOOM..
...RIGHT HERE!!!
HA! YOU'RE A FOOL. THIS IS A WINTER ISLAND. IT'S FREEZING COLD ALL YEAR ROUND!
CHERRY BLOSSOMS WILL NEVER BLOOM HERE!!
THEY WILL!!!
I WAS A WORTHLESS OUTLAW ON THE VERGE OF DEATH, BUT I RECOVERED AND LIVED.
I EXPERIENCED A MIRACULOUS CURE THAT CLEANSED MY VERY SOUL!!!

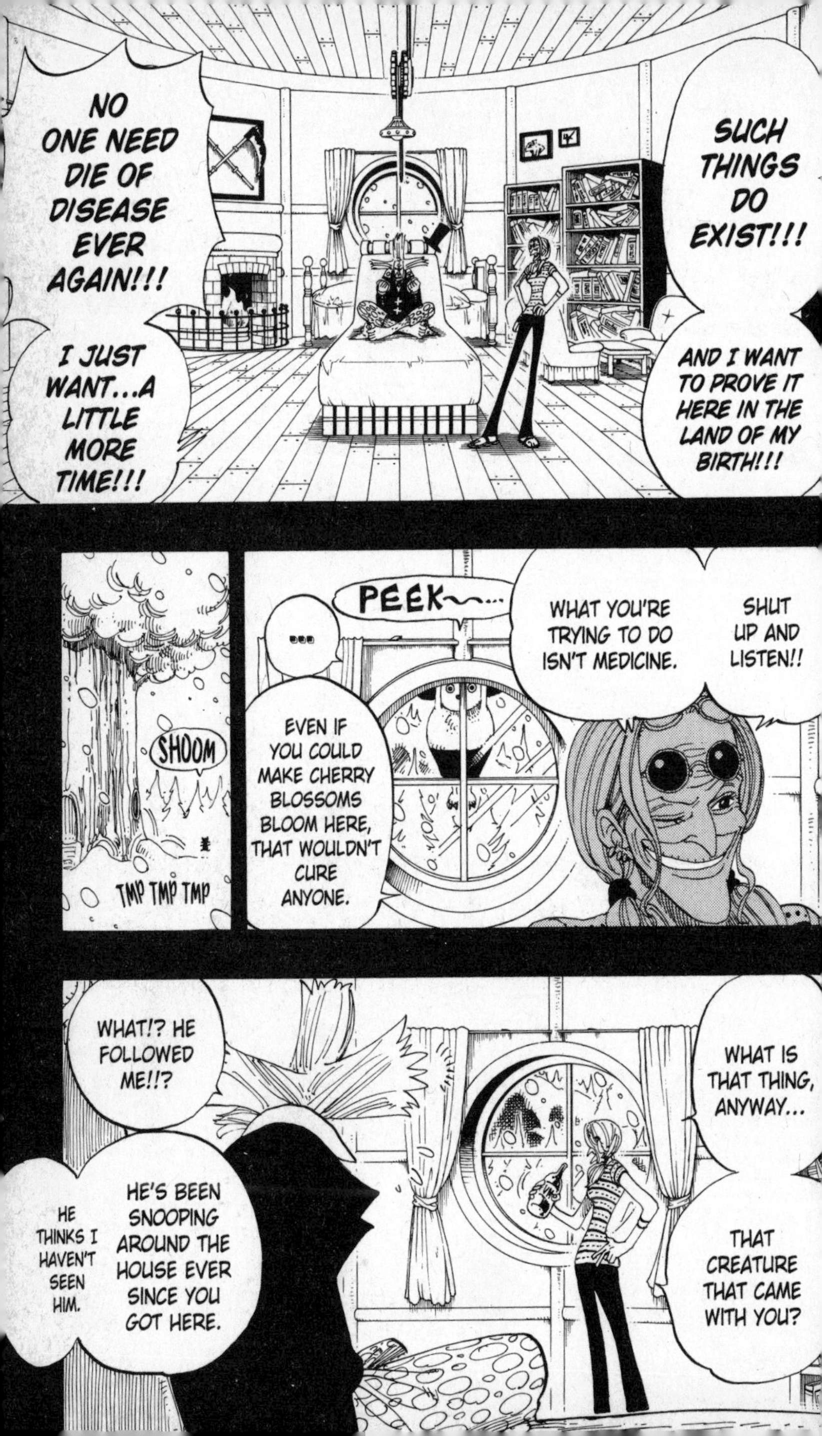
SUCH THINGS DO EXIST!!!
AND I WANT TO PROVE IT HERE IN THE LAND OF MY BIRTH!!!
NO ONE NEED DIE OF DISEASE EVER AGAIN!!!
I JUST WANT...A LITTLE MORE TIME!!!
SHUT UP AND LISTEN!!
WHAT YOU'RE TRYING TO DO ISN'T MEDICINE.
PEEK~~...
...
EVEN IF YOU COULD MAKE CHERRY BLOSSOMS BLOOM HERE, THAT WOULDN'T CURE ANYONE.
SHOOM
TMP TMP TMP
WHAT IS THAT THING, ANYWAY...
THAT CREATURE THAT CAME WITH YOU?
WHAT!? HE FOLLOWED ME!!?
HE'S BEEN SNOOPING AROUND THE HOUSE EVER SINCE YOU GOT HERE.
HE THINKS I HAVEN'T SEEN HIM.

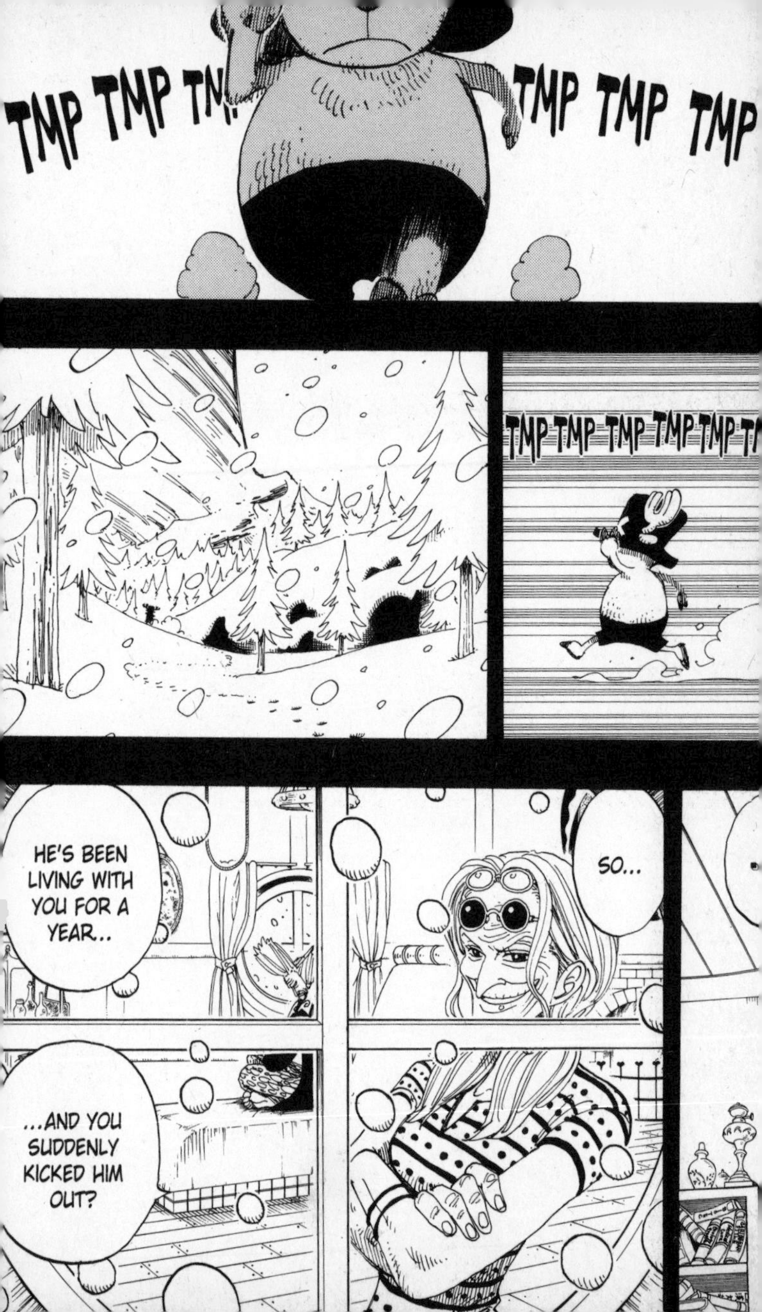
TMP TMP TMP
TMP TMP TMP
TMP TMP TMP TMP TMP
SO...
HE'S BEEN LIVING WITH YOU FOR A YEAR...
...AND YOU SUDDENLY KICKED HIM OUT?

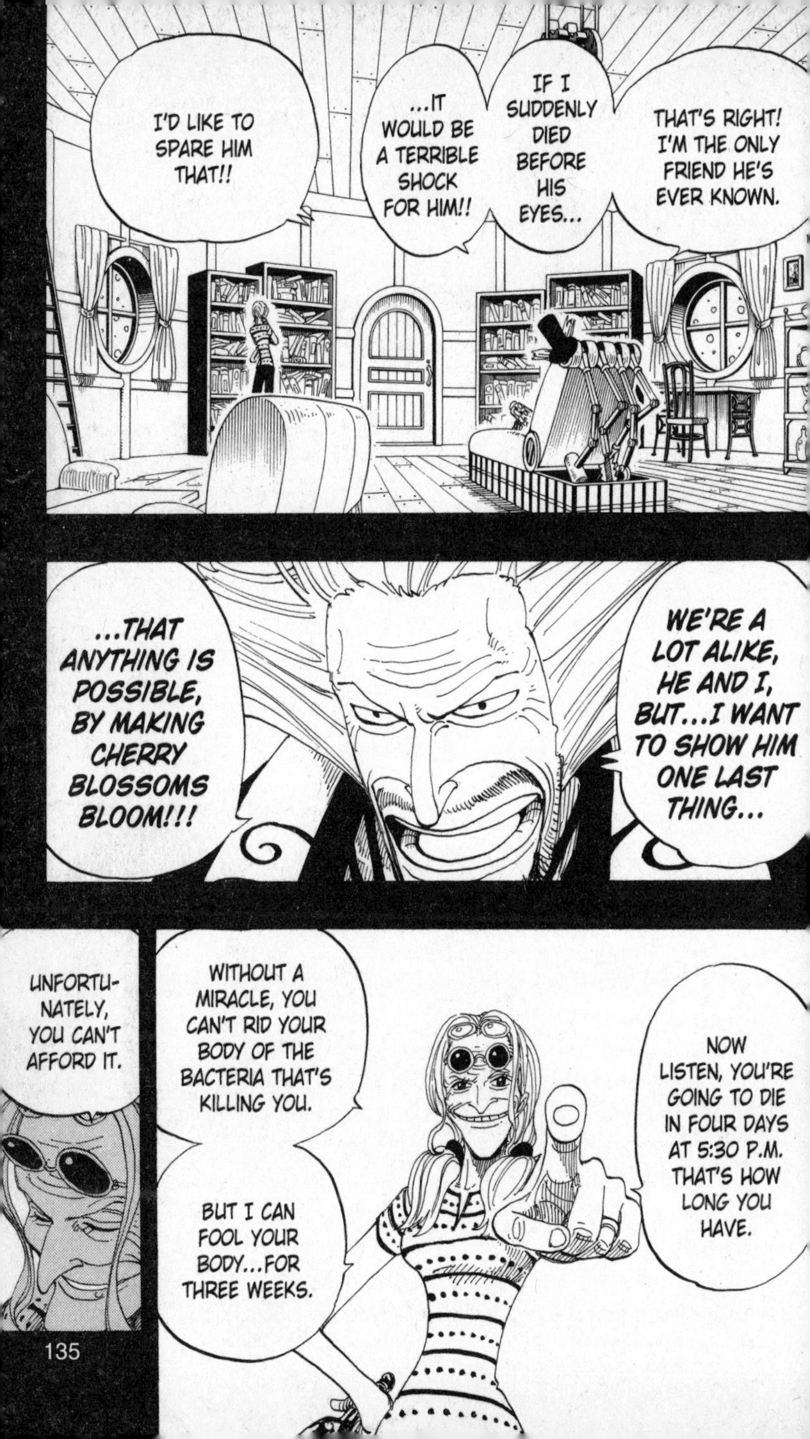
THAT'S RIGHT! I'M THE ONLY FRIEND HE'S EVER KNOWN.
IF I SUDDENLY DIED BEFORE HIS EYES...
...IT WOULD BE A TERRIBLE SHOCK FOR HIM!!
I'D LIKE TO SPARE HIM THAT!!
WE'RE A LOT ALIKE, HE AND I, BUT...I WANT TO SHOW HIM ONE LAST THING...
...THAT ANYTHING IS POSSIBLE, BY MAKING CHERRY BLOSSOMS BLOOM!!!
NOW LISTEN, YOU'RE GOING TO DIE IN FOUR DAYS AT 5:30 P.M. THAT'S HOW LONG YOU HAVE.
WITHOUT A MIRACLE, YOU CAN'T RID YOUR BODY OF THE BACTERIA THAT'S KILLING YOU.
BUT I CAN FOOL YOUR BODY...FOR THREE WEEKS.
UNFORTU-NATELY, YOU CAN'T AFFORD IT.

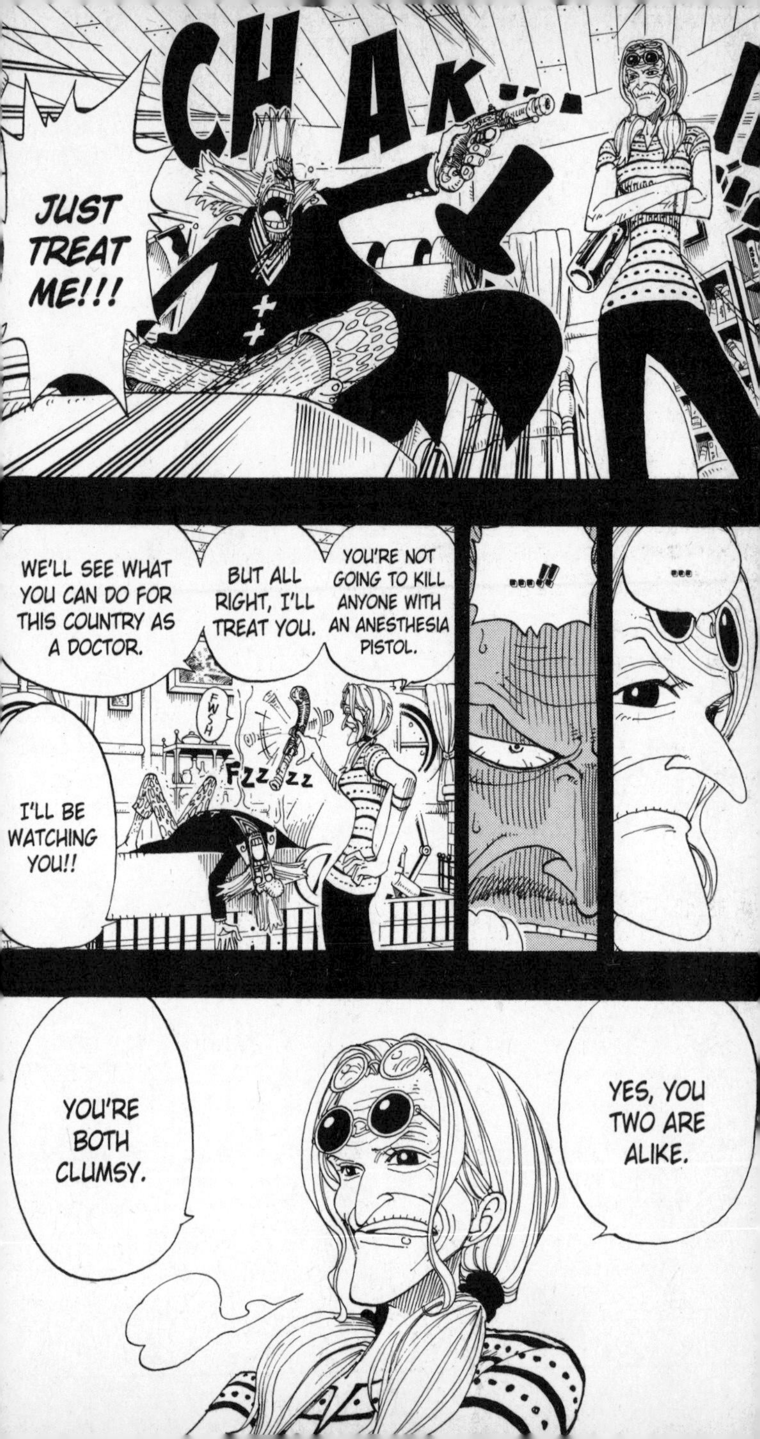

CHAK...!!
JUST TREAT ME!!!
...
...!!
YOU'RE NOT GOING TO KILL ANYONE WITH AN ANESTHESIA PISTOL.
BUT ALL RIGHT, I'LL TREAT YOU.
WE'LL SEE WHAT YOU CAN DO FOR THIS COUNTRY AS A DOCTOR.
FWSH
FZZZZZ
I'LL BE WATCHING YOU!!
YES, YOU TWO ARE ALIKE.
YOU'RE BOTH CLUMSY.

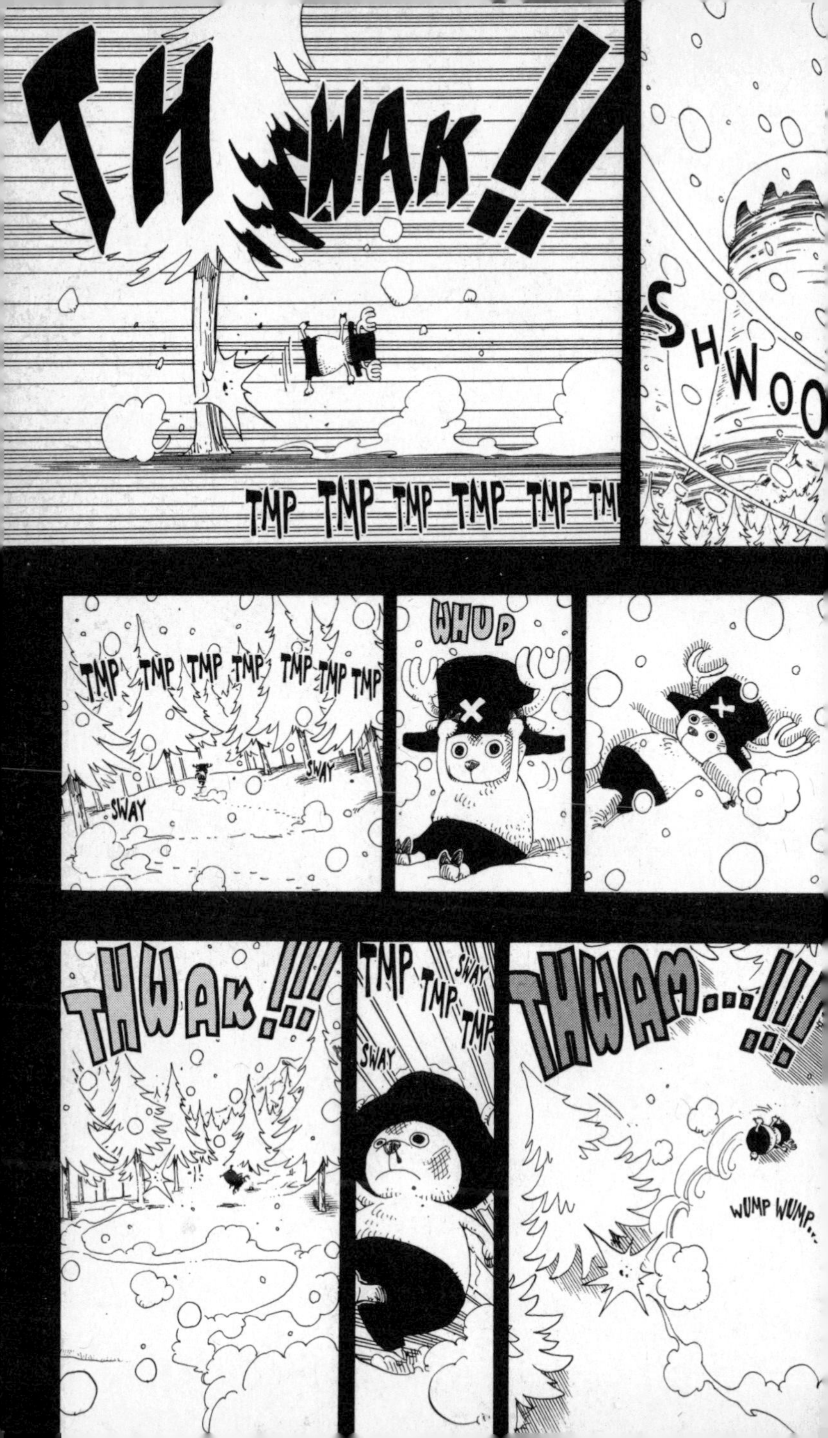
SHWOO
THWAK!!
TMP TMP TMP TMP TMP TM
WHUP
TMP TMP TMP TMP TMP TMP TMP
SWAY
SWAY
THWAM...!!!
WUMP WUMP...
TMP
SWAY
TMP
TMP
SWAY
THWAK!!!

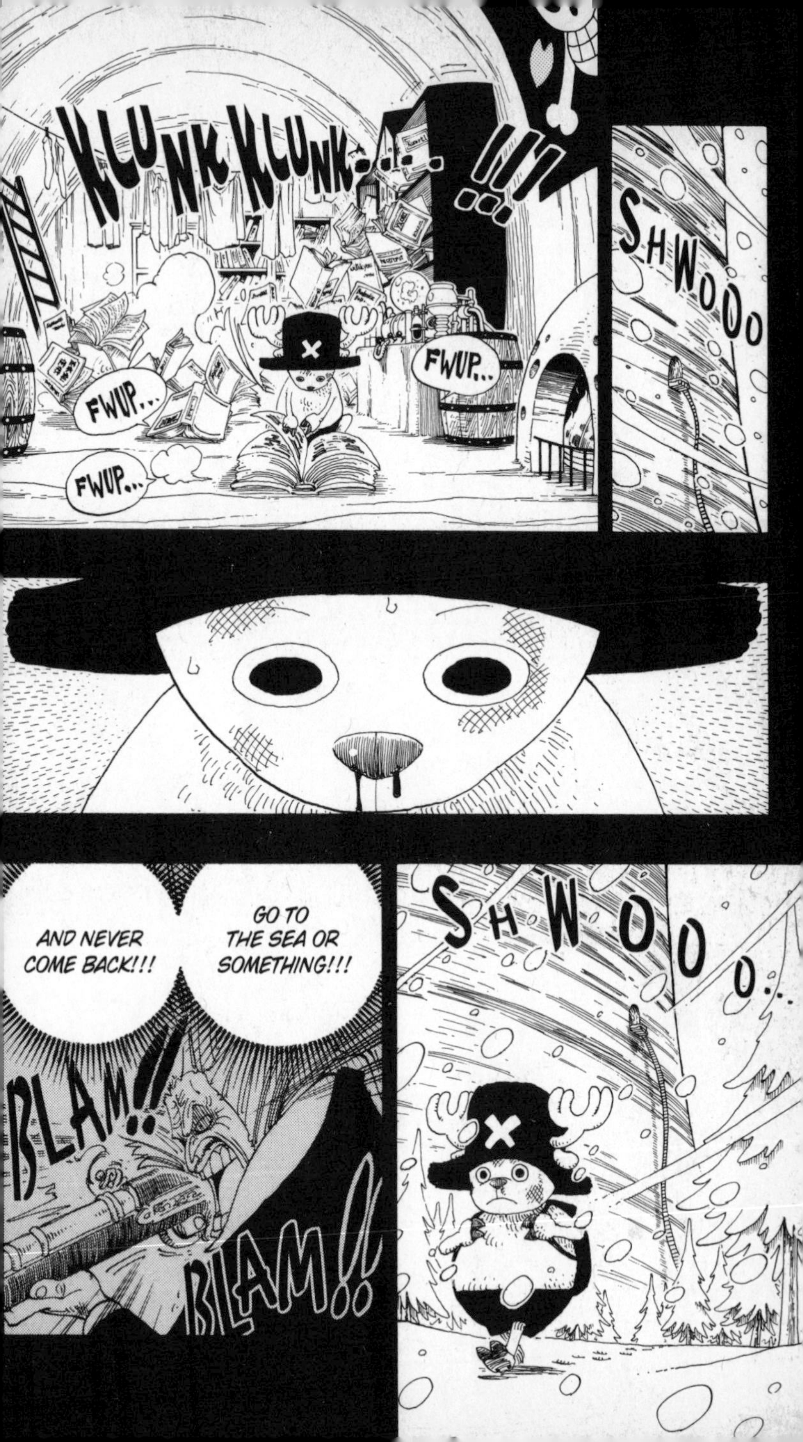

SHWOOO
!!!
KLUNK KLUNK
FWUP...
FWUP...
FWUP...
SHWOOO...
GO TO THE SEA OR SOMETHING!!!
AND NEVER COME BACK!!!
BLAM!!
BLAM!!

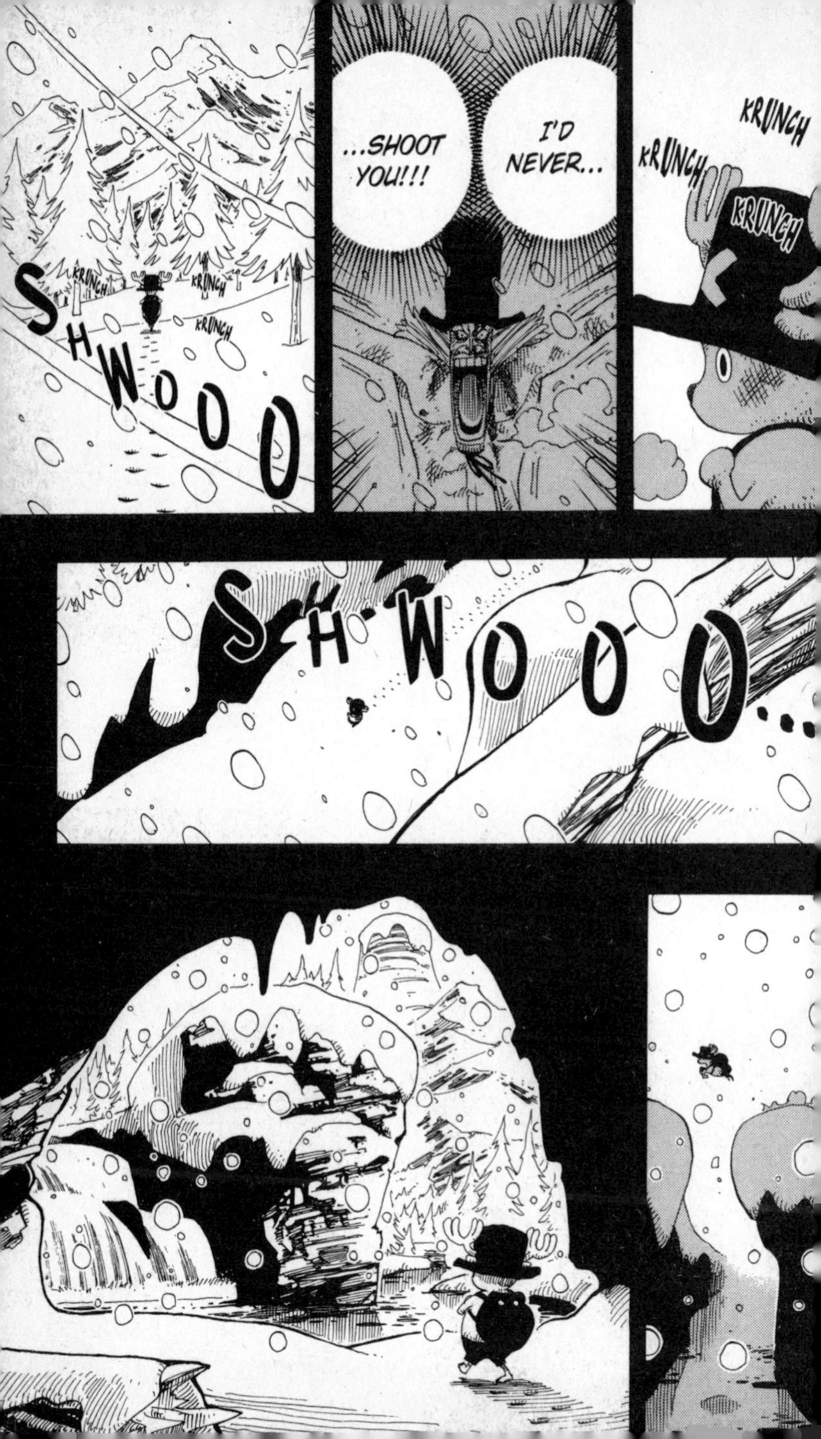
KRUNCH
KRUNCH
KRUNCH
I'D NEVER...
...SHOOT YOU!!!
KRUNCH
KRUNCH
KRUNCH
SHWOOO
SHWOOO...

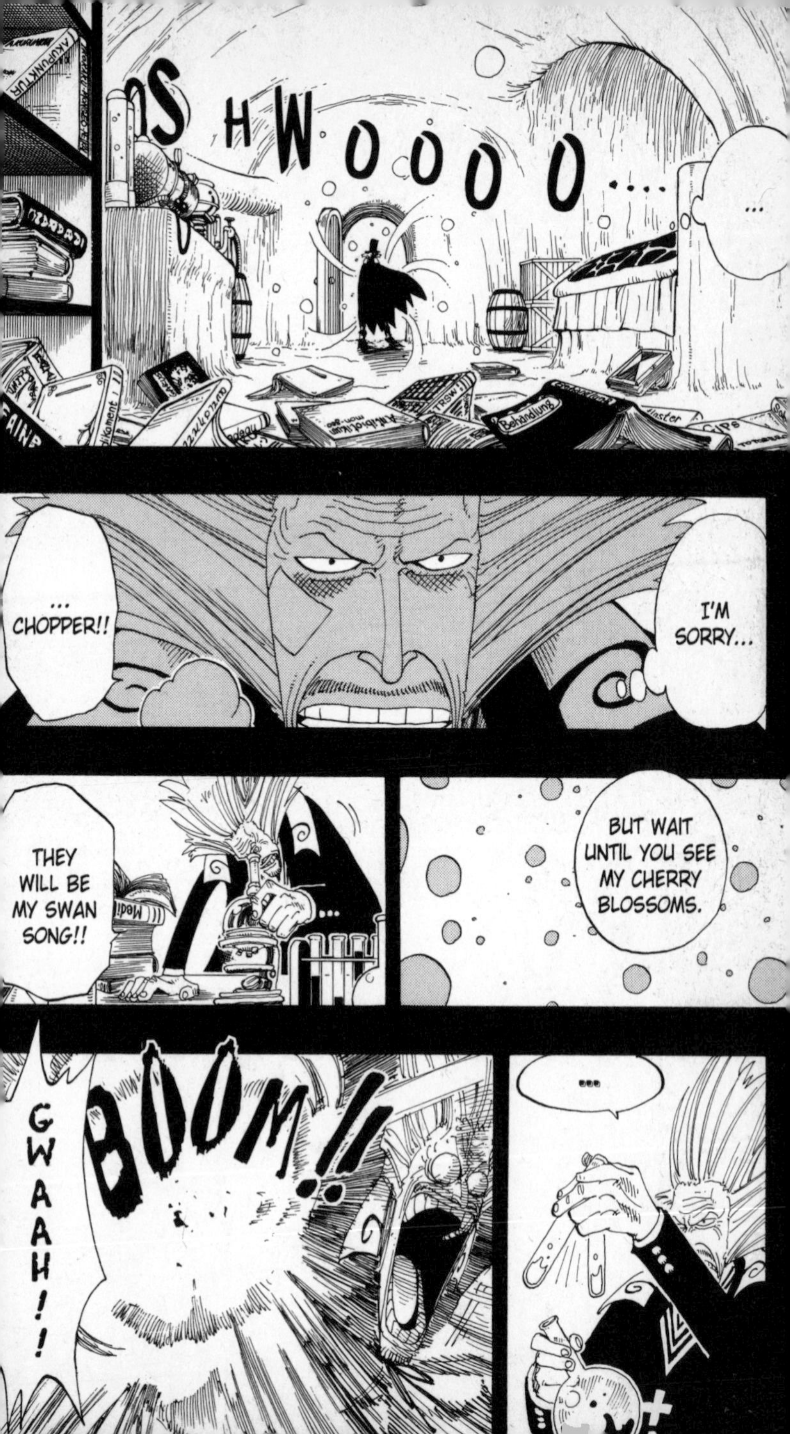
...
SHWOOOO...
I'M SORRY...
... CHOPPER!!
BUT WAIT UNTIL YOU SEE MY CHERRY BLOSSOMS.
THEY WILL BE MY SWAN SONG!!
...
BOOM!!
GWAAH!!!

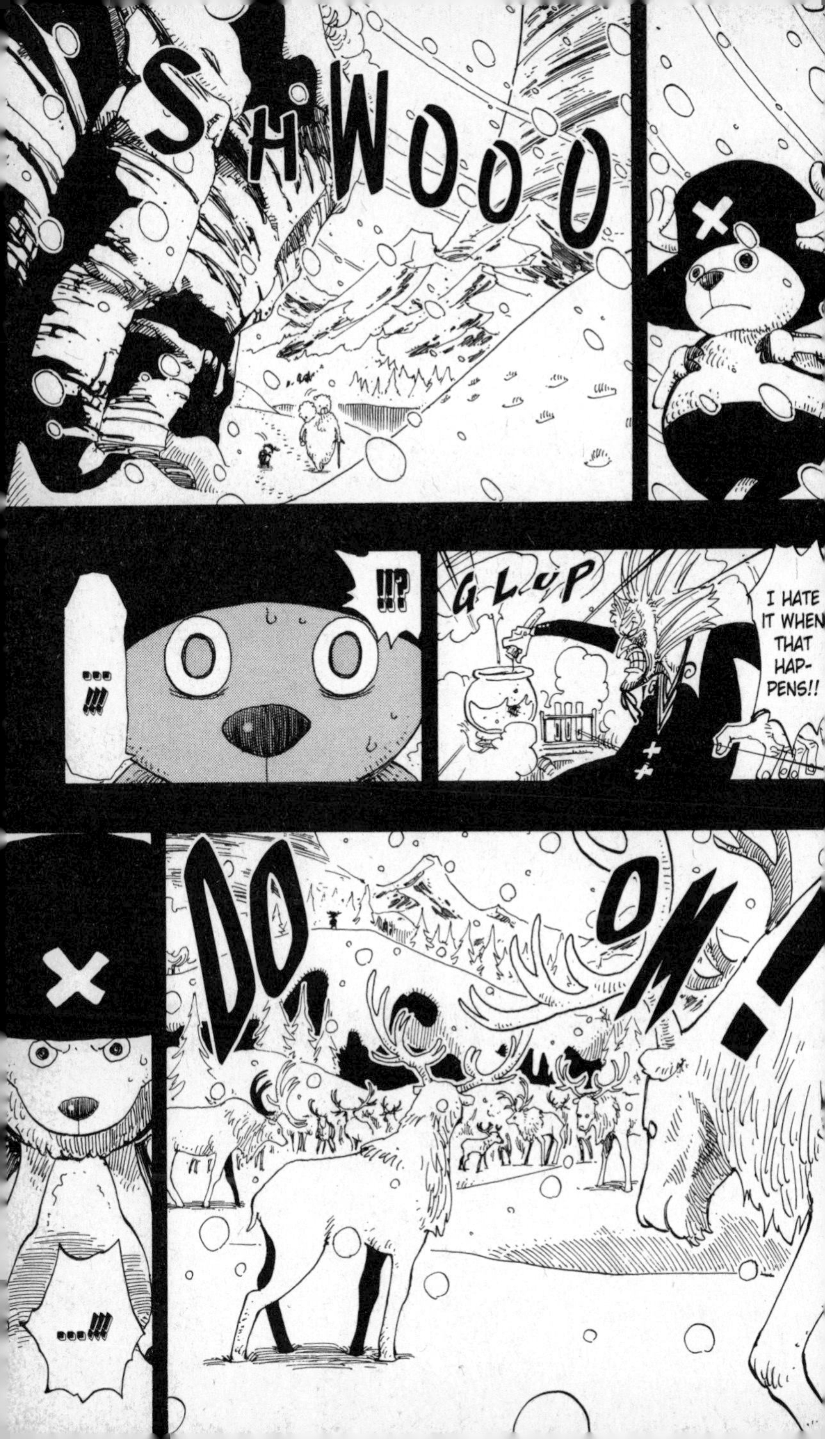
SHWOOO
I HATE IT WHEN THAT HAP-PENS!!
GLUP
!!?
...!!!
DOON!
...!!!

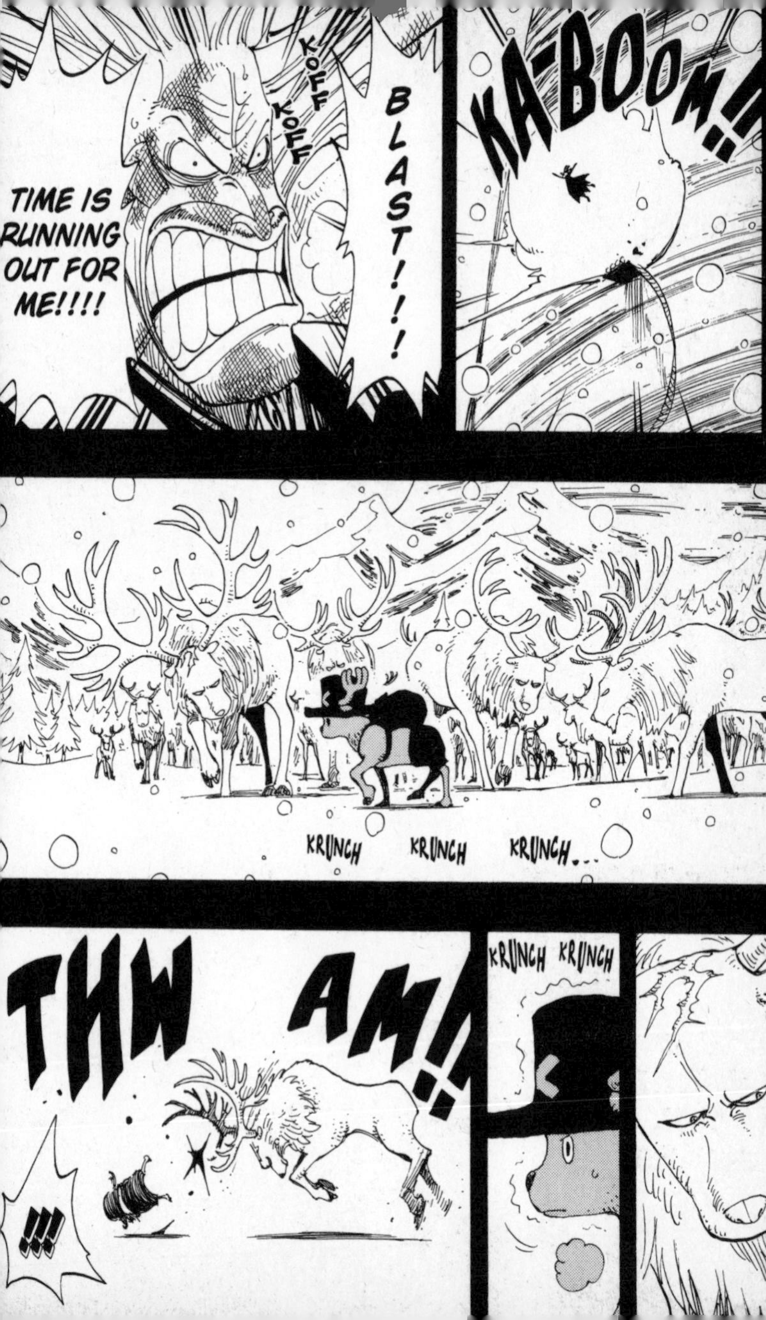
KA-BOOM!!
BLAST!!!
KOFF KOFF
TIME IS RUNNING OUT FOR ME!!!!
KRUNCH KRUNCH KRUNCH...
KRUNCH KRUNCH
THWAM!!
!!!

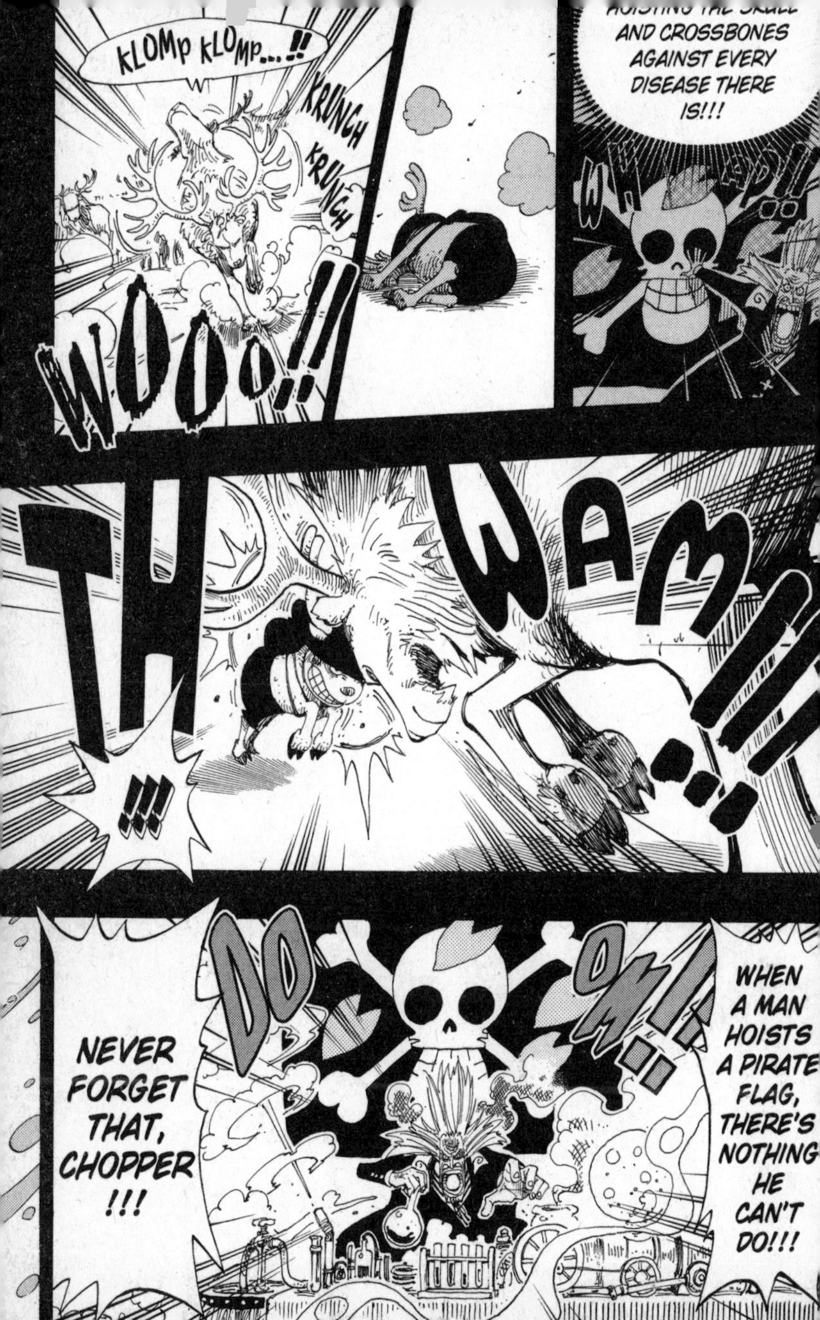
AND CROSSBONES AGAINST EVERY DISEASE THERE IS!!!
WHAP!!
KLOMP KLOMP...!!
KRUNCH
KRUNCH
WOOO!!
THWAM!!...
!!!
WHEN A MAN HOISTS A PIRATE FLAG, THERE'S NOTHING HE CAN'T DO!!!
DOOM!!
NEVER FORGET THAT, CHOPPER!!!

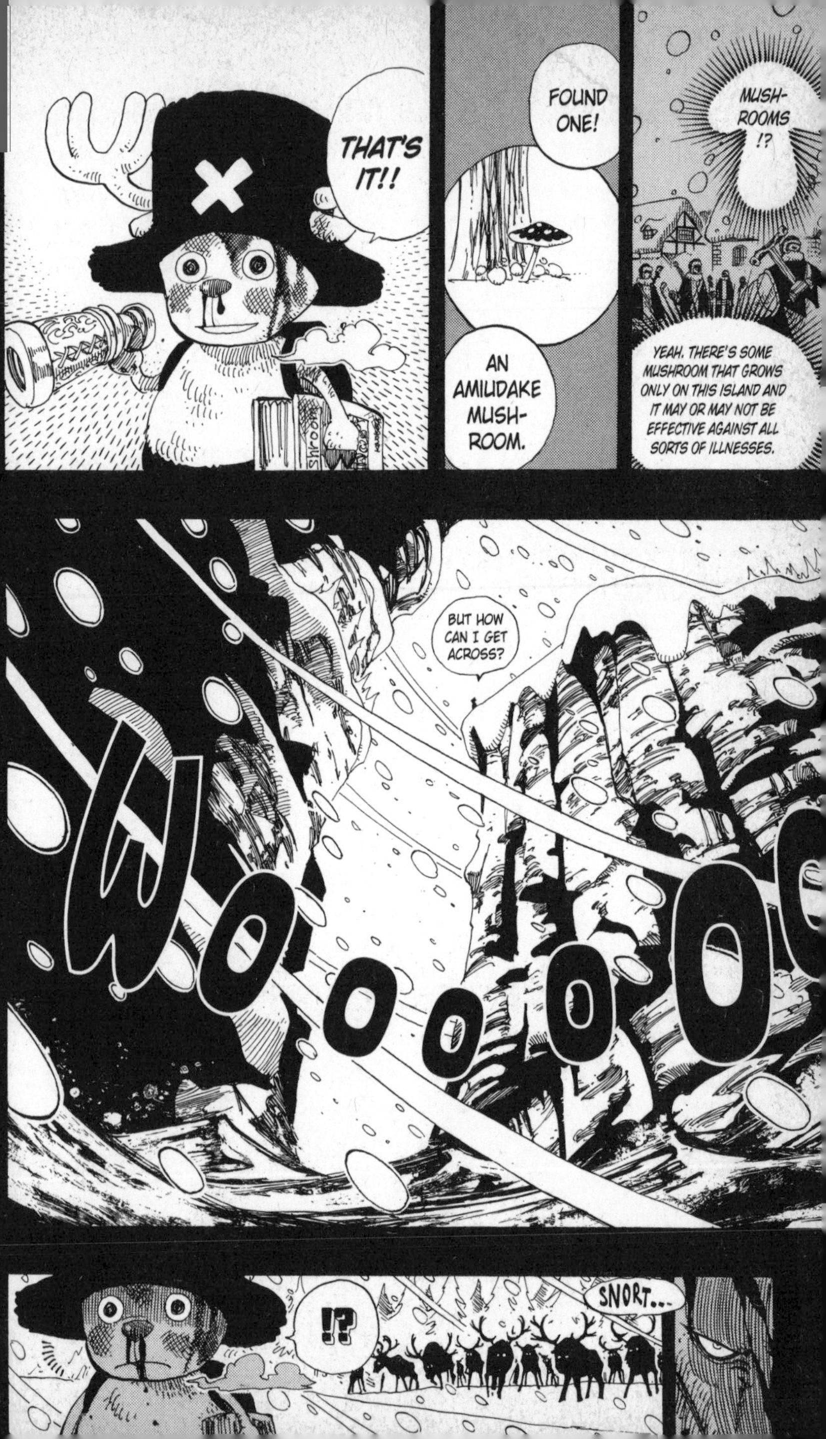
MUSH-ROOMS !?
YEAH. THERE'S SOME MUSHROOM THAT GROWS ONLY ON THIS ISLAND AND IT MAY OR MAY NOT BE EFFECTIVE AGAINST ALL SORTS OF ILLNESSES.
FOUND ONE!
AN AMIUDAKE MUSH-ROOM.
THAT'S IT!!
BUT HOW CAN I GET ACROSS?
WOOOOOOO
SNORT...
!?

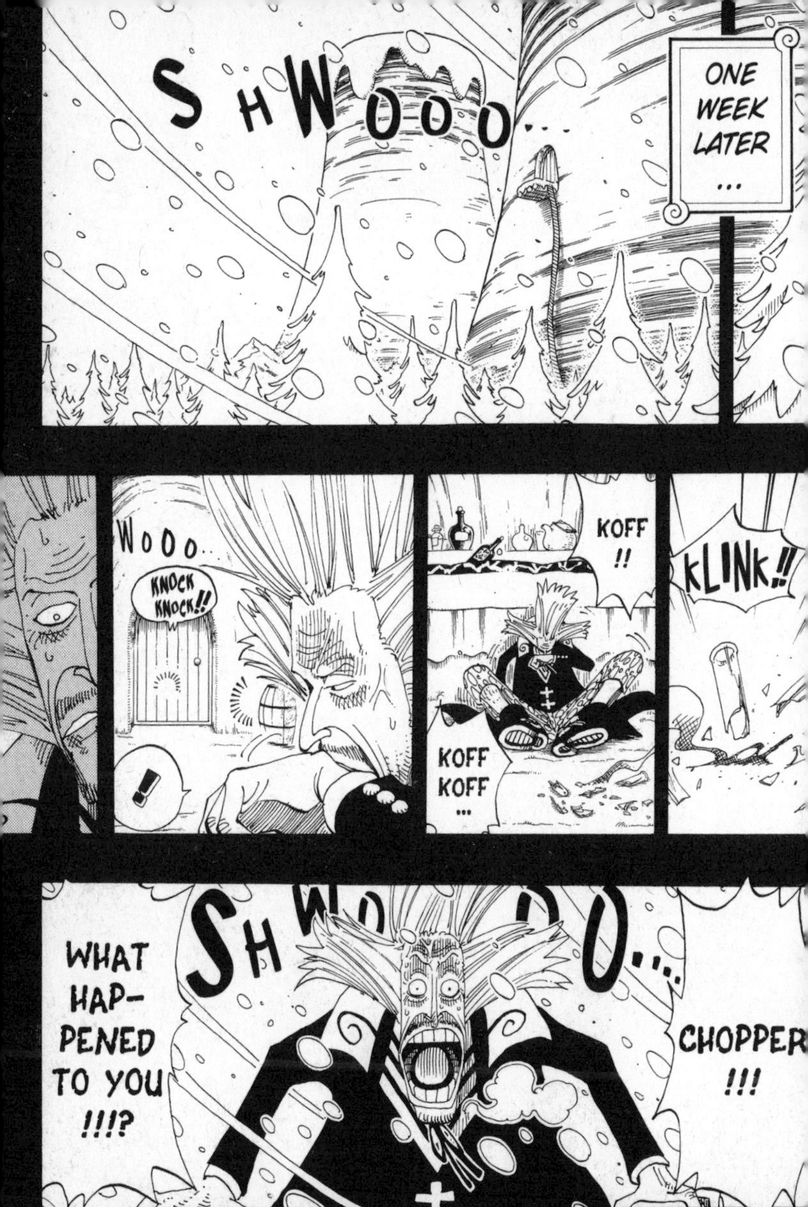

ONE WEEK LATER ...
SHWOOO...
KLINK!!
KOFF !!
KOFF KOFF ...
WOOO...
KNOCK KNOCK!!
!
CHOPPER !!!
WHAT HAP-PENED TO YOU !!!?

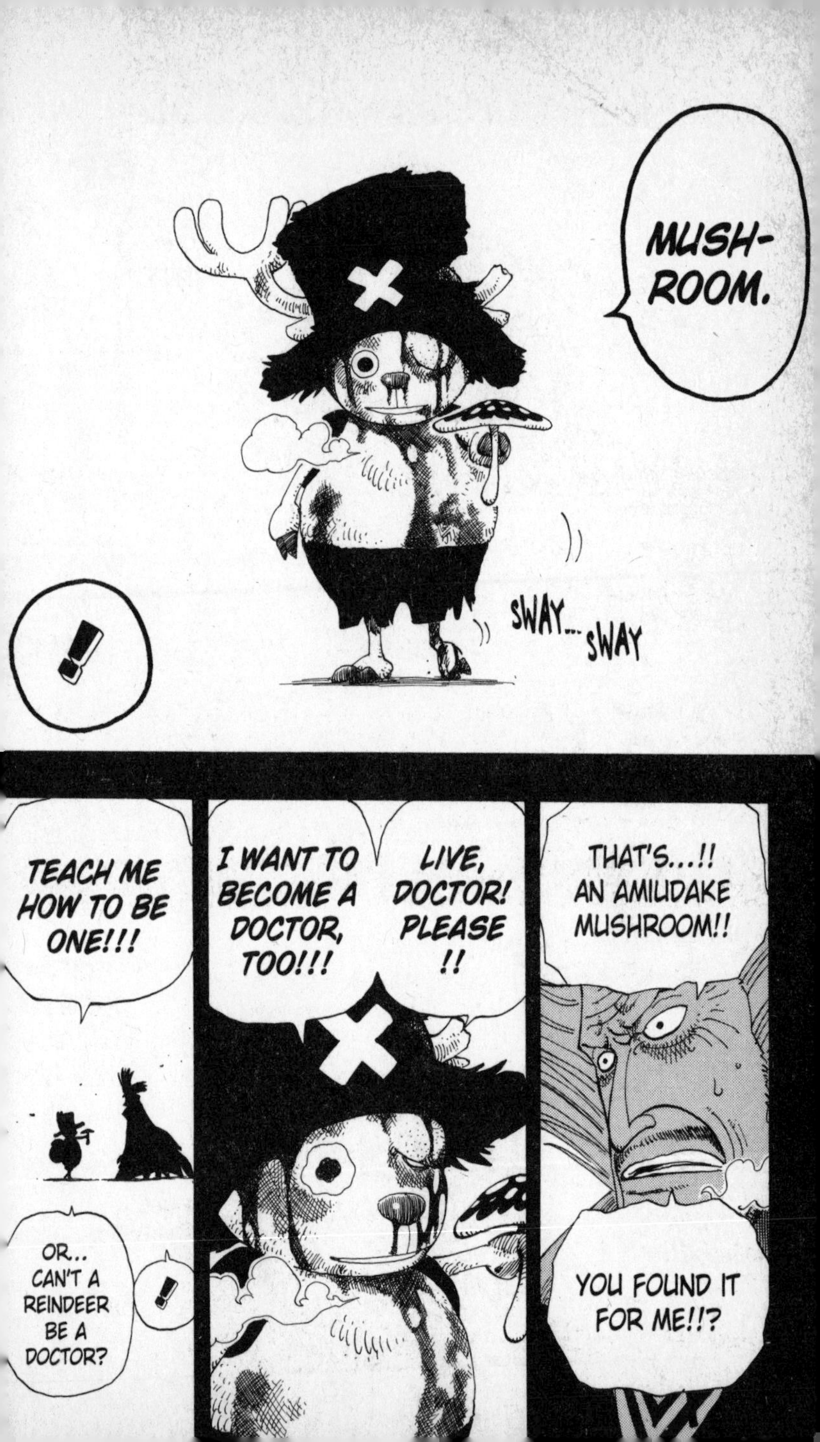
MUSH-ROOM.
SWAY... SWAY
!
THAT'S...!! AN AMIUDAKE MUSHROOM!!
YOU FOUND IT FOR ME!!?
LIVE, DOCTOR! PLEASE !!
I WANT TO BECOME A DOCTOR, TOO!!!
TEACH ME HOW TO BE ONE!!!
!
OR... CAN'T A REINDEER BE A DOCTOR?

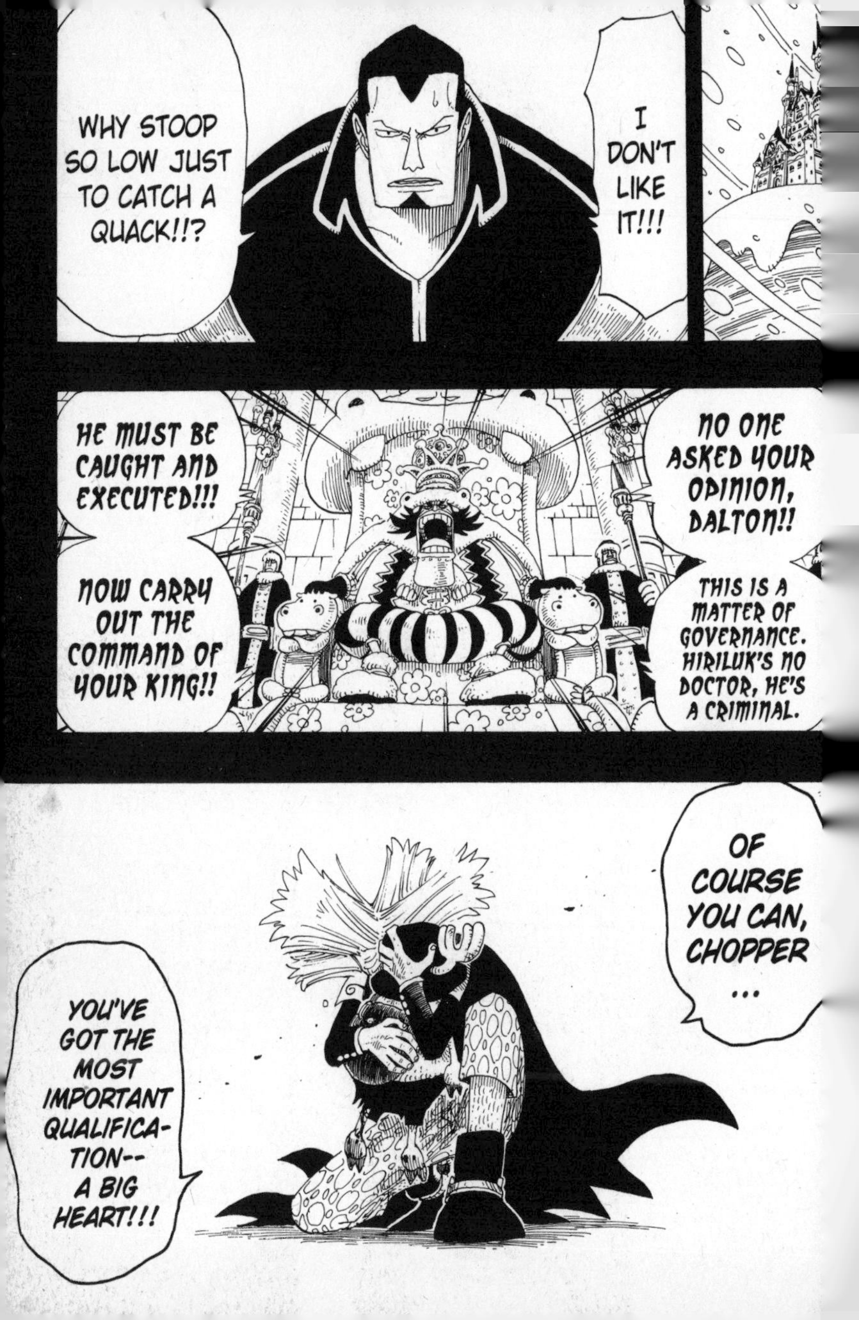
I DON'T LIKE IT!!!
WHY STOOP SO LOW JUST TO CATCH A QUACK!!?
NO ONE ASKED YOUR OPINION, DALTON!!
THIS IS A MATTER OF GOVERNANCE. HIRILUK'S NO DOCTOR, HE'S A CRIMINAL.
HE MUST BE CAUGHT AND EXECUTED!!!
NOW CARRY OUT THE COMMAND OF YOUR KING!!
OF COURSE YOU CAN, CHOPPER ...
YOU'VE GOT THE MOST IMPORTANT QUALIFICA-TION-- A BIG HEART!!!

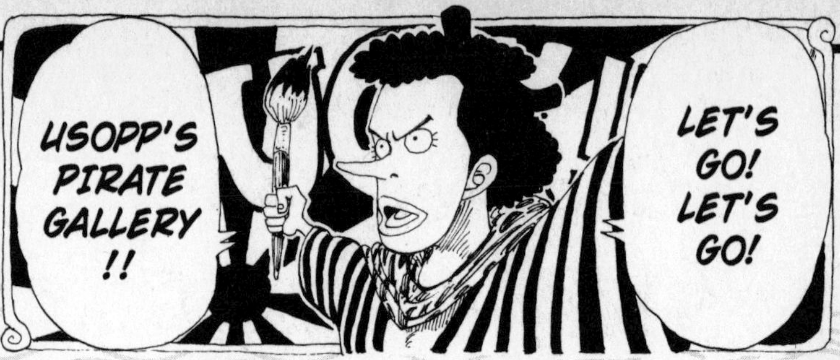
LET'S GO! LET'S GO!
USOPP'S PIRATE GALLERY!!

CHICKEN HEAD!

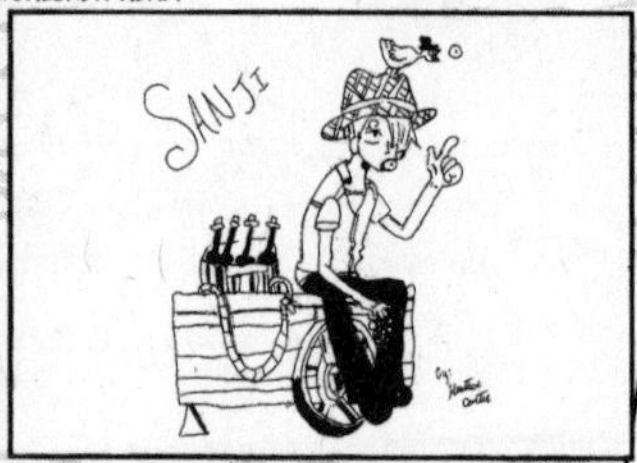
SANJI

HEATHER

STRAW HATS ATTACK!

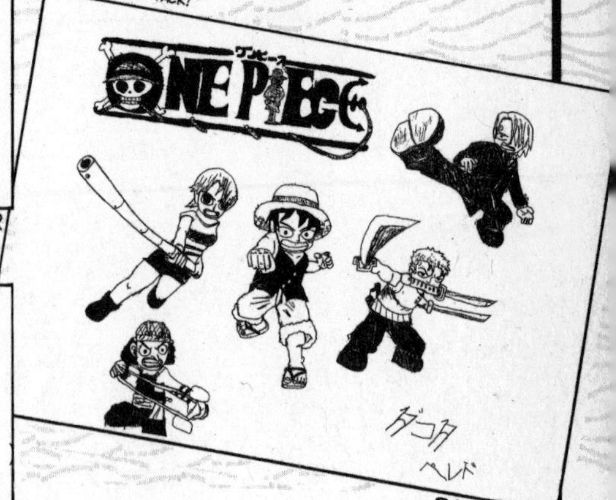

DAKOTA, 12

THERE'S A RUMOR THAT HER TEA IS GOOD.

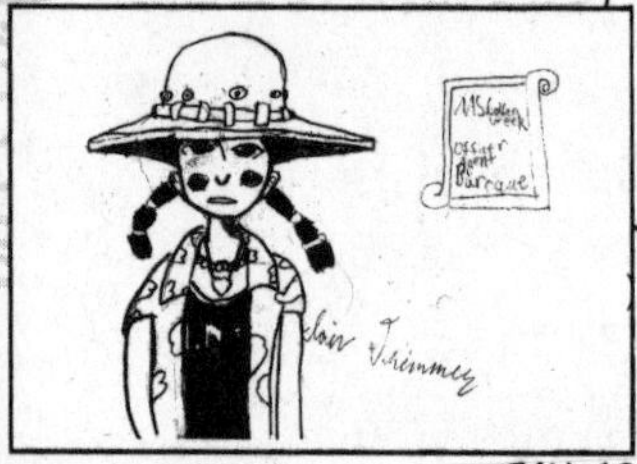

IAN, 10

SHE'S SMART TOO!

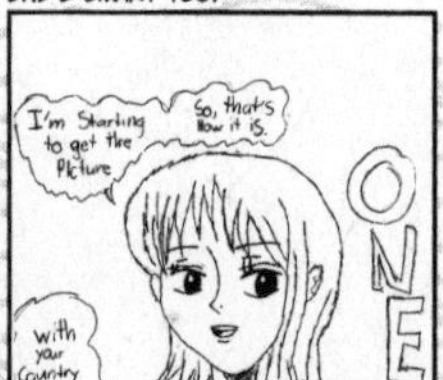
So, that's How it is.
I'm Starting to get the Picture
with your Country in Chaos. There is NO Money to Be Made There.
ONEPIE
Keisha Lewis

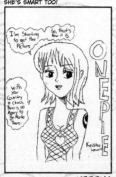

KEISHA

GREATEST SWORDSMAN ALIVE!

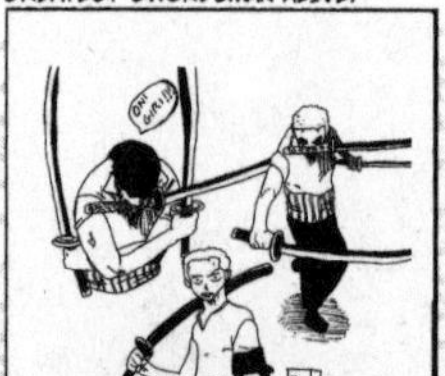

ALEX, 16

GOOD, LET YOUR ANGER FLOW.

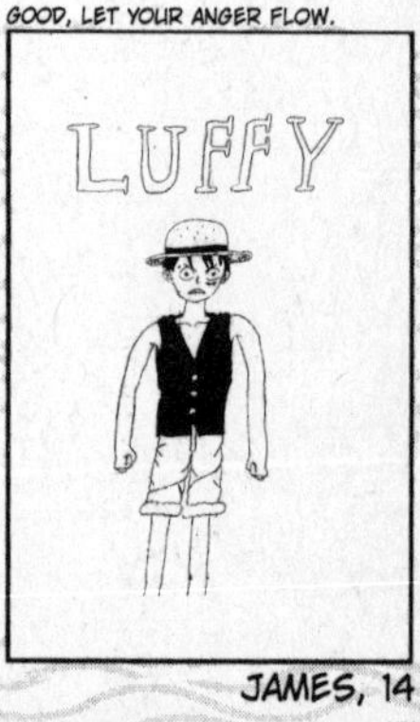
LUFFY

JAMES, 14

SUBMIT YOUR FAN ART TO:
SHONEN JUMP C/O VIZ. LLC P.O. BOX 77010, SAN FRANCISCO, CA, 94107
REMEMBER TO INCLUDE YOUR NAME AND AGE!!

USOPP'S COMMENTS WERE TRANSMITTED THROUGH THE U.S. SHONEN JUMP TEAM-*EDITOR*

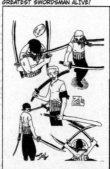

Chapter 144:
SNOW TALE

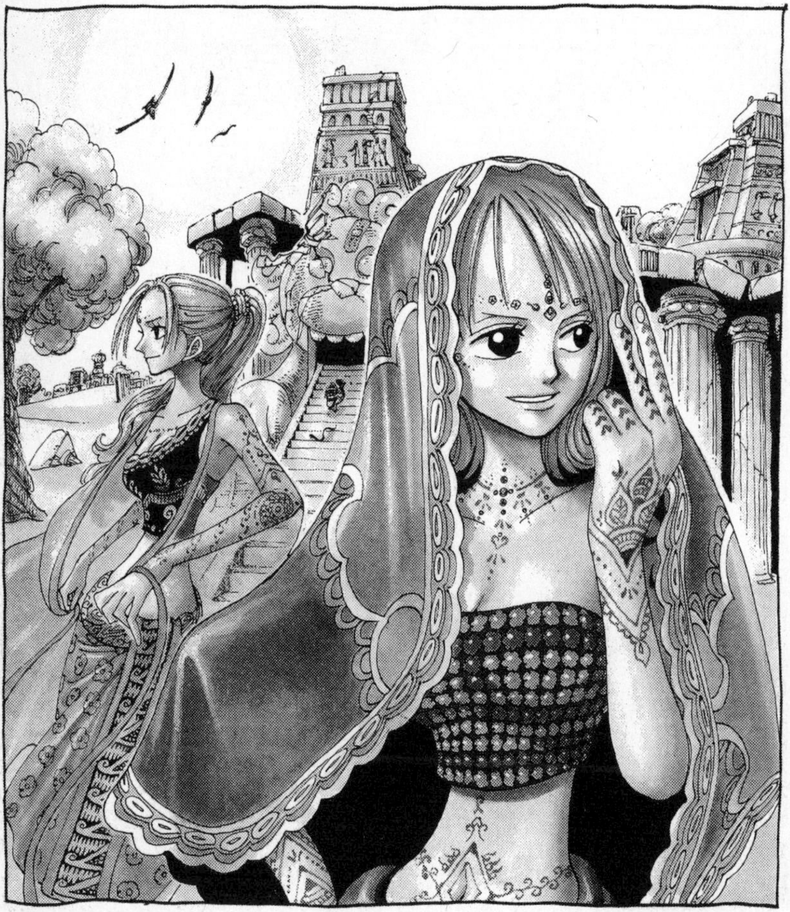

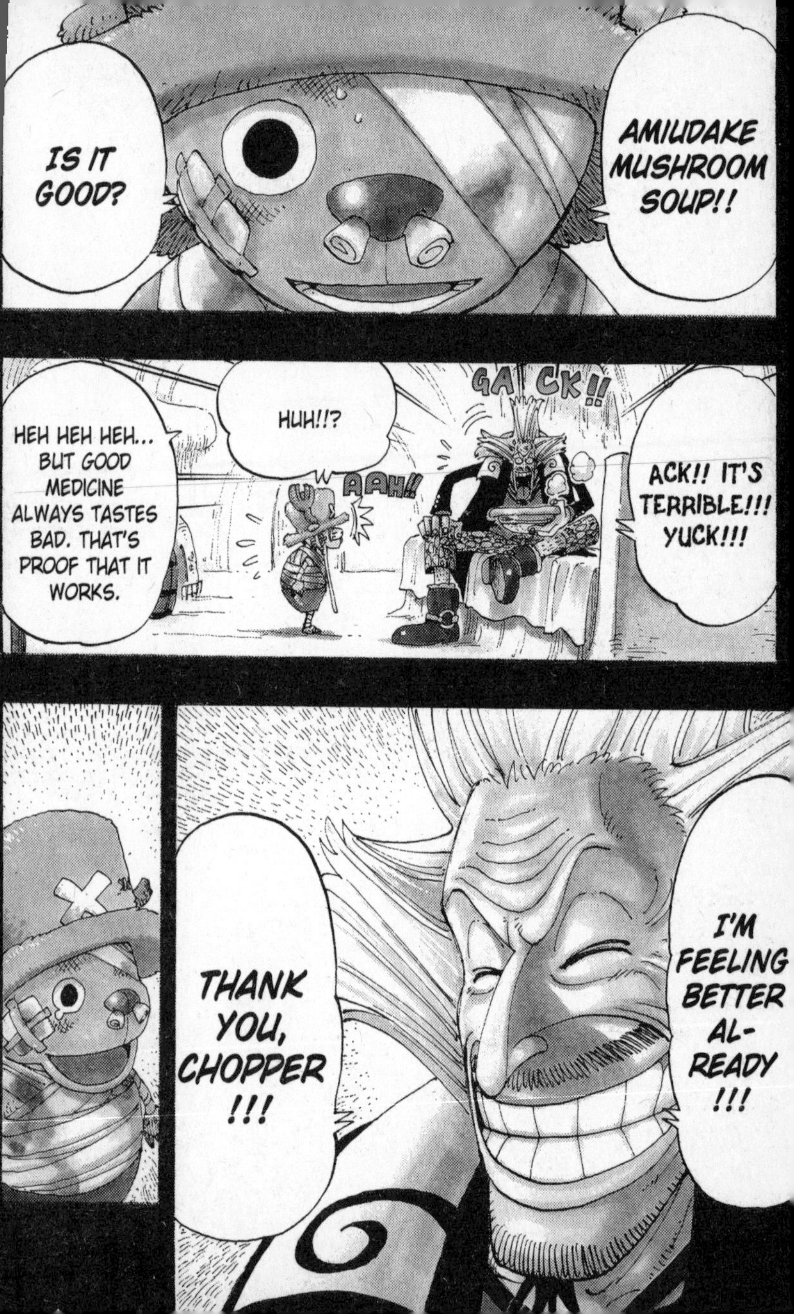
AMIUDAKE MUSHROOM SOUP!!
IS IT GOOD?
ACK!! IT'S TERRIBLE!!! YUCK!!!
GA CK!!
HUH!!?
AAH!!
HEH HEH HEH... BUT GOOD MEDICINE ALWAYS TASTES BAD. THAT'S PROOF THAT IT WORKS.
I'M FEELING BETTER AL-READY!!!
THANK YOU, CHOPPER!!!

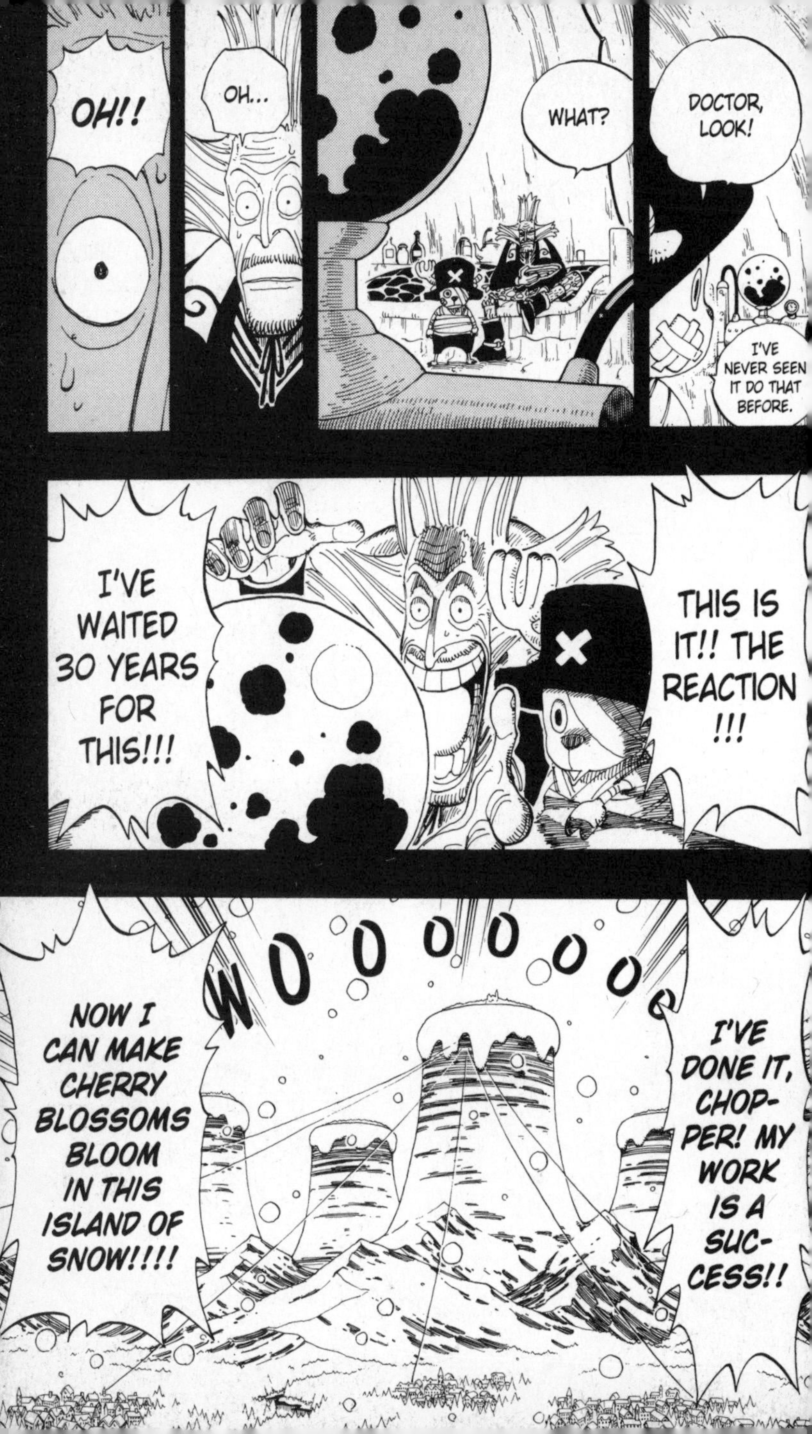
DOCTOR, LOOK!
I'VE NEVER SEEN IT DO THAT BEFORE.
WHAT?
OH...
OH!!
THIS IS IT!! THE REACTION!!!
I'VE WAITED 30 YEARS FOR THIS!!!
I'VE DONE IT, CHOP-PER! MY WORK IS A SUC-CESS!!
WOOOOOOO
NOW I CAN MAKE CHERRY BLOSSOMS BLOOM IN THIS ISLAND OF SNOW!!!!

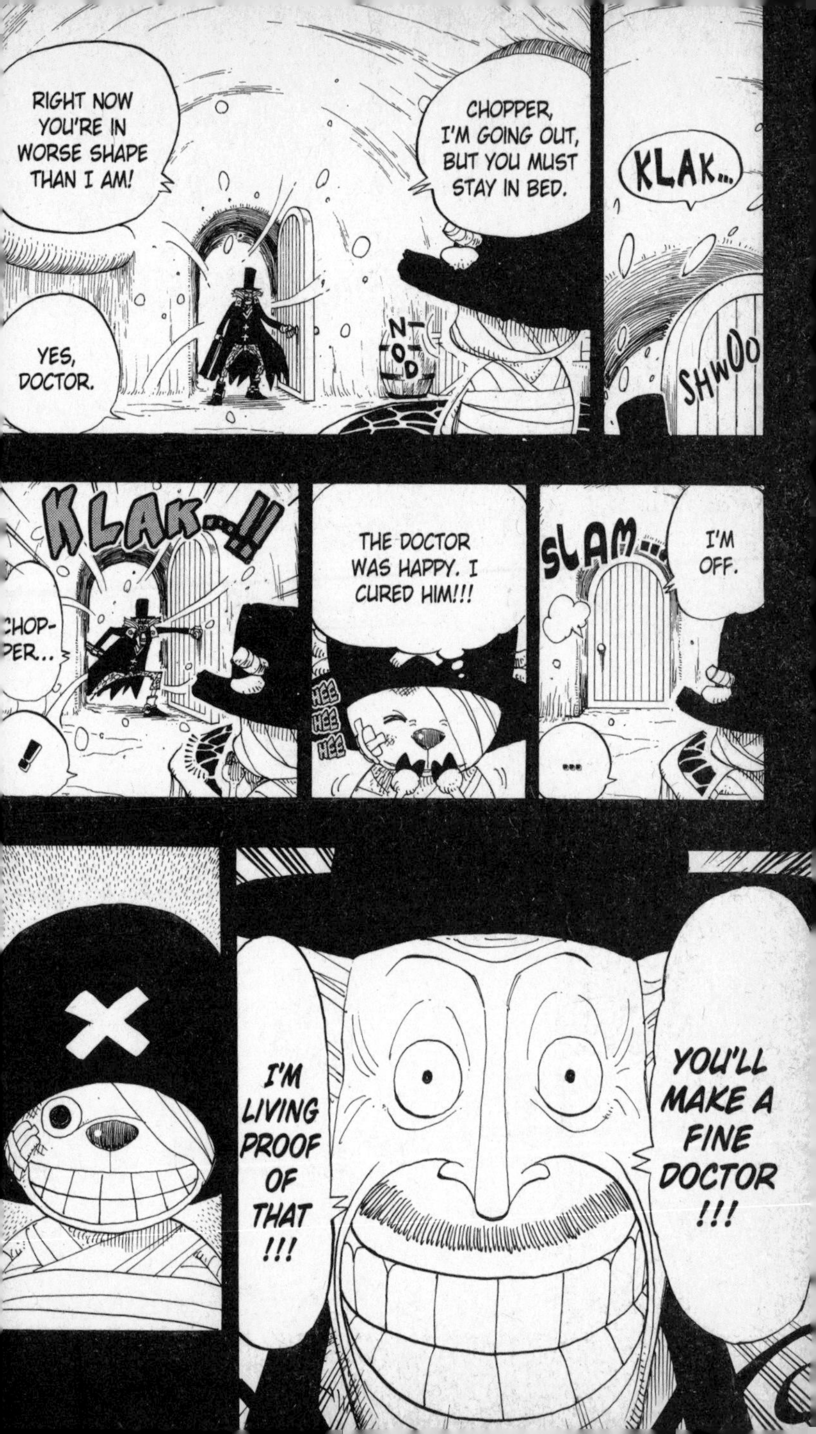
KLAK...
SHWOO
CHOPPER, I'M GOING OUT, BUT YOU MUST STAY IN BED.
RIGHT NOW YOU'RE IN WORSE SHAPE THAN I AM!
NOD
YES, DOCTOR.
I'M OFF.
SLAM...
...
THE DOCTOR WAS HAPPY. I CURED HIM!!!
HEE HEE HEE
KLAK...!!
CHOP-PER...
!
YOU'LL MAKE A FINE DOCTOR!!!
I'M LIVING PROOF OF THAT!!!

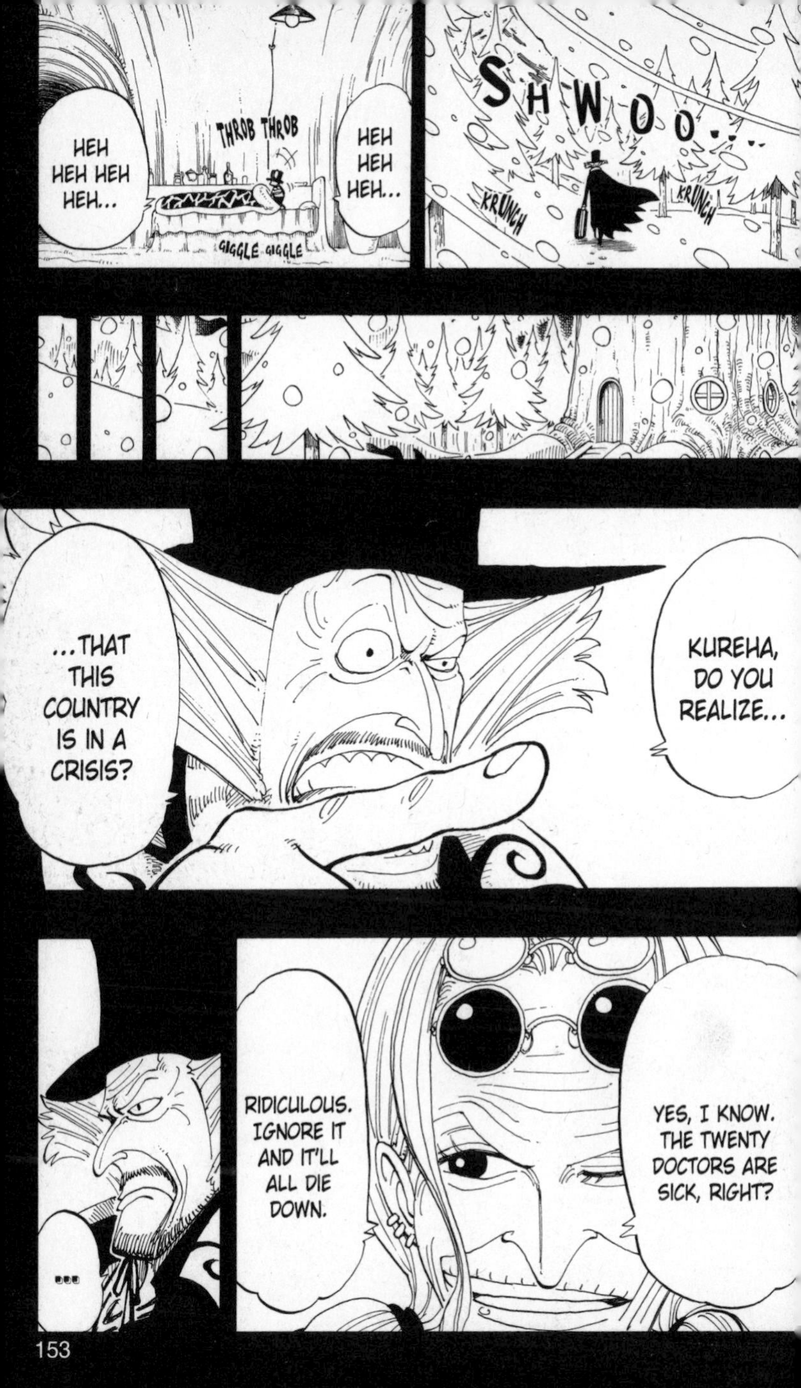
SHWOO...
KRUNCH
KRUNCH
HEH HEH HEH...
THROB THROB
HEH HEH HEH HEH...
GIGGLE GIGGLE
KUREHA, DO YOU REALIZE...
...THAT THIS COUNTRY IS IN A CRISIS?
YES, I KNOW. THE TWENTY DOCTORS ARE SICK, RIGHT?
RIDICULOUS. IGNORE IT AND IT'LL ALL DIE DOWN.
...

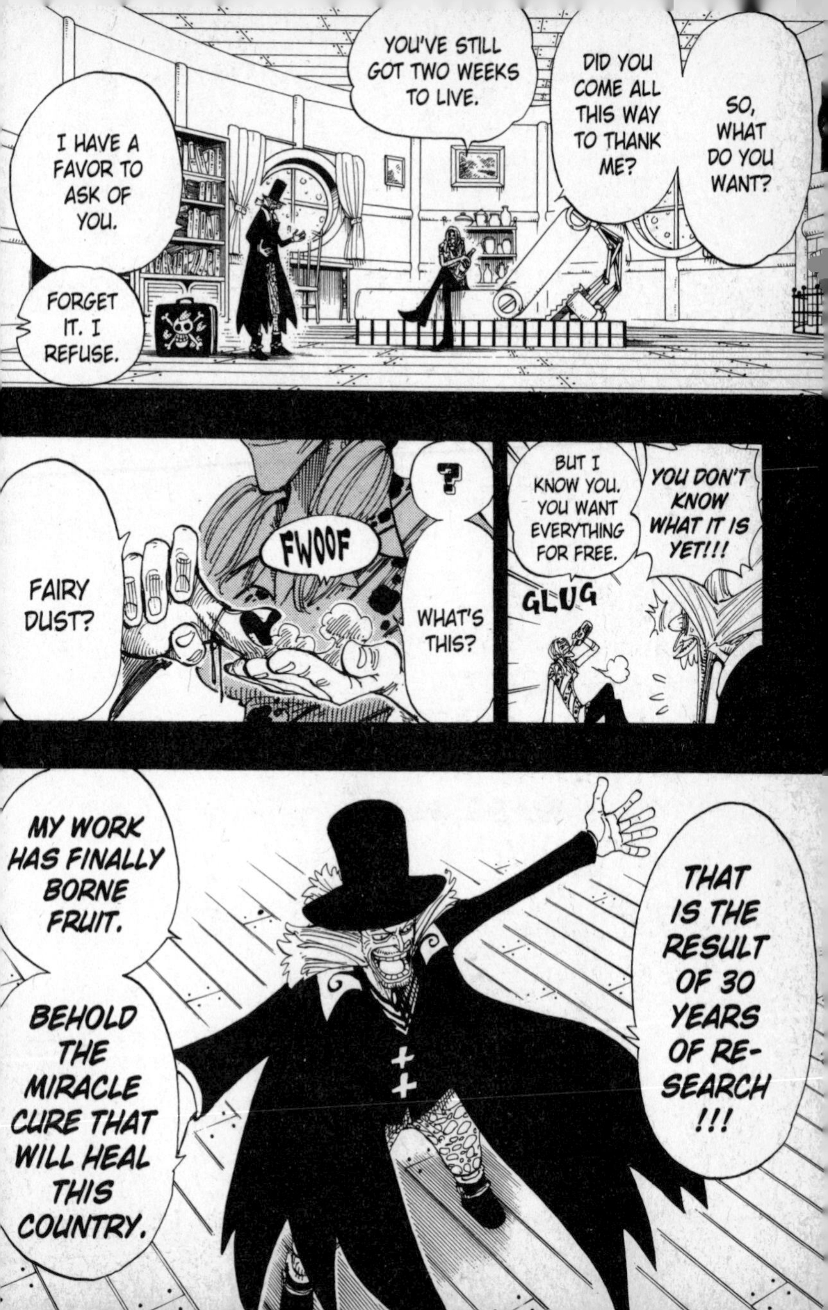
SO, WHAT DO YOU WANT?
DID YOU COME ALL THIS WAY TO THANK ME?
YOU'VE STILL GOT TWO WEEKS TO LIVE.
I HAVE A FAVOR TO ASK OF YOU.
FORGET IT. I REFUSE.
YOU DON'T KNOW WHAT IT IS YET!!!
BUT I KNOW YOU. YOU WANT EVERYTHING FOR FREE.
GLUG
?
FWOOF
WHAT'S THIS?
FAIRY DUST?
THAT IS THE RESULT OF 30 YEARS OF RE-SEARCH!!!
MY WORK HAS FINALLY BORNE FRUIT.
BEHOLD THE MIRACLE CURE THAT WILL HEAL THIS COUNTRY.

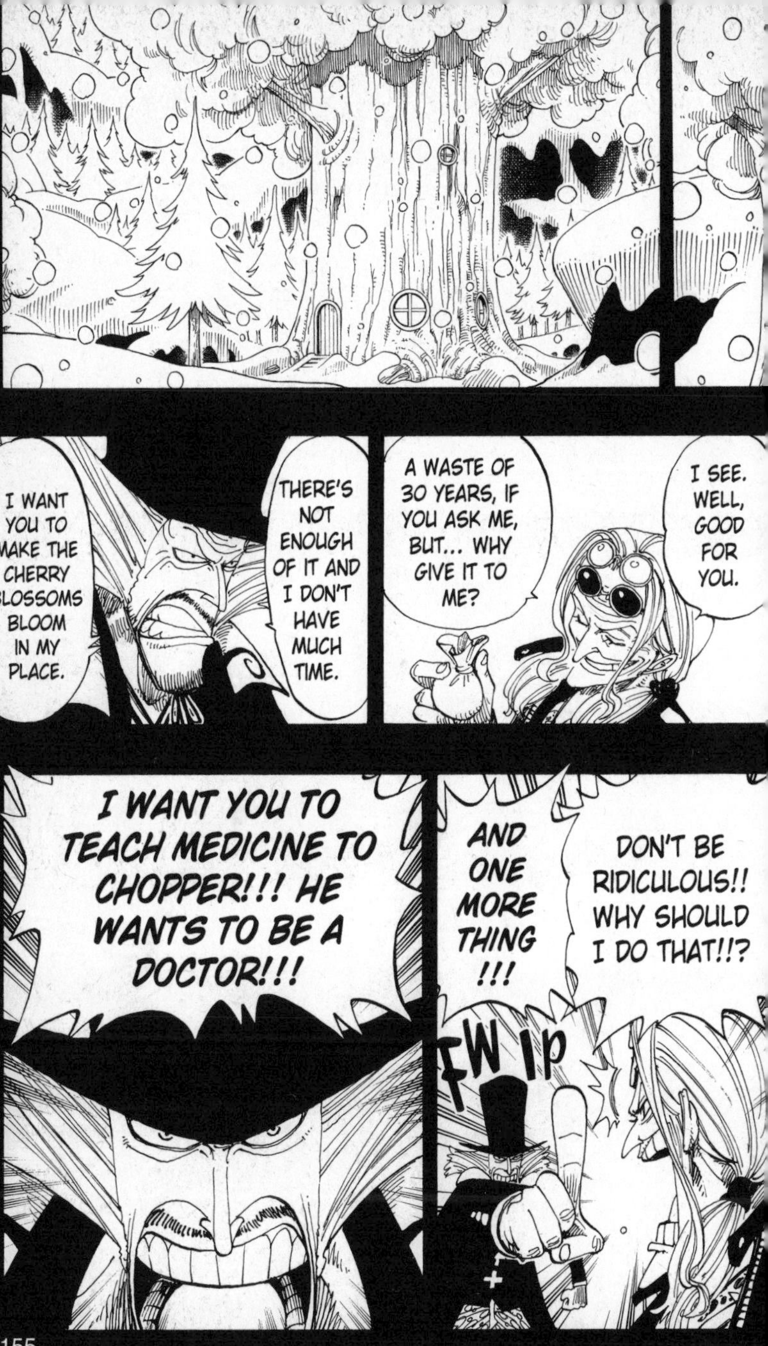

I SEE. WELL, GOOD FOR YOU.
A WASTE OF 30 YEARS, IF YOU ASK ME, BUT... WHY GIVE IT TO ME?
THERE'S NOT ENOUGH OF IT AND I DON'T HAVE MUCH TIME.
I WANT YOU TO MAKE THE CHERRY BLOSSOMS BLOOM IN MY PLACE.
DON'T BE RIDICULOUS!! WHY SHOULD I DO THAT!!?
AND ONE MORE THING!!!
FWIP
I WANT YOU TO TEACH MEDICINE TO CHOPPER!!! HE WANTS TO BE A DOCTOR!!!

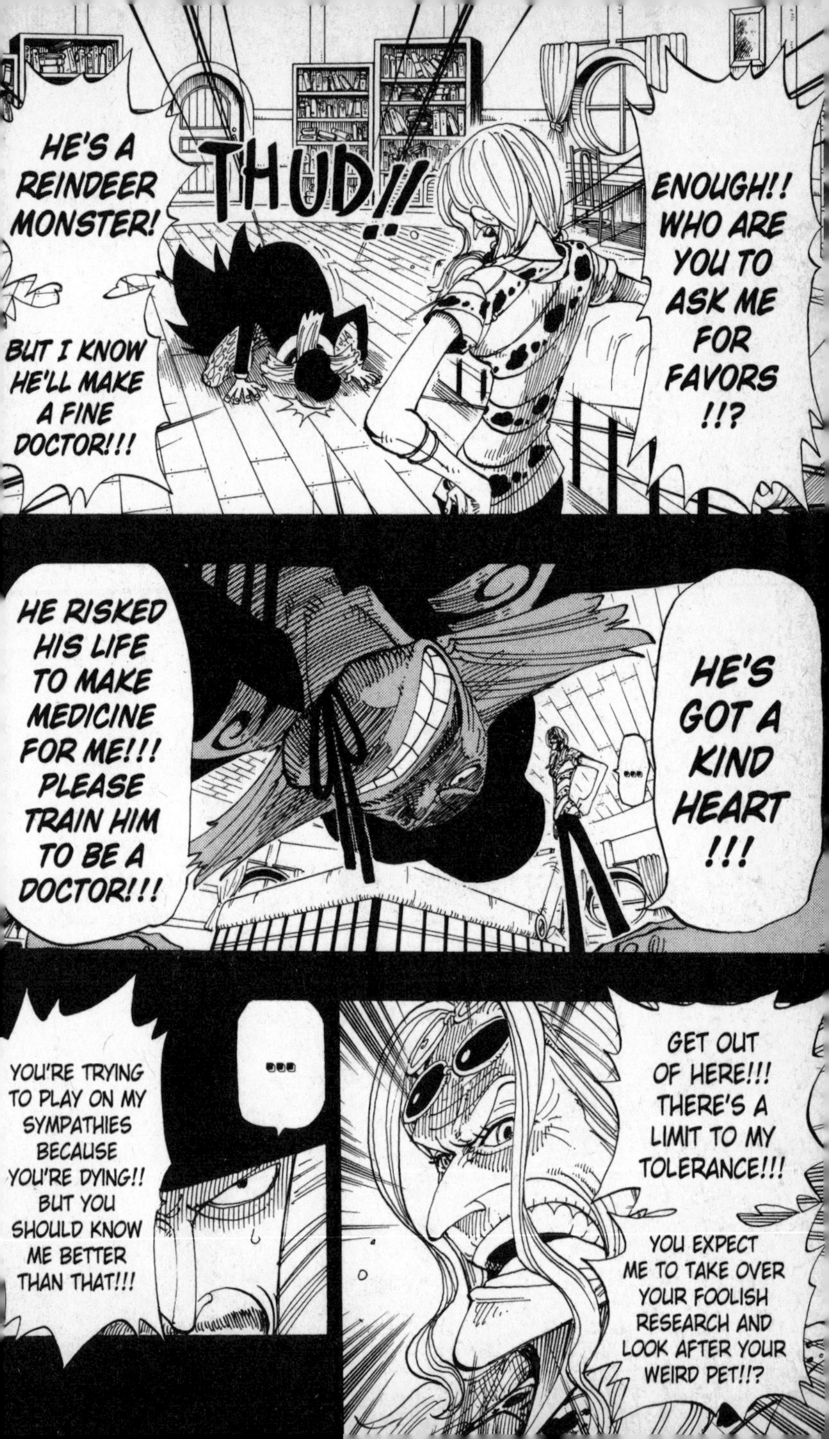
ENOUGH!! WHO ARE YOU TO ASK ME FOR FAVORS !!?
THUD!!
HE'S A REINDEER MONSTER!
BUT I KNOW HE'LL MAKE A FINE DOCTOR!!!
HE'S GOT A KIND HEART !!!
...
HE RISKED HIS LIFE TO MAKE MEDICINE FOR ME!!! PLEASE TRAIN HIM TO BE A DOCTOR!!!
GET OUT OF HERE!!! THERE'S A LIMIT TO MY TOLERANCE!!!
YOU EXPECT ME TO TAKE OVER YOUR FOOLISH RESEARCH AND LOOK AFTER YOUR WEIRD PET!!?
...
YOU'RE TRYING TO PLAY ON MY SYMPATHIES BECAUSE YOU'RE DYING!! BUT YOU SHOULD KNOW ME BETTER THAN THAT!!!

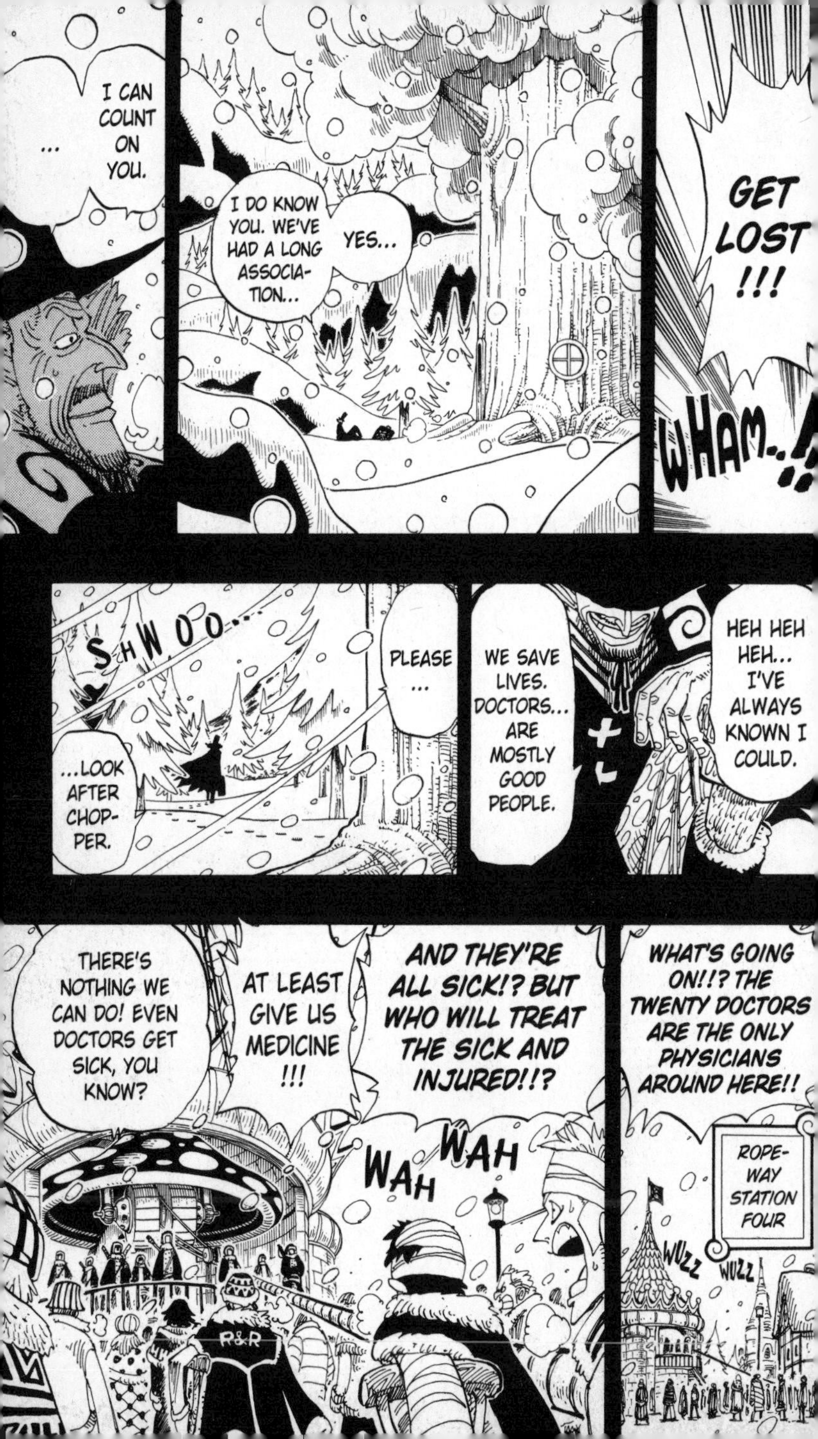
GET LOST!!!
WHAM..!!
YES...
I DO KNOW YOU. WE'VE HAD A LONG ASSOCIATION...
I CAN COUNT ON YOU. ...
HEH HEH HEH... I'VE ALWAYS KNOWN I COULD.
WE SAVE LIVES. DOCTORS... ARE MOSTLY GOOD PEOPLE.
PLEASE ...
SHWOO...
...LOOK AFTER CHOPPER.
WHAT'S GOING ON!!? THE TWENTY DOCTORS ARE THE ONLY PHYSICIANS AROUND HERE!!
ROPEWAY STATION FOUR
WUZZ
WUZZ
AND THEY'RE ALL SICK!? BUT WHO WILL TREAT THE SICK AND INJURED!!?
WAH
WAH
AT LEAST GIVE US MEDICINE!!!
THERE'S NOTHING WE CAN DO! EVEN DOCTORS GET SICK, YOU KNOW?

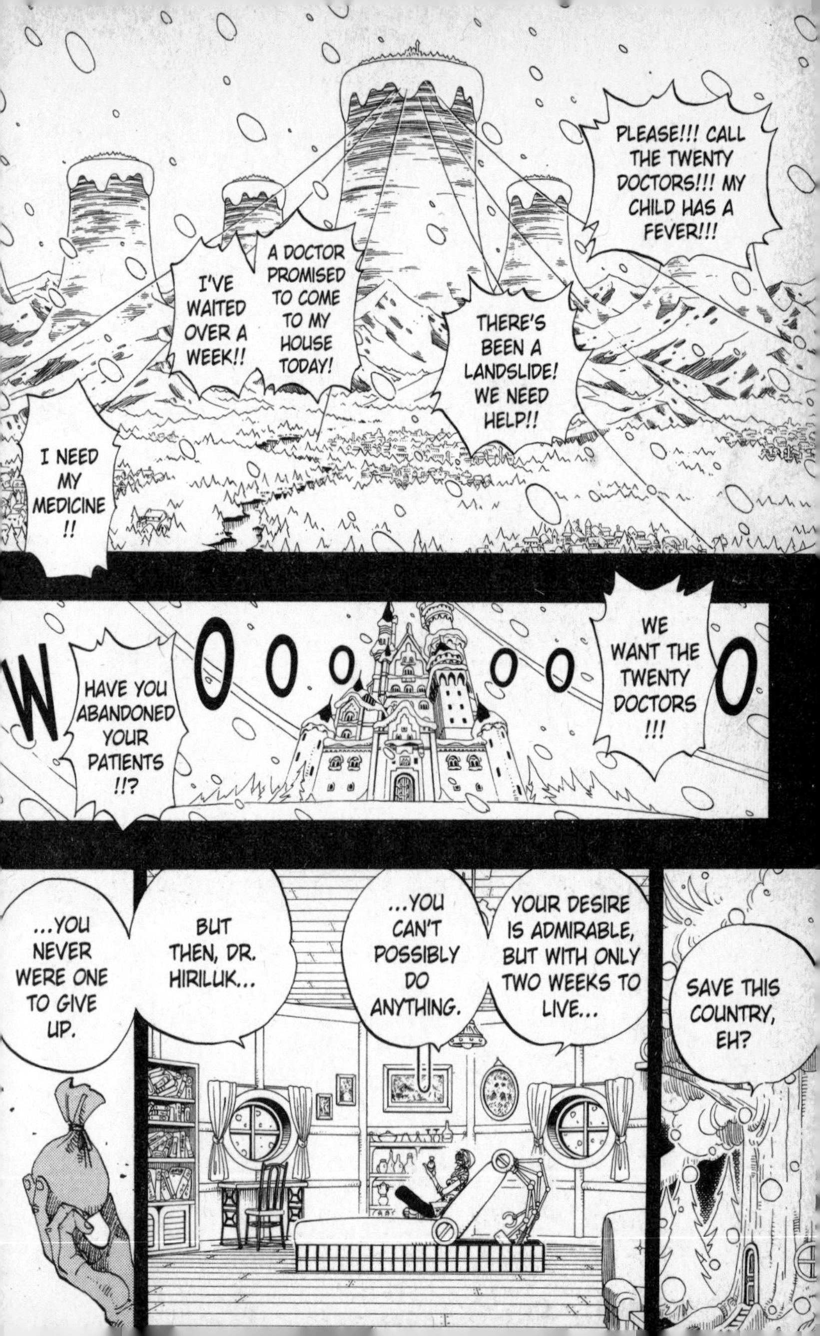
PLEASE!!! CALL THE TWENTY DOCTORS!!! MY CHILD HAS A FEVER!!!
THERE'S BEEN A LANDSLIDE! WE NEED HELP!!
A DOCTOR PROMISED TO COME TO MY HOUSE TODAY!
I'VE WAITED OVER A WEEK!!
I NEED MY MEDICINE!!
WE WANT THE TWENTY DOCTORS!!!
WOOOOOOO
HAVE YOU ABANDONED YOUR PATIENTS!!?
SAVE THIS COUNTRY, EH?
YOUR DESIRE IS ADMIRABLE, BUT WITH ONLY TWO WEEKS TO LIVE...
...YOU CAN'T POSSIBLY DO ANYTHING.
BUT THEN, DR. HIRILUK...
...YOU NEVER WERE ONE TO GIVE UP.

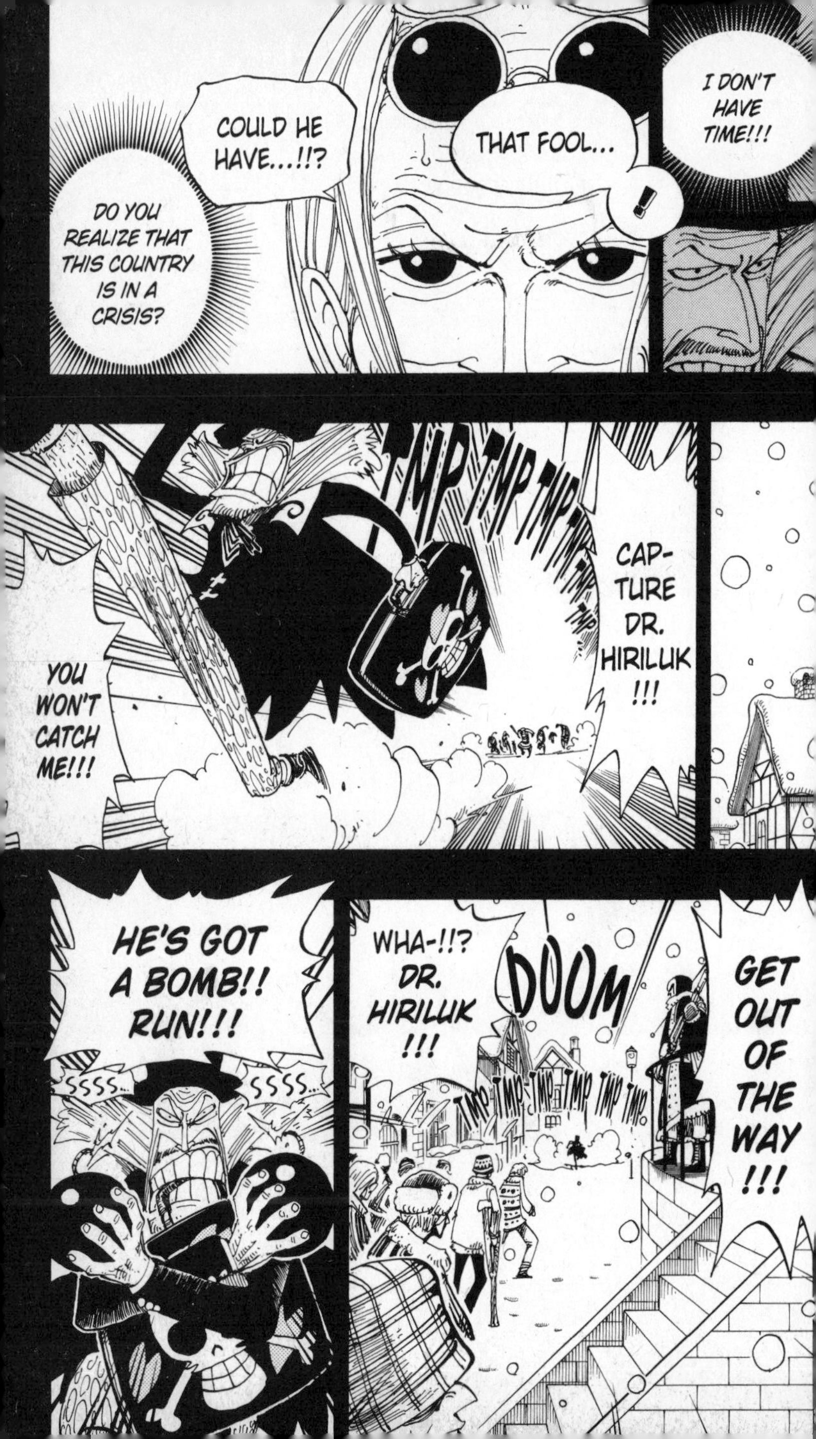

I DON'T HAVE TIME!!!
!
THAT FOOL...
COULD HE HAVE...!!?
DO YOU REALIZE THAT THIS COUNTRY IS IN A CRISIS?
TMP TMP TMP TMP TMP TMP TMP
CAP-TURE DR. HIRILUK!!!
YOU WON'T CATCH ME!!!
GET OUT OF THE WAY!!!
DOOM
WHA-!!? DR. HIRILUK!!!
TMP TMP TMP TMP TMP TMP TMP
HE'S GOT A BOMB!! RUN!!!
SSSS...
SSSS...

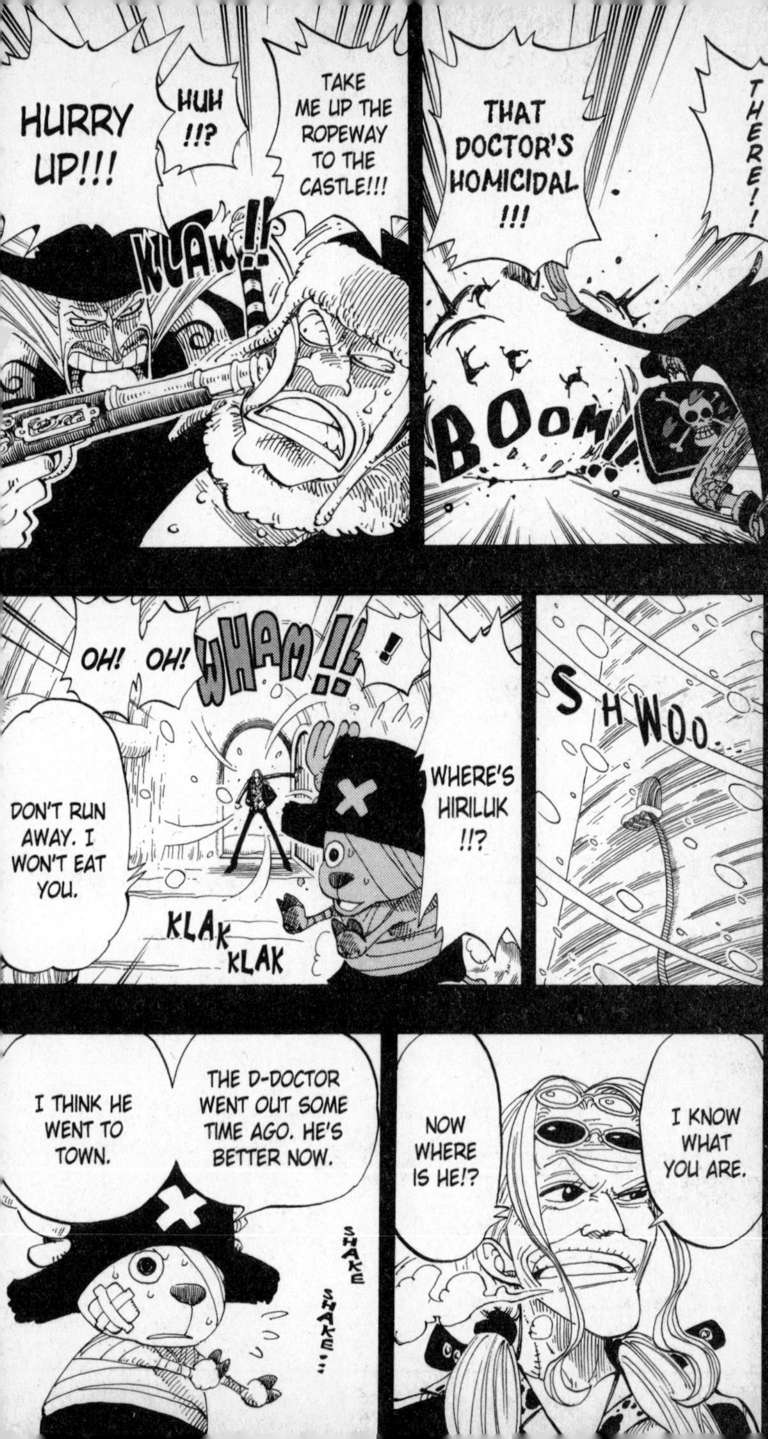
THERE!!
THAT DOCTOR'S HOMICIDAL!!!
BOOM!!
TAKE ME UP THE ROPEWAY TO THE CASTLE!!!
HUH!!?
HURRY UP!!!
KLAK!!
SHWOO...
WHERE'S HIRILUK!!?
!
WHAM!!
OH! OH!
DON'T RUN AWAY. I WON'T EAT YOU.
KLAK KLAK
I KNOW WHAT YOU ARE.
NOW WHERE IS HE!?
SHAKE
SHAKE...
THE D-DOCTOR WENT OUT SOME TIME AGO. HE'S BETTER NOW.
I THINK HE WENT TO TOWN.

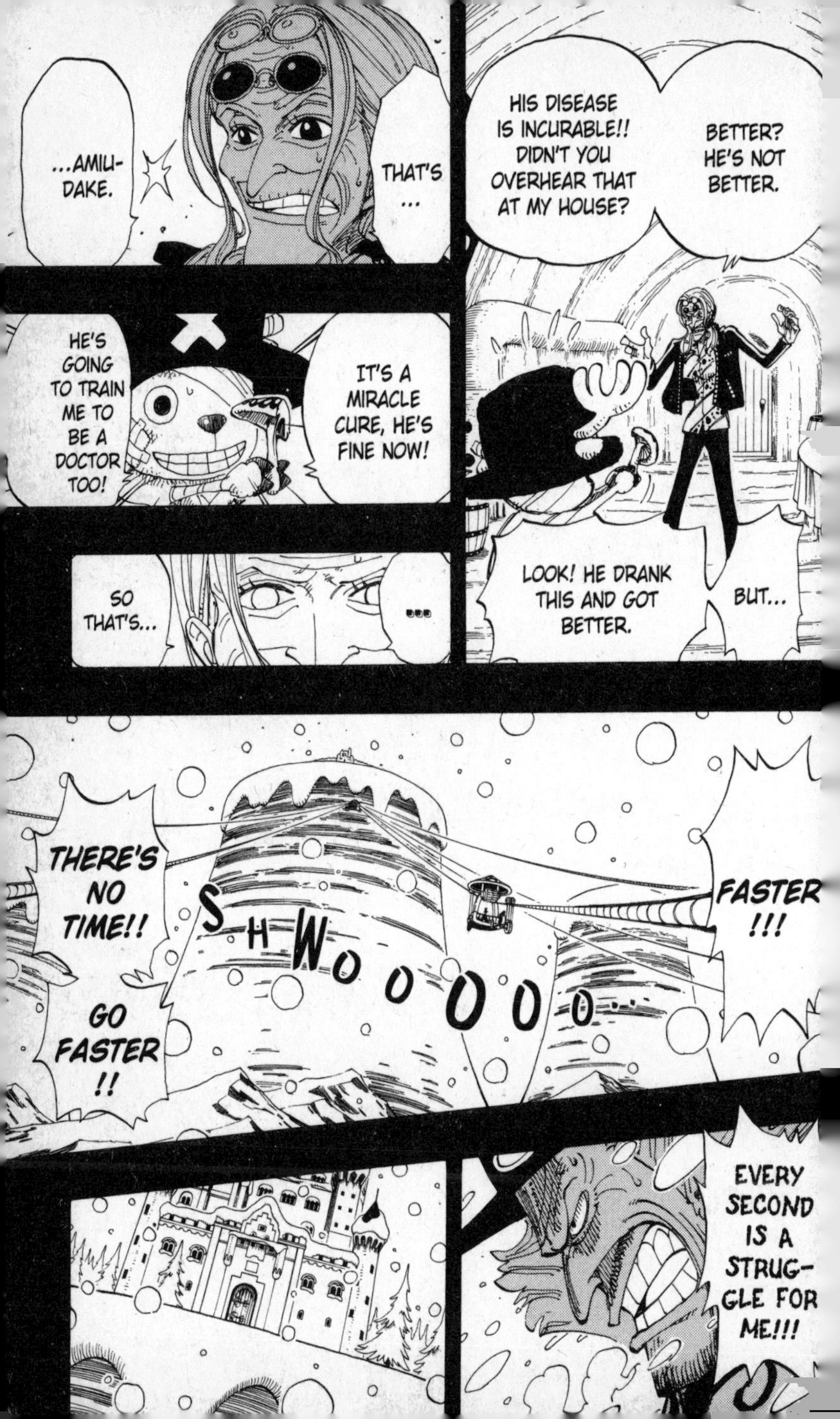
BETTER? HE'S NOT BETTER.
HIS DISEASE IS INCURABLE!! DIDN'T YOU OVERHEAR THAT AT MY HOUSE?
BUT...
LOOK! HE DRANK THIS AND GOT BETTER.
THAT'S ...
...AMIU-DAKE.
IT'S A MIRACLE CURE, HE'S FINE NOW!
HE'S GOING TO TRAIN ME TO BE A DOCTOR TOO!
...
SO THAT'S...
FASTER !!!
THERE'S NO TIME!!
SHWOOOOOO...
GO FASTER !!
EVERY SECOND IS A STRUGGLE FOR ME!!!

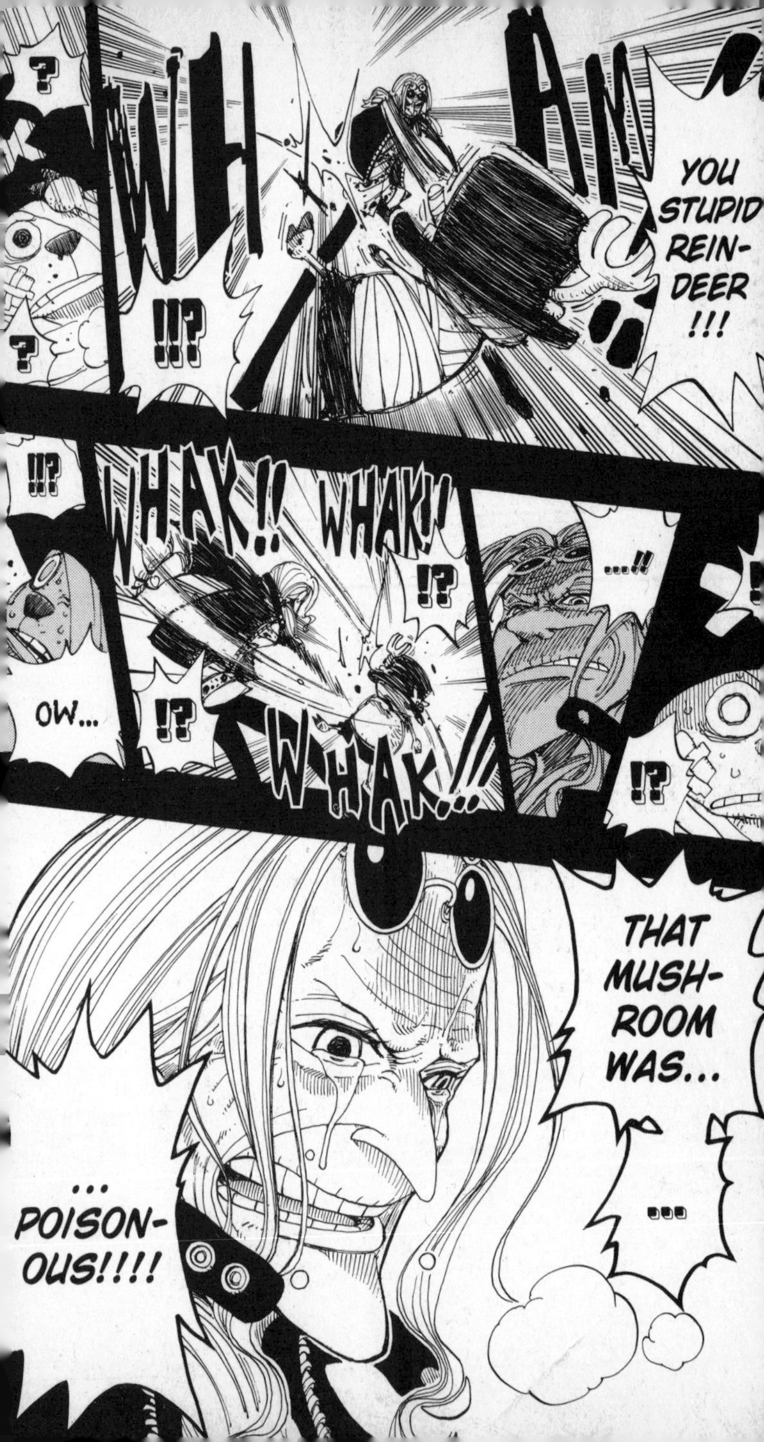
YOU STUPID REIN-DEER!!!
WHAM
!!?
?
?
!?
...!!
WHAK!! WHAK!!
!?
!?
WHAK...!!
!!?
OW...
THAT MUSH-ROOM WAS...
...
...POISON-OUS!!!!

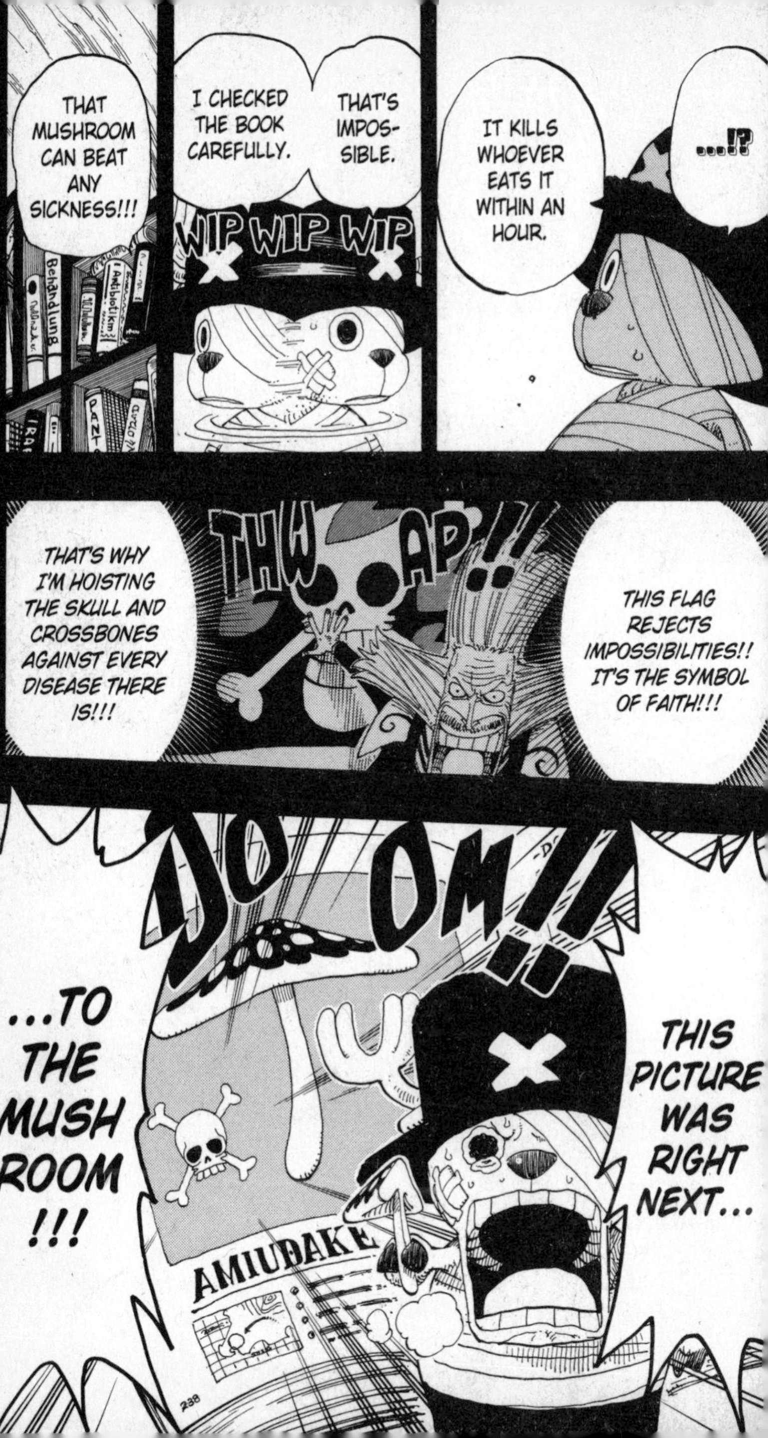
...!?
IT KILLS WHOEVER EATS IT WITHIN AN HOUR.
THAT'S IMPOSSIBLE.
I CHECKED THE BOOK CAREFULLY.
WIP WIP WIP
THAT MUSHROOM CAN BEAT ANY SICKNESS!!!
Behandlung
Antibiotikum
THIS FLAG REJECTS IMPOSSIBILITIES!! IT'S THE SYMBOL OF FAITH!!!
THWAP!!
THAT'S WHY I'M HOISTING THE SKULL AND CROSSBONES AGAINST EVERY DISEASE THERE IS!!!
THIS PICTURE WAS RIGHT NEXT...
DOOM!!
...TO THE MUSH ROOM!!!
AMIUDAKE

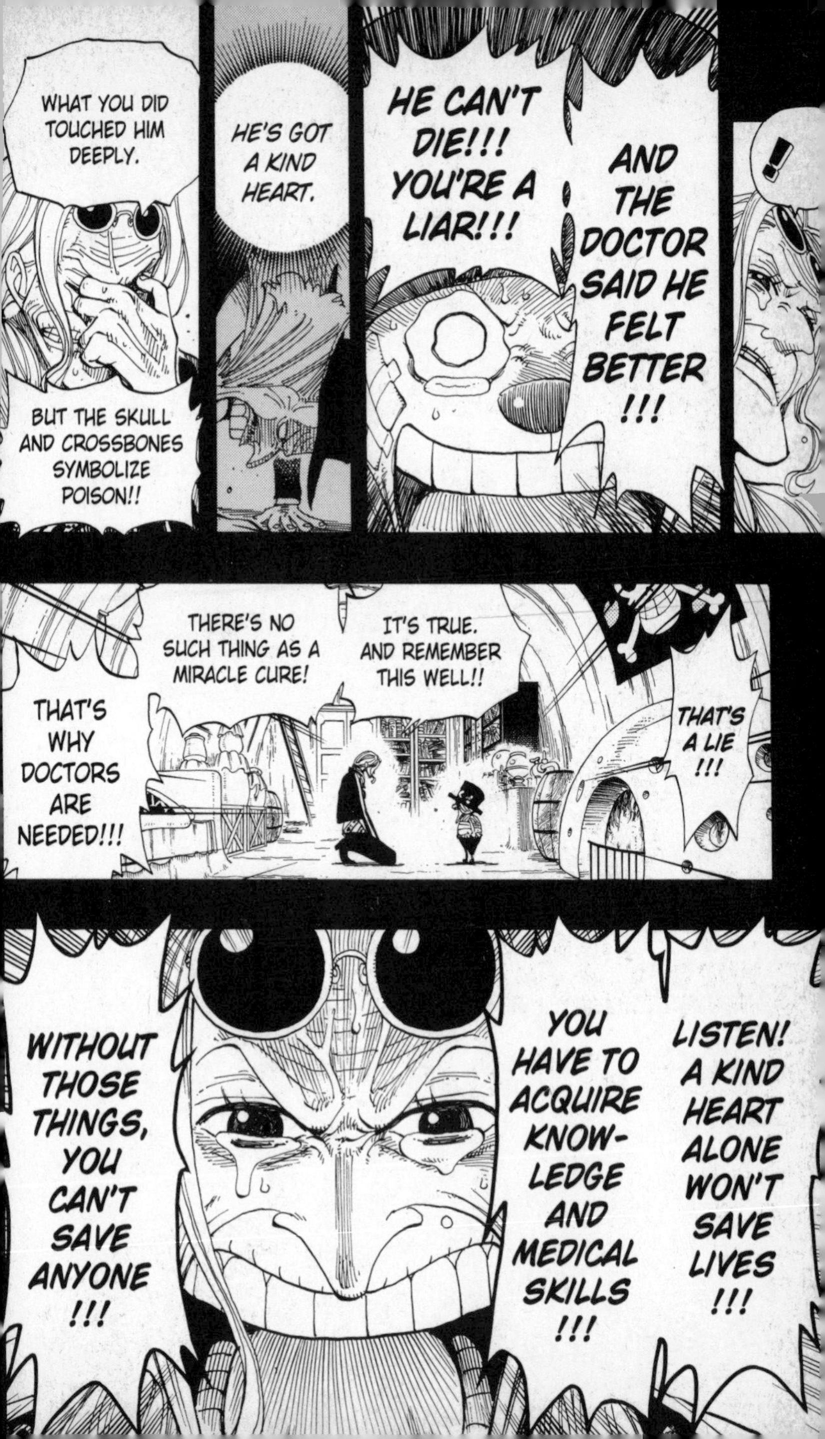
!
HE CAN'T DIE!!! YOU'RE A LIAR!!!
AND THE DOCTOR SAID HE FELT BETTER!!!
HE'S GOT A KIND HEART.
WHAT YOU DID TOUCHED HIM DEEPLY.
BUT THE SKULL AND CROSSBONES SYMBOLIZE POISON!!
THAT'S A LIE!!!
IT'S TRUE. AND REMEMBER THIS WELL!!
THERE'S NO SUCH THING AS A MIRACLE CURE!
THAT'S WHY DOCTORS ARE NEEDED!!!
LISTEN! A KIND HEART ALONE WON'T SAVE LIVES!!!
YOU HAVE TO ACQUIRE KNOW-LEDGE AND MEDICAL SKILLS!!!
WITHOUT THOSE THINGS, YOU CAN'T SAVE ANYONE!!!

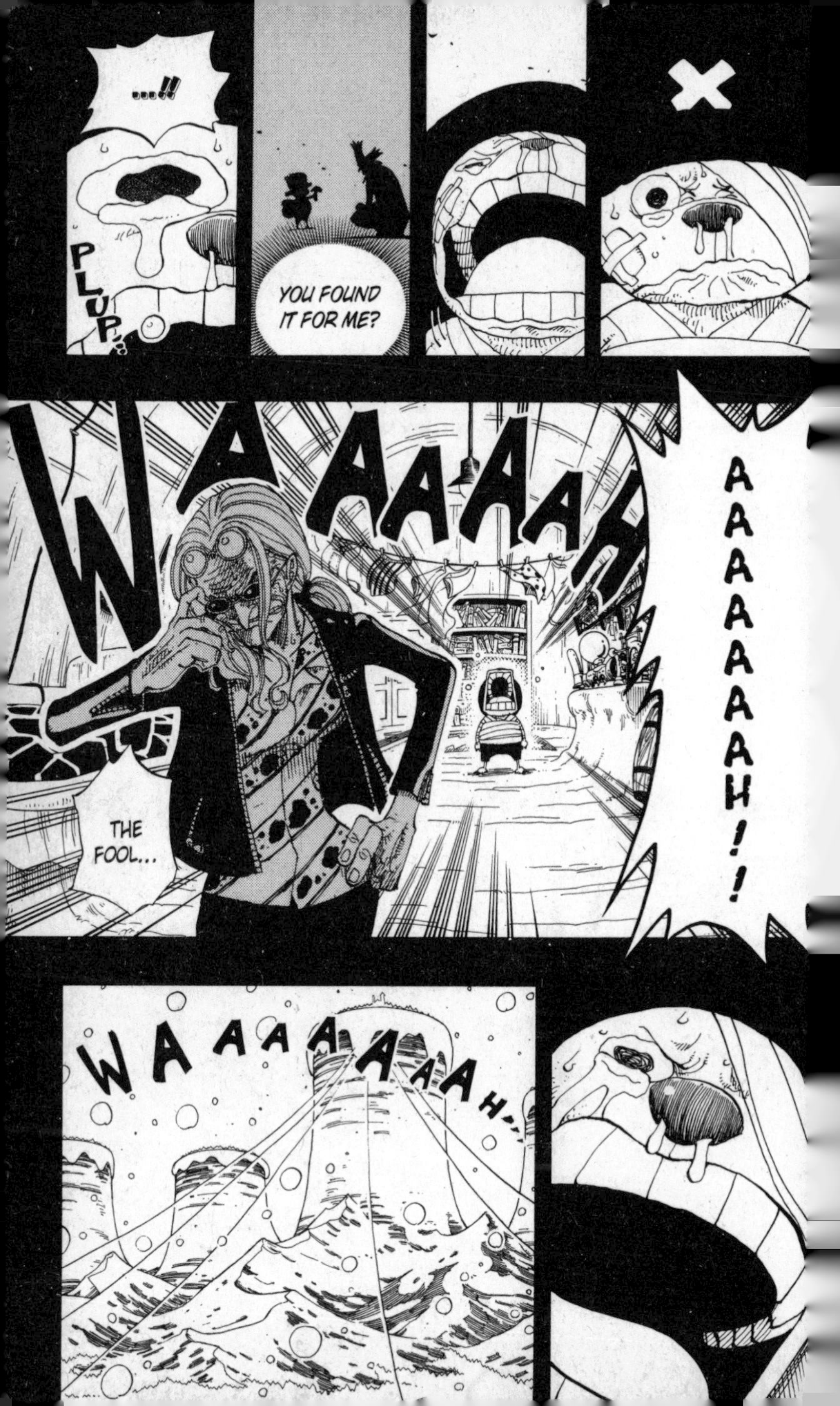

YOU FOUND IT FOR ME?
...!!
PLUP
WAAAAH
AAAAAAAH!!
THE FOOL...
WAAAAAAH-

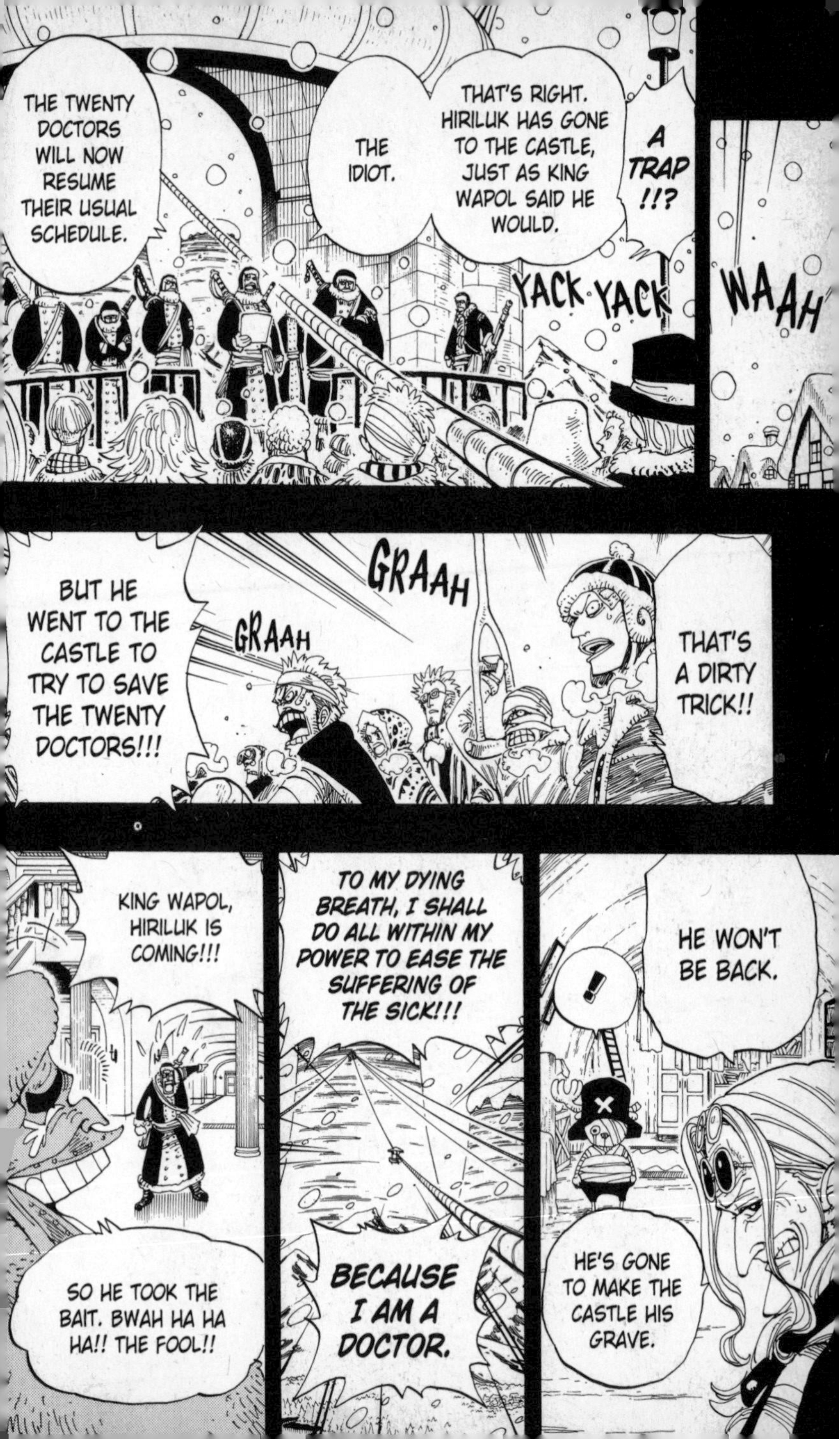
WAAAH
A TRAP!!?
THAT'S RIGHT. HIRILUK HAS GONE TO THE CASTLE, JUST AS KING WAPOL SAID HE WOULD.
THE IDIOT.
THE TWENTY DOCTORS WILL NOW RESUME THEIR USUAL SCHEDULE.
YACK YACK
THAT'S A DIRTY TRICK!!
GRAAAH
GRAAAH
BUT HE WENT TO THE CASTLE TO TRY TO SAVE THE TWENTY DOCTORS!!!
HE WON'T BE BACK.
!
HE'S GONE TO MAKE THE CASTLE HIS GRAVE.
TO MY DYING BREATH, I SHALL DO ALL WITHIN MY POWER TO EASE THE SUFFERING OF THE SICK!!!
BECAUSE I AM A DOCTOR.
KING WAPOL, HIRILUK IS COMING!!!
SO HE TOOK THE BAIT. BWAH HA HA HA!! THE FOOL!!

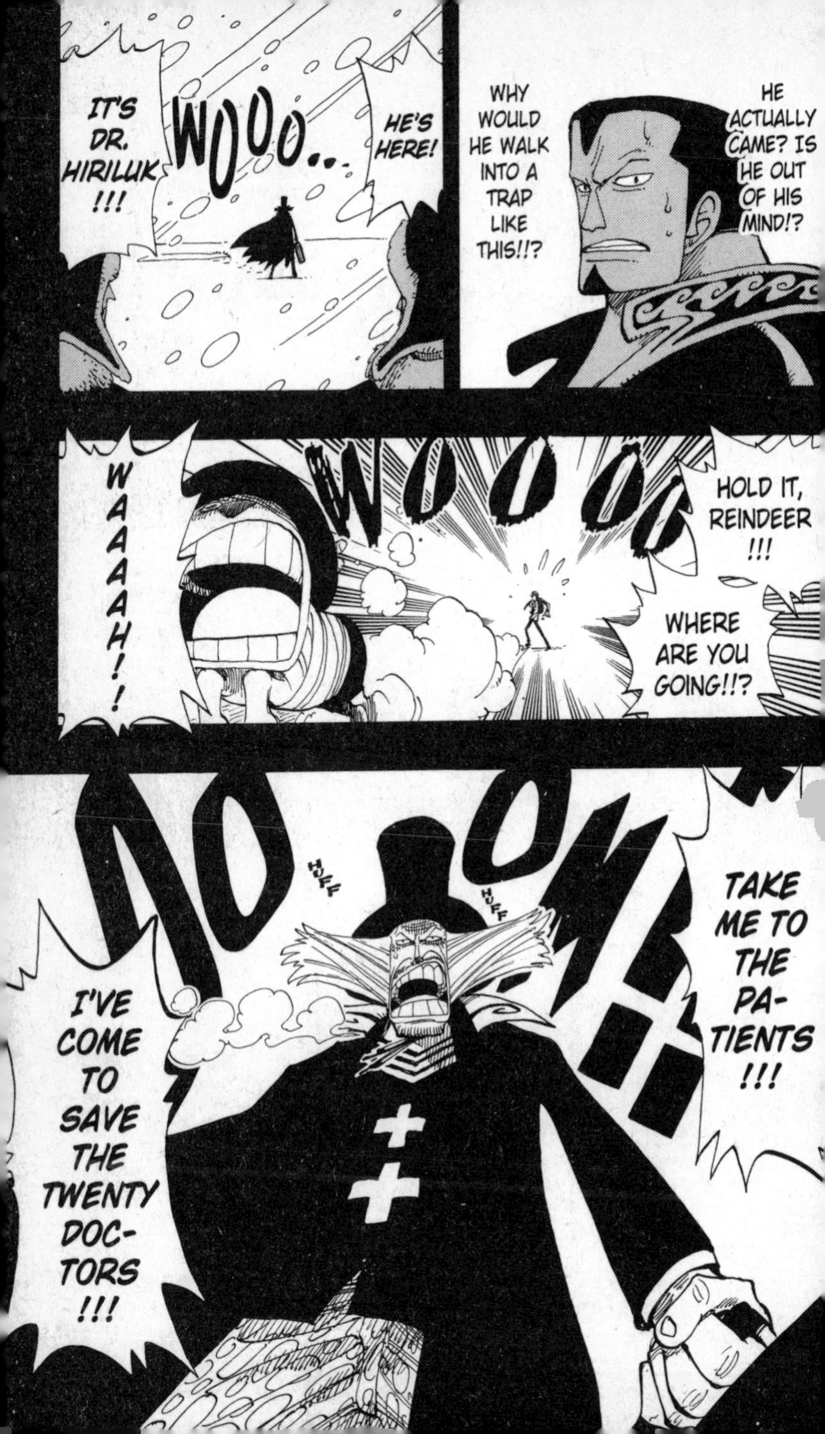
HE ACTUALLY CAME? IS HE OUT OF HIS MIND!?
WHY WOULD HE WALK INTO A TRAP LIKE THIS!!?
HE'S HERE!
WOOO...
IT'S DR. HIRILUK!!!
HOLD IT, REINDEER!!!
WHERE ARE YOU GOING!!?
WOOOO
WAAAAAH!!
TAKE ME TO THE PATIENTS!!!
HUFF
HUFF
I'VE COME TO SAVE THE TWENTY DOCTORS!!!

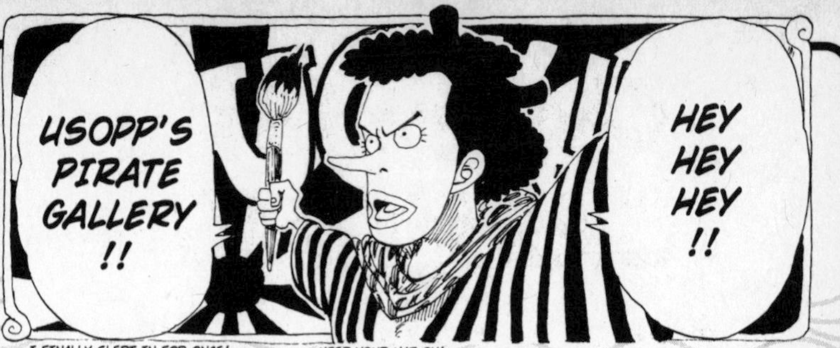
HEY HEY HEY !!
USOPP'S PIRATE GALLERY !!

ONE RUBBER FIST COMING RIGHT UP!

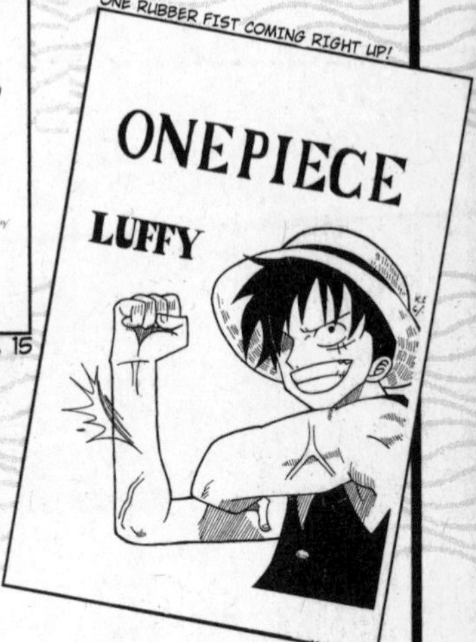
ONEPIECE
LUFFY

K.DO, 13

KEEP YOUR HAT ON!

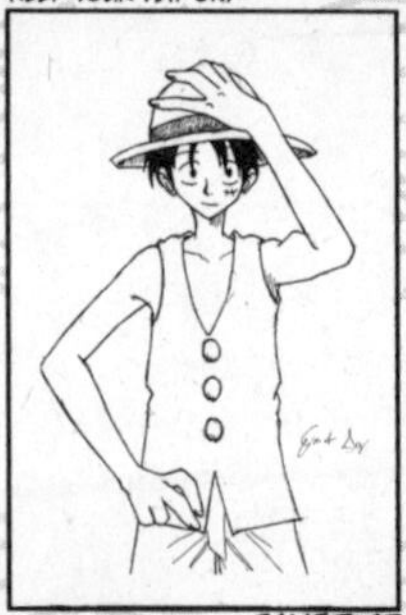

JANET, 15

I FINALLY SLEPT IN FOR ONCE!

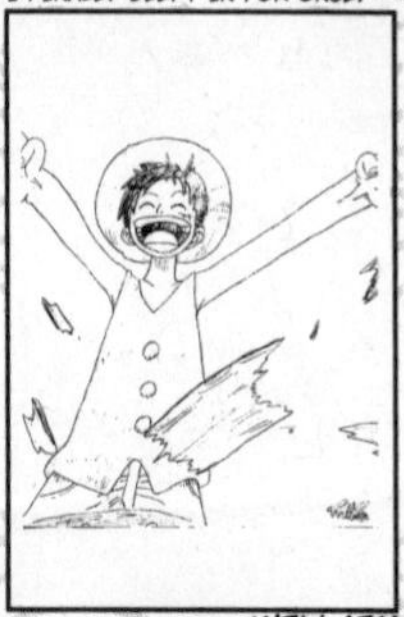

WILLAIM

I'M ALL FACE!

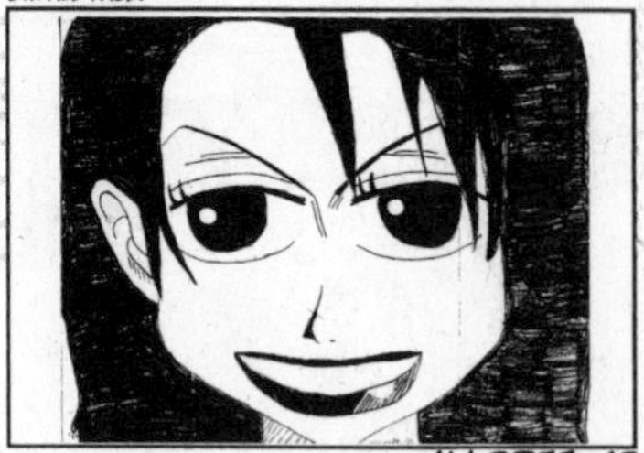

ALLBRIE, 13

IT'S GOOD TO BE THE KING!

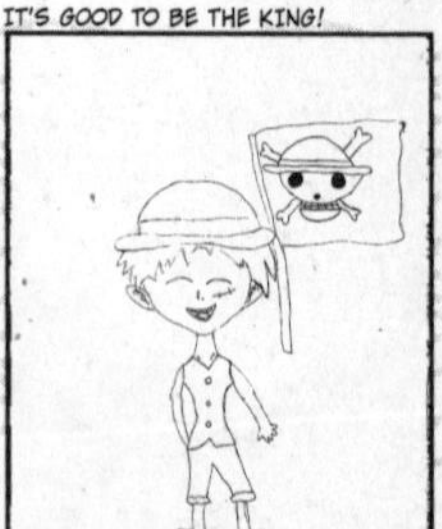
Luffy, King of the Pirates

CHRISTY, 13

WAKE UP ZOLO!

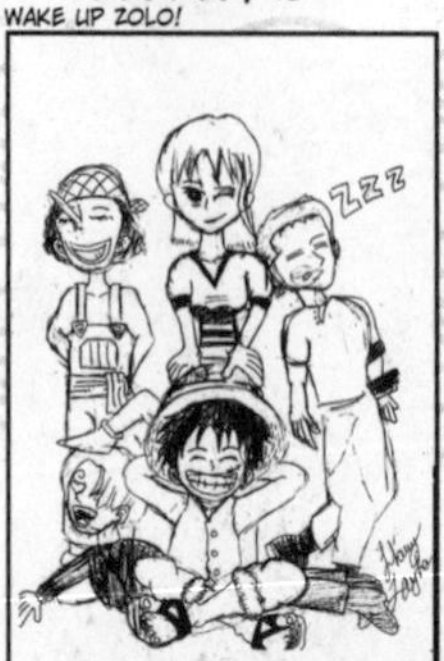
ZZZ

HARRY

I'M A PIRATE ON A WOODEN BOAT...

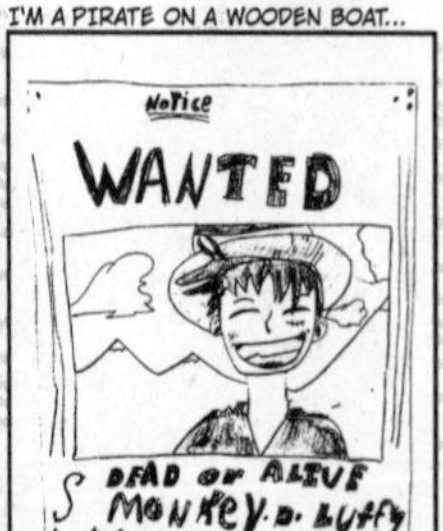
Notice
WANTED
DEAD or ALIVE
Monkey.D.Luffy
$100.000.000-
NAVY

BRIAN, 12

SUBMIT YOUR FAN ART TO:
SHONEN JUMP C/O VIZ. LLC P.O. BOX 77010, SAN FRANCISCO, CA, 94107
REMEMBER TO INCLUDE YOUR NAME AND AGE!!

USOPP'S COMMENTS WERE TRANSMITTED THROUGH THE U.S. SHONEN JUMP TEAM-*EDITOR*

Chapter 145:
CARRYING ON HIS WILL

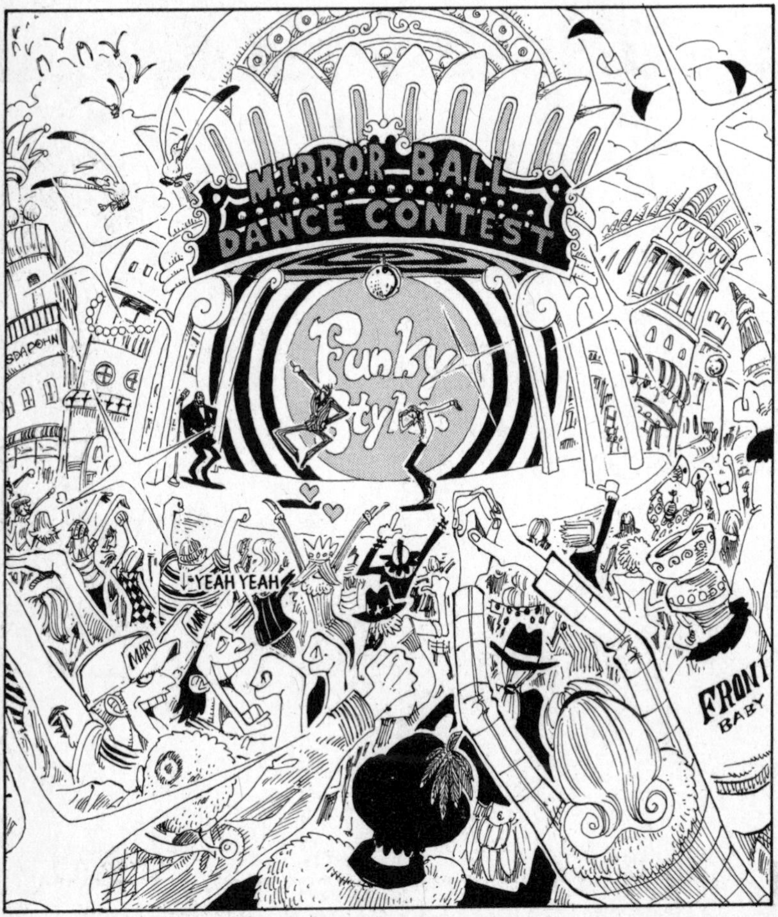
MIRROR BALL
DANCE CONTEST
Funky Style
YEAH YEAH
FRONT BABY

DJANGO'S DANCE PARADISE, VOL. 15:
"TOTALLY WHITE FEVER DANCE CONTEST"

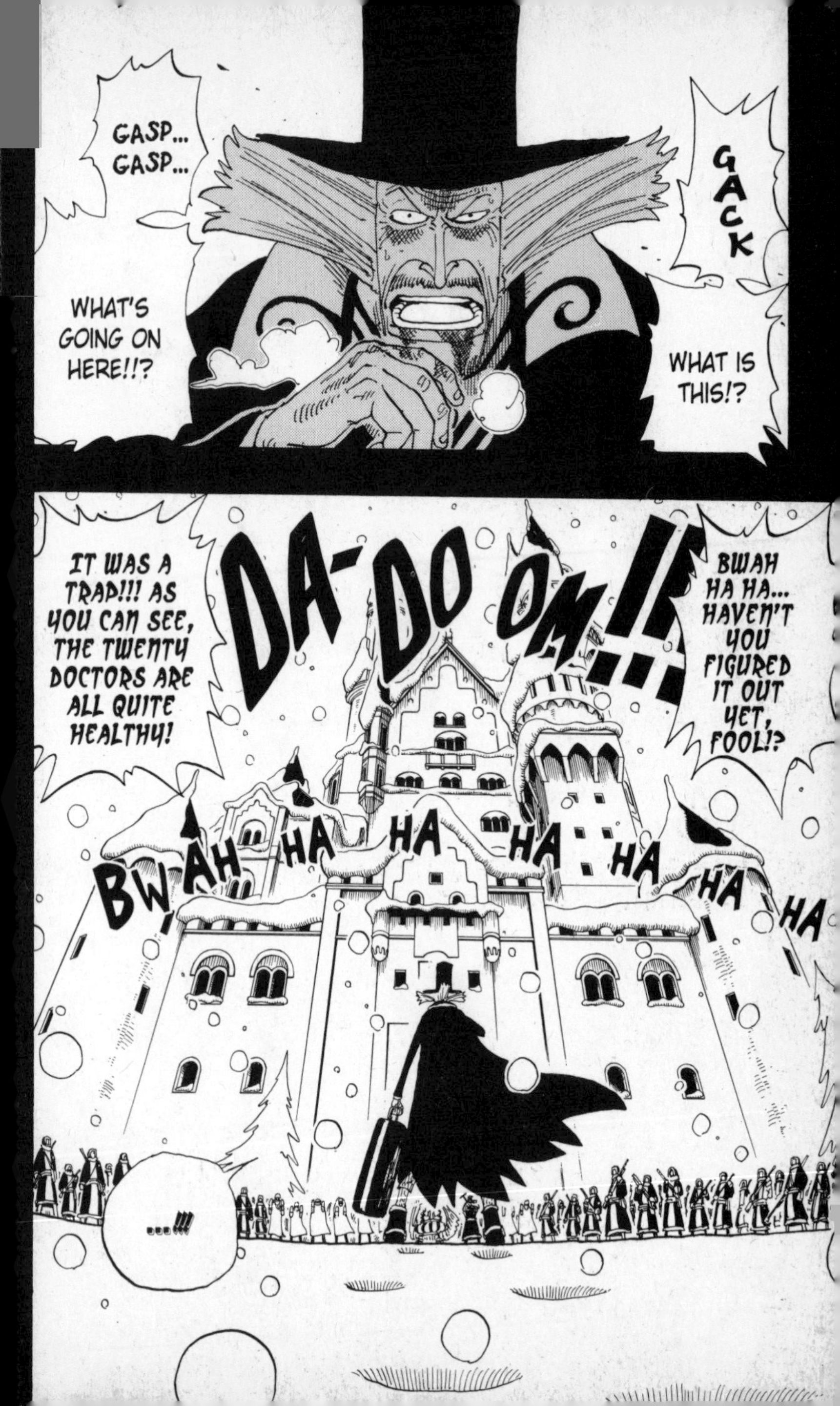
GACK
WHAT IS THIS!?
GASP... GASP...
WHAT'S GOING ON HERE!!?
DA-DOOM!!
BWAH HA HA... HAVEN'T YOU FIGURED IT OUT YET, FOOL!?
IT WAS A TRAP!!! AS YOU CAN SEE, THE TWENTY DOCTORS ARE ALL QUITE HEALTHY!
BWAH HA HA HA HA HA HA HA
...!!!

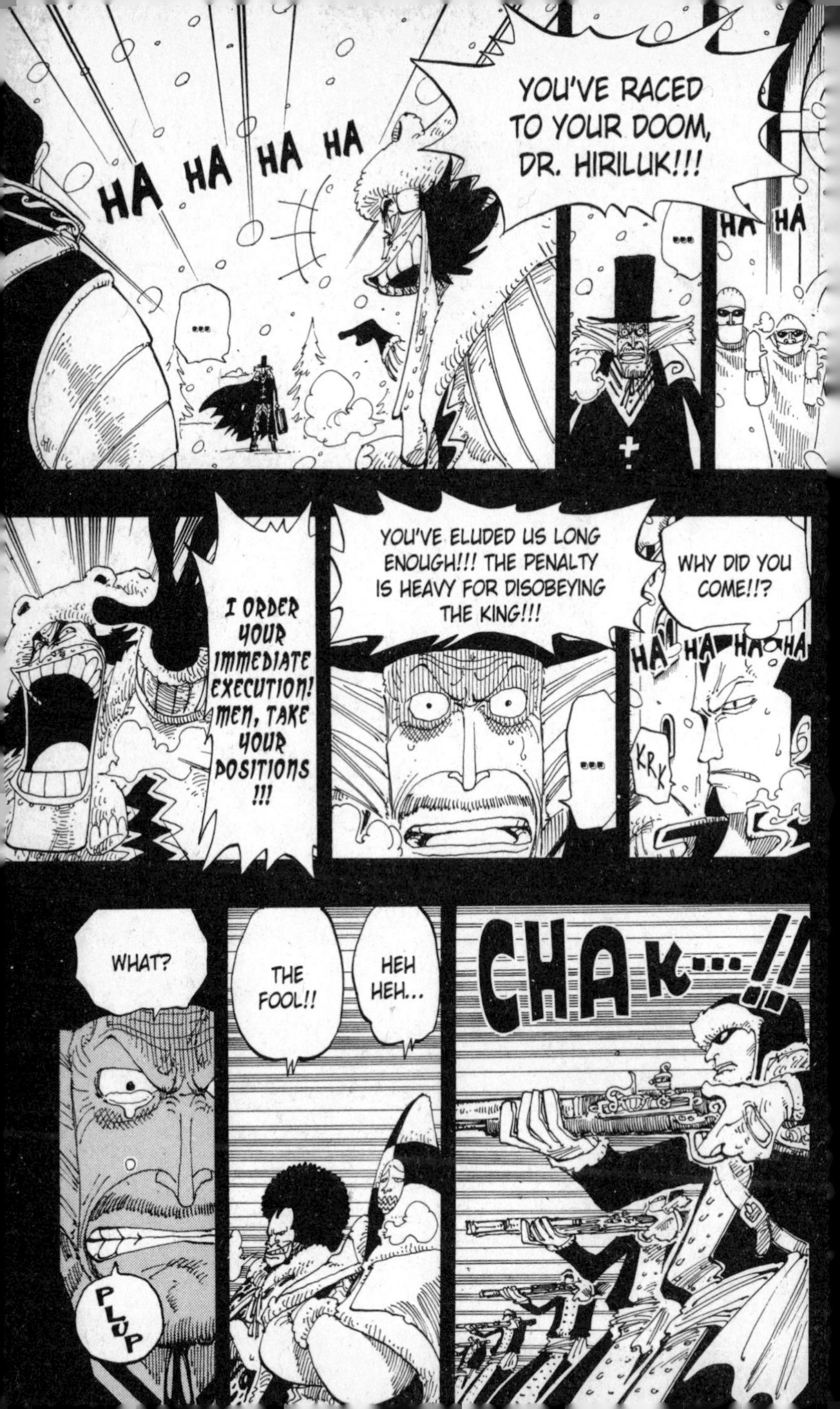
YOU'VE RACED TO YOUR DOOM, DR. HIRILUK!!!
HA HA
...
HA HA HA HA
...
WHY DID YOU COME!!?
HA HA HA HA
KRK
YOU'VE ELUDED US LONG ENOUGH!!! THE PENALTY IS HEAVY FOR DISOBEYING THE KING!!!
...
I ORDER YOUR IMMEDIATE EXECUTION! MEN, TAKE YOUR POSITIONS!!!
CHAK...!!
HEH HEH...
THE FOOL!!
WHAT?
PLUP

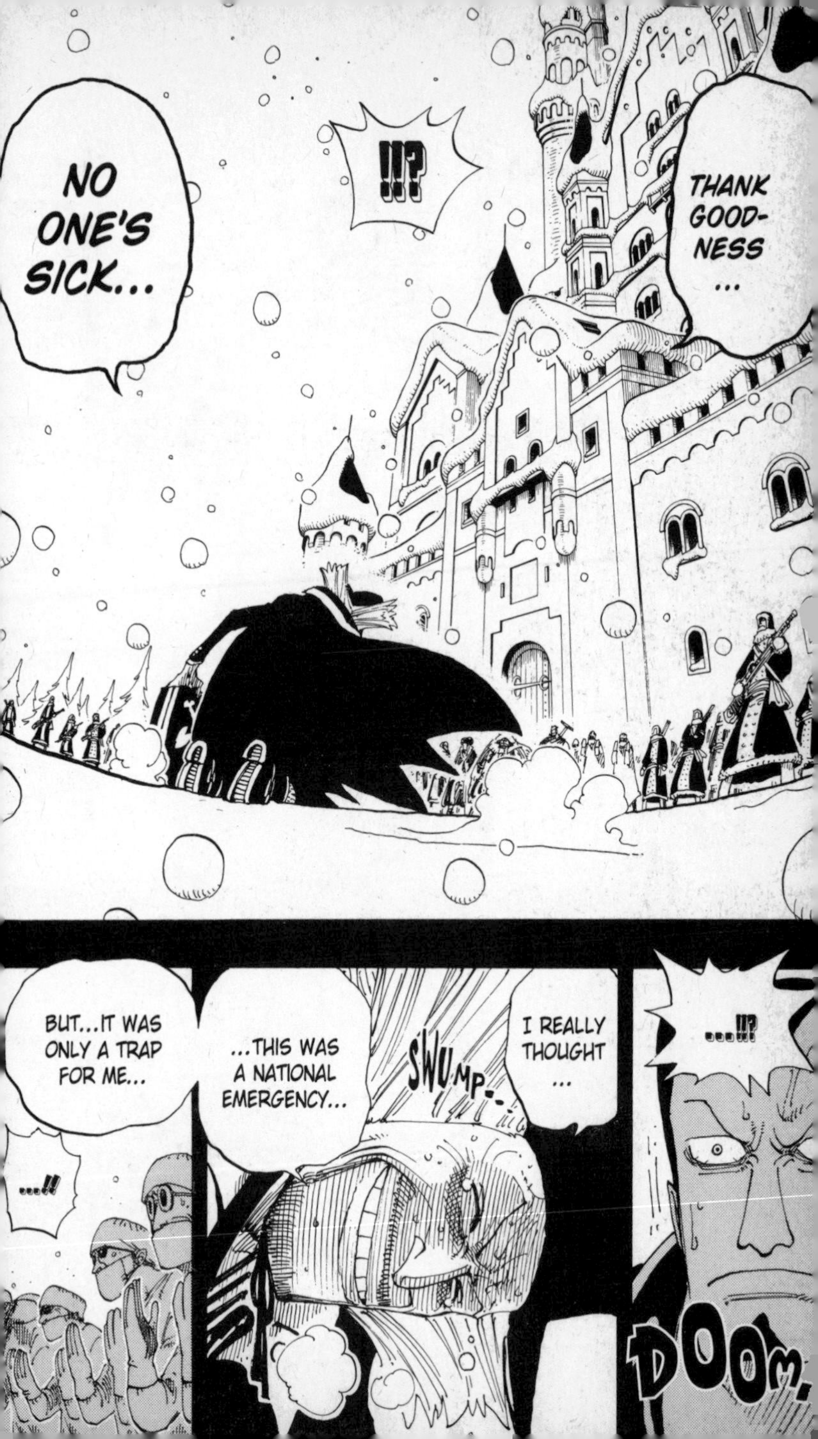
THANK GOODNESS ...
!!?
NO ONE'S SICK...
...!!?
DOOM.
I REALLY THOUGHT ...
SWUMP...
...THIS WAS A NATIONAL EMERGENCY...
BUT...IT WAS ONLY A TRAP FOR ME...
...!!

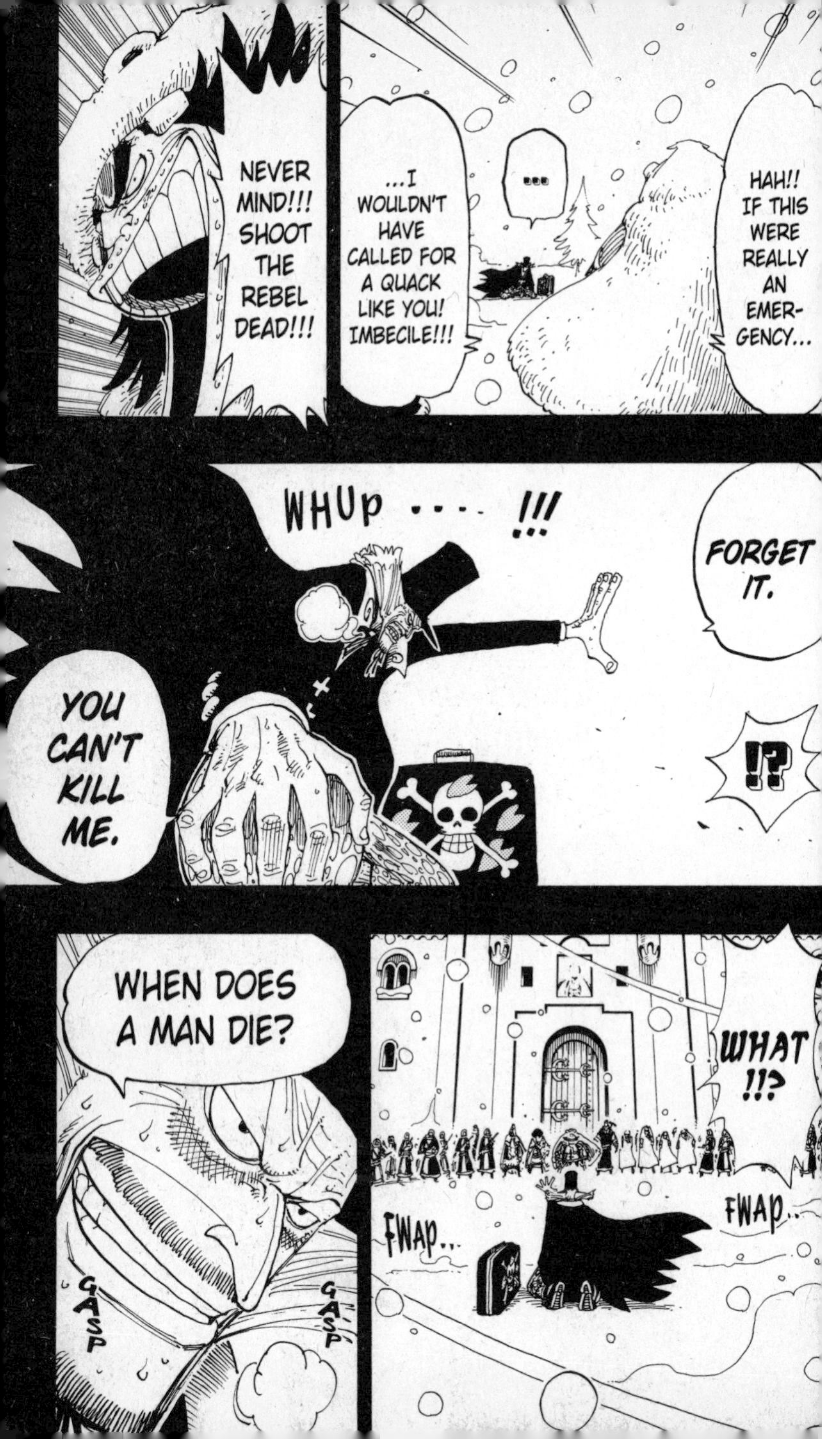
HAH!! IF THIS WERE REALLY AN EMERGENCY...
...
...I WOULDN'T HAVE CALLED FOR A QUACK LIKE YOU! IMBECILE!!!
NEVER MIND!!! SHOOT THE REBEL DEAD!!!
FORGET IT.
WHUp ....!!!
!?
YOU CAN'T KILL ME.
WHAT!!?
FWAp...
FWAp...
WHEN DOES A MAN DIE?
GASP
GASP

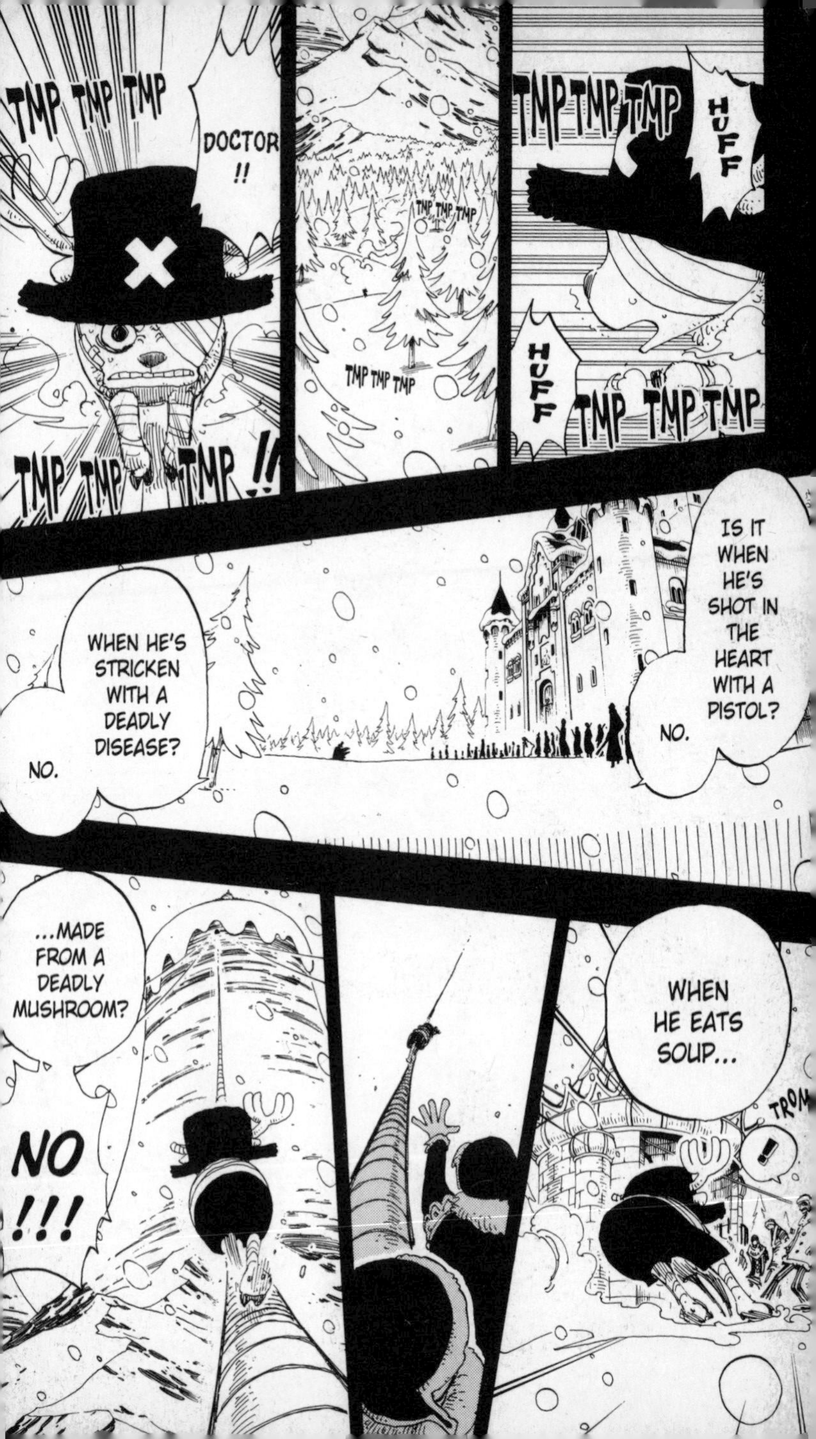
TMP TMP TMP
HUFF
HUFF
TMP TMP TMP
TMP TMP TMP
TMP TMP TMP
TMP TMP TMP
DOCTOR !!
TMP TMP TMP !!
IS IT WHEN HE'S SHOT IN THE HEART WITH A PISTOL?
NO.
WHEN HE'S STRICKEN WITH A DEADLY DISEASE?
NO.
WHEN HE EATS SOUP...
TROM
!
...MADE FROM A DEADLY MUSHROOM?
NO !!!

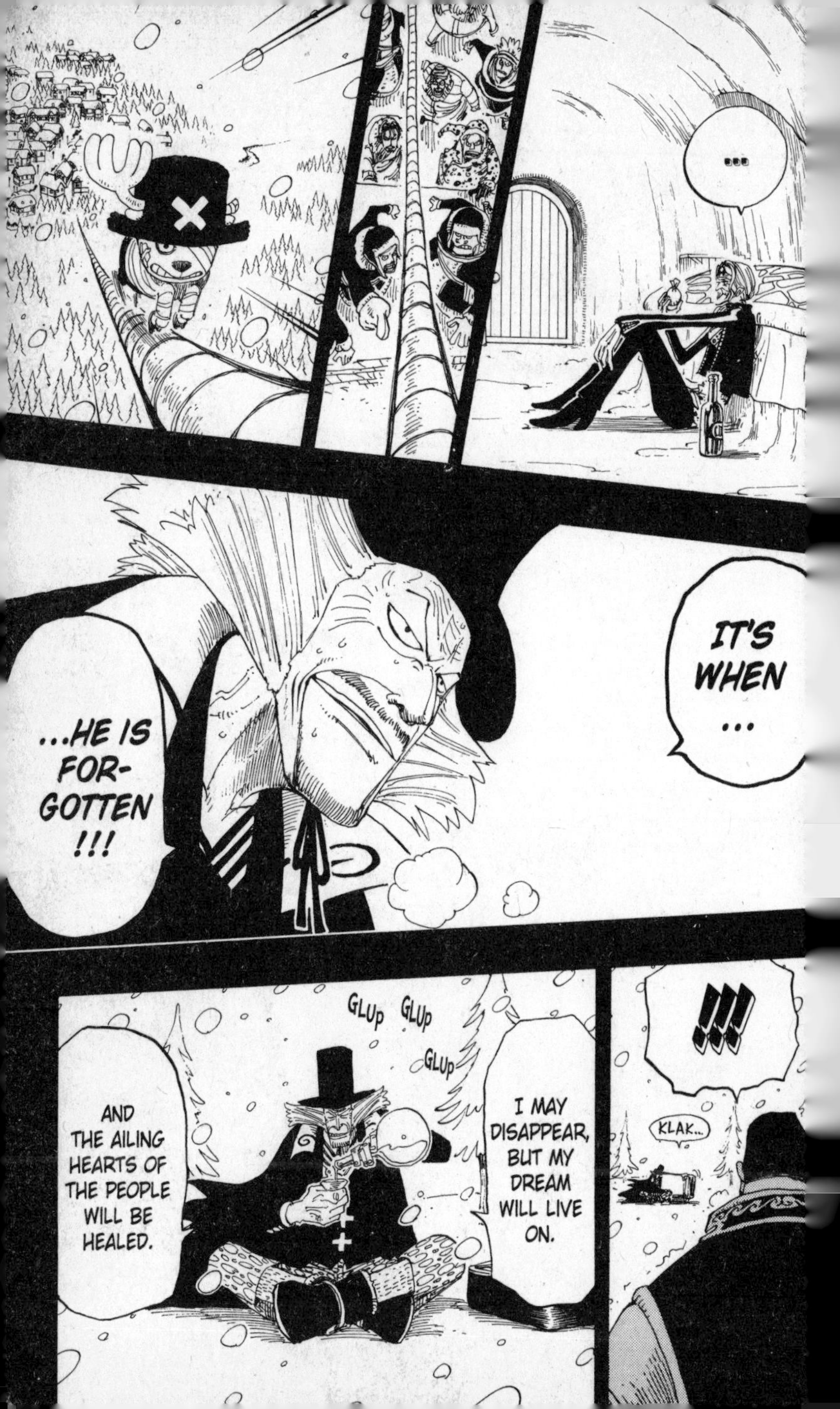
...
IT'S WHEN ...
...HE IS FOR-GOTTEN !!!
!!!
KLAK...
I MAY DISAPPEAR, BUT MY DREAM WILL LIVE ON.
GLUP GLUP GLUP
AND THE AILING HEARTS OF THE PEOPLE WILL BE HEALED.

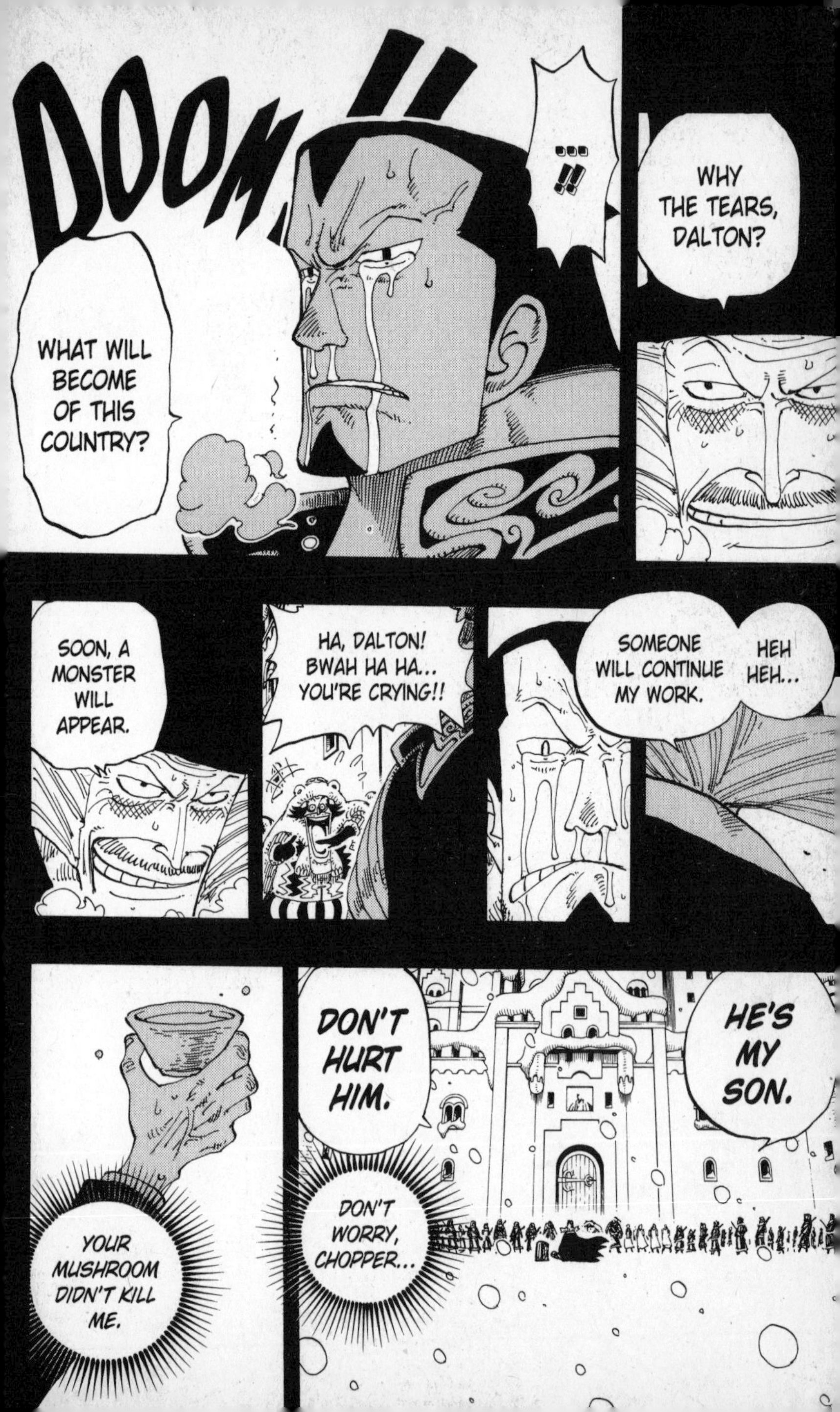
WHY THE TEARS, DALTON?
...!!
DOOM!!
WHAT WILL BECOME OF THIS COUNTRY?
HEH HEH...
SOMEONE WILL CONTINUE MY WORK.
HA, DALTON! BWAH HA HA... YOU'RE CRYING!!
SOON, A MONSTER WILL APPEAR.
HE'S MY SON.
DON'T HURT HIM.
DON'T WORRY, CHOPPER...
YOUR MUSHROOM DIDN'T KILL ME.

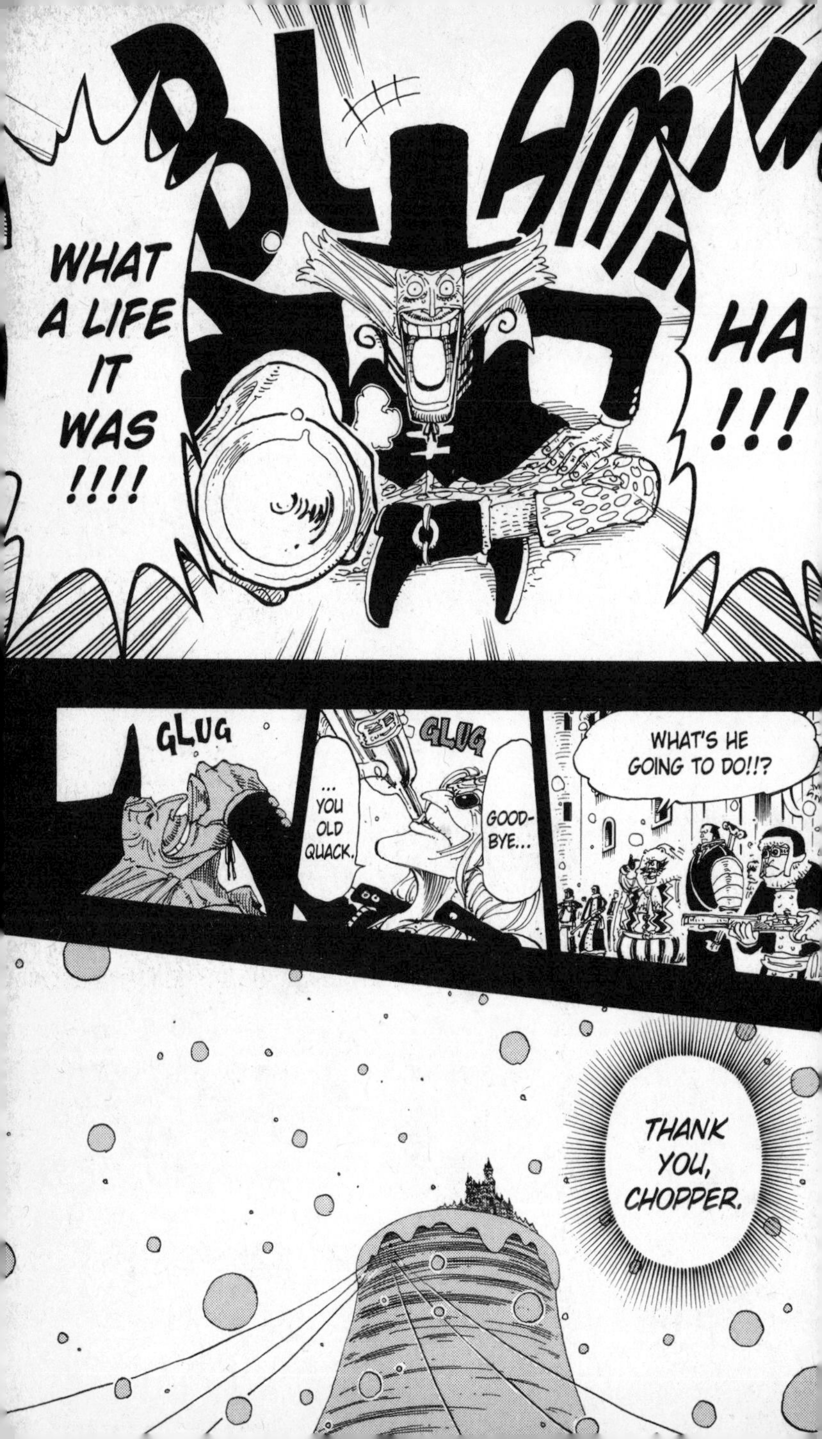
BLAM
HA!!!
WHAT A LIFE IT WAS!!!!
WHAT'S HE GOING TO DO!!?
GLUG
GOOD-BYE...
...YOU OLD QUACK.
GLUG
THANK YOU, CHOPPER.

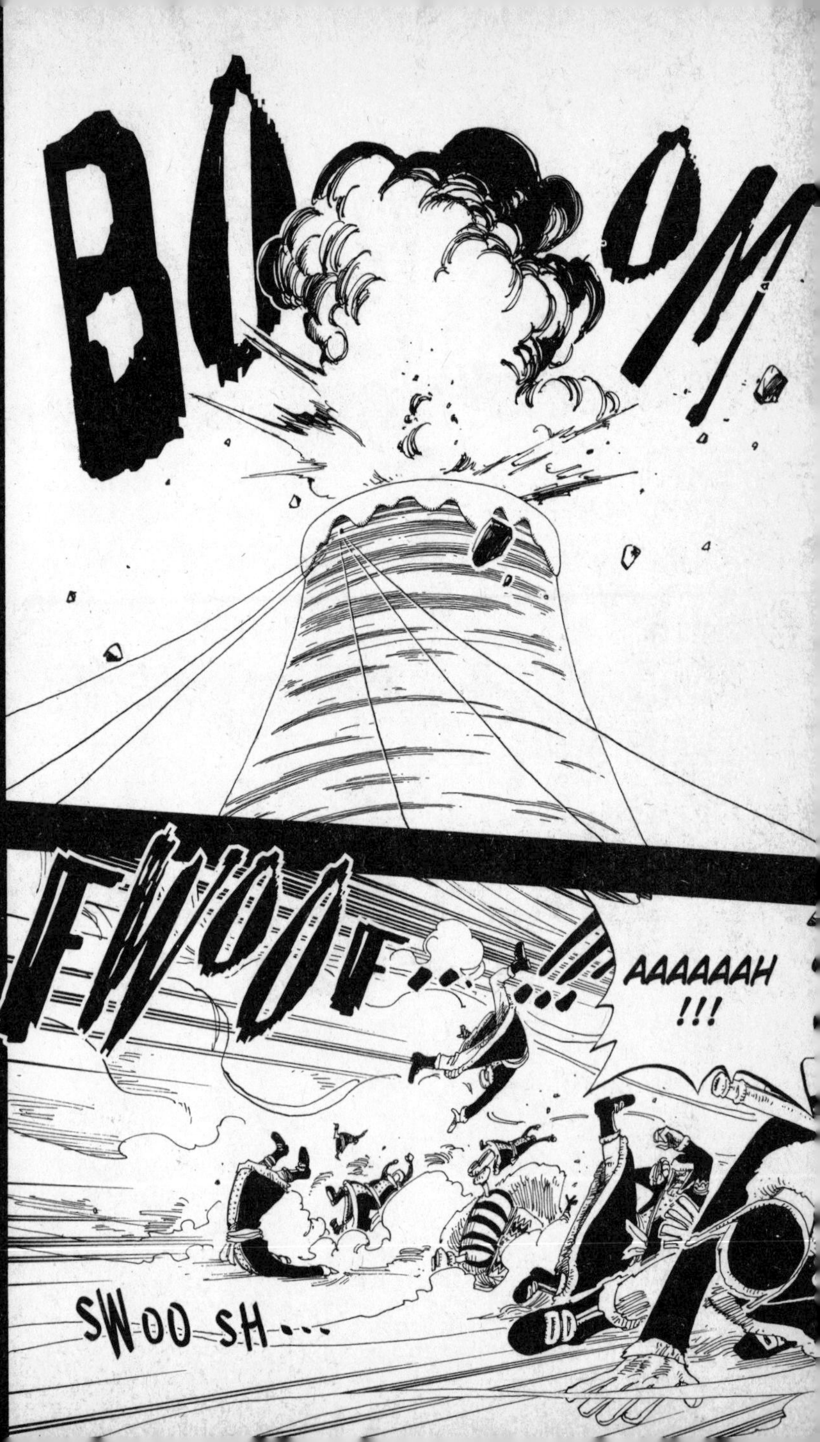
BOOOM
FWOOF...!!
AAAAAAH!!!
SWOOSH...

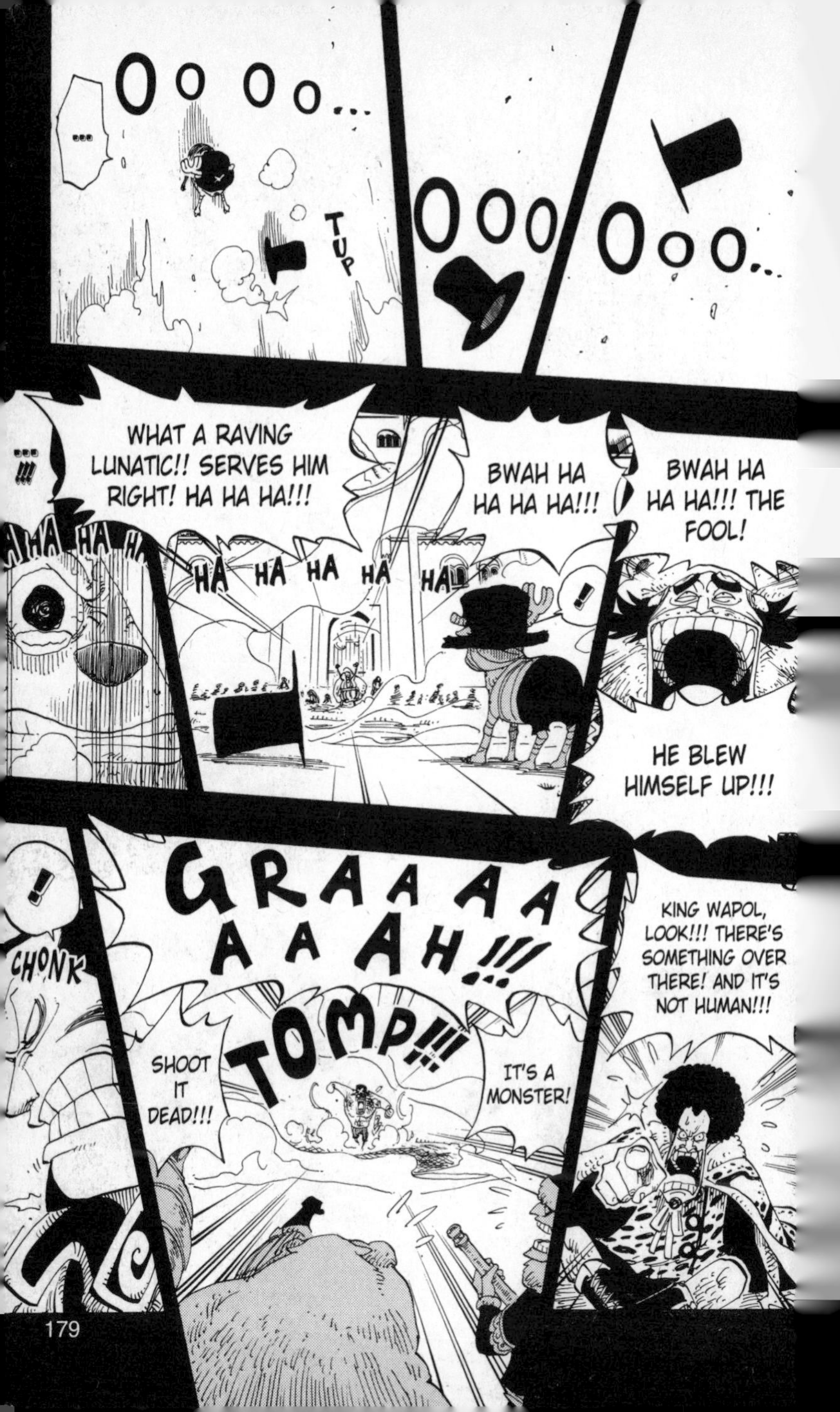
Ooo...
Ooo
...
Oooo...
TUP
BWAH HA HA HA!!! THE FOOL!
HE BLEW HIMSELF UP!!!
BWAH HA HA HA HA!!!
WHAT A RAVING LUNATIC!! SERVES HIM RIGHT! HA HA HA!!!
!
HA HA HA HA HA
...!!!
HA HA HA HA
KING WAPOL, LOOK!!! THERE'S SOMETHING OVER THERE! AND IT'S NOT HUMAN!!!
GRAAAAAAAH!!!
IT'S A MONSTER!
TOMP!!!
SHOOT IT DEAD!!!
!
CHONK

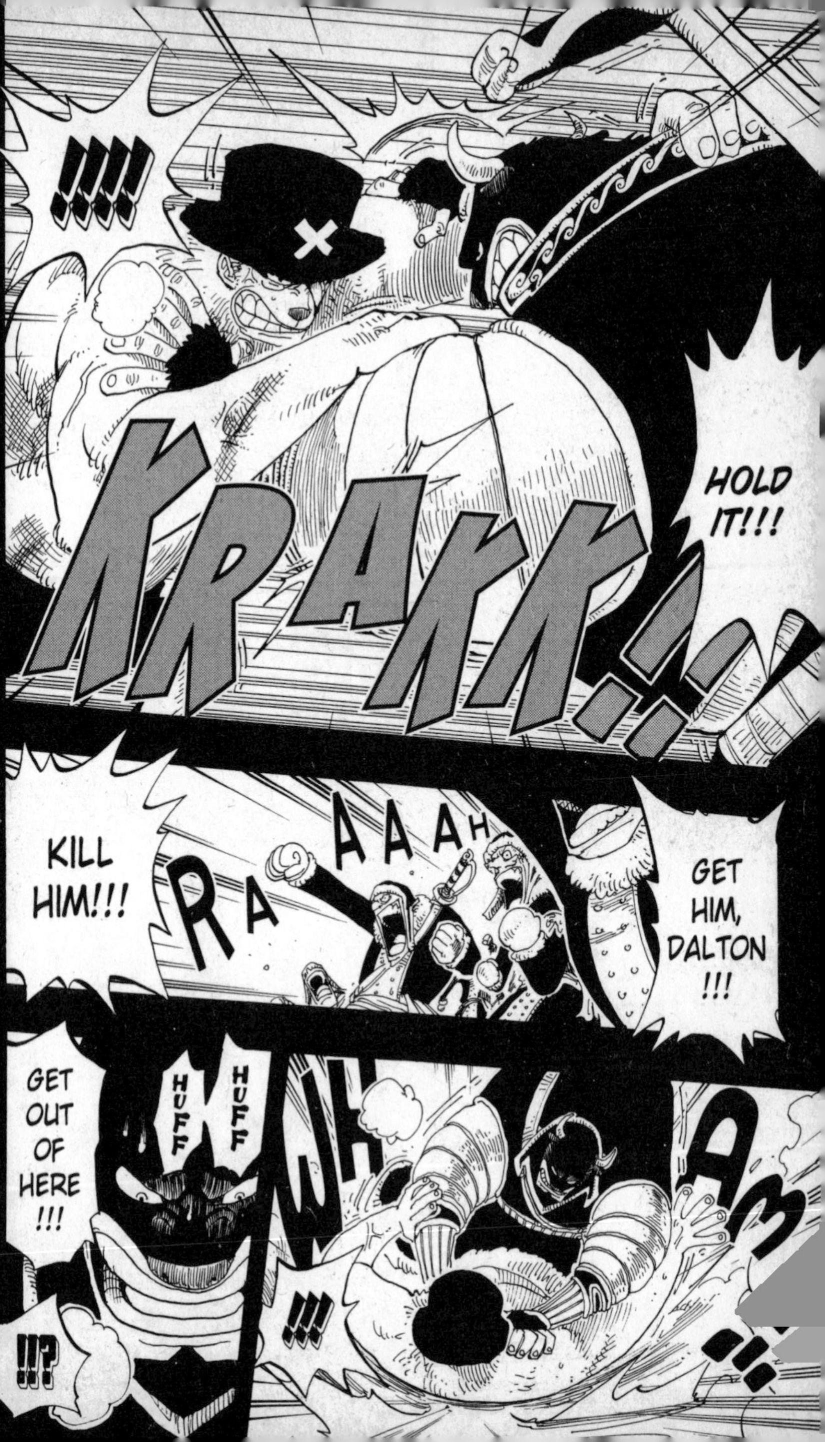
HOLD IT!!!
!!!!
KRAKK!!!
GET HIM, DALTON!!!
RAAAAH
KILL HIM!!!
!!!
HUFF HUFF
GET OUT OF HERE!!!
!!?

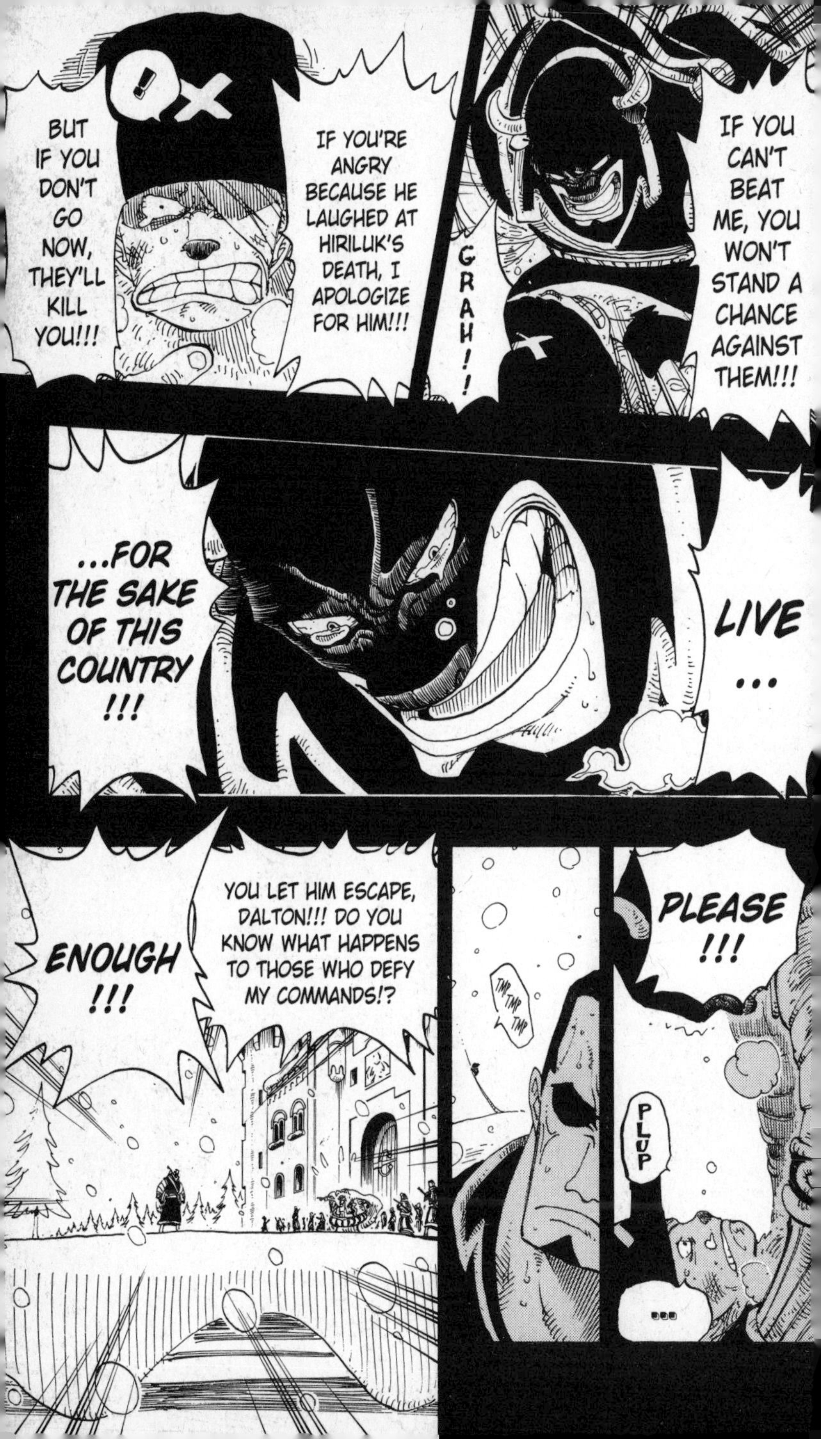
IF YOU CAN'T BEAT ME, YOU WON'T STAND A CHANCE AGAINST THEM!!!
GRAH!!
IF YOU'RE ANGRY BECAUSE HE LAUGHED AT HIRILUK'S DEATH, I APOLOGIZE FOR HIM!!!
BUT IF YOU DON'T GO NOW, THEY'LL KILL YOU!!!
LIVE...
...FOR THE SAKE OF THIS COUNTRY!!!
PLEASE!!!
PLUP
...
TMP TMP TMP
ENOUGH!!!
YOU LET HIM ESCAPE, DALTON!!! DO YOU KNOW WHAT HAPPENS TO THOSE WHO DEFY MY COMMANDS!?

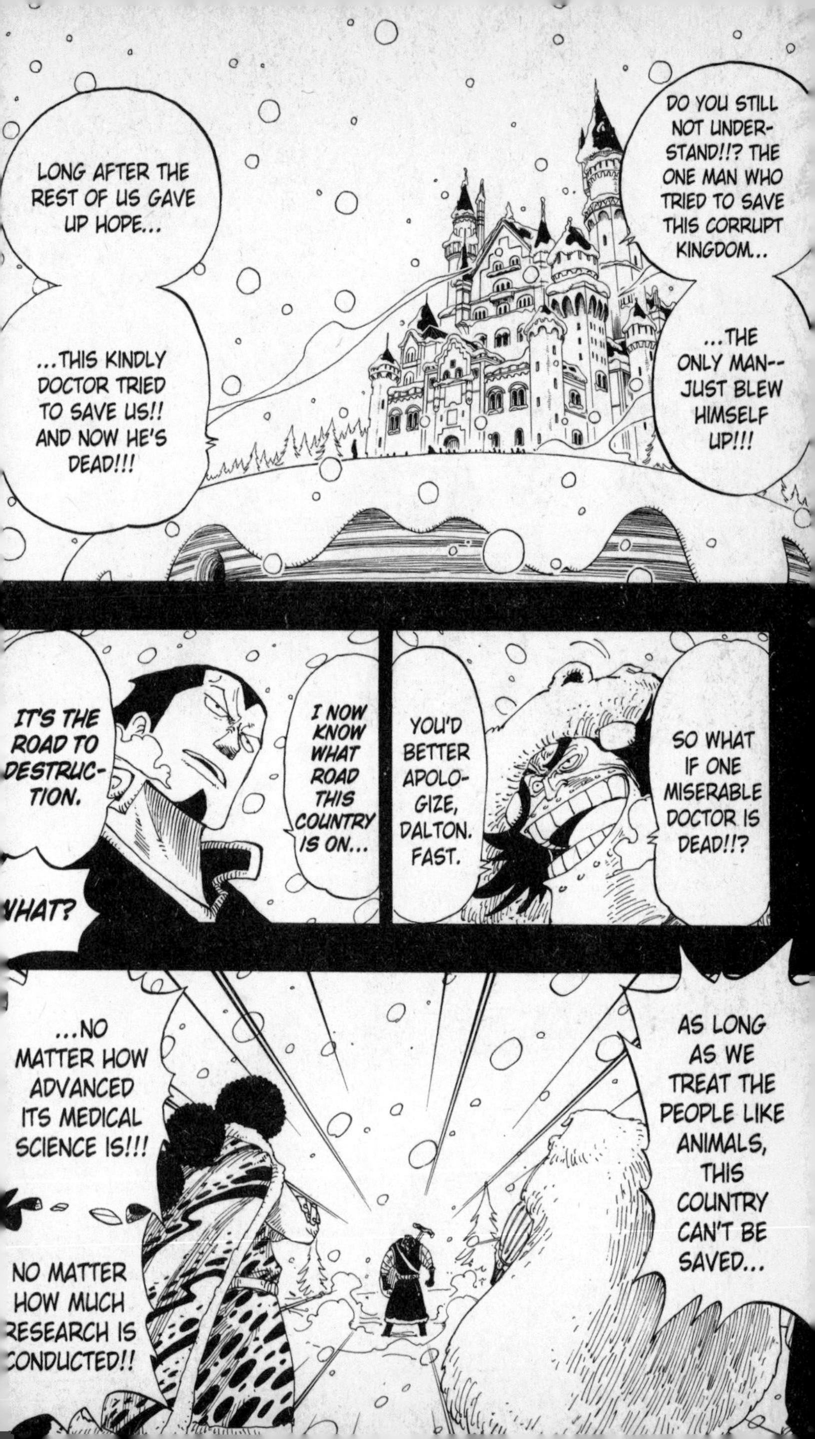
DO YOU STILL NOT UNDERSTAND!!? THE ONE MAN WHO TRIED TO SAVE THIS CORRUPT KINGDOM...
...THE ONLY MAN-- JUST BLEW HIMSELF UP!!!
LONG AFTER THE REST OF US GAVE UP HOPE...
...THIS KINDLY DOCTOR TRIED TO SAVE US!! AND NOW HE'S DEAD!!!
SO WHAT IF ONE MISERABLE DOCTOR IS DEAD!!?
YOU'D BETTER APOLOGIZE, DALTON. FAST.
I NOW KNOW WHAT ROAD THIS COUNTRY IS ON...
WHAT?
IT'S THE ROAD TO DESTRUCTION.
AS LONG AS WE TREAT THE PEOPLE LIKE ANIMALS, THIS COUNTRY CAN'T BE SAVED...
...NO MATTER HOW ADVANCED ITS MEDICAL SCIENCE IS!!!
NO MATTER HOW MUCH RESEARCH IS CONDUCTED!!

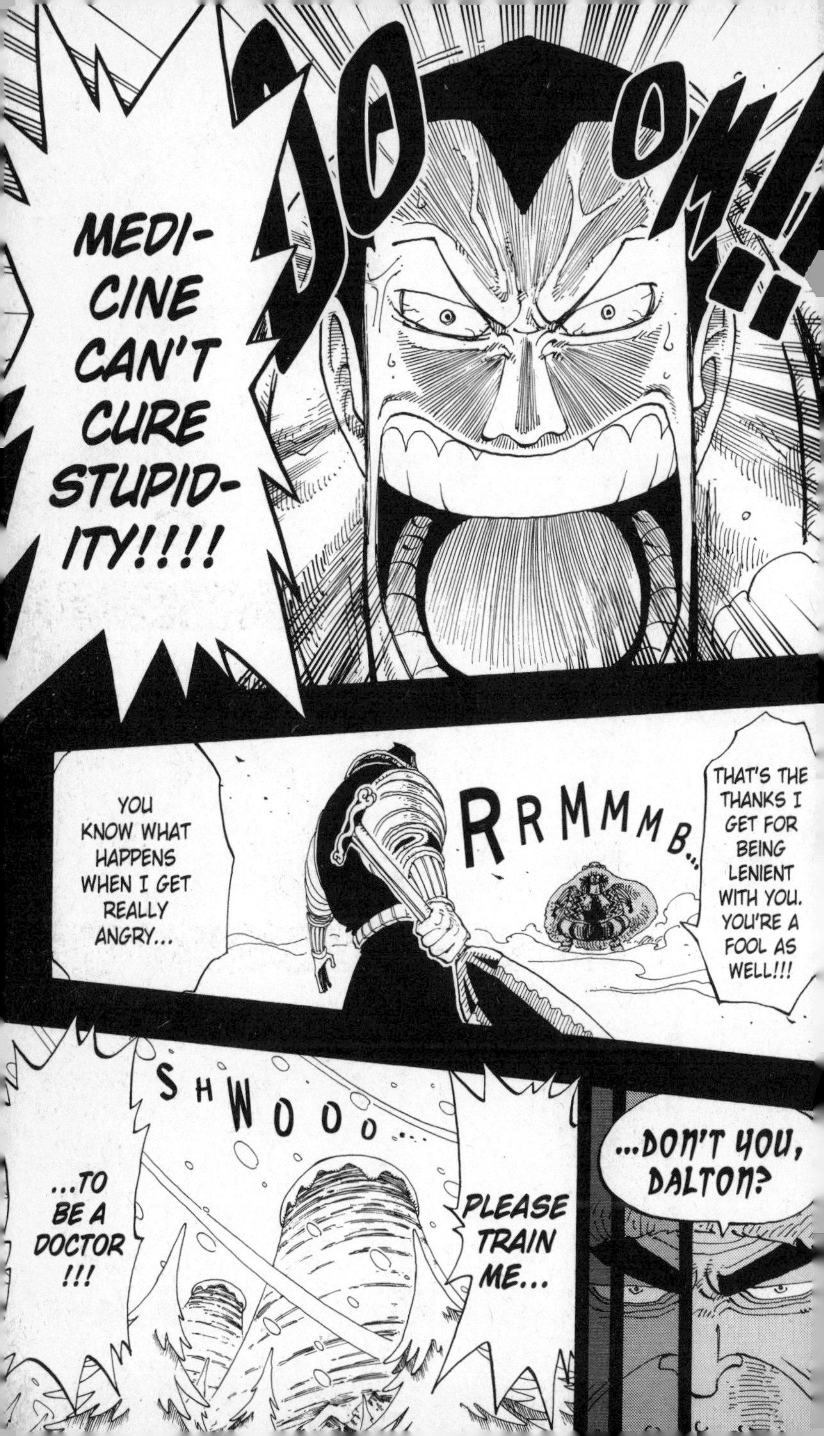
MEDI-CINE CAN'T CURE STUPID-ITY!!!!
THAT'S THE THANKS I GET FOR BEING LENIENT WITH YOU. YOU'RE A FOOL AS WELL!!!
RRMMMB...
YOU KNOW WHAT HAPPENS WHEN I GET REALLY ANGRY...
...DON'T YOU, DALTON?
SHWOOO...
PLEASE TRAIN ME...
...TO BE A DOCTOR!!!

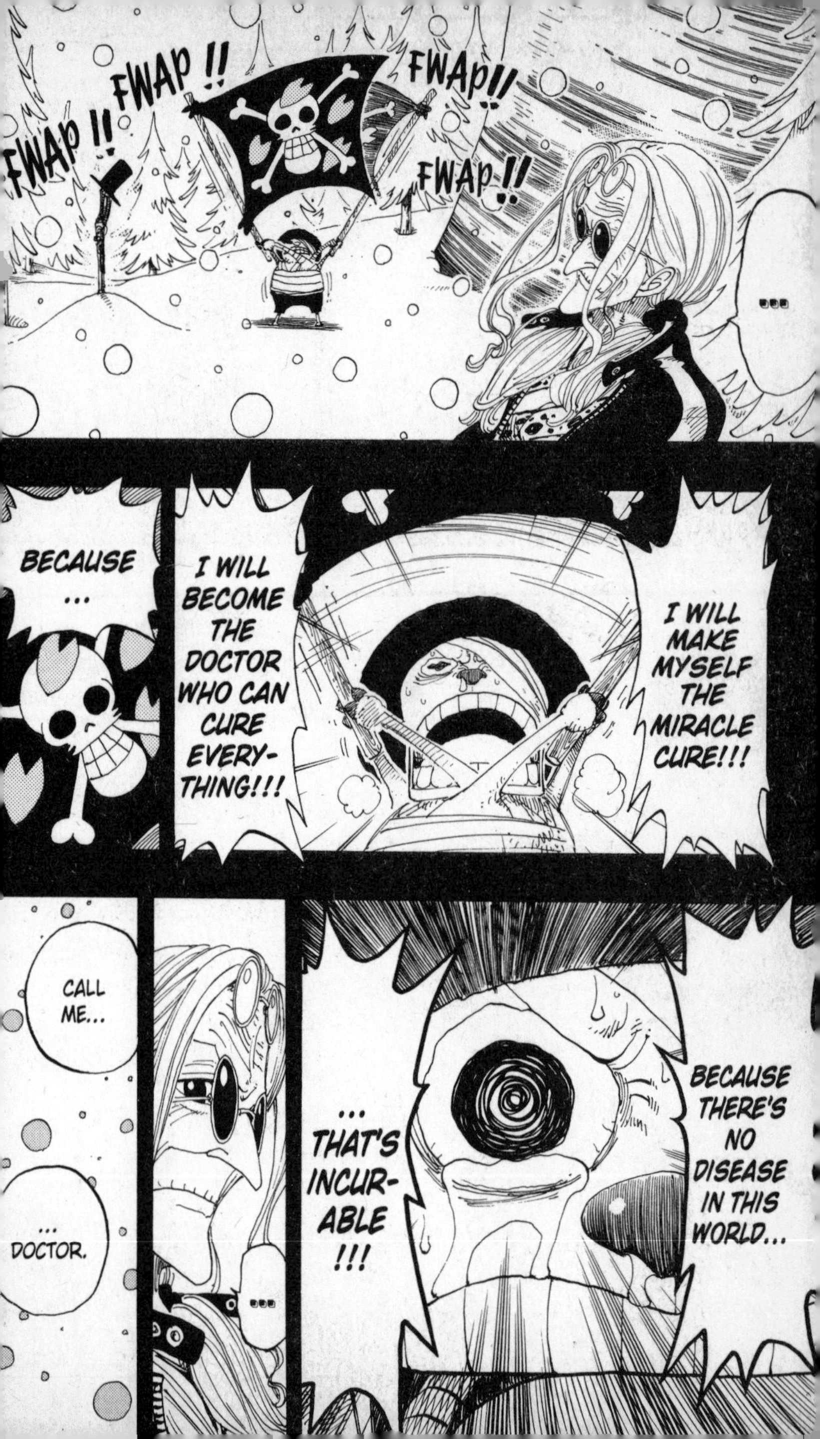
FWAp!!
FWAp!!
FWAP!!
FWAp!!
...
I WILL MAKE MYSELF THE MIRACLE CURE!!!
I WILL BECOME THE DOCTOR WHO CAN CURE EVERY-THING!!!
BECAUSE ...
BECAUSE THERE'S NO DISEASE IN THIS WORLD...
... THAT'S INCUR-ABLE !!!
...
CALL ME...
... DOCTOR.

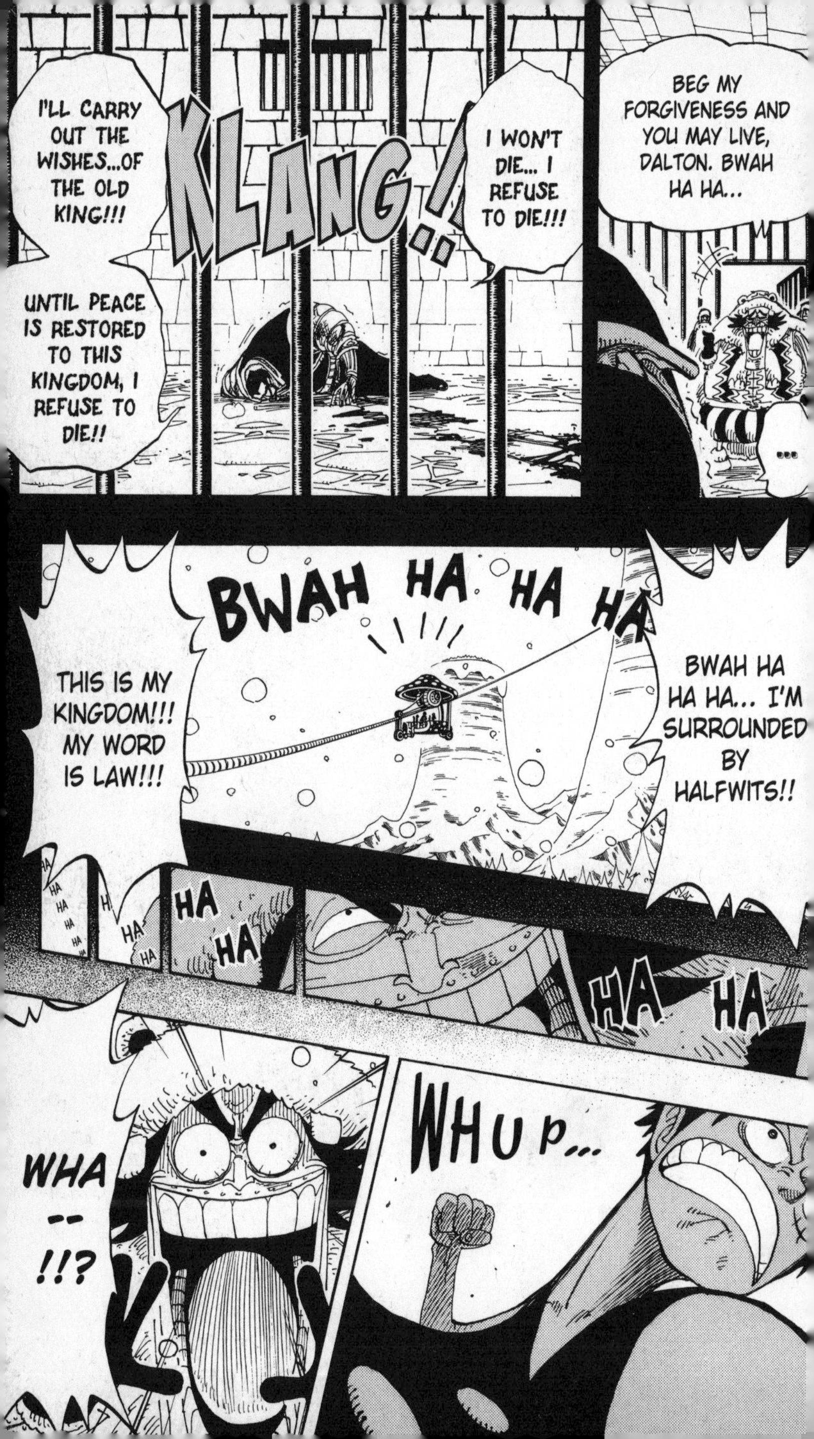
BEG MY FORGIVENESS AND YOU MAY LIVE, DALTON. BWAH HA HA...
...
I WON'T DIE... I REFUSE TO DIE!!!
KLANG!!
I'LL CARRY OUT THE WISHES...OF THE OLD KING!!!
UNTIL PEACE IS RESTORED TO THIS KINGDOM, I REFUSE TO DIE!!
BWAH HA HA HA
BWAH HA HA HA... I'M SURROUNDED BY HALFWITS!!
THIS IS MY KINGDOM!!! MY WORD IS LAW!!!
HA HA
HA HA
HA HA HA HA HA HA HA HA
WHUP...
WHA-- !!?

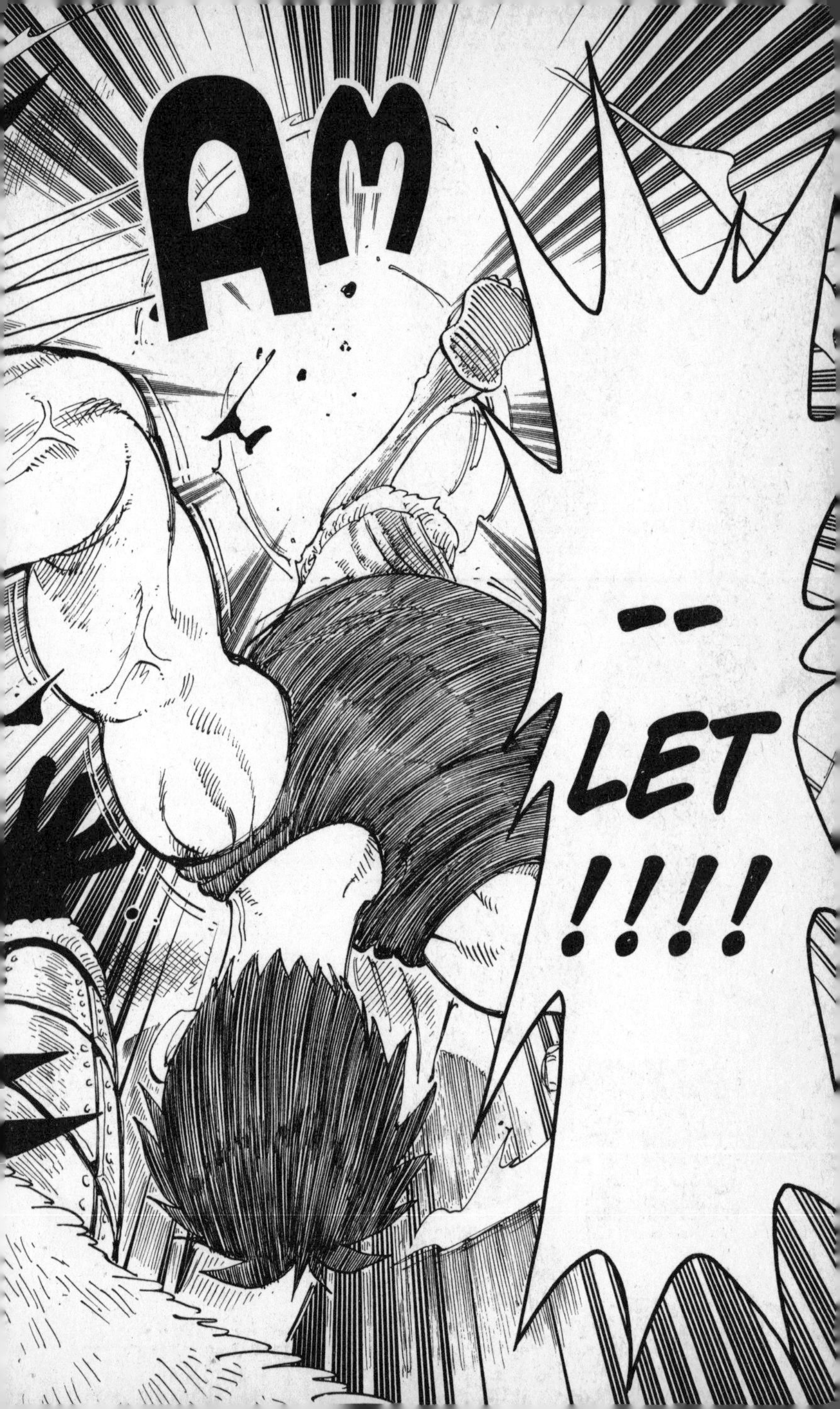
AM
-- LET !!!!

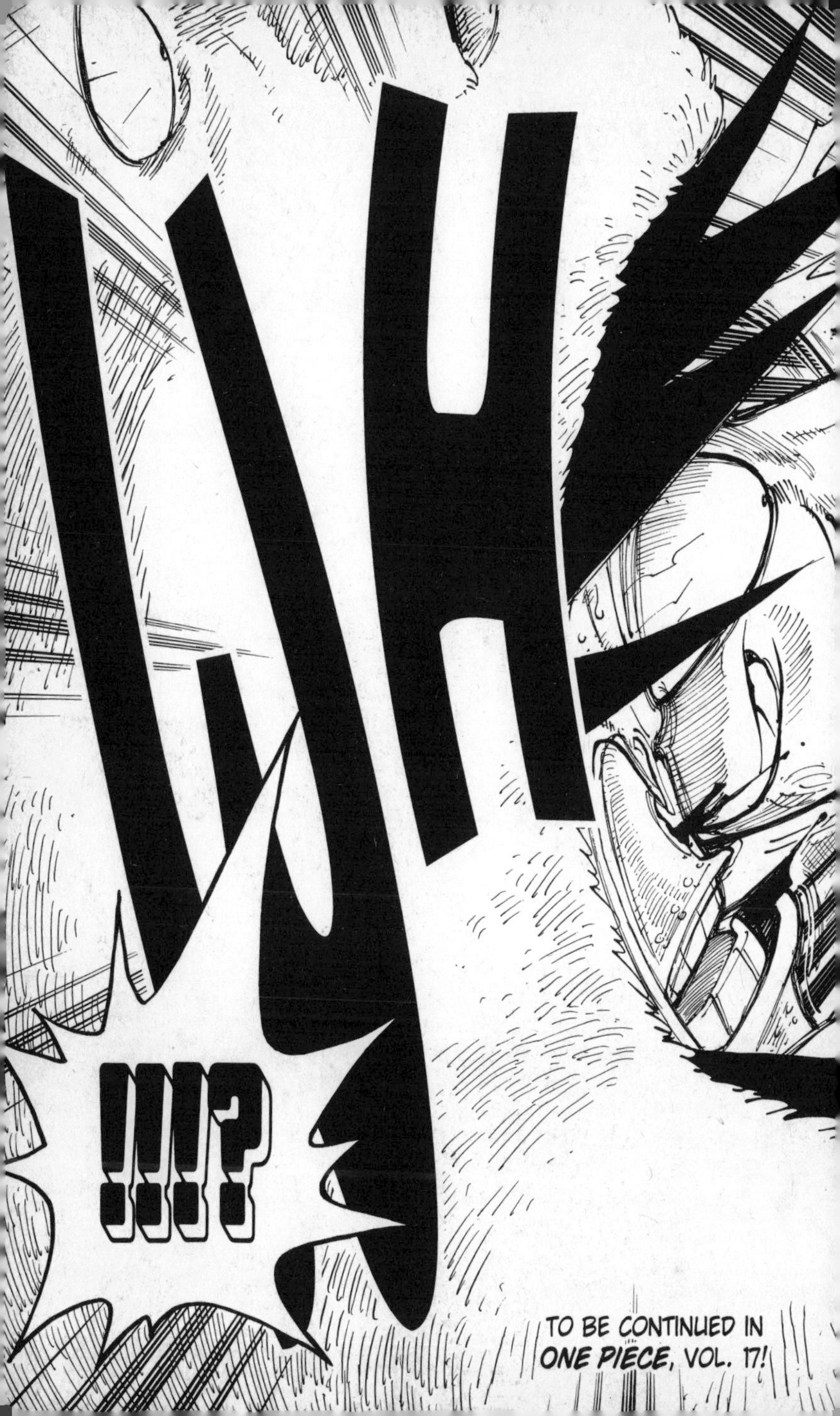
WH
!!!?
TO BE CONTINUED IN *ONE PIECE*, VOL. 17!

COMING NEXT VOLUME:

King Wapol wants his castle back and Luffy's not about to give it to him! It's the showdown you've been waiting for! Luffy and friends launch an all-out attack, forcing the metallic menace Wapol to eat his own henchmen, spit them out and produce the formidable combo of terror known as Chessmarimo! With Sanji out of commission, Tony Tony Chopper's on his own, but he's got a couple of tricks up his sleeve too!

ON SALE MARCH 2008!

Read it first in SHONEN JUMP magazine!

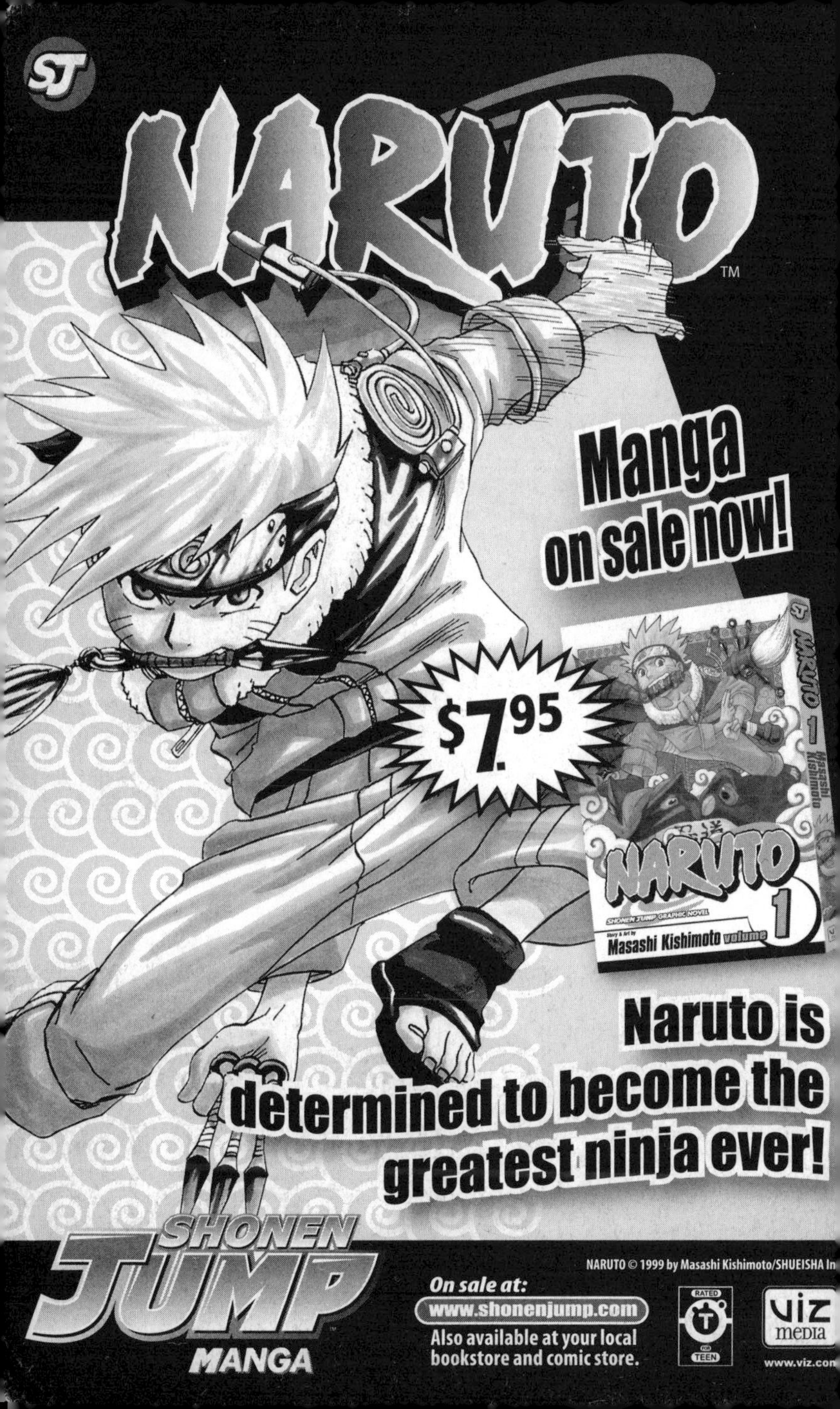
SJ
NARUTO™
Manga on sale now!
$7.95
NARUTO 1
SHONEN JUMP GRAPHIC NOVEL
Story & Art by Masashi Kishimoto volume 1
Naruto is determined to become the greatest ninja ever!
SHONEN JUMP MANGA
NARUTO © 1999 by Masashi Kishimoto/SHUEISHA In
On sale at:
www.shonenjump.com
Also available at your local bookstore and comic store.
RATED T TEEN
VIZ media
www.viz.con